SOLAR HOUSES
FOR A
COLD CLIMATE

SOLAR HOUSES FOR A COLD CLIMATE

A detailed study of 26 solar heated houses

Written by
DEAN CARRIERE
Photographed by
FRASER DAY

Published by
CHARLES SCRIBNER'S SONS
New York

Library of Congress Cataloging in Publication Data

Carriere, Dean.
Solar houses for a cold climate.

1. Solar houses—Climatic factors. 2. Solar houses —Cold weather conditions. I. Day, Fraser, joint author. II. Title.
TH7414.C37 690'.86'9 79-20930
ISBN 0-684-16288-1 (cloth)
ISBN 0-684-17424-3 (paper)

This book published simultaneously in the United States of America and in Canada—Copyright under the Berne Convention.

1 3 5 7 9 11 13 15 17 19 Q/P 20 18 16 14 12 10 8 6 4 2

Printed in the United States of America

Color slides of the twenty-six solar houses presented here are available from the author. For details, write Dean Carriere, Box 777, Wiarton, Ontario NOH 2TO, Canada.

CONTENTS

II CASE STUDIES OF SOLAR-HEATED HOUSES 29

APPENDICES

ACKNOWLEDGMENTS

We would like to thank our wives, Lin Carriere and Jinny Day, whose patience, cooperation, and assistance were immeasurable.

We are grateful to Gordon McNeil, Director, Mobile Intensive Learning Experience, Seneca College, Willowdale, Ontario, who has been an inspiration since the beginning.

The owners and builders of the homes we have featured overwhelmed us by their hospitality, generosity, enthusiasm, and honesty. Thanks largely to them the creation of this book has been an exciting and unforgettable experience.

Dean Carriere
Fraser Day

INTRODUCTION

Much has been written recently about the problems of overpopulation, pollution, resource depletion, and energy shortages, not to mention inflation, unemployment, and global economic inequities.

Writers report a growing social malaise and purposelessness and warn of the approaching apocalypse. Some feel that the physical basis of life is most acutely threatened in the industrialized world, where, propelled by an economic system dependent on unlimited growth in the material sector, we run the risk of drowning in our own wastes.

There is considerable controversy about the estimates of reserves of various resources. However, it has now become clear that there is a limit—a limit to resources and a limit to the carrying capacity of our planet. Realizing this, more and more people are becoming aware of the need to change from a consumer society to a conserver society, to live in harmony with nature, and to be concerned for the welfare of future generations.

Solar Houses for a Cold Climate is one response to such needs. Although solar space heating of houses is the central theme of the text, we take a more holistic approach by examining from an ecological perspective all aspects of dwelling design—including architectural features; technical support systems such as heating, power, water supply, waste disposal, and food production; and the building's relationship to the natural environment. We also investigate the reasons that each owner has chosen to live within a space heated by the sun.

Most of the solar-heated homes in Canada and the United States have been built in the last four years. Experts cannot yet agree on which systems are the best. Therefore, we have selected 26 homes that we feel are representative of the many solar space-heating systems operating in the temperate northeastern United States and central and eastern Canada. They include passive solar systems, in which the building itself collects and stores solar energy; active systems, using air or liquid to transport heat from collectors; and hybrid systems, having both passive and active components.

The homes are situated in rural, suburban, and urban areas. Several of the dwellings were built nearly 20 years ago, but most were built in recent years. Five of the examples are retrofits—that is, the houses were not initially designed for solar heating and thus had to be modified to accommodate the solar heating system.

Solar Houses for a Cold Climate is designed both as a practical manual for the do-it-yourself designer/builder and as a source of information for the "armchair" builder, the academic and the professional architect, the solar engineer, and the professional builder. Part I, Ecological House Design, provides an overview of ecological design principles and construction techniques and thus helps the reader understand the pictorial and narrative case studies which follow in Part II. A References section at the back of the book gives bibliographical information for many publications mentioned in the text and also lists other works and sources of information that may be helpful. The information content and order of presentation in Part II is consistent from one case study to the other, thus facilitating case-to-case comparison of similar components.

The text and photographs are sufficiently detailed that, after having carefully examined each example, you should be able to design your own ecological solar-heated house. It will be necessary, of course, to consult some of the books mentioned throughout and listed at the back of the book in order to determine exact engineering specifications for some components.

We hope that in addition to providing you with some of the tools to design your own home or to renovate an existing one, *Solar Houses for a Cold Climate* will inspire you to live a life more in harmony with the natural environment. To quote Adlai Stevenson, "We travel together, passengers on a little spaceship, dependent on its vulnerable resources of air and soil; all committed for our safety to its security and peace: preserved from annihilation only by the care, the work and—I will say—the love we give our fragile craft."

Dean Carriere
Fraser Day
Toronto

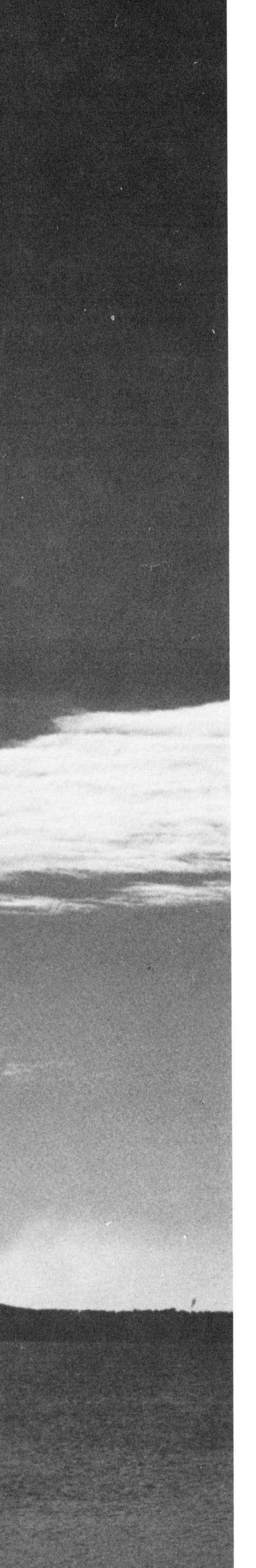

> The goal of alternative architecture is an end to resource depletion. But its successful adoption involved far more than facts and figures: a new relationship to our world is called for, characterized by both respect and reverence for the place we inhabit. We cannot "rule the world" without paying a heavy price; far better to enter into a symbiotic relationship and preserve both the world and ourselves.
>
> —Jim Leckie *et al.*, *Other Homes and Garbage*

Part I

ECOLOGICAL HOUSE DESIGN

We can better understand just what is meant by ecological house design by considering the so-called primitive architecture of past and present civilizations. It comes in many forms: the sod houses of the prairie farmers; the Cappadocians' cone houses hollowed out of spectacular erosion-created natural cones and minarets; the eight-sided horizontal-log and mud-plastered Navajo hogans; the traditional adobe houses of New Mexico; the houseboats of Kowloon; the dwellings of nomadic peoples, such as the Plains Indians' tepees, the yurts of various Asian tribes, and the igloo of the Eskimo. An almost infinite variety—yet we are struck by what they have in common. Invariably, natural, locally available materials are used, and usually the owners construct the dwelling themselves or at least assist in the construction. House orientation and space layout are dictated by climatic and site characteristics and specific functional requirements. The architecture is generally simple, devoid of excessive ornamentation, economical in use of materials and space. These architectural forms minimize harmful environmental impact while providing comfort and shelter, and thus by their existence define what we call ecological house design. The definition will become clearer as we examine specific aspects of ecological design.

CHOOSING A SITE

A search for a living space or a site upon which to build is usually most efficient in terms of time and energy spent (of whatever form) if you already live near the area in which you wish to settle and can investigate possible sites on foot, by bicycle, by public transit, or at least by relatively small use of environmentally wasteful modes of transportation. But frequently the area of search is not close by.

In this case a good deal of the preliminary work can be done by phone. For rural properties, it is helpful to then plot land that is available for purchase, on detailed 1:50,000 topographical maps. Many properties then can be eliminated as unsuitable on the basis of a thorough map analysis. Often it is less expensive and more energy-efficient to examine by small aircraft a number of properties that from their description and the map analysis seem appropriate. On one such search within a two-hour flight period, my wife and I examined 15 properties and were able to select three that met our criteria. It would have taken a week to accomplish the same amount by automobile, with the use of a lot more fossil fuel.

A main criterion in site selection should be the distance and time required to travel to work, school, church, shops, recreational centers, and other facilities. It would be ideal if you could walk, bicycle, snowshoe, cross-country ski, paddle, or travel by other environmentally harmless means to these activity areas. In Ottawa during winter months people skate to work along the Rideau Canal. More and more cities are creating roadways reserved for bicycles.

It is important to be aware of the man-made environment near a potential living space. In many cases, human ingenuity has complemented the natural beauty and the amenities of a certain area, but more often than not man's disregard of his dependence on the natural environment is painfully obvious. Through various government offices, environmental groups, local service organizations, and other sources, you can learn something about any existing and proposed developments in an area and their impact on the environment in the form of air, land, and water pollution. Sometimes the pollution is obvious, other times it is more insidious. The INCO refinery in Sudbury, Ontario, for example, increased the height of refinery smokestacks in an attempt to disperse air pollution more widely. Now sulfuric acid has been detected raining down on Prince Edward Island more than 1,500 miles away.

Little research has been carried out regarding the effects of road salt on the local environment. Tests along some major highways have shown roadside vegetation up to 10 yards from the highway had suffered major damage, and in some cases local wells have become contaminated with road salt.

People often overlook noise pollution when selecting a dwelling space. It is easy to overlook or underestimate noise from nearby factories or commercial activities in the excitement of buying land. It is generally not advisable to build near a hill on a busy highway; if cars have to power up the hill the noise could be disquieting. It is not advisable to build on the inside of a road curve; automobile lights will shine through house windows.

It is also important to consider proximity to hard, reflective surfaces. An area turned over to concrete parking lots, roads, sidewalks, and buildings is much less tolerable on a hot summer day than would be the same space covered with vegetation. (Reflective surfaces can be turned to an advantage. I know of one case where an ingenious builder gained permission to paint a neighbor's roof white in order to improve its reflectivity and thus the efficiency of the builder's nearby vertical collectors.)

Often neglected is the effect that man-made structures can have on the flow rate and direction of air currents. Downtown Bay Street, Toronto, is notorious for the strong winter north winds that funnel unmercifully down toward the lake between the tall office buildings. High-velocity air movement across a building surface increases the heat loss and decreases the longevity of the materials. Also, when strong winds are accompanied by moisture the probability of water leakage is increased.

Proximity to local utilities and essential services is a consideration. For many locations the cost of a wind generator will be less than the cost to hook up to the local electric power grid. The availability of heating and cooking fuels is of prime concern. Many parts of the United States suffered shortages during the severe winter of 1977 simply because poor road conditions made it impossible to deliver fuel. Particularly in more rural areas, a good woodlot or access to one is a great advantage. A woodlot is a renewable resource which if properly managed will supply fuel in perpetuity.

Another consideration is the proximity of centralized water- and sewage-treatment plants, not only for your own use—either desired or enforced—but for the impact that these plants might have on the environment. New Milford, Connecticut, is considering enlarging its local sewage treatment considerably and obliging rural folk to hook up to the centralized system. Many local people are fighting this because of the great increase in taxes that will result and because they feel that dumping all the treated waste into the river will seriously lower the local water table. If they are properly designed, decentralized sewage systems help to maintain the local water table without contaminating it.

The proximity to a fire station should be considered for two reasons: The distance will determine to some degree the type of fire-fighting equipment you should have on site, and often fire-insurance premiums are directly related to this distance.

Finally, zoning and building regulations for the area are important. Friends of mine bought a particularly beautiful piece of land on an island. They were very disappointed when a large cement plant was constructed on the mainland opposite their home, noisily spewing wastes into the air and visually contaminating the landscape. Often the rigid enforcement of antiquated building regulations makes life difficult for those experimenting with alternative building designs. Other friends nearly bought a beautiful old log house on charming country acreage. They discovered purely by accident that a large chemical firm was using a neighboring property for the dumping of waste chemicals.

Soil and Water

Of primary concern on any site are the soil characteristics. Strength or bearing capacity and moisture characteristics for drainage are particularly important for building. (Cole and Wing's *From the Ground Up*, listed in the References section, gives a good detailed treatment of this subject.) You should also determine the site water conditions, as these and the soil characteristics will determine the most appropriate foundation to use.

The high water table should be determined during the spring or periods of heavy rain, and of course natural water runoffs and extremely flat or depressed areas should be avoided where possible. Surface water in the process of evaporation tends to cool the surrounding air. This can be particularly advantageous during hot summer months if the dwelling is facing prevailing winds blowing across the water. However, depending on the building's orientation with respect to the sun and the water, discomforting glare could be a problem.

Vegetation

Vegetation is important in ecological home design for many reasons. Coniferous trees used as windbreaks can reduce fuel consumption by as much as 30%. Windbreaks are also an effective way of controlling snowdrifts on lanes and roads and in yards and fields. Deciduous trees in the summer provide shade and absorb solar radiation, which results in evaporation and subsequent cooling of the surrounding air. They lose their leaves in winter and therefore allow the sun to warm the house when heat is most needed. This is particularly important where solar collectors are used.

Too often overlooked is the impact that vegetation has on the psyche. Little research has been done in this area but it is certain that the forms, colors, and smells of vegetation and the changes that occur from season to season are healthful attributes of any site.

Natural Resources and Salvage Materials

You should become familiar with the uses of natural materials such as stone, earth, and wood for building construction and bear this in mind when assessing a site. Wood is a renewable resource that can serve a multitude of purposes—framing, siding, roofing, furniture, fencing, and heating.

An assessment should be made of the type, quantity, and quality of trees on any potential dwelling site. Some wood is better suited to some purposes than others. A cord of the densest hardwoods, such as hickory, maple, and white oak, is worth twice as much as a cord of softwood in terms of Btu. However, softwood trees of sufficient size can be much more useful for turning into timber and lumber than most hardwoods.

Local stone can be used to make foundations, walls, fencing, walks, and fireplaces. Earth, the most abundant construction material, is appropriate mostly for drier climates, although a rammed-earth home that was built near King City, Ontario, in the 1930s is still occupied and in good condition. The Cinva Ram press, a low-cost portable press for making blocks from a dampened mixture of humus-free soil and a stabilizing agent (usually Portland cement), has simplified earth-block construction considerably. Baled hay was a fairly common wall construction material in the U.S. Midwest around the turn of the century. House 19 in Part II demonstrates a modern use of straw bales in construction. Sod houses were particularly suitable to prairie conditions in early days where there was a shortage of fuel to heat uninsulated wood-frame structures. Today there are still hundreds of Nebraskans who live comfortably in sod homes built near the turn of the century.

An inventory of available salvage materials should be made. A foundation from an old house, factory, or barn might prove suitable to erect a new dwelling upon. An old barn no longer suitable or wanted for its original function might provide valuable and beautiful posts and beams for framing, barn board for board-and-batten siding, stone for foundations and fireplaces. House 17 in Part II was built almost entirely from salvaged materials. Salvage of used materials is generally very labor-intensive, but has obvious ecological advantages over the purchase of new materials. Several books listed in the References section, including Kern's *The Owner-Built Home* and *The Owner-Built Homestead*, and *Shelter* by Shelter Publications, illustrate various uses of natural and salvage materials for building construction.

Climate

Gaining an understanding of the climatic characteristics of a site is just another progression in our attempt to gain a greater understanding of our relationship to the natural environment. We must protect ourselves from the severity of the weather and take best advantage of its benefits in an environmentally appropriate way.

There are many sources that one can consult in order to obtain climatic information about a particular site. The local weather office will provide much information, but fuel and electric companies, insulation manufacturers, airports, air-pollution groups, the *ASHRAE Handbook of Fundamentals*, and those people whose professions depend on the weather, such as fishermen and farmers, are also good sources of information.

Temperature data is extremely important, as the temperature difference between the inside and outside of a dwelling is directly related to the rate of heat loss—that is, the greater the temperature differential, the greater the heat loss. A heating system should be designed to provide an amount of heat equivalent to the heat loss. From the sources mentioned above, one can determine what is generally accepted as the *minimum* outside design temperature for a certain locale. Temperature levels over time are expressed in "degree-days." A degree-day occurs for every degree the average outside temperature falls below 65° F. for a 24-hour period. For example, if the average outside temperature was 55° F. for 24 hours, 10 degree-days would have accrued. The severer the weather, the more degree-days. *The Solar Home Book* by Anderson, *Other Homes and Garbage* by Leckie *et al.*, and *The Nicholson Solar Energy Catalogue and Building Manual* by Nicholson and Davidson explain how to use these figures to determine heat loss and thus the required capacity of a heating system.

Wind is an important climatic consideration, as it has potential for ventilation, for increasing heat loss, for power generation, and for creating havoc. Wind speeds and directions during the various seasons should be taken into account when planning the orientation and design of your living space. Obviously it is desirable in cold, windy winter areas to present a low profile and minimal exposure to the wind. It is generally not advisable to build on top of a ridge or hill, as wind tends to increase in velocity as it passes over. Slopes facing away from the prevailing wind are generally warmer. Where winter cold is an important consideration it is advisable not to build in an open expanse, as wind will reach its maximum velocity; uneven terrain will tend to dissipate its strength. Windbreaks, fencing, unheated building space, protected airlock entrances not on the windward side, and tight construction will all reduce the impact of wind on a dwelling.

In my opinion, with proper design and orientation of buildings, and good insulation, in temperate climates there is no need for air conditioning. Usually good cross-ventilation can be provided by placing small vents low on the colder windward side of a dwelling and larger vents high on the warmer leeward side of the dwelling. Kern's *The Owner-Built Home* discusses this topic.

It is not the purpose of this book to go into any detail about wind power generation, although the discussion of House 17 explains how one owner gets 100% of his power needs from a wind generator. The References section includes books for those interested in pursuing the subject.

Precipitation data is particularly important for farming and gardening, and those interested in installing cisterns for in-house water use are also concerned. Frost data is also of interest to farmers and gardeners and is important to the builder when considering foundation type and depth.

Snow loads have to be taken into account when designing roof structures.

Having given careful thought to site characteristics, we can now turn our attention to some of the design principles of the ecological dwelling itself.

ECOLOGICAL DESIGN PRINCIPLES and SPECIFICATIONS

In a recent interview in *The Mother Earth News*, David Wright, one of the revolutionary architects of low-cost energy-efficient shelter, summarized his design principles in the following way: A dwelling should be built with its insulation on the outside just under the weather skin, keeping massive elements on the inside to act as a thermal flywheel, thus allowing you to coast through seasonal and daily temperature fluctuations that buffet the exterior of your abode. The building should face southward with large glass surfaces, and these surfaces should be well insulated with movable curtains or shutters. These principles are applicable both to new house construction and to modification of old houses.

Any ecological house must be designed to provide thermal comfort and aesthetic satisfaction while minimizing its impact on the environment. No decision, however, should be made regarding the design of the building—its size, layout, shape, and orientation—until the site characteristics, as outlined earlier, and your needs have been carefully considered.

Size

A small house is more economical of energy and resources than a large one. With proper layout of living spaces, letting them flow into one another and extend outward to the natural environment via view windows and decks, a small house can often meet the occupant's needs as well as a much larger one. For example, by using an open concept for traditional dining-room, living-room, and kitchen areas, more useful space can be created without the claustrophobic effect created by boxing these same rooms off into separate and totally distinct rooms. Instead of having a recreation room in a basement, why not use this kitchen/dining/living open-concept space for parties and games? It makes little sense to have two separate eating areas—one for formal occasions and one for everyday use. One area can be designed to be comfortable for both. Consider multiple use of rooms. Two children's rooms side by side could be designed with a movable partition, allowing them to be quickly converted to one large play area. By using an old desk-dresser and combining it with bookshelves above and filing cabinets on the sides, a friend turned a bedroom that was used only for sleeping into an efficient office/study/sleeping space. Bedrooms are often arranged so that a bed sits in the center of the room with the area around it largely unused. Better use of space can be made by building a bed into place, allowing access from one side only, and by building storage units underneath. Many families have two or more bathrooms where a single bathroom properly designed and located would be satisfactory. House 14 is an example of one good way of laying out a bathroom.

The need for a basement should be carefully weighed. In many houses this space is inefficiently and infrequently used. If it is used only for storage, the furnace, and the laundry equipment, these facilities could probably be placed in a much smaller space upstairs.

Room Layout

The open-plan concept was mentioned earlier. It is impossible to recommend an ideal layout, but some general guidelines will be useful. Hot rooms, such as the kitchen and laundry, should normally be kept away from the west side of the house, as during the summer this is the side that is exposed to the heat of the late-afternoon sun. It is recommended that sleeping areas be on the cool north side of the house and living areas be on the east and south sides.

The kitchen and bathroom, with the hot-water tank nearby, should be back to back; or, if they are on separate floors, piping from each should run down a common wall. This will minimize the amount of piping, installation costs, and the loss of heat through the pipes. If automatic washer and dryer are used, it is often possible to stack one on top of another within the bathroom or a hall space rather than having a separate laundry room. In order to minimize the danger of frozen lines, plumbing should not be installed on an exterior wall. Closets, pantries, and hallways placed along the north side of a home will reduce heat loss. Garages, woodsheds, toolsheds, and other such buildings placed on the cold, windward side will provide additional thermal buffering.

Shape

Ideally the house should present a low profile to the cold winter winds and expose a minimum of surface area to the outside, yet allow good ventilation during summer and a pleasing view. I have seen designs that resemble the low-resistance profile of an airfoil; however, in many cases the materials available, the builder's skill, costs, and other factors may rule out such an exotic design. A circular shape encloses the most area for the least perimeter and thus uses less material and has less heat loss, and it is better at fending off strong winds than other shapes. (A circular house plan in two sizes [804 and 1,134 sq. ft.] is available from the U.S. Government Printing Office, Washington, D.C. Order Plan No. FS-SE-5. Price is $2.)

One would think that domes would be ideal. However, Lloyd Kahn, editor of *Domebook 1* and *Domebook 2*, has become somewhat disenchanted with domes, as there are too many unsolved problems with them. Many of the modern materials used in their fabrication have a shorter life span than anticipated; there are problems with weatherproofing and with shading, curtaining, or shuttering windows. Many people cannot adjust to the curved living space. Kahn and the other people who have since published *Shelter* have discovered that "there is far more to learn from the wisdom of the past, from structures shaped by imagination, not mathematics, and built of materials appearing naturally on earth, than from any further extension of white man technoplastic prowess." The *Shelter* people are not against modern technology, but against its misuse. Domes do cover the maximum area with the least amount of material, but how much energy and resources are consumed in the extraction, processing, fabrication, and transporting of that material?

You might like to consider an underground or partially underground house. The feasibility of this type of structure will depend to a considerable extent on the site characteristics. Some sites are more suited to it than others. The best and most comprehensive book on this subject is *Alternatives in Energy Conservation: The Use of Earth Covered Buildings* (Proceedings and notes of a conference held in Fort Worth, Texas, July 9-12, 1975, and sponsored by the University of Texas/Arlington. Editor: Frank L. Moreland. Available from the Superintendent of Documents, U.S. Government Printing Office, Washington, D.C. 20402. Stock No. 038-000-00286-4. $3.25).

Malcolm Wells is probably the single most authoritative architect on the subject. Refer to his ten-page article entitled "Underground Architecture" in *Co-Evolution Quarterly,* Fall 1976, and his own book, *Underground Designs*, available for $6 from the author (Box 183, Cherry Hill, N.J. 08002).

A square house plan is 12% to 15% more efficient than a rectangular plan. There is less surface on a square, and therefore there is less heat loss and less material is used.

A two-story house is more efficient than a bungalow of the same floor space, as it requires only half as much roof and foundation. Material use and heat loss are therefore less.

Orientation

When we consider insulation data for houses with different sizes, shapes, and orientations at various latitudes at different times of the year, available in the *ASHRAE Handbook of Fundamentals* tables, we find that the square house is *not* the optimum form in *any* location and that the optimum shape in every case is one elongated along an east-west axis, as it absorbs the most solar radiation from the low winter sun. Houses elongated along a north-south axis are less efficient than a square. One expert suggests an orientation somewhat east of due south in order to take advantage of the early-morning sun when it is most needed.

Materials

Materials were mentioned earlier in discussing site characteristics, but it is worth reemphasizing that for all construction it is very important that you give careful consideration to the use of locally available materials that require a minimum of energy in extraction, processing; fabrication, and transportation. You should look also for ways compatible with energy-efficient design to minimize the quantity of materials used in building.

For example, an alternative to standard flooring is tongue-and-groove boards 2" or 3" thick to serve as a floor for one level and as a ceiling for the level below. Salvaged brick on a sand base makes a substantial floor with high thermal capacity and thermal lag. In 2 x 4 studwall construction, why should the interior walls be constructed the same way as exterior walls if the former are not load-bearing? Consider using 1" or 2" shiplap or tongue-and-groove rough-sawn boards set vertically and secured at top and bottom on both sides with horizontal members. Another possibility is the use of insulated floor-to-ceiling curtains that can section off or open up various parts of the house for different functions as well as insulate one section from another for zone temperature control. Board-and-batten construction makes good use of rough-sawn boards for exterior siding. The vertical boards allow water to drain down the grain and the boards to dry quickly. Painting is not recommended, because of the constant maintenance required and because paint can trap moisture and thus encourage wood rot. The most common wood preservative used where it is required at all is Cuprinol. Cypress, cedar, and redwood do not require any preservative. Ken Kern recommends single-pitch shed-type roofs, as they can be attractive and are easier to build, require less material, and offer better solar and ventilation controls than the traditional gable roof.

Insulation, Weatherstripping, and Caulking

Some of the materials that one might use for insulation, weatherstripping, and caulking will either be petroleum-based or energy-intensive in their manufacture, but it can be a sensible use of a nonrenewable resource, as in the long term there will be considerable savings in the use of nonrenewable resources for space heating. In some cases, such as House 16, the application of rigid polystyrene foamboard insulation to the exterior of massive concrete walls makes passive solar heating feasible. The only backup heating source in House 16 is a wood stove that burns about a cord and a half of wood per year. Some people who have renovated older uninsulated brick houses have used this system. They expose the interior brick, which is aesthetically very pleasing but also serves the very practical function of absorbing heat and slowly radiating it back at night.

The Thermal Resistance Value (R-value) is the rating commonly used for insulation. The higher the R number, the greater the insulation value. There is a bewildering array of insulation materials on the market. Many of the books listed in the References section include tables summarizing the R-values, applications, and advantages and disadvantages of the many types of insulation now available. New materials and techniques will doubtless soon be developed now that the building and home-improvement industries have had to focus attention on insulation. When pricing types of insulation it is important to consider the cost per unit (R) of insulation value, and not the cost per inch of thickness.

An advantage of foamboards such as used in House 16 is that they form a continuous envelope of uniform R-value around a house. This reduces infiltration losses and eliminates the hot spots that one gets at the lower R-value studs with standard studwall construction. Some foamboards have tongue-and-groove edges for tighter joints. Many builders use two layers of foamboard and stagger the joints. Foamboards should not be used on the exterior of studwalls without a breather strip at the top as the insulation could act as an additional vapor barrier and thus cause structural damage by trapping vapor within the studwall.

The University of Illinois has proposed a double 2 x 4 studwall construction with a 2″ spacing between the walls. The 2 x 4s are placed on 24″ centers and staggered so that they are not opposite one another, thereby reducing heat loss by conduction. Insulation is 10″ batts which are installed between the walls and extend down to the floor and right up to the ceiling between the plates. For complete details of this method, write: Small Homes Council—Building Research Council, University of Illinois at Urbana-Champaign, One East St. Mary's Road, Champaign, Ill. 61820 and ask for Council Notes, Lo-Cal House C2.3 Vol. 1, No. 4, Spring 1976 (25¢).

Foam insulation has received considerable promotion lately. However, on a recent visit to a Pennsylvania energy consultant I was shown an old frame farmhouse that had been insulated with ureaformaldehyde six months previously. Just before my visit some plaster had been removed from one exterior wall to facilitate renovations. Between the wood lath we could see that the foam in curing had shrunk about 3/16″ away from each stud. From his observations, the consultant was of the opinion that the claimed R-values of foam insulations would be considerably reduced when investigations are completed.

Cellulose fiber is one of the least expensive insulations, has relatively high R-value, is easy to install, and uses a minimum of largely renewable resources. It is manufactured from old newspapers, cardboard boxes, and other kinds of waste paper and treated with some readily available and inexpensive chemicals to make it self-extinguishing and verminproof. *The Mother Earth News* No. 48, November/December 1977, features an article on how to manufacture your own cellulose fiber from waste paper and cardboard, employing a feed-grinding hammermill that many farmers use. Borax is used as the fireproofing agent, and aluminum sulfate is used as a rodent and insect repellent.

How much insulation do you need? Ontario Hydro recommends a minimum of R-30 in the ceiling and R-16 in the walls. Dr. D.G. Stevenson of the Natural Research Council of Canada recently completed a study showing that in some areas it is economical to use R-20 in the walls at *today*'s fuel prices. If you compare the insulation used in House 6 to the size of its solar system, it is readily apparent that it is cheaper to add more insulation than to increase the solar collector area and the storage volume.

In determining the amount of insulation, Anderson's *The Solar Home Book*, Leckie's *Other Homes and Garbage*, and Nicholson's *The Nicholson Solar Energy Catalogue* are very useful. They give detailed information on how to compute heat loss, using the R-value for the insulation and other materials used, and thus determine the heat output required from a heating plant, be it solar or otherwise. As well, "The Overselling of Insulation," *Consumer Reports*, February 1978, is very useful. It features a step-by-step worksheet designed to help the consumer determine whether installation of insulation will pay for itself within a reasonable period. A good text on installation of insulation is *Keeping the Heat In: How to Re-Insulate Your Home To Save Energy and Money (And*

Be More Comfortable), published by Energy Mines and Resources, Canada (available free of charge by writing to: Keeping the Heat In, P.O. Box 900, Westmount Postal Station, Montreal, Quebec H3Z 2V1).

Unless the insulation itself includes a good vapor barrier, one must be added. Vapor and airtightness are needed on the side of the insulated surface that is closest to the interior living space. Polyethylene film is commonly used; however, aluminum foil with an airspace between it and the interior wall sheathing has the added advantage of radiating some of the shortwave radiation back into the room.

Infiltration losses can amount to 30% of the heat loss in an average home. Therefore it is particularly important to ensure that all windows and doors are properly weatherstripped and that the cracks are thoroughly caulked. *Keeping the Heat In,* Eccli's *Low-Cost, Energy-Efficient Shelter*, and Wade and Ewenstein's *Thirty Energy-Efficient Houses You Can Build* give good how-to details.

Latex, silicone, and butyl caulking compounds are the best, but each has different properties, so check the manufacturer's instructions. After insulation has been stuffed into all inside cracks, caulk them very carefully. Check cracks at the foundation and sill plates, ceiling fixtures, water pipes and drains, furnace flue, plumbing vents, pipes and air ducts in the attic, attic entry, and between heated and unheated areas. It is important to caulk all outside cracks as well, not only to minimize infiltration losses but to avoid water leaks.

Doors

The location of doors is particularly important during winter months. If possible they should not be located on the windward side, as the positive pressure forces the air inside, nor on the leeward side, as the negative pressure there tends to suck air out of the house. Double doors with a small vestibule between will create a still-air space, which will reduce air infiltration. For existing houses this can be achieved by building such a vestibule within an existing hall or by building a small addition onto the outside. Exterior doors should be insulated and weatherstripped. Commercial insulated doors are available but are quite costly, so it is worth considering manufacturing your own. Interior doors can be installed to facilitate lowering the temperature in some rooms when they are not in use. These will be more effective if weatherstripped. Good-quality salvage doors can often be procured for a fraction of the cost of new doors.

Windows

Windows are generally designed to serve four functions: view, light, ventilation, and solar-heat gain. Often, however, the location ideal for one function may not be ideal for another. For example, to obtain good natural ventilation small openings should be placed low on the windward side of the house and larger openings high on the leeward side. If view windows are also used for ventilation, the screens required in summer can reduce visibility by 30%. In many cases it would be wiser to have separate vent openings that can be closed off and insulated for the winter, and fixed window sashes, except where for psychological, social, or fire-safety reasons it is better to have windows that can open. In general, of course, you should have as few windows as possible on the side buffeted by the cold winter winds, usually the north, and the largest window area to the south, to take advantage of passive solar-heat gain. Decide what view is important and you might find that windows facing this way alone provide all your lighting requirements.

House 19's site has a spectacular view of a part of Lake Ontario to the north. Most builders might be tempted to place a large picture window facing that direction, or possibly face the "front" of the house that way; however, House 19 has one small window in the kitchen at eye level which provides a beautiful view that subtly makes one aware of the site's relationship to the waters. Tall, thin windows next to a white wall can be effective in allowing light to sweep the wall and reflect into the room. A room will always maintain higher levels of illumination when ceiling and walls are light-colored. For sashes, I prefer wood, as it is a better insulator, is warmer to the touch, and does not have the condensation problems that metal windows do. Wood also has the additional advantage of being a renewable resource. Insulated, thermopane glass is recommended for all heated spaces. Sometimes patio glass can be purchased at a reasonable cost, as it is in relatively abundant supply. For those who would like to make their own double-pane windows, Cole and Wing's *From the Ground Up* gives good instructions.

Skylights and Clerestories

Skylights and clerestories are particularly effective for natural lighting. However, because of their generally high location they can be a source of considerable heat loss, and the high location also complicates the use of insulated shutters and curtains. Attempts should be made to insulate them at night. House 19 has ingeniously designed shutters for the clerestory windows.

Alex Wade (*Thirty Energy-Efficient Houses You Can Build*) designed a very low-cost effective skylight. He uses Plexiglass (acrylic plastic) sheet, applies it like a large shingle, and uses clear silicone sealant and screws to secure it. Velux manufactures very good-quality insulated skylights with wooden sashes. (Contact Velux-America Inc., 78 Cummings Park, Woburn, Mass. 01801.)

Shading

Summer shading is necessary to minimize summer overheating in an ecological home. Proper shading, ventilation, and good insulation obviate the need for an air conditioner. An overhang is the best way of shading the southern exposure; however, it is useless on the east and west sides because of the low sun angle. On these sides deciduous trees have been shown to be seven times more effective than shades or drapes. In designing shading devices and windows it is essential to have an understanding of the position of the sun during different times of the day and different times of the year. Values of solar altitude above the horizon and solar azimuth measured from the south are given for various latitudes in the *ASHRAE Handbook of Fundamentals*, published by the American Society of Heating, Refrigerating and Air-Conditioning Engineers. Similar tables for latitudes of particular relevance in Canada are included in *Tables of Solar Altitude, Azimuth, Intensity and Heat Gain Factors for Latitudes from 43 to 55 Degrees North*, by D.G. Stephenson, published by the National Research Council of Canada (NRC 9528). A very good NRC publication entitled *Walls, Windows and Roofs for the Canadian Climate* by J.K. Latta clearly illustrates the use of these tables. Refer to *Solar Control and Shading Devices* by Aladar and Victor Olgyay (Princeton: Princeton Univ. Press, 1976) or *Architectural Graphic Standards* by C.G. Ramsey and H.R. Sleeper (6th ed., New York: Wiley-Interscience, 1970) for a more detailed treatment of shading techniques.

Insulated Shutters, Shades, and Curtains

Insulated shutters, shades, and curtains are an effective way of minimizing heat loss through glass surfaces. Eccli's *Low-Cost, Energy-Efficient Shelter* describes how to construct your own insulated shutters. Steve Baer (at Zomeworks, Box 712, Albuquerque, N.M. 87103) has invented several ways of insulating windows. In the simplest case, magnets are used to secure foamboard insulation to the window frame. Another of his inventions, Skylids, are employed in the greenhouse of House 26. A third design, the Beadwall, functions by blowing polystyrene beads between two panes of glazing when required at night and pumping them out during the day.

Even an ordinary light-colored opaque roller shade mounted inside a window frame can reduce heat loss through a window by as much as 30%. It can also be quite effective in reducing summer heat gain. The Insulating Shade Company Inc. (Blue Hills Rd., Box 689, Durham, Conn. 06442) manufactures a three-layer and a five-layer roller shade with thermal resistance values of R-6 and R-10 respectively.

A good insulated drape can be made by lining existing drapes with the insulation material used for quilts or sleeping bags. These can be made more effective by securing the sides and bottoms with Velcro tape. The Appropriate Technology Corp. (22 High St., P.O. Box 975, Brattleboro, Vt. 05301) manufactures an insulated curtain made of two layers of polyester fiber fill separated by a vapor barrier and enclosed in a protective and decorative covering of Dacron. Conservation Concepts, Down Under Company (P.O. Box 138, Bondville, Vt. 05340) manufactures a curtain composed of a double-layer fabric curtain liner enveloping a layer of the plastic air-bubble material commonly used in packaging.

"Space blankets" of the type readily available in camping-supply stores can be easily adapted to form insulated curtains. The Shelter Institute (Bath, Maine) stocks a very similar material in rolls 54" wide.

WATER SUPPLY

We in the United States and Canada have been accustomed to thinking that our water supply is practically limitless. Water shortages in recent years on various parts of the continent have convinced many people of the folly of this way of thinking.

Typically, the average household's *indoor* water consumption is about 60 gallons per day. Consumption for various facilities is generally broken down as follows: toilets, 40%; lavatories, 3%; bathing, 33%; laundry, 12%; utility sink, 2%; and kitchen, 10%. There are many fixtures on the market designed to reduce consumption; however, what is most needed is a change in attitude and behavior. We must make a conscientious effort to reduce water consumption. The benefits are much greater than the conservation of our water resources. Reduced consumption lightens the load on our water-supply and waste-handling systems. We can make do with smaller conduits and smaller water-treatment and waste-handling systems. As we discuss the various facilities and fixtures we will mention possible conservation techniques.

Kitchen faucets should be selected with a flow rate of no more than 2 gallons per minute.

Lavatory faucets that combine a low flow rate with a wide spray pattern should be used. A flow rate of half a gallon per minute with this type of faucet is sufficient, compared to 2 or 3 gallons per minute with a normal lavatory faucet. For existing kitchen and lavatory faucets flow-control values can be installed in the hot and cold supply lines.

Showers are recommended over tubs, as they generally use less water. For example, a ten-minute shower using a shower head with a flow rate of 2 gallons per minute uses 20 gallons of water, whereas a standard bathtub with 5″ of water amounts to 30 gallons. Considerable savings can be made if one has a "navy shower" (mandatory on board naval ships where fresh water must be manufactured by desalinating sea water); that is, wet, turn off the shower, lather with soap, turn on the shower, and rinse. A single tap mixing hot and cold water with a push-pull on-and-off device is most practical for this type of shower. A number of good low-cost water-conserving shower heads are now on the market. For existing shower heads a flow restrictor can be installed just behind the head. *Consumer Reports*, September 1977, featured the results of a study done on four water-flow restrictors tested in conjunction with two shower massagers, one with a normal flow rate of 5½ to 6½ gallons per minute and the other with a range from 4 to 5½ gallons per minute. The American Standard Aquamizer 34626-02 ($4) proved to be the most efficient water saver, cutting flow rate to 2¾ gallons per minute with both massagers.

The Japanese soaking tub and the Finnish sauna are two other examples of water-conserving methods of cleansing the body.

A domestic hot-water heater can consume a considerable amount of energy. Heat losses can be reduced by wrapping extra insulation around the outside of the tank. House 5 has its tank wrapped with fiberglass batts covered with cotton muslin. Consider a heat exchanger in your wood stove or fireplace connected to your domestic hot-water supply. Solar hot-water heaters will be discussed later in this part.

To cut down on water consumption outside the home, when doing any landscaping consider the use of indigenous vegetation that requires only rainwater. Later, we will discuss a gardening method that can require as little as a quarter of the amount of water that a typical garden requires. When washing vehicles or equipment, use the navy-shower technique.

Kains' *Five Acres and Independence* gives a good account of cisterns for the purpose of collecting and utilizing rainwater. Caution must be advised near industrial areas, as the rain could be contaminated with pollutants.

WASTE SYSTEMS

As mentioned earlier, the flush toilet is the heaviest consumer of water in a typical household. Every flush uses 5 to 7 gallons of formerly pure water to transport perhaps a pint of excrement, or 10,000 gallons per year for the average flush-toilet user. This is an incredible waste of water resources and has, particularly in the case of centralized systems, caused immeasurable environmental damage. According to Barry Estabrook, writing in *Harrowsmith* (November/December 1976), the St. Lawrence River, receiving all of Montreal's raw sewage, now ranks as the world's third most polluted river, following the Mississippi and the Rhine.

There are ways of conserving water in the standard flush toilet. For example, water-saving types are now on the market that consume only 3 to 3.5 gallons per flush. The Gerber Co. markets a flush toilet that uses 1 gallon for flushing urine and 3 for feces. Bricks can be placed in the tank of standard existing flush toilets, or inexpensive rubber dams can be installed. Water-conserving flush valves can also be retrofitted.

According to Sim Van der Ryn, California State Architect and Director of the Office of Appropriate Technology (P.O. Box 1677, Sacramento, Calif. 95808), *Waste Water Treatment Systems for Rural Communities* (Commission on Rural Water, 1973; available from Information Clearing House, Demonstration Water Project, 221 Lasalle St., Chicago, Ill. 60601) is the best single sourcebook on septic tanks and why current standards have little scientific basis. The report states that "from just about every environmental point of view a privy of sound construction which is properly maintained represents an excellent solution to the disposal of human excreta."

There are other ecological waterless-toilet alternatives too, the best known of which is the Clivus Multrum composting toilet. Basically the Clivus is a large inclined box which accepts both kitchen scraps and excrement, which decompose in the presence of oxygen to form a compost suitable for garden use. There are now smaller forced-draft heated models such as Mullbank, Mull-Toa (also known as Humus), and Bio-Loo on the market. There are also medium-sized inclined-box types such as Toa-throne with optional but recommended fan for forced draft.

The Manitoba Department of Northern Affairs has been testing three Clivus Multrum and nine Mull-Toa toilets. An interim report in August 1976 concluded that the Clivus Multrum "can provide simple and effective sanitation when properly installed and adequately loaded. . . . It is the very large size of the system that provides its greatest advantage, its ability to withstand underloading, overloading, and shock loading." The report also concluded that "the small electrically-assisted mouldering (composting) systems have less inherent utility in northern and rural communities. In particular, the Mull-Toa appears to be extremely sensitive to any type of perturbation, especially hydraulic overloading. In addition, the waste mass cannot be effectively aerated internally and anaerdrosis soon results. . . . Of the nine units only one, serving a three-person family, is operating well. It is maintained by a gentleman fully conversant with the variabilities in managing microbial systems."

Dr. Witold Rybizynski, author of *Stop the Five-Gallon Flush*, is also conducting experiments with the Clivus Multrum toilet. There have been problems with odor on sultry days, and a plague of fruit flies at one point; however, Rybizynski feels that a fan installed in the exhaust vent until the toilet reaches an ecological balance will eliminate these problems. The manufacturer says that there is a two-year break-in period with any Clivus Multrum before this balance is reached. Rybizynski and the McGill group are also experimenting with a low-cost cement-block version of the Clivus Multrum type of composting toilet.

Composting Toilets and Graywater Disposal . . . Building Your Own, by Zandy Clark and Steve Tibbets (The Alternative Waste Treatment Association, Star Route 3, Bath, Maine 04530), features good description of commercial composting toilets plus plans for building your own. AWTA also publishes a quarterly newsletter called *Compost Toilet News*. The Office of Appropriate Technology, referred to earlier, publishes plans for a do-it-yourself composting pit privy that is suitable either for a detached outhouse or for incorporation into the house.

Some areas where composting toilets are installed allow for a reduction in the size of the septic system. The state of Maine, for example, allows a 40% to 50% reduction in field size and up to a 20% reduction in tank size.

The conventional decentralized method for treatment of graywater (waste water other than toilet water, which is called blackwater) is a septic tank, distribution lines, and a soil seepage system. It is time-proven and materials are readily available. It is efficient, inexpensive, and environmentally appropriate provided proper installation and maintenance procedures are followed.

Different experiments are being conducted to determine alternate methods of treating graywater. Note the system initially built into House 19. Bold experiments in alternative sanitation systems such as this are needed if we are to find more ecological ways of handling this waste resource.

When thinking about solid-waste disposal we should consider the three Rs—reduce, reuse, and recycle. We must first think in terms of reducing our consumption, then in terms of reusing goods, and finally in terms of how to recycle that "waste." Every decision to acquire additional goods should be examined with these thoughts in mind. Our houses should be designed to facilitate the reuse and recycling of consumer goods. For example, facilities to accommodate recyclable tins, bottles, and newspapers could be built in.

LIGHTING

The first step in designing ecological lighting is to make the best use of natural light. A home should be designed so that there is no need for artificial light during daylight hours. Some ways of accomplishing this were mentioned when we discussed windows. Nearly all useful light in a room comes from above. Clerestories and skylights therefore provide very good lighting, whereas windows close to the floor provide very poor lighting. Of course, light transmission will be better if windows and lighting fixtures are kept clean. Light-colored interior surfaces, especially for ceilings, walls, and draperies, reflect light and thus make more efficient use of both natural and artificial light.

Fluorescent lighting fixtures are three to five times more efficient than incandescents; they generate less heat, and they usually last seven to ten times longer. As fluorescents have a slight pulsation that annoys some people, it is recommended that they be installed behind baffles. They are therefore best suited for general lighting, whereas incandescents are best suited for task lighting—that is, concentrated lighting for desks, workbenches, kitchen work areas, sewing areas, etc.

Increased efficiency can be achieved by locating lights in a corner and thus reflecting light off two walls. You can get even further efficiencies by using light-colored lampshades with white liners or by using the G-40 globe-type bulbs that require no shades at all. Coupled with good lighting-system design, and all designs, should be a conscientious effort to conserve. We should all get in the habit of turning off unnecessary lights if we are planning to be out of the room for more than a few minutes.

APPLIANCES

When buying appliances, first attempt to determine what your real needs are and then shop for the most durable and energy-efficient ones. We have become accustomed to owning a wide variety of appliances that we consider absolutely essential. Elsewhere in the world, people get along quite well with much less. For example, among poorer Mexican people food is often cooked on a single small charcoal burner. On a visit to that country I used this method for several months and found it to be perfectly satisfactory. I adjusted my diet so that I ate more uncooked foods than I had been accustomed to. As a result, my diet no doubt improved, as certain vitamins and minerals are lost during the cooking process.

Refer to magazines such as *Canadian Consumer, Consumer's Bulletin*, and *Consumer Reports* to assist you in your selection. Factory seconds or used appliances can often be purchased for a fraction of the cost of new ones. Often appliance repairmen can be helpful in advising you which goods are the most trouble-free and the least costly to repair.

Consider the use of manually operated appliances wherever possible. It makes little sense to use an electric can opener when there are excellent manually operated ones that perform just as effectively, are manufactured from less resources, and of course use no electrical energy. Small appliances can save money and energy if used efficiently. For example, small broilers and toasters are more efficient than an oven broiler for some purposes, and coffee makers are more efficient than range tops for brewing coffee.

Cooking Appliances

When choosing a gas or electric range on the basis of energy efficiency, the choice will depend to a certain degree on how the electricity that you use is generated. Although the surface unit of an electric range is about 60% efficient compared to a 40% efficiency for a gas range, when fossil fuels are used to generate electricity, only about 33% of the energy in the fuel is converted to electricity; the rest is wasted.

About 5% to 10% (some people estimate as much as 30%) of the natural gas in homes is used by pilot lights. Electric ignition systems replace the pilot lights on new appliances and thus conserve energy. On some of the older gas models that do not have pilot lights, save matches by using a flint spark igniter (commonly used for welding torches). For electric range tops the rod-type surface elements are the best for good thermal contact. Ceramic tops are not nearly as efficient. Many people think that because electric self-cleaning ovens use a high-heat method to reduce grime to a residue, they use more energy than a regular oven. In fact, because of their extra insulation, self-cleaning ovens use less energy. Based upon 400 hours of baking, a self-cleaning oven uses about 250 kilowatt-hours of electricity compared to 350 kilowatt-hours for a conventional unit. Some people purchase a self-cleaning oven and then disconnect the self-cleaning unit after the warranty expires. General Electric has now produced a "Rapid-Clean" self-cleaning oven which the company claims further reduces energy consumption by 40%.

Microwave ovens use about a quarter as much energy as a conventional oven and can be used for nearly all your cooking needs; they should be carefully considered.

Some of the standard wall ovens will allow the addition of more insulation around the outside perimeter, increasing their efficiency.

VITA (Volunteers in Technical Assistance) has tested twelve different solar cookers, four of which have been rated very good. (Details can be obtained by writing Volunteers in Technical Assistance, 3706 Rhode Island Ave., Mt. Rainier, Md. 20822.)

Where you have access to either free or reasonably priced fuel wood, a wood cookstove is an environmentally appropriate alternative for cooking. Shelton and Shapiro's *The Woodburner's Encyclopedia* lists thirty-three different wood-burning cookstoves available in the United States. Specifications are included for each. Some Canadian firms also manufacture wood cookstoves, including Enterprise Foundry Co. Ltd. (Sackville, New Brunswick EOA 3CO), Enheat Ltd. (100 East Main St., Sackville, New Brunswick EOA 3CO), and Lunenburg Foundries and Engineering Ltd. (16 Brook St., Lunenburg, Nova Soctia BOJ 2CO). A fourth company, Elmira Stove Works (Elmira, Ontario), formed two years ago, has revived the famous Findlay Oval wood cookstove.

No independent studies have been done on the relative merits or efficiencies of wood-burning cookstoves, but a recent import from Ireland, the Stanley No. 8, is purported to be the most efficient such stove now on the North American market. It is precision-engineered, airtight, and well insulated, allowing it to fit close to other appliances and furnishings.

Another alternative is the combination fuel range. Malleable Iron Range Co. (Beaver Dam, Wisconsin 53916), for example, produces Monarch ranges which utilize coal/wood/gas, coal/wood/oil, or coal/wood/electric. House 19 has an Enterprise combination oil/wood cookstove.

Properly located, a wood cookstove can also serve as a valuable source of space heating and a cheerful focus around which to enjoy cold winter evenings.

Refrigerators and Freezers

The efficiency of a refrigerator varies depending on its overall size, amount of insulation, methods of defrosting, and the freezer compartment's location, size, and temperature. Choose a size to suit your needs. If it is too large you will be cooling unused space. If it is too small you will be making extra trips to the store and thus possibly wasting more nonrenewable energy.

Insulation can be added to the sides and top of the refrigerator and often between the coils and the box. Automatic-defrost models typically use 55% to 60% more energy than manual-defrost ones; however, the latter should be defrosted when frost is ¼" thick. It is best to have a freezer section with a completely separate door. There should be plenty of air circulation around the coils, or the compressor will be required to work overtime. The condenser should be kept clean for maximum efficiency; therefore it is helpful to have either casters or a removable grill to facilitate cleaning. The refrigerator should also be kept away from direct sources of heat such as air registers, stoves, and direct sunlight.

Most of the guidelines with respect to selection and maintenance of refrigerators are also applicable to freezers. The chest-type freezer is more efficient than the upright, as less cold air is lost when the door is opened. The freezer will be more efficient if it is kept filled and the food rotated.

Using some of the "old-fashioned" methods of preserving, such as root cellaring and drying of foods, will allow you to reduce the size of your refrigerator and freezer. The old-fashioned pantry is also a worthwhile feature to bring back. Often many things are kept in a refrigerator that need not be kept there at all.

Washing Machines and Dryers

The motor in an automatic washer actually uses only a small amount of energy. It is the hot water used that is the energy hog. In the average house, hot-water heating accounts for about 15% of the energy bill, and clothes washers consume a considerable portion of this. *Consumer Reports*, October 1974, reported that tests found that cold water cleans as well as hot and may prolong fabric life. Some types of washers are more conserving than others. For example, front-opening rotating-cylinder types use less water than top-loading agitator types. Those with a "sud saver" feature which allows wash water to be reused can save 20 of the normal 35 gallons used. Wash only full loads unless the washer has a water-level or load-size device.

The most ecological way of drying clothes is on a clothesline. A cleverly designed sun-tempered porch on the south side of a house can make the task of hanging clothes outside on cool days more pleasant. A greenhouse integral to the main house is an ideal place to dry clothes in the winter. For those who insist on using an automatic clothes dryer, it is best to have one with a moisture-sensing shutoff valve so that heat is supplied only when the clothes are damp. This feature can save from 10% to 15% of the energy otherwise consumed. For gas dryers, electric ignition systems to replace pilot lights are recommended. A bypass damper and an extra lint filter will allow warm air to exhaust into the house in winter; however, this could create excessively high humidity levels for some areas.

FURNITURE

The furnishings within should mirror the ecological ethic of the house itself. Again it is worthwhile to consider the way in which our ancestors lived. In the winter, wing chairs were set before the fireplace or wood stove. They held the heat of the fire and enfolded the sitter, protecting him from drafts. Open-armed chairs were placed in front of the window only in summer. Heavy carpets and drapes were brought out for the winter months, and warm-colored, soft fluffy material was used to cover furniture, whereas in summer, light-colored, smooth, absorbent fabrics were used. Beds were kept away from outside walls, and often curtains were draped around them at night. Many of these features are worth incorporating into a modern home.

FOOD SYSTEMS

It seems reasonable that any design for an ecological home should include plans for the provision of wholesome natural foods at a minimal cost to the natural environment. The best way, of course, is to grow your own. Not only are homegrown foods likely to be healthier for you, but it eliminates the vast expenditures of energy and resources required to bring produce from the grower to the consumer. It has been estimated that the Chinese wet-rice agricultural system produces more than 50 Btu in food energy for every Btu of human energy expended, but that the North American mechanized and centralized agricultural system produces only a fifth of a Btu in food energy for every Btu of fossil-fuel energy expended.

There are many excellent books on the market dealing with the subject of organic (meaning biological or ecological) gardening and farming, several of which have been included in the References section. It is not within the scope of this text to discuss the various organic methods in detail; however, I would like to mention a few recent developments.

In Berkeley, California, the Farallones Institute has established the Integral Urban House, an ecological urban homestead. On a 125 x 60′ lot six residents raise fish, chickens, and rabbits and grow their own fruits and vegetables. They also recycle most of their wastes and solar-heat their hot water. Crops are sown in raised beds surrounding the house and in rooftop containers filled with compost.

Laying chickens provide eggs and fryers, and rabbits provide meat. Honey bees provide several dozen pounds of honey per year, while a small fish pond serves for experiments in the raising of a native California fish. The food-raising system is detailed in the Olkowskis' *The City People's Book of Raising Food* (see References). Information about the Integral Urban House in general can be obtained by contacting Helga Olkowski, c/o Farallones Institute, 1516 Fifth St., Berkeley, Calif. 94710.

Ecology Action of the Midpeninsula (2225 El Camino Real, Palo Alto, Calif. 93406) began experimenting with the biodynamic/French intensive method of food production in 1972. Basically this involves double-dug raised beds, intensive planting, companion planting, and composting. Using simple low-cost manual tools, the experimenters have achieved yields two to four times the U.S. average. In addition, they use one-half to one-eighth as much water and one-half to one-sixteenth as much added nitrogen per pound of food produced as commercial agribiz. Jeavons' *How to Grow More Vegetables Than You Ever Thought Possible on Less Land Than You Can Imagine* gives a detailed how-to description of this method of organic gardening.

The Institute for Local Self-Reliance (1717 18th St., N.W., Washington, D.C. 20009) was established "to investigate the technical feasibility of community self-reliance in high-density living areas and to examine the implications of such decentralization," to quote from its April 1976 newsletter. The institute is also experimenting with biodynamic/French intensive gardening. It has successfully helped residents establish rooftop hydroponic gardens and a community commercial sprouting operation. A newsletter and various institute publications describe their methods.

The New Alchemist Institute has constructed on Cape Cod and Prince Edward Island what it describes as bioshelters or Arks—that is, shelters inspired by biological systems and able to provide their own energy and food and treat their own wastes. The Arks are comparable in size to small, family-operated commercial greenhouses but rely on solar, wind, and wood-fuel energy to function. The Cape Cod Ark is strictly a vegetable and fish production facility; the Prince Edward Island Ark also has a residential area for a family of six. The activities of the New Alchemists and a description of the Arks are thoroughly detailed in the *Journals of the New Alchemists*, available from the New Alchemy Institute (P.O. Box 432, Woods Hole, Mass. 02543).

Dr. Stuart B. Hill is establishing an institute at Macdonald College, McGill University, for research into alternatives to chemical agriculture. At the present time the institute has a resource center stocked with books, periodicals, and reprints on ecological agriculture and plans to establish research, teaching, and extension programs.

The Brace Research Institute, also at Macdonald College, has developed a new design for a greenhouse for colder regions. Basically, the greenhouse is oriented on an east-west axis; the south-facing roof is transparent, and the north-facing wall is insulated with a reflective cover on the interior face. A reduction has been found in the heating requirement of 30% to 40% compared to a standard double-layer-plastic greenhouse. A complete description is contained in *The Development and Testing of an Environmentally Designed Greenhouse for Colder Climates*, by Law *et al.*, published by the institute.

Cloudburst 2, edited by Vic Marks, features a chapter on the Sunpit Greenhouse built by Hal and Judy Hinds in New Brunswick, Canada. Their sun-heated sunken greenhouse, or sunpit, is basically a rectangular hole 4′ deep, 9′ wide, and 19′ long, running along a northeast-southwest axis within which a concrete foundation is constructed. The gable roof and gable ends are insulated all around except the southeast side, which is fitted with plastic. By using local and recycled materials and contributing their own labor, costs were kept to a minimum. A small blown-in electric space heater thermostatically set at 40° F. comes on occasionally during cold overcast days; however, the Hindses feel that with careful management there would be no need for this supplemental heat, as when the heater had been left disconnected and outside temperatures dropped to -20° F. the sunpit temperature never dropped below 35° F. So far the Hindses have successfully grown several varieties of salad greens all winter, forced many pots of bulbs, overwintered and propagated tender herbs and other plants, and started flowers and vegetables from seed for summer gardens.

Consider planting fruit trees and gardens wherever you are. Not only will you be rewarded with wholesome foods, but the challenge of growing your own, particularly in seemingly barren surroundings, will nourish your spirit and mind.

CONVENTIONAL SPACE-HEATING SYSTEMS

The vast majority of the population in Canada and the United States will continue to be dependent on conventional space-heating systems for a number of years. It is important therefore that serious measures be taken to conserve our quickly diminishing fossil-fuel resources.

A small, compact, airtight, well-insulated home with south-facing windows and insulated shutters will use considerably less fuel than a typical poorly built one. Similarly retrofitting an existing building can result in immense savings.

Oil and Gas Heating

You can conserve oil and gas by first ensuring that you know how your heating system functions and then ensuring that it runs at optimum efficiency.

The *Toronto Star* and the *Canadian Homes Magazine* conducted a survey in the fall of 1976 in order to determine the effectiveness of oil-furnace servicing and concluded that the servicing is largely a sham. The Canadian government estimates that it takes about an hour and a half to do an annual servicing, but of the fifty Toronto homes tested the serviceman was usually finished in half an hour with no improvement in furnace efficiency. Most oil companies sell service contracts to their customers and then subcontract the work. The more service calls the subcontractor makes, the more money he earns, and the less efficient the furnace, the more fuel the oil companies sell.

You must either do the servicing yourself or have the knowledge to ensure that the serviceman does it properly. In order to assist the consumer the Department of Energy Mines & Resources, Ottawa, has published a good book entitled *The Billpayer's Guide to Furnace Servicing* that shows all the steps a serviceman should go through. The book is available free of charge from Furnace Book, P.O. Box 2010, Weston, Ontario M9N 3R4.

Further fuel savings can be made by learning to live in cooler surroundings. The National Research Council of Canada has stated that for a typical southern-Canada location a thermostat setback of 1° F., assuming the setback is for eight hours every night during the heating season, will result in a 1% reduction in annual fuel consumption. An around-the-clock setback of 5° to 8° can reduce fuel consumption 15% to 20%. The setback can be done manually or by an automatic timer, which can be purchased at many heating-supply stores.

New high-speed flame-retention oil burners can reduce fuel consumption by as much as 10%. And automatic flue dampers have been developed which close immediately after the heat cycle, thus reducing heat loss up the chimney. These are availabe for use with oil-fired furnaces, but approval for use with gas furnaces is still pending.

The February and June 1976 issues of *Popular Science* magazine describe outside venting of oil and gas furnaces. Normally air is taken from the area immediately surrounding the furnace. With a very tightly sealed building the furnace often has difficulty "breathing," so outside air must be provided. The retrofitting of older buildings with outside venting typically results in fuel savings of from 15% to 25%.

It is important to ensure that the size of the furnace is compatible with the heat loss of the home. Oversized systems cycle more often than those designed just to meet the load and therefore lose more heat up the chimney. For small, energy-efficient houses the typical oil or gas furnace is much too large; however, small furnaces manufactured for house trailers are ideal and cost much less than a standard furnace.

Electric Heating

The efficiency of fossil-fuel-fired systems—that is, the amount of energy in the fuel that is available as useful heat output—is typically 65% to 80%. Electric heating in the home has an efficiency of 100%. However, a modern thermal generating station achieves an efficiency of only 35% to 40%. When line losses are considered, the overall efficiency of electric heating in the home is not likely to reach 35%. In addition, coal-fired generating stations, which produce most electricity in the United States, are among the main industrial sources of air pollution. Except for temporary, localized heat, electric space heating is therefore not recommended where the power is produced at thermal generating stations. It makes more sense to use electricity for space heating where power is derived from hydroelectric plants. However, it is generally not recommended as a backup to solar space heating because of the peak-load problems inherent in electricity.

There are several ways of making more effective use of electricity if it is used for space heating. The first is a little-known radiant heater which Alex Wade describes in his book *Thirty Energy-Efficient Houses You Can Build.* Basically it is a flat plate of tempered glass with a heating element fused to its back. One 1,500-watt unit placed high and angled down toward the occupants is usually adequate for one large room of a well-insulated house.

Some people choose to install infrared lights in small otherwise unheated spaces in order to provide instantaneous heat. In spite of the high wattage of these lamps the overall efficiency is quite high because of the relatively brief on time. Heat pumps are another effective way of using electricity. They work like a refrigerator by extracting heat from one space or object and pumping it to another. For space heating, heat can be extracted from low-temperature heat sources such as the ground, water, or air. Heat pumps can be reversed in summer to provide cooling to the home. The efficiency ratio of a heat pump averages about 2:1 to 4:1 compared to 0.65:1 for a typical oil furnace; however, it is most efficient when the temperature difference between the heat source and the home is minimal. Since most parts of Canada and the northern United States experience temperatures well below freezing for much of the heating season, water-to-air or ground-to-air systems are more efficient in these regions than air-to-air systems.

The National Film Board of Canada's film entitled *Heat Pump* describes Bill Loosely's ground-to-air heat pump that was installed in his Burlington, Ontario, home in 1951. It works so well that even today his heating bill is under $100 per year.

Heat pumps can be particularly effective with solar systems. A good example of this is House 8, which uses a solar-heated water-storage system from which the heat pump extracts heat for space heating at very low cost.

The main disadvantage of the heat pump over electric-resistance heating is its high initial cost and the generally higher maintenance costs.

WOOD HEATING

More and more people in various parts of Canada and the United States are turning to wood as either a primary or a secondary source of space heating. This movement is particularly noticeable in rural areas where wood is free or competitive in price with conventional fuels. The October 1977 issue of *Yankee* magazine featured an article on how one can easily determine whether wood heat is a good economic investment. It showed, for example, that in New England families would be better off heating with good hardwood at $80 per cord, in a high-efficiency stove (60% efficiency), than with oil at 53¢ per gallon; or better off heating with wood at $364 per cord than with electricity at 9 cents per kilowatt-hour.

Wood has many advantages over conventional fuels. It is a renewable resource, provided the forests and woodlots are properly maintained. It is a form of solar energy, as through the process of photosynthesis the sun's energy is stored in the trees.

Wood contains very little nitrogen and sulfur compared to coal and oil, and thus the emissions of polluting sulfur and nitrogen oxides are minimal. Wood stoves do emit a substantial amount of smoke; however, very little research has been carried out on the possible harmful effects of these emissions. Certainly if a large number of people in a densely populated area use wood heat, visual pollution can be a serious problem.

There is much speculation about the effect that carbon dioxide, a product of the combustion of both fossil fuels and wood, will have on the earth's climate. Whether wood is burned or is allowed to rot on the ground the net effect is the same—the same amount of CO_2 is emitted. The same is true for oxygen consumption and heat generation during combustion. The process is speeded up slightly, but there is no difference in the net effect.

The disadvantages of heating with wood are well known; however, many of them are much less a problem than in the old days. A chainsaw can cut down 500 Btu of wood energy for every Btu of gasoline energy expended, and with it one man can do the work of three men of another era. Modern high-efficiency airtight stoves use as little as one-quarter the wood that some of the old stoves used. The amount of labor involved could therefore amount to one-twelfth of what it was in the past. The amount of wood burned and thus the labor involved can be further reduced by ensuring that the space to be heated is small and well insulated. Larry Gay, the author of *The Complete Book of Heating with Wood*, heats his five-room Vermont home with two cords of wood per year. Since an acre of good hardwood, managed on a sustainable yield, can produce one cord of firewood per year, one does not need a large woodlot to be self-sufficient in terms of fuel.

Fireplaces

Of the many ways of heating with wood, the traditional fireplace is the least efficient. If used continuously, net efficiencies from 10% to 30% are probable; however, since with small fires or none at all and the damper open there is a net heat loss, the actual net efficiency of a traditional fireplace in a typical home is much lower. The efficiency can be improved somewhat in a number of ways. Various types of flue heat exchangers that extract heat from the hot flue gases are available or can be owner-built. These are quite effective, but care must be taken to ensure that the flue-gas temperature is not lowered to the point where the draft is adversely affected.

Tube grates, usually made of a series of U-shaped steel tubes, draw cold air in at the bottom of the fireplace and exhaust hot air near the top. In some designs circulation is speeded up by the use of a small blower.

Glass doors can be installed to restrict the flow of room air up the flue. These are probably most effective if the doors are left open when a strong fire is burning at a steady state so that radiation is not absorbed by the glass and if the doors are closed as the fire dies down.

Fireplaces are also more efficient if the chimney is inside and exposed to the space to be heated. Chimneys on exterior walls conduct considerable amounts of heat to the outside.

If the chimney is located so that solar heat from south-facing windows strikes it, a considerable amount of heat can be stored in the mass and be radiated into the living space as it cools later in the evening.

Although these ways of improving the efficiency of the traditional masonry fireplace do work, no careful objective testing has been done to measure their effectiveness.

Some prefabricated fireplaces of the heat-circulating design could be as efficient as freestanding stoves; however, as far as I know, no objective testing of these units has been done either. Water or air circulating in the fireplace walls effectively extracts some of the heat that would otherwise go up the flue.

In some prefabricated units, such as Northern Heatliner, outdoor air is heated within a double metal wall and circulated into the room. Some of this heated air then becomes the supply air for combustion in the fireplace. In addition to providing the fireplace with adequate combustion air, uncomfortable floor-level drafts are eliminated.

Kern's *The Owner-Built Home* gives plans for a low-cost do-it-yourself steel heat-circulating fireplace.

Wood-Burning Stoves

There are many good wood stoves on the market. One has to weigh the energy-efficiency, heating capability or power, ability to generate steady heat over a long period of time without refueling or adjustment, durability, ease of handling, amount of ash produced and ease of removing it, and cost. An assessment of the many models on the market can be mind-boggling. Fortunately, John W. Shelton, at Williams College, has been conducting independent efficiency tests on many models.

Where occasional quick heating is desired, Shelton recommends a lightweight thin-walled stove such as a drum or barrel stove, the Yankee, and the Ashley models 23 and 25. For long burns with a fairly steady output. stoves like the Riteway or one comparable to the Jøtul 118 and the Independence are best. High-energy-efficiency stoves like the Sevca, Lange 6303, or double drum are more desirable where the availability or cost of wood is the main concern.

Detailed results of the tests are included in the very excellent book *The Woodburner's Encyclopedia*, which Shelton wrote with Andrew B. Shapiro.

Recently the Canadian federal government's Combustion Research·Laboratory has also been conducting efficiency tests on wood-burning stoves. The results of these tests should soon be available. For information write: Combustion Research Laboratory, Bell's Corner, c/o Energy, Mines and Resources Canada, 555 Booth Street, Ottawa, Ontario K1A OT1.

Wood-Burning Furnaces and Boilers

Wood or multi-fuel furnaces or boilers can offer more comfort and convenience than a stove and are likely to be as efficient, although no independent tests have been conducted to confirm this. The multi-fuel units automatically switch to the conventional fuel when the wood burns out, thus allowing a person to go away for the weekend without worrying about water pipes freezing. Furnaces like the Valley Comfort will carry a charge of wood for over 14 hours on the coldest of days and up to 24 hours if desired.

Add-on wood-burning units that attach to an existing furnace are available and are inexpensive, but one must be careful to ensure that the sizing and placement of ducts, blowers, and flue are adequate.

In my opinion *The Woodburner's Encyclopedia* is the best wood-heating book on the market. In addition to covering all aspects of heating with wood, it includes comprehensive manufacturers' specification charts for most cookstoves, space-heating stoves, fireplaces, and furnaces as well as accessories, hot-water heaters, barrel stove kits, and wood splitters.

Lists of Canadian manufacturers and suppliers are included in Bruce McCallum's *Environmentally Appropriate Technology* and in *The Sun Builders* by Argue *et al.*

If you plan to heat with wood, make sure that you make use of the References section. Wood can be an enjoyable and effective way of heating a house, but you must understand the technology in order to optimize its effectiveness, minimize the chances of fire damage, and minimize impact on the natural environment.

SOLAR ENERGY FOR HEATING

Solar-energy technology has been around for many years. However, because of the availability of inexpensive fossil fuels it has been ignored by most until very recently. Now with the increased cost and current and predicted shortages of fossil fuels, interest in solar energy has become widespread.

Advantages over Conventional Energy Sources

Solar energy has many advantages over conventional and other alternative fuels. It is an abundant, nondepleting, nonpolluting resource. It lends itself to the establishment of small-scale, decentralized manufacturing units and thus can make use of local capital and labor. Though in some cases solar hardware is initially quite costly, the operating costs on a good system are quite low.

William A. Shurcliff, the foremost cataloguer of solar-heated buildings, thinks that perhaps 80% or more of the buildings he has surveyed are not economic when measured against today's gas and oil prices. Amory Lovins, one of the world's leading experts on nuclear energy and a strong proponent of "soft technologies," points out that we should not be comparing the cost of solar energy with that of conventional nonrenewable fossil-fuel energy but rather with that of the other alternatives. Solar energy is much less expensive than energy from the tar sands or nuclear reactors and much less demanding on the environment.

It is very difficult to generalize about the economic feasibility of solar energy in any case, as it depends on such variables as the design of the solar system, the initial purchase price of the solar system, interest charges, maintenance costs, the future cost and availability of other sources of energy, geographic location, and building type.

Tables 1 to 4, excerpted from Bruce McCallum's

Environmentally Appropriate Technology, will serve to illustrate the way in which estimates of economic feasibility are commonly arrived at. The figures are McCallum's estimates. Not included in this accounting is the possible appreciation in house value as time progresses and conventional fuels become costlier and less available, nor the cost savings to society through the use of a nonpolluting, renewable resource.

Before reaching any decision regarding the type and size of heating a system, be it solar or otherwise, you should first attempt to minimize heat loss by using insulation, multiple-glazed windows, insulated shutters or drapes, insulated and double doors, weatherstripping, caulking, and other energy-conserving methods as discussed in previous sections. Conservation methods are usually less costly than solar-system installation. In selecting a solar system you must look at more than just the economies of the system. Some attempt must be made to assess the environmental impact of the processing, manufacturing, and transport of the system materials and components. A very high-efficiency collector may be less environmentally appropriate than a lower-efficiency one.

It is not possible here to discuss all of the developments in the solar-energy field. The purpose of this book is primarily to give a detailed photographic and narrative description of a number of working solar-heated homes. However, in order to increase your understanding of these descriptions, a brief discussion of the principles of solar energy and various solar systems applicable to domestic use is in order.

Table 1: Oil or Gas Heating System

1,500 sq. ft. house
Oil or gas furnace—provides 100% of total requirement
$1,000 Capital cost
400 Fuel cost (20%/yr. inflation)
130 Principal and interest (at 12%)
20 Operating cost (20%/yr. inflation)

550 = Year heating costs
50 = Hot-water heating (electricity, gas, or oil)
$ 600 = Yearly heating costs (for yr. 1)

Year	Operating cost Oil or gas—20%/yr. inflation		Principal and interest		Total heating cost/yr.
1	$ 470	+	$130	=	$ 600
2	564	+	130	=	694
3	677	+	130	=	807
4	812	+	130	=	942
5	974	+	130	=	1,104
6	1,169	+	130	=	1,299
7	1,403	+	130	=	1,533
8	1,684	+	130	=	1,814
9	2,021	+	130	=	2,151
10	2,425	+	130	=	2,555
11	2,910	+	130	=	3,040
12	3,492	+	130	=	3,622
13	4,190	+	130	=	4,320
14	5,028	+	130	=	5,158
15	6,034	+	130	=	6,164
16	7,241	+	130	=	7,371
17	8,689	+	130	=	8,819
18	10,427	+	130	=	10,557
19	12,512	+	130	=	12,642
20	13,014	+	130	=	13,144

Table 2: Solar and Electric Heating System

1,500 sq. ft. house
Solar-heating system—provides 65% of total heat requirements
South-facing windows with shutters—provide 10% of total heat requirements
Supplement heat—electricity—provides 25% of total heat requirements, 20%/yr. inflation
$6,000 Capital cost
778 Principal and interest (at 12% interest)
40 Operating cost (electricity to power pumps and fans—20%/yr. inflation)

818 Solar heating and cooling system costs/yr.
120 Supplementary heating costs (25% of total heat requirements)

$ 938 Yearly heating and cooling costs (for yr. 1)

Year	Supplementary heat (electricity —20%/yr. inflation)		Operating cost (electricity —20%/yr. inflation)		Principal and interest		Total heating cost/yr.
1	$ 120	+	$ 40	+	$778	=	$ 938
2	168	+	48	+	778	=	994
3	202	+	58	+	778	=	1,038
4	242	+	70	+	778	=	1,090
5	290	+	84	+	778	=	1,152
6	348	+	97	+	778	=	1,223
7	418	+	116	+	778	=	1,312
8	502	+	139	+	778	=	1,419
9	602	+	167	+	778	=	1,547
10	722	+	200	+	778	=	1,700
11	866	+	240	+	778	=	1,884
12	1,039	+	288	+	778	=	2,105
13	1,246	+	346	+	778	=	2,370
14	1,495	+	415	+	778	=	2,688
15	1,794	+	498	+	778	=	3,070
16	2,153	+	598	+	778	=	3,528
17	2,584	+	718	+	778	=	4,079
18	3,109	+	862	+	778	=	4,741
19	3,731	+	1,034	+	778	=	5,543
20	4,477	+	1,241	+	778	=	6,496

Table 3: Hooper Solar-Heating System

1,500 sq. ft. house
Solar-heating system—provides 90% of total heating requirements
South-facing windows with shutters—provide 10% of total heat requirements
$10,000 Capital cost
1,300 Principal and interest (at 12% interest)
60 Operating cost (electricity for pumps and fans, 20%/yr. inflation)
$ 1,360 Yearly heating (and cooling) costs (for yr. 1)

Year	Operating cost (electricity —20%/yr. inflation)		Principal and interest		Total heating cost/yr.
1	$ 60	+	$1,300	=	$1,360
2	72	+	1,300	=	1,372
3	86	+	1,300	=	1,386
4	103	+	1,300	=	1,403
5	124	+	1,300	=	1,424
6	149	+	1,300	=	1,449
7	179	+	1,300	=	1,479
8	214	+	1,300	=	1,514
9	257	+	1,300	=	1,557
10	308	+	1,300	=	1,608
11	369	+	1,300	=	1,669
12	443	+	1,300	=	1,743
13	531	+	1,300	=	1,831
14	637	+	1,300	=	1,937
15	764	+	1,300	=	2,064
16	917	+	1,300	=	2,217
17	1,100	+	1,300	=	2,400
18	1,320	+	1,300	=	2,620
19	1,584	+	1,300	=	2,884
20	1,901	+	1,300	=	3,201

Table 4: Solar and Wood Heating System

1,500 sq. ft. house
Solar-heating system—provides 65% of total heat requirements
South-facing windows with shutters—provide 10% of total heat requirements
Supplementary heat—wood—provides 25% of total heat requirements
$6,000 Capital cost (assuming wood is available free)
778 Principal and interest (at 12% interest)
40 Operating cost (20%/yr. inflation)
818 Solar heating and cooling system costs/yr.
30 Supplementary heating costs (25% of total heat requirements)
000 (Wood is free at nominal cost for chainsaw fuel and
000 maintenance, 5%/yr. inflation)
$ 848 Yearly heating and cooling costs (for yr. 1)

Year	Supplementary heat (wood—5%/yr. inflation)		Operating cost (electricity —20%/yr. inflation)		Principal and interest		Total heating cost/yr.
1	$30	+	$ 40	+	$778	=	$ 848
2	32	+	48	+	778	=	858
3	34	+	58	+	778	=	870
4	36	+	70	+	778	=	884
5	38	+	84	+	778	=	900
6	40	+	97	+	778	=	915
7	42	+	116	+	778	=	936
8	44	+	139	+	778	=	961
9	46	+	167	+	778	=	991
10	48	+	200	+	778	=	1,026
11	50	+	240	+	778	=	1,068
12	53	+	288	+	778	=	1,119
13	56	+	346	+	778	=	1,180
14	59	+	415	+	778	=	1,252
15	62	+	498	+	778	=	1,338
16	65	+	598	+	778	=	1,441
17	68	+	718	+	778	=	1,564
18	71	+	862	+	778	=	1,711
19	75	+	1,034	+	778	=	1,887
20	79	+	1,241	+	778	=	2,098

Principles of Solar Energy

Of the solar energy striking the earth, 7% is in the ultraviolet range, 47% is in the visible-light range, and 46% is in the infrared (heat) range of the spectrum. This energy is absorbed, reflected and deflected, and can pass right through various substances. There are three ways that it is used. First, it can be used to generate chemical conversions, of which photosynthesis is the best example. Second, it can be used to generate electrical conversions. One example of this is solar energy striking crystalline forms of certain elements, such as silicone, to free electrons which generate electrical direct current. Considerable research and development is being done in this area, particularly in the United States, and although costs are presently prohibitive for residential electrical-supply purposes, many scientists feel that these solar cells will be economic within two or three years. Third, solar energy is used for thermal conversion—the collection and use of solar energy as heat energy. It is this last use which is the concern of this text.

Brightly polished surfaces reflect most solar radiation, while snow reflects about 85%. Transparent surfaces allow nearly all the shortwave solar radiation to pass through, while very dark surfaces absorb nearly all. Heat energy is then re-radiated in the form of longwave radiation. These long waves heat air molecules and other objects that they come in contact with, but do not readily return through the transparent surfaces. This is known as the greenhouse effect. In the case of domestic solar heating, this trapped heat is then transported to living spaces or to a shortage bin for later use.

Solar energy can be collected for use in space heating by passive or active means or by a combination of both.

Passive Systems

The most commonly accepted definition of a passive solar-heating system is one in which the thermal energy flows occur by natural means. In other words, no external power is needed for it to function.

Often passive solar systems are categorized into three basic types: direct gain, indirect gain, and isolated gain. In direct-gain types the solar radiation enters the living space through south-facing glazing and then strikes massive building components such as stone, concrete, or brick fireplaces, floors, or walls. These components absorb the solar radiation during the day and re-radiate warmth to the cooler rooms at night. Without proper design, excessive glare and temperature fluctuations can result.

In the second type, indirect gain, some massive element intercepts the solar radiation and then transfers it to the living space. The mass Trombe wall made famous by Felix Trombe of France is a good example of this. It consists of a south-facing, black-painted concrete wall behind a layer of glazing. Air is heated between the concrete wall and the glass, rises, and enters the living space through vents at the top of the wall. Cooler air from the house is returned by natural convection through vents at the bottom of the wall. Heat also migrates through the concrete and radiates into the dwelling from the wall's interior surface.

A water Trombe wall of the type used in the house of another famous solar pioneer, Steve Baer, illustrates another kind of indirect-gain passive solar system. Here 55-gallon oil drums are stacked horizontally behind a vertical south-facing glass wall. The drums absorb solar radiation and then re-radiate heat into the living space when the large exterior insulated panels are closed at night.

A third kind of indirect-gain system is the water pond developed by Harold Hay. Here water bags in the structure absorb solar radiation during the day. When movable insulated covers are slid across the roof to cover the bags at night, the water bags give up stored heat to the living space below. The house can also be cooled during the summer by allowing the water bags to absorb house heat during the day and then radiate it to the cool night sky. This system is more suitable to warm climates where freezing conditions and snow do not occur.

In the third basic type of passive solar system, isolated gain, solar radiation is collected in an area distinct from the living space and then transferred either directly to the living space or first to a storage mass. Attached solar greenhouses are a good example of this concept.

Examples of all of these types are given in the case studies.

A good passive solar system will demonstrate an appreciation of the relationship of spatial arrangement to efficient energy-flow patterns, the unique thermal properties of various building materials, and the climatic characteristics of the site.

Hybrid Systems

In the interest of system efficiency, often a mechanical assist to natural energy flows is employed. The American Institute of Architects Research Corporation in its recent "Survey of Passive Solar Buildings" defines as "hybrid" any solar system where this assist is from collector to storage, or from storage to living space, but not from both. When all the energy flow within a system is forced, it is classified as an active solar system.

Active Systems

Most of the efforts to date in solar technology have been directed toward active systems—that is, systems composed of a solar collector, a heat-transfer medium (usually air or water), devices for heat storage and heat distribution, and a control system. The heat-transfer medium is used to transfer heat from the collector to storage or directly to the dwelling. The flat-plate collector, either the liquid or air type, is used for nearly all domestic applications.

Liquid-Type Flat-Plate Collectors

A typical flat-plate collector is composed of one or multiple glazings, an absorber plate, a fluid transfer medium, insulation, and a shallow box to house these components.

The glazing, which traps sunlight using the greenhouse effect, is a transparent material such as glass, acrylic, fiberglass-reinforced polyester, or a thin plastic film such as Mylar, Tedlar, Teflon, or Lexan. The plastic and fiberglass glazings are lighter and easier to handle than glass, in many cases are less subject to breakage, and usually are less expensive. Their disadvantage is that they are generally more subject to deterioration from high temperatures, ultraviolet radiation, and weather. The efficiency of glazing can be improved in many ways. For example, certain coatings applied to the exterior reduce reflectivity, low-iron glass will reduce absorption losses within the glass, evacuating the space between two adjacent layers of glazing will reduce conduction, and convection losses and installing a nonabsorbing egg-crate honeycomb between glazings or between glazing materials and the absorber will further reduce convection losses.

There are three types of absorber plates commonly used: the open-faced type, in which the water trickles down over the front surface; the tube-in-plate type, in which the liquid passage is integral to the plate; and the sandwich type, in which the metal tubes transporting the heat-transfer medium are fastened on either side of a flat plate.

Generally, the absorber plate is made of sheet steel, copper, or aluminum and painted flat black. Efficiency of the absorber can be increased by chemically bonding, electroplating, or painting a selective surface onto the plate in order to reduce the amount of re-radiation from the plate, by applying a microgrooved structure to the plate which discourages emission of longwave radiation without discouraging absorption of solar radiation, and by keeping the absorber plate cooler.

However, the plate designer must always ask if these attempts to increase efficiency are worthwhile. Nearly every change made in the interest of increasing efficiency results in increased costs, decreased reliability, or both.

Insulation is required to minimize heat loss out the back and sides of the collector. Care must be taken to ensure that the type of insulation is appropriate for the operating temperature of the collector. Savings can be made on insulation and roofing if the collectors are designed to be an integral part of the roof. The glazing then serves the same function as roof shingles.

Air-Type Flat-Plate Collectors

Experts cannot agree on which system is best—the fluid-type or the air-type flat-plate collector. Air-type collectors have many advantages. They are not subject to corrosion and freezing. Air leakage and thermal contraction and expansion are only minor problems compared to liquid systems. The main disadvantage of air is its low heat capacity. About 3,500 cu. ft. of air are required in order to transport the same amount of heat as 1 cu. ft. of water. Air systems therefore require large ductwork with the subsequent loss of space, and generally require larger storage volume than fluid systems. There are three common designs of air-type flat-plate collectors.

Alternatives to Flat-Plate Collectors

Evacuated tubes looking somewhat like banks of fluorescent tubes have been developed by some companies. Although they are very efficient, their cost at this time is quite high, often twice as much as for typical flat-plate collectors.

Various types of concentrating collectors have been developed which focus a concentrated beam of sunlight on the heat-transport medium, creating high temperatures. Most of these are incapable of focusing diffuse light and require mechanical devices to track the sun. As a result they are more costly and more subject to mechanical breakdown than low-technology systems. A notable exception is the Compound Parabolic Collector developed at the U.S. Argonne National Laboratory by Dr. Roland Winston. It is capable of performing at 50% efficiency and developing temperatures 150° F. above that of the outside air. Basically this collector is composed of a series of troughs whose sides are sections of a parabolic cylinder. Both direct and diffuse radiation are concentrated on copper tubes containing the heat-transfer fluid at the bottom of each trough, without the need of costly tracking devices.

There are literally hundreds of approaches to solar-collector design, and the race is neck and neck. No one knows which approach, or which dozen approaches, will eventually gain a decisive lead.

Collector Orientation

According to J.R. Sasaka in *Solar-Heating Systems for Canadian Buildings* (Building Research Note No. 104, Division of Building Research, National Research Council of Canada), the optimum orientation of the collector is due south, but if the collector is mounted 15° from south there is only 3% less energy collected. At 30° from true south, only 10% less energy is collected.

He goes on to state that the optimum altitude is the latitude +20° but an altitude of latitude +5° or latitude +30° will yield energy collection within 3% of the optimum. A vertical wall will collect 10% below the optimum, although reflection from snow or a man-made reflector will increase the energy collected.

Heat Storage

For active systems there are basically two ways of storing heat. The first, termed the "sensible" storage of heat, uses rocks or water, both of which will rise in temperature as heat energy is transferred from the heat-transfer medium. If water is the heat-transfer medium, it is usually used as the storage medium too, as this combination reduces the size and number of heat exchangers, thus improving efficiency and decreasing costs. With air-type collectors, rocks or crushed gravel are most often used, thus making heat exchangers unnecessary. The case studies give detailed descriptions of the construction and operation of various storage systems.

The second method of storing heat relies on the heat of fusion when substances experience a change of phase in the temperature range associated with space heating—that is, between 90° and 120° F. Certain salt hydrates and paraffin waxes have been used which, when they undergo a phase change, absorb or release considerable amounts of latent heat per unit volume, thus permitting storage volumes much smaller than those for water. There are some problems, such as heat exchange during change of phase because of volume changes, component separation (salts separating out of solution and unable to recycle or continue phase changes), and supercooling and fire hazards with some materials. These problems still have to be fully resolved before phase-change storage mediums can gain wide acceptance.

Heat Distribution

The main criterion for a heat-distribution system is that it be compatible with the existing or proposed conventional system.

When rock storage is used, a thermostatically controlled damper allows air to blow through the rock storage, become heated, and enter the conventional air-distribution system. When water storage and a conventional forced-air system are used, often a heat-exchange coil similar to a car radiator is installed in the hot-air-supply duct.

System Controls

One temperature sensor is placed in the collector and another in the storage tank. When the temperature in the collector is warmer than in the storage tank by a preset amount (usally 10-15° F.), a differential thermostat activates the pump or blower which transports the heat-transfer medium through the collector.

Similar sensors and thermostats activate valves or dampers which allow the solar heat from the collector to be supplied either to storage or directly to the house, or they allow heat to pass from storage to the house. They also activate the switchover to the conventional system, if one exists.

Sizing the System

It is difficult to generalize about the amount of solar-collector area for a building, as it will depend on the collector performance; insulation for the area; building heat demands; the type, size, and heat-loss characteristics of the storage; and on the percentage of total heat requirements one expects to derive from the solar system. A rule of thumb often used is that for systems that can supply two or three days of storage, the collector areas should be roughly one-half of the heated floor area of the building. However, House 6, located near Ottawa, Ontario (8,830 degree-days), has a heated floor area of 1,850 sq. ft. and only 200 sq. ft. of collector area. The secret is super insulation, weather-stripping, and caulking.

This illustrates the need to make detailed calculations for each unique building, location, and solar system. Anderson's *The Solar Home Book*, Leckie's *Other Homes and Garbage*, and Montgomery's *The Solar Decision Book* detail how these calculations can be made.

For the storage size, again it is difficult to generalize, as this will depend on the heat losses of the building and the storage container, the heat capacity of the storage medium, the efficiency of the heat-transfer medium, and the upper and lower limits of the storage temperature.

Another rule of thumb often applied to short-term storage systems is that from 1 to 2 imperial gallons (1.2 to 2.4 U.S. gallons) of water storage (or its equivalent heat capacity) be used for every 1 sq. ft. of collector. Long-term storage is possible, but the cost in terms of space and material is a deterrent to many builders. Most experts feel that seasonal storage is more suitable to larger buildings and multiple-housing units, which can accommodate the larger storage tanks and which usually have less heat loss and thus less heat demand for any given area than a single-family unit. It is recommended that specific calculations be made in accordance with the details given in the books just mentioned.

Solar Domestic Hot-Water Systems

Solar domestic hot-water systems have been used in Florida, Japan, Israel, and Australia for decades. The main features of any system are basically the same as those of solar space-heating systems. Rather than having a separate collector for the hot water, however, many systems simply install a heat exchanger within the space-heating system's storage. In some cases a small steel tank is simply placed within the rock storage, allowing the water inside to be heating by conduction.

A very simple system works on the thermosiphon principle. The water-storage tank is installed above the collector so that the temperature difference between the water in the hot top and the cold bottom of the tank causes water to circulate through the collector without the need of a pump.

Part II

CASE STUDIES OF SOLAR-HEATED HOUSES

The houses selected in this study were chosen to illustrate the wide variety of solar-heated buildings in the colder regions of North America. Although because of financial and time limitations we restricted our study to homes in central and eastern Canada and the mideastern and northeastern regions of the United States, we feel that the climatic characteristics of these areas are sufficiently varied to make the studies applicable to most temperate regions of the globe.

Most were also chosen because they had gone through a shakedown period—a period in which the owners sometimes had to make substantial modifications to render the buildings and their systems more energy-efficient. Some are still not quite complete, but the growing pains their owners have experienced are as important to report as the satisfaction of owners and builders of homes that have been relatively trouble-free.

The format for each case study was designed to be consistent from one case to the other, thus making it easier to make comparisons. Also, if you are interested at one point in studying only one aspect of building design, such as windows, the format facilitates this; there is a heading for windows for each case study. Some headings—such as for food supply, landscaping, and household appliances—do not occur for houses where the information is of insufficient interest. There is also some case-to-case variation in the number and detail of drawings explaining solar systems and in the breakdowns of initial costs and yearly savings resulting from solar heating, because the data available were often scanty. However, in each case we have done our best to provide enough detail to permit an adequate understanding of the house. Every effort has been made to ensure that the information presented here is accurate and up to date.

ACTIVE SYSTEMS

HOUSE 

Little of our effort goes for our survival. Most of it in some complex way goes to satisfy or stimulate our fantasies—toward our feeling good. Yet we spend less effort making where we live beautiful and good feeling than we do traveling to other places to get away from our bad ones. Travel less—give more to making where you are a paradise.

—*Rainbook*

Solar Manor

NEIL and KATHY SWITZER

Neil and Kathleen Switzer have researched, designed, and built one of Canada's first generation of solar-heated homes. Their house, in Ontario in the heart of the Niagara Peninsula, has been conscientiously and comprehensively designed by ecological principles.

Neil and Kathy see themselves as part of a larger future movement: "People are beginning to recognize their social responsibility to live within our planetary means," according to Neil, "and in the process of learning how to do more with less, they are realizing that an outwardly simple life can also produce an inwardly more rewarding and rich life-style."

"We're especially proud," says Kathy, "to think that our son Abraham—Abe—is part of a new generation that will always have lived in a solar-heated home and will grow up with an appreciation for the natural independent energy forces."

Supporting their beliefs, they will point out the various social scientists and futurists who have recognized and identified the emerging social movement as a potential means of resolving many of the present economic, social, and environmental predicaments plaguing us today. Central, dominant values in this growing movement include material simplicity, human-scale organization, self-determination, ecological awareness, and personal growth. As Neil says, "We can all afford to start living for the future." Their example should inspire us as to what can be done with limited means, and a lot of dedication toward living in harmony with the natural environment.

When asked about the design parameters which determined the building of their home, Neil replied, "Since I'm trained in environmental planning and design as a landscape architect, it was only natural that our house should exemplify a strong environmental bias. The following environmentally appropriate design parameters upon which our design would evolve were set back in 1974:

"First, incorporation of energy-efficient architectural features—that is, compact design, microclimatic orientation, optimum insulation, minimum glazing strategically located, double glazing with storms and shutters, airlock entry, proper caulking and weatherstripping, and so on.

Smithville, Ontario
1,400 sq. ft. living area

"Second, utilization of appropriate technology, including solar space- and water-heating systems, wind generator, energy-efficient appliances, and composting toilets.

"Third, low-impact building materials—minimizing use of nonrenewable resources or materials requiring high-energy inputs for manufacture, and maximizing use of recycled materials.

"Fourth, economy of design, permitting simple do-it-yourself construction techniques, and recognition of total costs of construction or manufacture.

"Fifth, the art of design—by which I mean the qualitative value of design which crafts the personal living environment to suit the individual's total being."

The product of the above design process eventually became known as Solar Manor. Construction began in the spring of 1975, and the Switzers moved in in the spring of 1977. "We could have built faster if we'd mortgaged, or received a portion of the government assistance that others received for similar projects, but without these we proceeded in the owner-built style of building on nights, weekends, and holidays as time and funds permitted."

The Switzers have successfully completed a major portion of their original goal, as the accompanying text will attest, with the remaining portions still intended, only now at a "little more of a reasonable pace."

Solar Manor is a very fine example of ecological design. It is nestled into the south edge of a 2-acre woodlot and is thus well protected from winter storm winds.

LOCATION AND ORIENTATION

The house is located on RR#1, Smithville, Ontario. Neil used his professional landscaper's skills to site it on the rural 18-acre lot to take best advantage of the micro-climatic and physical features of the property. The open agricultural lands have been preserved for farming, while the house has been tucked into the south-central edge of a mixed oak, hickory, and pine woodlot. The shelterbelt effect of the 2-acre woodlot effectively dissipates winter wind velocities by approximately 50%, so that the Switzers enjoy "a relatively tranquil serenity on even the stormiest of winter nights." Exposure to the summer southwest breezes provides pleasant summer ventilation. Neil has not had time to really begin his low-maintenance natural-garden concept, but the preservation of the existing vegetation alone gives the house a most pleasant woodland setting.

The house axis is positioned east-west to provide ample southern roof exposure for the solar collectors. Geographically, the house is situated at 43° N. Lat.

ARCHITECTURAL FEATURES

The two-story building contains 1,400 sq. ft. of living area over a 32 x 26′ concrete-block basement. The attached garage, measuring 15 x 22′, has an unfinished attic space above which will be suitable as an extra bedroom if required later.

Situated on the northwest corner of the house, the garage is strategically placed to act as an effective thermal buffer from prevailing northwest winter winds. The main-entry deck and patio on the west side of the house is protected by the garage and leads to a vestibule with two doorways, which provides an airlock as well as a wet area. Inside, an open central hallway runs from the entry, between the living room and bathroom, to the kitchen and dining room on the east side. The kitchen, dining room, and hallway are all floored with antique quarry tile on a 2″ concrete base to provide not only a low-maintenance floor, but also an additional heat mass within the building to moderate temperature fluctuations in both winter and summer. The Fisher stove is located in the central hall. The hall wall is faced in recycled red brick to provide additional thermal mass and fire protection.

The L-shaped second floor contains two open-concept work areas—one for Kathy's sewing and crafts and the other for Neil's drafting equipment. The open concept allows them to work comfortably in a small space while being able to observe what is happening in the rest of the house.

The Switzers chose to accept the slight inconvenience of having only one bathroom in order to use less materials during construction and to reduce the building's heat load. The building's capital and operational costs were thus reduced. The bathroom was located on the first floor next to the kitchen in order to min-

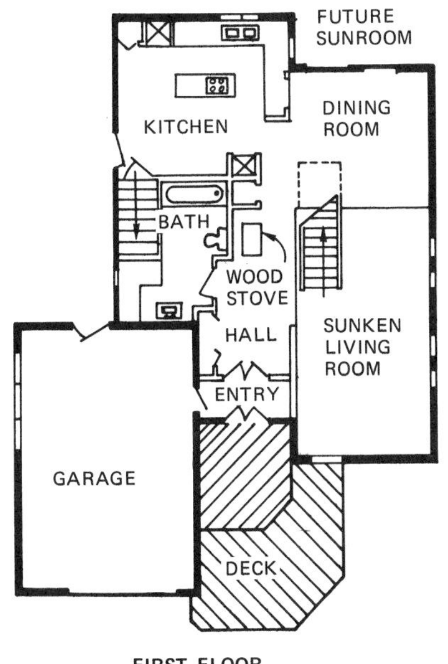

FIRST FLOOR

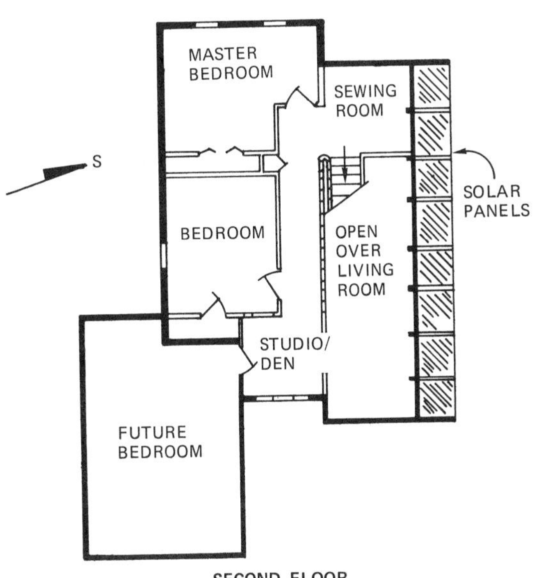

SECOND FLOOR

imize overall plumbing pipe runs and to minimize the distance that hot water has to flow from the domestic hot-water tank in the basement. Also the Switzers felt that since more of their waking hours would be spent on the lower level, the first-floor location would be more convenient for them and guests than a second-floor location near the bedrooms.

Construction is post-and-beam with 2 x 4 frame infill, with the exception of the low south wall, which has been constructed of 2 x 6s to accommodate the hidden duct run to the collector. The posts and beams are original hand-hewn barn beams, with some coming from a local barn, others bought at an auction, and still others obtained from a landscape-contractor friend. The 3 x 14 ceiling joists of British Columbia Douglas fir were salvaged from a century-old school in nearby Hamilton. The rough-sawn 2 x 8 floor joists on the second level and the 1″-thick random-width oak floorboards were also salvaged from the same school.

Sixteen-foot lengths of 4′-wide acrylic twinskin are used for the collector glazing.

Exterior Walls

The Switzers wanted to use wood for the exterior siding, as it is a renewable resource. Of the many alternatives available, 4 x 8′ sheets of redwood paneling were chosen for a number of reasons. There are fewer joints with 4 x 8′ sheets than with typical shiplap or board-and-batten siding, which thereby minimizes infiltration. Furthermore, redwood is naturally resistant to rot and termites, and the panels come with a factory-applied water repellant. In any case, the redwood paneling was locally in stock and was the cheapest siding available that had the rough-sawn look that Neil and Kathy desired. Acknowledging the dwindling stocks of redwood, Neil says, "Perhaps we bent our rules somewhat on this one, but we went for the better product at the cheapest price. Cedar should be the logical choice, but it is extremely knotty, is more expensive, and was not available at the time." (According to a Club of Rome report, based on existing reserves and present rates of consumption, we will run out of redwood by 1983.)

Detail of collector glazing material.

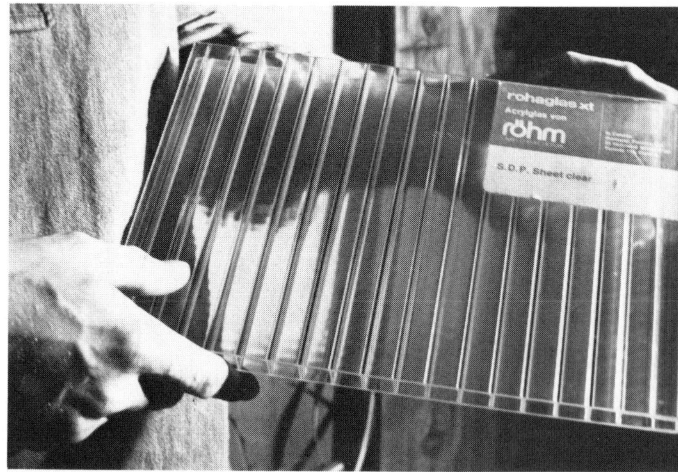

Interior Walls and Ceilings

Gypsum board ⅜″ thick is used throughout and is accented by the exposed ceiling joists and hand-hewn barn beams and posts. As mentioned, reclaimed brick is utilized in the central hall and kitchen.

Roof

The ⅜″ exterior-grade plywood sheathing is covered with simulated-cedar asphalt shingles. Real cedar was preferred, but the cost was four times greater than the asphalt. The glazing on the roof's south pitch doubles as collector glazing and the roof's weathertight skin. The exterior wood struts at the roof peak are described by Neil as pure embellishment. He explains that he felt the sharp roof angles would have appeared harsh had he not offset and balanced them with the struts.

Insulation Summary

Ceiling: R-30; fiberglass batts
Walls: R-18; fiberglass batts and exterior Styrofoam. This combination is billed by the manufacturer as the "Super Insulation System," for it provides a continuous thermal barrier, thus reducing heat loss through studs and joints.
Basement: R-12; 2 x 4 studwalls filled with 3½" fiberglass batts

All insulation is covered on the inside with polyethylene vapor barrier, and the house is carefully weatherstripped and caulked throughout.

Doors

The double entrance doors, garage doors, and all interior doors are all pre-1900 pieces, and with refinishing add a special class from an age of craftsmanship in everyday skills and trades. The wood kitchen door and storm as well as the wood-frame Mason sliding glass door off the dining room on the east side of the house are all new, and were chosen for their weathertight qualities. Eventually some form of insulated curtain or shutter will be used over the sliding glass door during the winter.

Windows

Mason wood-sash thermopane windows are predominantly used throughout; with their placement and the open-concept building design they permit good cross-ventilation. Two custom thermopane windows were designed and constructed—one angled to match the roof slope floods the study with light, while the other contains an old stained-glass window that transforms the afternoon sunlight into a kaleidoscope of color on the living-room walls.

SOLAR-HEATING SYSTEM

Neil designed and built the solar system himself, with help from Kathy and their families.

Collector

The 500 sq. ft. of Solarfoil air-type collectors were designed and fabricated on site by Neil and face due south, sloped at 60° to the horizontal. The collector glazing material is SDP-16 acrylic twinskin manufactured by Chemachryl Plastics of Toronto. While recognizing the limitation of acrylic, Neil says advantages include good light transmittance, light weight, good structural stability, low breakage hazard, and better insulating properties than double glass. Drawbacks include a high coefficient of expansion (up to 1" in a 16' length), a maximum operating temperature of 160°, and an eventual optical deterioration. The beauty of 4 x 16' panels, says Neil, was the ease of installation with a minimum of joints and internal supports to provide maximum effective collector area. The high coefficient of expansion is provided for in the aluminum-channel clamping bar, in which the glazing floats between butyl gaskets greased with silicone lubricant. Silicone sealant is also used around the clamping bar, providing flexibility without breaking the bond. The glazing and sealant are thoroughly examined every fall and spring when a protective tarp is removed and installed.

The unique collector absorber plate has been pioneered by Neil in Canada. He has trade-named it Solarfoil. It consists of slit and expanded aluminum foil (.003" thick), primed, painted flat black, and layered six deep to form a mesh to absorb incoming solar radiation in depth. The advantage of this system is that high collector efficiencies result from the high ratio of heat-transfer area to volume, and high heat-transfer capability results in relatively lower matrix surface temperatures. This provides quicker heat extraction, thereby minimizing typical surface heat losses from the absorber. Expensive selective coatings are not required, because of the inherent selective property of structurally capturing the sun in depth. The 16' length of absorber plate is split into three sections, each a little longer than 5' and set diagonally across the 4" collector cavity. The air is blown upward in a serpentine path, over, through, and under the first, second, and third sections, and thence ducted to storage or the living space. The collector is backed with a sealed wood panel painted flat black and insulated with 2" of beadboard and 3½" of fiberglass.

Important to note, says Neil, is the provision for an upper-limit or fail-safe unit in emergency situations, where hot stagnation temperatures must be vented off to protect the system from overheating. "On one occasion our system malfunctioned—our vent door was installed, but the automatic weighted opening device wasn't. Our maximum design temperature was 160° F., but we knew the stagnated temperature was well over 200° F., as the beadboard began melting. Fortunately the high internal pressure kept the softened acrylic from slumping in, and actually bowed it out slightly." The system was designed for flow rates of 2 cu. ft. per minute per sq. ft. of collector, with an operating temperature from 90° to 150° F.

It was first intended that awnings could roll down from the roof peak to protect the solar panels in the event of a system failure; however, the cost of such awnings proved prohibitive, so individual awnings are snap-fastened over the panels during the summer months, when space heating is not required. Nylon, canvas, and cotton tarps were considered; cotton was chosen as it was the cheapest. Custom cost was only $125, and the minimum life expectancy should be six to eight years. In addition to closing down the system when heat is not required, the tarp will extend the life expectancy of the acrylic.

Storage

Sixteen tons of ¾″ clear gravel is contained in an 8 x 10′ insulated frame storage bin located in the basement. Heat transfer is by forced vertical air flow. The advantage of this, states Neil, is that he gets increased usable heat because of the natural stratification of heat at the top, from which heat can still be extracted even after the bottom and core has cooled, plus collector efficiency is increased by returning the coolest air off the bottom of storage for heating. Typical water-storage systems exhibit a mean temperature throughout, because of water's high conductivity, whereas rocks lower conductivity and void spaces promote heat stratification. "It's an amazing sponge, for we can blow a thousand cubic feet per minute of hundred-and-forty-degree air into the top, with eighty-degree air exiting off the bottom."

The bin has R-27 insulation on the top, R-20 walls, and an R-10 floor, with the 5′ depth of gravel supported on wire mesh and spaced bricks.

"The storage size, shape, rock particle size, and air velocity are all critical factors to be figured in storage unit design," explains Neil. The unit must provide a minimum standard pressure loss of 0.15 SWG (Standard Water Glass); if it is too low heat transfer is decreased, if it is too high exceedingly large fans must be employed. For rule-of-thumb guidelines, Neil recommends consulting the *Solaron Application Engineering Manual* or see the Solaron article in the September 1978 issue of *Solar Engineering Magazine.* Solaron has found both round pebble or crushed gravel to be suitable. Neil chose gravel, as it is only a sixth to a seventh the cost of round pebble in his area.

Heat Distribution

The air-handling system consists of typical standard galvanized ductwork (taped and insulated to R-12 in the attic), a standard two-speed duct blower, and two motorized dampers. It is controlled by a Solartrol (Carl Pepper) differential thermostat (modified to adapt to the Switzers' 24-volt system), and a standard house thermostat. The blower's low speed is used for house heating; the high speed is used for collection. The system operates in three separate modes: (1) collector to house, (2) collector to storage, and (3) storage to house.

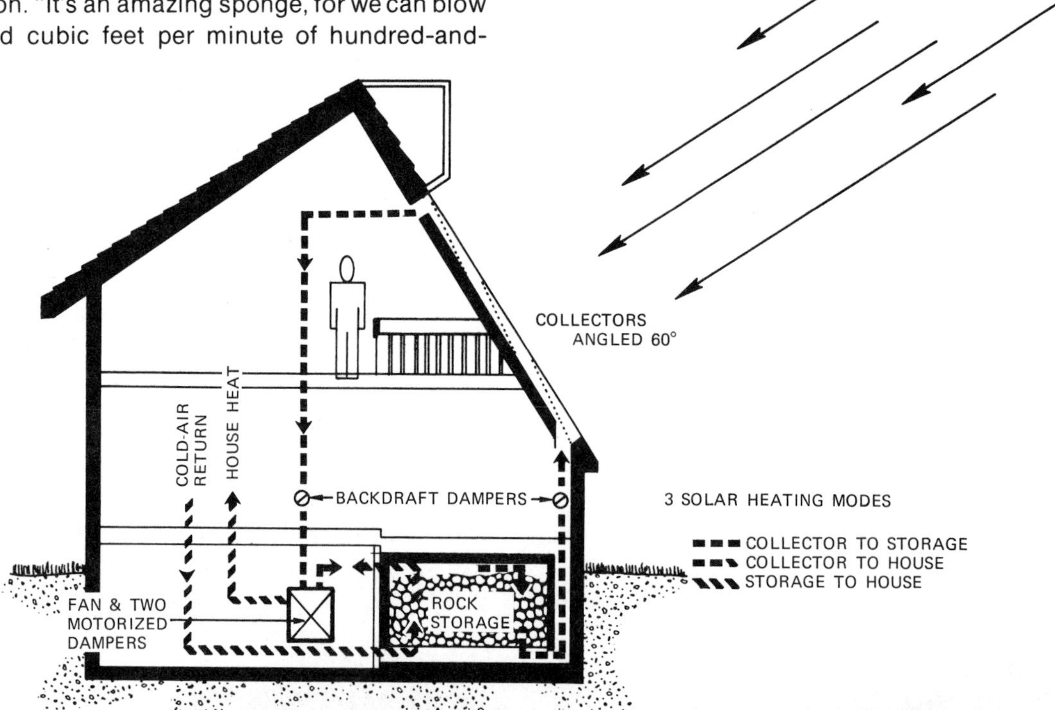

AUXILIARY HEATING

Wood is the Switzers' sole source of auxiliary heat. They use a Fisher Mama Bear stove and state that they are most happy with its performance. It's rated for heating 10,500 cu. ft. and can easily maintain embers for ten to twelve hours. They have found that in its central location the stove can comfortably heat the whole house on only a low draft or slow burn. Their only caution to those using airtight stoves is, "Use properly seasoned wood, or otherwise you'll have problems with condensation or creosote formation in the relatively cool chimney stack."

Anticipating considerable heat stratification with the open-loft concept, the Switzers also built a small recirculating system within the walls, but it is rarely used. Neil attributes this possibly to the low infiltration rates and minimum drafts from proper design and construction.

PERCENT SOLAR-HEATED

The original design was calculated to provide 60% to 70% of the total space-heating load. Unfortunately, official performance validation is not yet available, for, as Neil states, he has not received "a hell of a lot of help from various contacts within the provincial or federal governments." He hopes to conduct performance tests in the near future. (Ironically, three years after Neil began his work, a major study conducted jointly by Electrohome and the University of Waterloo in Ontario reiterates the advantages of the matrix-type collectors mentioned earlier and suggests they are a good concept.) Neil estimates that they burned a cord of well-seasoned hardwood last winter but hopes to keep better records during the 1978-79 heating season.

COOLING SYSTEM

No means of artificial cooling has been needed for the house to date. Operable windows for catching summer breezes and the open concept provide for good cross-ventilation. Deciduous trees give shade in summer, and the placement of the garage relative to the west entrance makes a funnel for cool summer breezes. The insulation and architectural features mentioned earlier also effectively act as thermal buffers. It would be possible to run the solar space-heating system in reverse and use the rock storage for extracting heat from the house; however, the features designed to cool the house work so effectively that neither this or a standard air-conditioning system is necessary. "Typically during the hottest weather we let the house cool off at night, and then close it up tight the next morning, which then keeps it pleasantly cool all day."

An 8x10′ rock storage bin is located in the basement. A roll of Solarfoil used for the collector absorber sits near the author (right).

WATER SUPPLY AND WASTE SYSTEM

Presently a well is the sole source of water, but since the water is extremely hard they intend to install an exterior cistern for rainwater in the near future. Domestic hot water is solar-preheated by passing the water through a buried tank in the rock storage bin, with final temperature boosting provided by a standard 40-gallon electric hot-water tank. A complete solar hot-water system will be installed sometime in the future. A regular tub has been sunk into one end of the bathroom. The cavity underneath and around the tub is insulated with fiberglass insulation to retain the heat longer for comfort without adding more hot water. Further utilization of this heat can be made by allowing the heat to dissipate into the room before pulling the plug. A salvaged old-fashioned pedestal sink with separate hot and cold faucets encourages one to fill the sink with just the right amount of water required to wash, rather than leaving the faucets running with the stopper open, which is often the tendency with single-faucet units.

The flush toilet is a 3-gallon-capacity water-saver type. Neil had considered installing a composting toilet; however, he changed his mind when the Ontario Ministry of Environment refused to allow for any reduction in the size (and thus cost) of the septic-bed system for the remaining graywater wastes. "We couldn't afford both," he explains.

ELECTRICAL POWER SYSTEM

A wind-generating system was originally planned, but because of the high initial capital costs, standard 100-amp service was installed. This meant that all wiring must conform to Ontario Hydro regulations, which Neil describes "as a little heavy. Certainly safety is an important factor, but the extent or number of things like outlets are geared for the extreme electrical consumer, which is certainly what we are not. Never will we need six complete separate circuits in the kitchen alone, for just an example."

The use of fluorescent lighting was considered because of its relatively high efficiency, but was ruled out because of its apparent harshness and coldness, except for one fixture in the kitchen. Elsewhere, incandescent lights are used (some on dimmers).

FOOD SYSTEM

Neil grew up on his parents' neighboring farm, and has a rich agricultural background, which he intends to put to good use at Solar Manor. Complete food self-sufficiency is not an immediate goal, for Neil knows that basic Canadian consumer foods are still an unbeatable bargain (particularly in their area), unless one's time is extremely cheap. Neil and Kathy are concentrating on improving their gardening skills and do put away considerable foodstocks in their basement chest freezer or built-in cold-storage room. The majority of their land is still farmed as part of Neil's father's farm, but a modest garden is always planted, and the adjacent 3 acres are under organic management techniques to rebuild the somewhat depleted intensively farmed soil.

COSTS

Solar Manor, being 98% complete in autumn 1978, has incurred total construction and material costs of approximately $26,000, which includes $5,000 for servicing (hydro, septic system, well) and $4,500 for the solar system. Actually, the solar system cost only an additional $2,000 when one subtracts the costs of a typical furnace system, ductwork, and 500 sq. ft. of roofing materials. The collectors cost $4 per sq. ft. to construct, and $2,060 in total. The storage system cost $470, while the mechanics, controls, and ductwork cost $2,050. A similar commercial system should cost between $8,000 and $10,000.

"We could have built the house a lot cheaper, but we wanted to do it right the first time. We also appreciate qualitative value, and some of the most durable products are also the most expensive, but nonetheless still a good buy over the long run."

Looking east from the living room to the dining room at the far end. All the woodwork shown in the photo was recycled from buildings in the local area.

CONCLUDING THOUGHTS

Future works envisioned at Solar Manor include a solar greenhouse, solar entry porch, a sunroom off the dining room, a stocked artificial pond, and associated small outbuildings for eventual self-sufficient living.

In Neil's work in the field of environmental planning and design in general, and solar energy in particular, he has been "appalled at the Canadian apathy toward the future which is already unfolding before us (limited resources, environmental degradation, spiraling costs, social unrest, and so on." He warns that we must begin to use our knowledge and remaining nonrenewable resources in ways that will facilitate a sane, orderly transition to a conserver society. To this end, Neil has formed a consulting firm which will specialize in "designs and systems for self-reliant living." Through this firm he plans to act as a catalyst for people wishing to make the transition but lacking the necessary skills in research and design.

Pursuing their material and philosophical goals in creating Solar Manor has been most rewarding for the Switzers; however, the biggest reward Neil feels is that their life-style has taken them to a point where they feel that through the consulting firm they will have a greater impact on the shaping of future society.

Sudbury, Massachusetts
2,300 sq. ft.
including family room

WALTER and LESLIE STRONG

Walter Strong is a young mechanical engineer who works for Stone & Webster Engineering Corporation, a firm that designs and constructs power plants, process plants, and industrial plants. A group of twenty to fifty company engineers meet informally once a week on their lunch hour to discuss solar projects. Walter belongs to this group and to the Boston Chapter of the New England Solar Energy Association. It seemed only fitting, therefore, that when he decided to build a new house it would be solar-heated. Walter describes why he chose solar: "I like to be as self-sufficient as I can, although I have to temper that to the society around us. Most of the houses that were built five or ten years ago and even those under construction today are obsolete. While solar-energy technology is considered new, it's been around for a long time. The state of the art is such that I think that if a person is building a house he should definitely use solar energy, as it will pay for itself if done properly."

LOCATION AND ORIENTATION

Walter and Leslie's solar home is located at 200 Hudson Road, Sudbury, Massachusetts. They got the number 200 because the house was started in 1976—the United States bicentennial year. Walter designed the house himself, with a little help from an architect who works with him at Stone & Webster, and in doing so, attempted to create a design that was aesthetically and functionally compatible with the site, while satisfying the family's comfort requirements. Their acre of land borders a great deal of forested land that cannot be developed. The neighbors that have developed property seem to share the same healthy respect for the forest as the Strongs and thus have retained woodlots around their homes. The house is oriented 22° west of south—a position which is a compromise between the optimum due-south orientation for solar gain, the required driveway swing into the garage, and the aesthetics of the site. The house is situated about two-thirds of the property length back from the road and is set into the south brow of a small hill. The north side of the basement is thus buried, but the house sits up high enough so that trees at the front of the property filter traffic noise and pollution without shading the collectors. Walter selectively cuts trees from the property so as to minimize their house's impact on the environment. Some tall pine trees were left near the south and west sides of the house to provide summer shade. Much of the surrounding mixed forest is pine, so the house has an excellent windbreak from the winter northeast winds. The forest also protects the house from the scorching heat that often develops at the end of a summer day.

The south side of the house was backfilled to create a plateau with a slight slope that reflects winter sun into the sunporch. The grass provides a nonreflective surface in summer.

ARCHITECTURAL FEATURES

The modified-hip-roof two-story house has 2,300 sq. ft. of living space, including the family room located in the southeast quarter of the basement. A south-facing greenhouse is entered from the family room. A built-in garage on the west side, the solar storage bin, the furnace room, and the workshop occupy the rest of the basement. The open-concept kitchen and dining/living area give the illusion of greater space, and facilitate natural lighting, heat circulation, and ventilation. The master bedroom with its adjacent dressing room is located on the cooler northeast side of the house; the morning sun coming in the east windows serves as an environmentally appropriate alarm clock. The half-bath/laundry is located near the kitchen and immediately under the second-floor main bath to minimize the amount of piping. A dramatic cathedral ceiling above the living room extends to the roof peak.

A wooden circular staircase leads to the second floor. The second-floor rooms surround the open balcony, which looks down on the living room. The bath is centrally located for convenience. Leslie's sewing room is located on the warm and bright southwest corner of the house. A sundeck permits her to sew outside when she wishes and also provides access to the solar collector. Walter's office is on the northwest corner. The view to the forest serves as a constant reminder of the natural environment.

The deck on the first floor extends from the screened-in porch to the north side of the dining room, along the west wall to the sunporch at the south side of the house. The west deck shelters the garage doors from snow. The deck floorboards are a 2 x 6 pressure-treated southern yellow pine called Outdoor Wood. Walter feels that this wood is preferable to redwood, as the grades of the latter available on the East Coast are not very good and also the redwood has become a threatened species. He feels that it is as good as or better than cedar at half the cost.

The foundation was poured September 3, 1976, after Walter had spent much of his spare time for the previous year clearing the land and digging the foundation hole himself. The foundation walls are 10" reinforced poured concrete. The post-and-beam framing was put up by a company called Beam House from Exeter, New Hampshire. The timbers are all native north-eastern white pine. The heavy beams were selected out of the forest by Walter. They are rough-sawn and came right from the New Hampshire sawmill to the site. Contrary to most construction practices, green wood was used for the framing; however, the way it is held together it is not allowed to twist anywhere. In fact, it is designed so that as it dries out it will provide some tension and hold things together even better. Following colonial building practices, gunstock posts are used at the corners. They taper from a relatively small base to a larger bearing area at the top. These

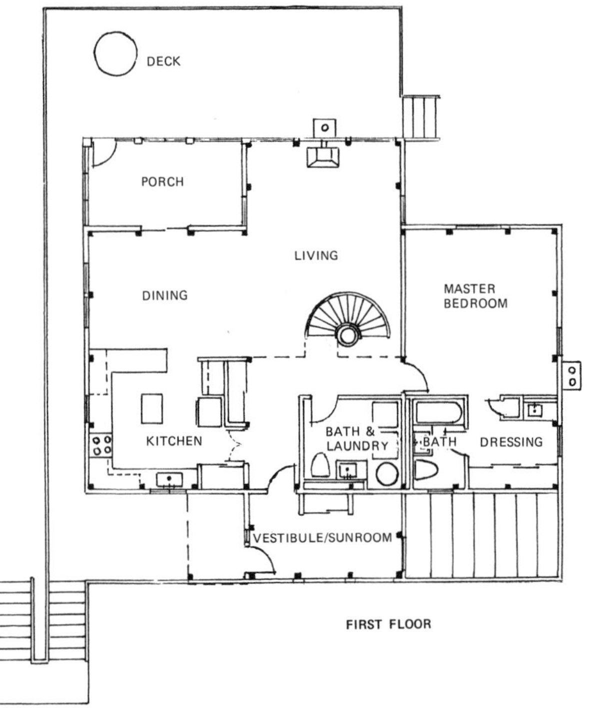

FIRST FLOOR

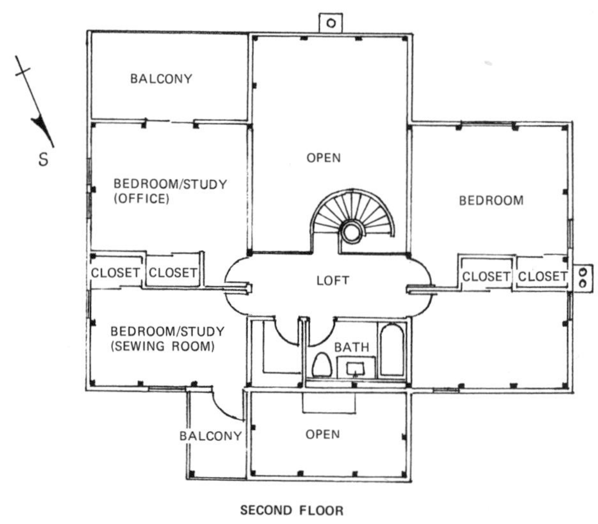

SECOND FLOOR

and intermediate posts are notched into the 6 x 6 top plate beams and secured with octagonal oak pegs. The posts are simply toenailed into the flooring and match up with the 4 x 10 floor joists. The joists were layed on 30″ centers and covered with 1″ tongue-and-groove pine and then ⅝″ plywood.

Exterior Walls

The exterior walls were built using an old-style balloon-framing technique whereby the framing extends beyond the floor joists and joist headers. The sills are 2 x 12s; these provide bearing surface for the floor joists and extend 6″ beyond the floor joists to accommodate non-load-bearing 2 x 6 framing members. Most of the 2 x 6s were used horizontally, although some were placed vertically to help tie the two floors together. This technique was used so that the posts and beams would all be fully exposed and because Walter calculated that the material costs were about one-half those of conventional framing. Also, outside foamboard insulation for the foundation walls was intended to tuck in under the sill and be secured to the foundation; however, Walter later decided not to insulate the outside of the foundation because of time constraints and opted instead to insulate only the inside walls of the living area. The exterior of the walls is clad with vertical ¾″ cedar shiplap boards with a reverse-board-and-batten appearance. It is treated with Cuprinol wood preservative. Six inches of fiberglass batts, a polyethylene vapor barrier, and two layers of ½″ gypsum board complete the exterior-wall construction.

BASEMENT

Interior Walls and Ceilings

All interior partition walls were constructed using standard 2 x 4 studwall framing techniques. A single layer of ⅝″ gypsum board was used to panel these walls. The exposed floor joists and knotty-pine floorboards of the second level serve as the ceiling of the first level. The exposed rafters and roofboards serve as the ceiling of the second level.

Roof

The roof was built from the inside out. The roof trusses on 5′ centers were covered with 4 x 10′ sheets of ⅝″ plywood running horizontally and spanning two trusses. A polyethylene vapor barrier was laid over the plywood; then 1¾ x 8″ rough-cut pine boards on edge, on 2′ centers, were framed to run horizontally. The cavities were filled with 10″ of fiberglass batts. The roof was insulated right to the eaves, so they have had no problems with ice dams. One oversight that could possibly lead to moisture problems within the insulation is the lack of soffit venting. The roof was sheathed with ½″ plywood and weatherproofed with tarpaper and GAF Timberline asphalt shingles. Walter chose these shingles because they are guaranteed for thirty years. Their color is similar to that of weathered cedar shingles, and because they are thicker than regular asphalt shingles, from a distance they also have the texture of wood shingles. As well, they present less of a fire hazard than cedar shingles.

Insulation Summary

Basement:	R-4; ¾″ beadboard
Garage/workshop ceiling:	R-19; 6″ fiberglass batts
Exterior walls:	R-19; 6″ fiberglass batts
Roof:	R-30; 10″ fiberglass batts

Doors

The main entrance is through the sunporch on the south side of the house. The insulated steel door with magnetic weatherstripping is located on the west side of the sunporch, where it is protected from the northeast winter winds and by the deck above. No storm door is used, as the steel door forms a perfectly weathertight seal and doesn't warp. The sunporch acts as an airlock before one enters the main house through a similar steel door. There are two Pella wood-frame insulated patio doors on the north side of the house; however, they are quite well protected from winter winds by the pine windbreak, and to minimize heat loss through them Walter will probably install insulated shutters or drapes. A Dutch door links the family room aesthetically and functionally with the greenhouse. The garage door is a commercial-grade overhead type with factory-installed beadboard insulation on the inside.

Windows

Walter describes some of the thinking that went into the window layout. "We have a nice lot, so we wanted to take advantage of all the views. There is a good view of woods to the north, so we have a lot of window area there. We have a very efficient wood stove to offset heat loss and have a good windbreak to the north; however, if necessary we will install inside shutters. I made my own window-trim boards, which I designed to facilitate the addition of shutters. Another good feature is that in most rooms we placed tall windows opposite a door so that when you walk into a room you are looking outside and the interior space therefore looks bigger than it is." As in most solar-heated houses, there is a large amount of south-facing window, most of which is built into the sunporch. An added benefit of the post-and-beam construction is that the beams act as a valance above the windows, thus counteracting heavy drafts up and down over the window surface.

Operable clerestory windows at the peak of the cathedral ceiling provide venting and lighting to the living room and the second-floor balcony.

There is a large Pella insulated thermopane picture window that gives a view of the greenhouse from the family room and provides additional light to the living spaces.

The other basement windows are operable Andersen thermopane awning-type windows. All other windows are Pella wood-frame windows that have been stained Navajo red to contrast with the cedar siding and trim, which is stained transparent gray to ensure a uniform color when aged. Most are casement windows, though combination fixed and awning are used in the sunporch and living room. The Pella double-pane windows are used rather than regular insulating glass because they permit one to take out the inner glazing during the warm season and because they offer better insulating value.

The Strongs opted for considerable glazing on the north because of the view of the forest. The south side, shown in the opening photo, has 500 sq. ft. of air-type collector, a sunroom, and south-facing windows to provide solar heat for this house; a foundation has been poured on the southeast corner to accommodate a planned greenhouse.

SOLAR-HEATING SYSTEM

This solar-heating system has both passive and active components. The insulated south-facing sunroom with its ample window area provides substantial solar-heat gain. The sunroom's cathedral ceiling has a vent at the top, so that excess heat can be bled off into the main part of the house. Similarly, the greenhouse is designed to collect solar heat, which can be either directed into the family room through the doorway or ducted by natural convection into the sunroom and then to the main part of the house. The greenhouse will use the same Kalwall glazing and the same framing and glazing pattern as the active collectors, so from a distance they will look the same. The concrete walls and floors were poured at the same time as those of the main structure.

Collector

The 500 sq. ft. (about 475 sq. ft. net) of air-type solar collector was built almost single-handedly by Walter following the DIY-Sol do-it-yourself plans. The design is similar to that used on House 22 except Walter used the two-pass system as described in the concluding remarks on House 22. Also he used the new Tedlar 400 XRB 160SE as an inner glazing and Kalwall Sun-Lite Premium as an outer glazing. Cedar battens were used to match the siding. The orientation and tilt of the collector were a compromise between optimum solar-collector angles, aesthetics, and other functional requirements of the building as mentioned earlier. Walter did not want a house that looked as though it had a drive-in movie screen in front, so he integrated the collector into the house design and tilted it at 42° from the horizontal because that angle looked best for the site and the house. It is oriented 22° west of south.

When I asked him why he chose the DIY-Sol system, he replied, "I wanted to design my own system, but since I had to design the house too, I just didn't have the time. The DIY-Sol system is probably the closest to what I would design myself. I studied the performance

An airtight Danish Morsø #1125 combination fireplace/stove is located on the north wall of the central living area.

Detail of post-and-beam construction.

of other collectors through the library that my company's solar group has and found that DIY-Sol is as good as any on the market. It is a sophisticated, high-performance collector, but one that a do-it-yourselfer can construct." Walter built the collector in place on the roof by himself, which was rather difficult. Because the roof is so steep, he usually could not find anyone who was willing to go up with him. It might have been easier and faster to have assembled the collector on the ground.

Storage

A total of 1" of gypsum board on the exterior walls and ⅝" on interior walls provides some passive storage capability, as does the 1/2" clay tile in the sunporch. Concrete walls, four 55-gallon water-filled drums, and the planting soil provide thermal mass for the greenhouse.

The rock storage bin is located in the basement under the sunporch. The 7 x 15 x 5′ high (rock depth) structure was built according to DIY-Sol specifications. Three sides were constructed of 10" poured concrete; the north side, facing into the garage, is 2 x 4 studwall framing with ⅝" plywood on the inside. In this way, if a better storage medium becomes available, the system can be easily retrofitted. Urethane slab insulation 2" thick is installed around the inside perimeter of the storage bin and then laid on the concrete floor, with all edges sealed with silicone. A hardboard sheet was laid over the urethane floor slab, and for air distribution concrete blocks were laid in place with a ½-¾" space on all sides. The bin has a ½"-thick Homasote lining to protect the urethane foamboard. The bin was filled to a depth of 5′ and to within 6" of the cover with 28 tons of 1¼" to 1¾" round rock. Before Walter poured the foundation cement, he made sure that a rectangular hole was built into the outside wall so that a chute could be used to pour rocks in from outside the building.

Heat Distribution

Heat distribution within the passively heated sunporch and greenhouse has already been described. The venting of the sunporch through natural convection is designed to be integrated with the cathedral-ceiling vent/heat-recovery manifold of the main part of the house. Hot air can be exhausted at the top of the roof through this vent or it can be drawn down into the rock storage or directly back to the house through the integrated hot-air-recovery manifold. The forced-air active solar system operates in the three modes typical of air systems—collector to storage, collector direct to house, storage to house. All ductwork consists of factory-made lightweight, one inch thick, compressed, foil-backed fiberglass insulation.

A Thermolator kit composed of the same components as shown in the solar schematic for House 22 was purchased from DIY-Sol. This is the heart of the control system.

AUXILIARY HEATING

An oil furnace located in the basement is automatically integrated with the solar system. This Blue Ray furnace (Long Island, N.Y.) is one of the new energy-conserving, low-pollution types that is about half the size of a conventional oil furnace and burns at about 80% efficiency.

A Danish Morsø 1125 combination fireplace/stove is intended as the principal backup to the solar system. It is of heavy cast-iron construction with a firebrick base and lining. Bricks on the floor and on the wall behind the stove help to store some of the stove's radiant heat. The high-efficiency Morsø with a full load of 20" logs will burn up to sixteen hours, heating 10,000 cu. ft.—in this case about half the house. Excess convective heat rises to the 28′-high cathedral ceiling, where the hot-air-recovery manifold pulls it down to the basement for recirculation.

PERCENT SOLAR-HEATED

The solar-system storage, automatic controls, and distribution were not installed, nor was insulation complete for the 1977-78 heating season. During that season the Strongs burned 600 gallons of fuel oil and two cords of oak and maple. Walter calculates that at this 6,000-7,000 degree-day site the solar system will provide between 60% and 70% of the house's heating needs and anticipates that the oil-furnace backup will be used only when the house is unoccupied for extended periods of cloudy weather.

Excess heat in this room can be vented to the main part of the house.

Master bedroom with views to the north (left-hand side) and east.

COOLING SYSTEM

The vents at the top of the cathedral ceiling create a chimney effect that encourages a good draft when windows are open during the summer. Even the sun-porch with its low awning-type vent windows is kept cooler in the summer than the outside. The natural forest provides good shade, and the lawn diffuses sunlight that would otherwise reflect onto the house. As well, the good insulation helps to keep the house cool. Cool night air could be drawn from the outside into the rock storage and then ducted to the living spaces during the day, but this has not been required.

The collector fan is operated during the summer to preheat the domestic hot water and then vented. This protects the collector from overheating.

WATER SUPPLY AND WASTE SYSTEM

Water is supplied from the town line. About 80% of the Strongs' hot-water needs are supplied by the DIY-Sol fin-tube heat exchanger located in the hot-air-supply duct. The exchanger is connected to a 50-gallon pre-heat tank. The water temperature is topped up if required in the conventional 80-gallon electrically heated hot-water tank.

Single-lever control faucets are used throughout the house in order to get the right control quickly and thus minimize water wastage. For the same reason, a vol-ume-control shower head was used. It has the same effect as a low-volume shower head but is more con-trollable—if one wants a forceful blast now and then, the option is there. High-quality, durable Kohler fiber-glass tub-and-shower units were built into the master and second-floor bathrooms. Both hot- and cold-water pipes were insulated throughout the house. The waste lines have noise-control insulation. The inte-riors of the toilet tanks are factory-insulated so that the tanks do not sweat and thus damage the flooring. The insulation also decreases interior volume and thus conserves water. The bathrooms feature a com-bination light, heater, and exhaust fan in one unit.

Blackwater and graywater wastes are disposed of in

Note detail of flashing and greenhouse foundation wall.

a septic system, which is standard except for the septic tank, which has a 1,500-gallon capacity—larger than was required by the health regulations. The Strongs plan to recycle as much of their solid wastes as possible by composting, but they have been spending so much time trying to get their house fully operational that waste recycling has regrettably received low priority.

ELECTRICAL SUPPLY SYSTEM

The house is hooked up to the local electrical utility grid; however, Walter has a gasoline-powered combination 3,500-watt generator/arc welder that can be used in emergencies.

In designing the lighting system, Walter made a conscientious effort to minimize power consumption. The house takes advantage of natural lighting through the use of ample windows and the clerestory windows at the roof peak. The light-painted gypsum board improves illumination quality. The house features a mixture of light fixtures. Valance-type fluorescent lights are used for general lighting in work areas, and high-wattage incandescent lights are used infrequently for task lighting such as for reading. In the hallways, low-wattage colonial-style sconce lighting is used to provide just enough light to get from one activity area to another.

MAJOR HOUSEHOLD APPLIANCES

"We purchased appliances we think are the most energy-conserving on the market," said Walter. The Strongs based their decision on a study of manufacturers' data and *Consumer Reports* magazine. "The Frigidaire electric double-oven unit is well insulated and has an on/off timing feature. It is a self-cleaning unit as opposed to a continuous cleaning, which means that the owner controls *when* the oven is cleaned. The electric Frigidaire countertop cookstove has temperature sensors built into the burner elements to prevent overheating. The Thermodor vent hood has variable-speed air-exhaust control so that no more air than is necessary is exhausted to the outside.

"The Maytag dishwasher has a drying cycle that can be turned off. The Frigidaire washer and dryer, which we located on the first floor for convenience, were rated well by *Consumer Reports* as being water- and energy-conserving."

FOOD SYSTEM

The Strongs plan to grow some vegetables in the greenhouse year-round. As Walter's father used to run a commercial greenhouse operation, Walter is experienced in the growing of greenhouse produce. This greenhouse requires little auxiliary heat because there is substantial storage mass within the concrete walls, the water barrels, and the soil of the elevated growing beds.

An outside organic garden is planned to be terraced down the face of the south-sloping hill in front of the house and will therefore be well protected from the north while having a southern exposure.

COSTS

The completed house cost between $60,000 and $70,000, not including the cost of the land. Walter did a great deal of the work himself, including most of the excavating, all of the interior, and all of the heating ductwork and the solar system. The money thus saved was used to buy top-quality materials.

The materials for the entire solar system cost less than $3,000, a relatively small amount considering the system's contribution to the heating requirements. If the Strongs had contracted out the solar-system installation, the cost would have tripled.

CONCLUDING THOUGHTS

The DIY-Sol system is one of the best and most cost-effective do-it-yourself commercial solar systems on the market. The builder must still be prepared to work out a lot of details that might be unique to his particular situation and be prepared to invest a considerable amount of time, as the installation is very labor-intensive. Walter spent about two months working alone on just the collector installation. He advises anyone contemplating a similar project to get his house livable first and then build the solar system rather than living in the midst of the construction of the house interior as long as his family did.

New Boston, New Hampshire
2,500 sq. ft. living area

DANIEL and KARI ZWILLINGER

Daniel and Kari Zwillinger started construction of their solar-heated home in December 1974. They were motivated by a deeply ingrained conviction that people have to become more self-sufficient. "Services have become too costly, and we are living under the threat that they could be cut off." Daniel readily admits that the savings in conventional fuel costs may never pay back his capital investment in the solar system, but since he is trying for 90% solar contribution he never expected the system to be economical. "Our energy-conscious house began with survival in mind, but turned into a solar-energy-development project, as we began to discover how poor the then-available solar products were, which might serve as an explanation why our solar system is still unfinished."

LOCATION AND ORIENTATION

The Zwillinger home is located on Laurel Lane, New Boston, New Hampshire. They wanted a smaller parcel of land than the 160 acres they purchased; however, they were unable to find a suitable one. They are slowly selling off parts of the land in order to help pay off the mortgage and fund solar-energy technological developments.

The house is oriented 5° west of south and is built just below the brow of a gently sloping south-facing hill. During excavation, care was taken to save trees that would be beneficial in controlling the microclimate. Many deciduous trees were cut out of the woodlot to the north and east to allow the pine trees to grow better and faster and thus provide a good windbreak against winter winds. Some deciduous trees were left immediately to the east and west of the house in order to provide shade. Daniel attempts to practice good woodlot-management techniques in order to ensure that their trees remain healthy and strong.

ARCHITECTURAL FEATURES

This 3,000-sq.-ft. wood-frame, split-level structure with 2,500 sq. ft. of heated living space is composed of five levels, including an attic space. It was intended to convert the attic into two bedrooms for the children, but it has remained an attic as the improvement would have increased local taxes excessively.

With the split-level construction the stairs were designed to act as corridors, thus saving valuable space. According to Daniel, "People still do not realize what horrendous expenditures can result from poor space utilization such as long corridors between rooms." He has calculated that the building-cost increase to install a clothes dryer beside a washing machine instead of over it, unless the intallation is in the basement, can be as much as $700.

A sunroof, reached from the attic, is an excellent place to sunbathe, meditate, or contemplate the constellations. The north end of the house has an entry porch and living, dining, and kitchen areas on one floor over a mostly underground basement with a day room, office, sauna, and root cellar. The entire south face of the house is composed of solar collectors.

The foundation is poured concrete over continuous footings. The inside of the foundation is insulated with 2" of urethane tongue-and-groove foamboard. A 5"-thick slab with only a #10 wire 6 x 6" mesh rests over 4" of polyurethane foam and 7' of crushed stone (thermal storage). Cars have parked on the slab for four years and no cracks have appeared. At the time of construction, wood was relatively inexpensive, so it was used generously. Oak flooring was used over plywood subflooring throughout, except in the porch, lower bath, and adjacent hall, where durable, easy-maintenance ceramic tile was used; in the kitchen, where vinyl linoleum was used; and in the downstairs day room, where vinyl flooring was used directly over the slab.

Exterior Walls

Standard 2 x 4 studwall construction techniques were used with 4" of fiberglass insulation in some wall cavities and 2" of continuous tightly fitted urethane foamboard secured to the exterior of other studwalls. The three-story south wing has cedar shingles, which make that part of the building appear lower; the two-story north wing has vertical pine board-and-batten, which makes that wing appear taller, thus creating a better visual balance between the two wings. All exterior siding is treated with Cuprinol wood preservative and has been allowed to age naturally.

Interior Walls and Ceilings

All interior walls and the flat ceilings were sheathed in ½" gypsum board. All ceilings except the north-wing cathedral ceiling were painted white to enhance illumination.

Kari is Norwegian; so, in keeping with Norwegian building traditions, the north-wing interior is sheathed in wood. The walls of the porch, living room, dining room, kitchen, and day room are ¾" tongue-and-groove solid-pine boards. All south-wing walls are sheathed in real-pine-veneer plywood, except the bathroom walls, which are plastic laminate. The cathedral ceilings in the living room, dining room, and kitchen are 2" tongue-and-groove spruce.

Roof

The shed-type roof of the south wing is composed of 2 x 10" rafters and 8" fiberglass batt insulation, ½" plywood sheathing, building paper, and cedar shingles to match the wood motif of the exterior siding. The gable roof over the north wing is insulated with 2" of polyurethane foamboard over the 2" spruce decking and then topped with ½" plywood, another 1" of polyurethane, plus tarpaper and shingles. Daniel recommends the use of tongue-and-groove insulation rather than the butt-end type he used.

Insulation Summary

Foundation:	R-10; 2" polyurethane foamboard
Walls, south wing:	R-11; 2" polyurethane foamboard
Walls, north wing:	R-18; 4" fiberglass batts and 1" polyurethane
Ceiling, south wing:	R-28; 8" fiberglass batts and 1" polyurethane
Ceiling, north wing:	R-18; 3" polyurethane and approx. 3" of wood

Daniel states that these R-values were advanced in 1974, but the main emphasis was on careful detailing and installation to achieve airtightness.

Doors

The small glassed-in front porch is insulated both from the outside and from the living areas. It can therefore be efficiently heated, when required, to a minimum temperature. The exterior wood-frame door and aluminum storm door are weatherstripped to minimize infiltration losses. An insulated, thermopane patio door connects the porch to the living room. While providing a certain amount of thermal buffering, the porch provides a substantial amount of natural light to living spaces that otherwise have small window areas.

The other entranceway is through the garage/workshop, so it too is well buffered from the elements. Both entrances act as airlocks, reducing the heat loss due to air exchange.

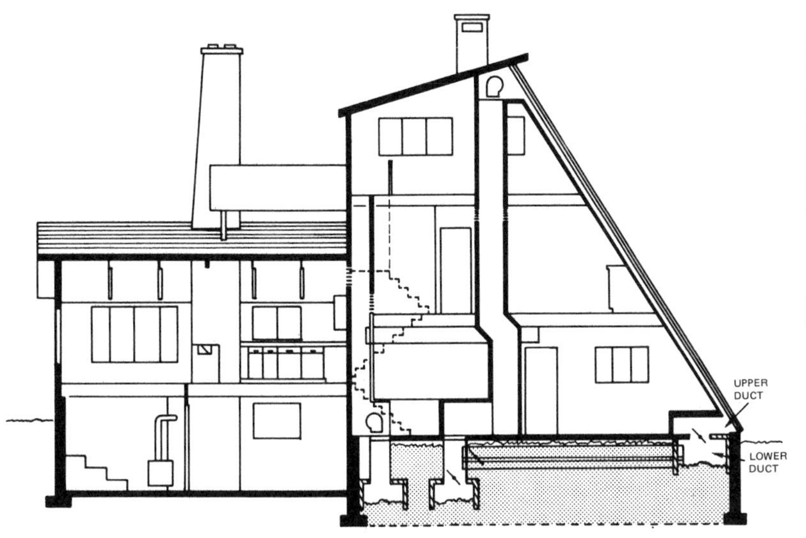

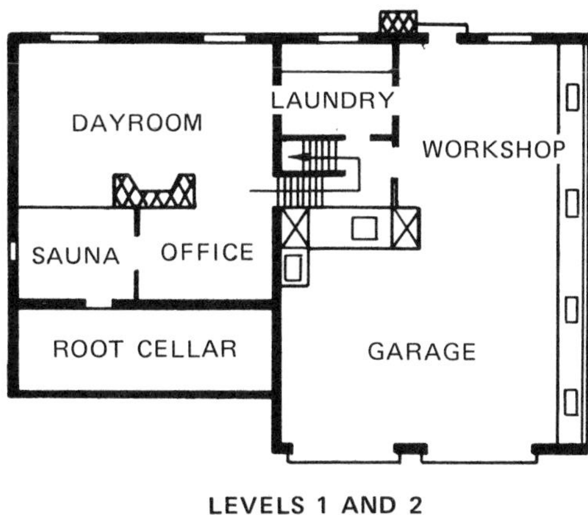

LEVELS 1 AND 2

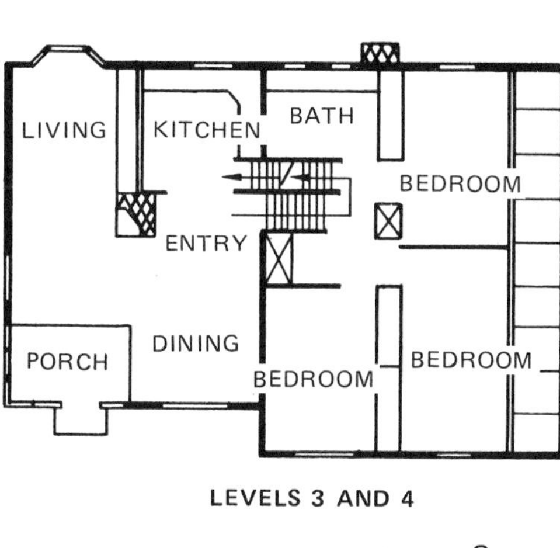

LEVELS 3 AND 4

S

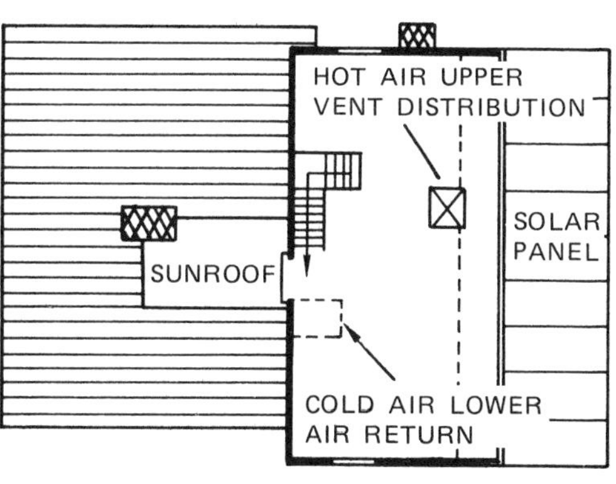

LEVEL 5

Windows

All of the windows are Andersen thermopane wood-frame awning or casement windows. Daniel chose the vinyl-covered type because they require no maintenance. Most of the glazing is on the east and west walls. There are no windows on the south wall, as that area is entirely covered with collector; therefore, there will be little passive solar gain when the collector is finished. The east and west windows are shaded by deciduous trees. The window area of the north walls is very small. There is no system of insulated shutters; however, Daniel and Kari do plan to install some type of heavily insulated curtains. Daniel offers the following suggestions for window design: "Windows facing the sun should actually have only one pane of glass, and a good curtain to pull over, for best results. All glazings—I'm not referring just to glass—pass direct spectral light better than diffused light, but they all create diffusion, so two layers are always bad. A polyethylene film on the inside or, for better quality, a Teflon film would be the best way of creating dead-air space. A curtain larger than the window, fitting well into a window niche, would also do, and if the curtain has an aluminized surface outward, it would produce the best 'primitive' passive solar system. A triple-pane window, curtain arbitrary, should be used on sunless walls only. Thermopanes on part-time solar exposed walls would still be the most convenient, but good curtains would be advisable there."

The west entrance is through a sunporch. Note the large central chimney.

SOLAR-HEATING SYSTEM

Daniel chose an air-type active system because he prefers the controllability of active systems and because he does not believe in water systems. He feels that water systems generally have too many problems—leakage, corrosion, plugging of pipes, the costs of antifreeze, and the need to run antifreeze through a heat exchanger (not a problem with trickle-type collectors) and thus the need to channel the collector heat-transfer mediums to a central station. "By going to my type of system," he says, "air can be channeled off the collector at any point, bypassing the central system and thus saving the temperature in storage. For example, in the early morning when the air temperature in the collector is colder than the storage temperature but still warm enough to supply house heat, this air can be channeled into the living spaces without touching the storage."

Collector

The Zwillinger collector, which has a gross area of 1,300 sq. ft. and a net area of 1,200 sq. ft., covers the entire three-story south face of the house and is oriented 5° west of south. It is tilted at 57° from the horizontal. Daniel points out, "The tilt is only reasonably critical with regard to sun absorption when a glazing like Tedlar, which is less angle-of-incidence-dependent than glass, is used. However, sliding off snow is very important—mainly sticky wet snow and sleet. A frequent hazard is caused by placing doors under panels, so that someone's neck could be broken by a snow avalanche from the panel."

The collector array measures 36 x 36′ and is composed of nine panels, each measuring 4 x 36′ high. There is a 1¼″ space between the two Kalwall Sun-Lite Regular fiberglass-reinforced plastic glazings. A rectangular 2′ aluminum mesh separates them, acts as a stiffener, and reduces convection losses.

Daniel received U.S. patent approval on March 21, 1978, for a unique collector design which he has not installed in his home yet. He may decide to replace the Kalwall when the final installation is made because he does not think that its solar energy transmission properties are as good as he had been led to believe.

Daniel stated, "A single layer of transparent cover coupled with a selective finish on the absorber plate is, we believe, the only way to collect solar energy for our latitude. An additional one-mil-thick layer of Teflon may be the most I would settle for. The transparent film that I would like to bet on the most, although not the only one that may be meritous, is DuPont's four-mil-thick Tedlar—their new material that is rated to withstand one hundred degrees Centigrade of continuous temperature; the old material rated only seventy degrees. As it now stands, the cost of the Kalwall transparent panel that we now have would have paid for the new collector panel, with the glazing as well."

The absorber plate will be a selectively coated aluminum extrusion with a finned underside giving a surface area three or four times that of a plain surface. "The selectivity of the surface is created not only by the special oxidation process that produces a crystalline structure which is selective between infrared and visible electromagnetic energies, but combines this with a geometric macro-shape which in itself is selective. The chemical-dip finish costs pennies a square foot, and a complete collector panel using this system with a Tedlar glazing is expected to cost in the neighborhood of five dollars a square foot." It has a transmittance of 85-90% and an emissivity of 10-15% at 200° F. He claims the system is very unsophisticated and suitable for site-built application for the do-it-yourselfer.

Vertical board-and-batten on the low north wing and horizontal cedar shingles on the south wing provide a visual balance between the two sections of the house.

In his house, as in his patented design, air will pass between the rafters (4′ O.C.) and behind the absorbers in an approximately 6″-deep airspace that is tapered from the bottom to the top. This taper will cause the cool air to linger longer and thus absorb more Btu. "At the top of the panel, the temperature difference between collector-panel and thermal-medium air is decreased, thus higher air velocities than at bottom become more exchange-effective. Also due to the inclination, rising hot air is pressed up against the underside of the absorber, thereby absorbing more heat from a front-pass system, where the air would have to be turbulent to make contact with the top side of the absorber plate. This turbulence leads to greater heat losses out through the glazing. In my case, the extra layer of stagnant air between the glazing and the absorber will act as another insulation space."

The back of the airspace will be covered with gypsum board as a precaution against flash fires. (The system has very good heat-distribution characteristics, and flame spread, therefore, has to be considered carefully.) The back of the gypsum board will be insulated with 2″ of tongue-and-groove polyurethane foamboard. Daniel would prefer to use more inert ureaformaldehyde, but the polyurethane was purchased in bulk in 1974 before he knew about the former. Another layer of gypsum board behind the insulation completes the collector construction.

Storage

The 30 x 30 x 6′ high poured-concrete storage bin (1,800 cu. ft.) contains 200 tons of 1½″-diameter crushed stone and is located under the garage. "This volume is about two or three times the quantity generally recommended for the size of the panel, but I felt I could increase efficiency better with just a small increase in cost for storage than by trying to increase the temperature of the air produced by the panel. Due to the low air velocity—about a tenth that ordinarily used in air solar systems—it will go through the pit well, with improved heat-transfer efficiency over high-velocity

View from dining room looking east. The extensive use of wood is typical of homes in Kari Zwillinger's native Norway.

air. As well, dust will be minimized." The outside perimeter and the top of the storage reservoir is insulated with 4′ of polyurethane foamboard. There is no insulation between the bottom of the bin and the rock ledge, as the seventh foot of stone, below the lowest air-circulation level, is for insulation from the gound. It is not likely that air blown horizontally through the bin will get below a foot above the rock ledge, although Daniel feels that the rock ledge could store usable heat if water does not contaminate it. In anticipation of possible water infiltration, footing drains were installed around the perimeter of the bin.

Heat Distribution

Daniel describes the air-circulation system as follows: "One portion of louvered closet doors is for the cold-air-return ducts. Bathroom doors are also provided with a small louvered section, because no air returns are provided directly in baths, to reduce circulation of bathroom steam. Our kitchen has no warm-air supply nor return, because of circulation of food aroma and less of a need to solar-heat the kitchen. The warm-air supply emanates from metal louvers just below the ceiling line. This last factor is like the old-fashioned gravity heat circulation, because we are talking of large air volume that should come out warm at the top and return below after giving heat to the room. Nowadays, both heat supply and heat return are in floors, because we are dealing with relatively warm air—concentrated heat—that is given a chance to mix with room air as it rises to the ceilings, and then descends back to the register across the room to return. This does not become the case when we are actually almost replacing the entire air in the room with air just a little bit warmer; thus the outdated circulation pattern.

"In the large gypsum-board-lined main chute, air moves in a forward and reverse direction. Air comes down this chute during sunshine, and space air distribution takes off to the side ducts; or, when no direct sun heat is present, the air flow is upward out of the storage, for distribution throughout the house. With the exception of this one duct, air flow always follows just one direction. There is a double duct just under the solar panel, the lower one to collect air from the storage space and either send it through a bypass duct into the house, or into the upper duct for distribution into the collector panel. This upper duct can also be fed directly from the bypass duct when no energy storing takes place. I will make up the dampers. Almost all if not all of them will be gravity-operated, and the only items requiring control will be two blowers of variable velocity, one at the top of the main supply chute, the other at the bottom of the return of the return chute. The pressure differential between these ducts ought to control the gravity dampers most of the time. In the advanced passive system I shall use on the next-model house, the system will not even require these fans."

At the present time and until the collector is finished, the only way solar heat is distributed is by opening doors to rooms on the panel side of the collector when the sun is shining. (As only the glazing has been fitted to the collector array, the adjacent rooms are heated passively.) At night or when the sun is not shining these doors are simply closed.

AUXILIARY HEATING

Electric baseboard heating in the upper level of the north wing and wired-in-ceiling radiant heat in the rest of the house are capable of carrying the full midwinter load. Electricity is the most expensive of the conventional heating sources, but it was the cheapest to install, and Daniel rarely expects to use it once the solar system is completed.

The modified Rumford-style masonry fireplace located in the center of the living space is capable of heating the living room, dining room, and kitchen. Because of its central location and geometry, the efficiency is probably better than most traditional fireplaces; however, its net efficiency could be increased substantially with outside venting and fire doors with draft controls.

Another fireplace located in the dayroom conforms exactly to the Count Rumford specifications. Its flue runs up the same chimney as that of the upstairs fireplace.

"I am staying away from glass doors," says Daniel, "even though these would improve the combustion characteristics of the fireplaces—although a Rumford fireplace is already a considerable improvement over a conventional one—because with them the energy density of the radiation produced by flames is cut by two-thirds, leaving most of the fireplace heating to the convection process, which works only from the ceiling down, and our ceilings in the north wing are cathedral and quite high. A lot of the fireplace atmosphere gets lost, and I shun that as long as I can justify this.

"I recently tested air-pipe grates in my fireplaces and discovered that they do not work with a properly designed Rumford fireplace to any advantage. Even if constructed high enough so that the hot air they produce is prevented from flowing back up the chimney, they decrease the radiation output of the firewall in back of the hearth, both by cooling and by bringing the flames forward and away from the firewall; both have considerable effect on proper combustion by cooling the combustion. A proper Rumford fireplace works best by pressing the burning side of wood, between at least two logs, against the back firewall for highest possible combustion temperature. Thus proper grating for such a fireplace should have a straight back to prevent it from sliding forward, have a rather narrow bottom, and have the front slant upward and forward, quite high. In this way, large logs can be placed, and by gravity they will be kept in contact with each other as they burn. We have had a pair of dry oak logs twelve inches in diameter burn with a small blue flame for almost twenty-four hours. Smoldering is, of course, a waste of energy and creates a lot of smoke. A flame along full lengths of the logs is necessary, no matter how small, and the arrangement I describe is necessary for this condition. Infrared radiation, the main output of a Rumford fireplace, does not require dark surfaces in order to be absorbed, as does sunlight, so any room finish except shiny metal is okay. Warm-air generation is just a remedy for a bad fireplace. It is quite amazing how many square feet of living area we can heat in the cold of winter, with this one corner fireplace.

"I am also working on a gravity-operated damper that will adjust according to the amount of exhaust that is required—a very tricky proposition. Montgomery Ward markets an electric-controlled 'heat saver vent damper' that could be coupled to a smoke detector at the mantelpiece to do the trick. A lot can be saved if the flue accompanies the exhaust need."

The sauna's only source of heat is a wood-burning Nippa Sauna Heater, Model WB-22 (from Bruce Mfg. Co., Bruce Crossing, Mich. 49912). This unit has water jackets as well and can be hooked into the hot-water system. To heat the sauna room to adequate temperature takes half an hour at the most. The sauna stove has its own flue, which could be shared with the optional wood-burning kitchen range. This flue shares the fireplace's chimney. A completely separate chimney serves a wood stove in the garage, with optional future hookups for the bedroom space.

Typically the Zwillingers have been burning six cords of wood, which they harvest from their 10-acre well-grown hardwood woodlot.

The separate shop receives a lot of direct-gain passive solar heat.

PERCENT SOLAR-HEATED

When the system is completed, Daniel predicts that 90% of his heating requirements will be provided by the solar system. He calculates that if the rock pile is fairly uniformly heated, 10° F. of temperature drop of the storage pile will heat the house for an average of 24 sunless hours, provided the temperature of the rock pile is still a few degrees above the desired room temperature.

COOLING SYSTEM

The vertical air shafts in summer can be used to create a chimney effect to exhaust warm house air to the outside, as can the central chimney in the north wing. Good insulation, strategically located vent windows, deciduous shade trees on the east and west, and ground cover all contribute to summer cooling.

WATER AND WASTE SYSTEM

Water is supplied by a 150′ drilled well. Domestic hot water is heated in electric heaters. Eventually solar preheating will be done by hanging plastic tubes along main-shaft walls to perform as air-to-water heat exchangers, with control valves to stop reverse gravity flow when no heat can be added to the hot-water system. The hot-water system has a gravity return loop that circulates the hot water to keep it warm near the taps, and into this return will be hooked the solar-heated water supply, with circulation through the solar heat exchanger taking place only when this can provide at leat 150° F. water, or, when water is being used extensively, a differential thermostat will shut off the cold-water intake to the electric heater, to receive water through the heat exchanger, during the heavy use of the hot water, letting the flow of the water to be used provide the circulation flow pressure.

A water-saving toilet uses 3 gallons per flush rather than the usual 5. Daniel installed the plumbing to the toilet so that a little hot water is mixed with the cold to prevent condensation. (I have found that a toilet tank insulated on the inside achieves the same results while incidentally reducing the water volume.)

Blackwater is disposed of in a 1,000-gallon septic tank with a leaching field, while graywater is disposed of separately in a drywell. Daniel separated the two effluents so that detergents would not contaminate the blackwater should he decide to experiment with methane. An experimental composting toilet will be installed in the barn. It will be built out of impregnated wood lined with DuPont Hypalon lining and will have exterior insulation.

Organic household wastes are run down the electric disposal in one of the sinks. In this way they can be useful in the proposed blackwater methane generator. Vegetables from the garden are trimmed at the garden, onto the compost pile. Paper is saved for the winter, to burn, unless it is soiled, in which case it goes to the dump together with glass, metal, and plastics—a once-a-month trip.

ELECTRICAL POWER SYSTEM

The Zwillinger home receives its power from the local utility company. "I am working on a wind-generator design that will operate in gusty conditions, thus making it possible to install it closer to the ground, just far enough away not to hurt anyone. In this way higher wind velocities close to buildings can be utilized. Batteries can be charged in very intermittent fashion and space heating in conjunction with solar can be handled the same way." Daniel is also considering plans to operate the motorized dampers and fans for the solar system on 24 volts with a bank of storage batteries hooked in between them and the external power lines. In this way the solar system can still function during power failures.

A combination of incandescent and energy-efficient fluorescent lights are used throughout the house. Natural illumination is particularly good in the living areas. Window area is small in the bedrooms, but the white-painted ceilings improve the quality of illumination.

MAJOR HOUSEHOLD APPLIANCES

Most of the appliances were bought in or before 1973 when little was written about energy-conserving appliances and when few were available. The Zwillinger home has all the standard major appliances, including an electric stove, refrigerator, and a chest-type freezer. Their purchase of a General Electric dishwasher was based on hearsay. They only use it once a day in order to conserve hot water. They have an automatic washer and dryer but do not use the latter. The "solar dryer" (clothesline) in the attic will be used until the collector is completed.

FOOD SYSTEM

The Zwillingers' first garden was planted in 1978, but "our biggest problem was replanting several times due to marauding chipmunks and birds, delaying our season by one month. Blinking Christmas lights might be the solution to both groups—a project for next year." They have been trying to improve the quality of the garden soil through the addition of compost and some sand to improve the drainage. An area of the forest has been cleared and sewn to rye grass, as Daniel is considering raising some sheep or goats in the future. A concrete root cellar integral to the basement will be used to store much of their produce.

COSTS

Daniel and Kari did their own design work and acted as their own general contractors. When they built their house the building industry was in a slump, so they were able to have the contract work done cheaper than normally. They were thus able to build the house for $35,000 exclusive of the cost of land and solar equipment.

The solar system was expensive, as the Zwillingers were aiming for 100% energy independence and their dissatisfaction with the existing technology led them to spend a considerable amount of money on research and development. The solar components—including the storage, built-in ductwork, and other features unique to the solar system but excluding the collector panels—cost $4,000. The 1,200 sq. ft. of collector glazing cost $5,000. Daniel estimates that another $4,000 will have to be spent on additional ducts to the north wing of the house, on the motorized dampers and the control system.

To complete the collector using the existing tooling for Daniel's new patented extruded aluminum absorber plate will cost $12,000 more. However, $8,000 of this was for research and development, which included the materials and tests for tooling up four times.

With the recent refinements that he has made to the extrusion design Daniel estimates that if he invested $3,000 for new tooling he could cut the cost from $12,000 to $6,000 for 1,200 sq. ft. of absorber. When he gets into high-volume production of the aluminum extrusions, unit costs will be reduced by about one-half again.

None of the costs quoted above for the development of Daniel's collector unit includes the great deal of time and effort that he has devoted to the project.

CONCLUDING THOUGHTS

By and large Daniel is satisfied with the house and the solar system, as there have been no severe pitfalls. He is a bit disappointed that the estimated energy outputs for the collector quoted to him during the design phase were so low that he did not bother to run ducting more into the north wing of the house. If his calculations are correct his patented absorber plate's efficiency will be much better than anticipated, thus making additional ducting feasible. Although snow does not actually stick to the collector, it has had severe ice buildup on its exterior surface from the bottom up, when Daniel was not present to remove it—easy enough, as the bottom of the collector is so close to the ground. Daniel may excavate down beside the foundation to rectify this problem and is also considering expanding the excavation work to create a parabolic shape that, with snow on the ground, will reflect a considerable amount of solar radiation onto the collector.

Daniel, who has degrees in physics and mechanical engineering and has done graduate work in computer science and electronic engineering, has followed interesting and varied career paths related to his fields of study. However, he has become so engrossed in solar-energy development that he is now devoting full time to it. Patent approval for his collector design has been applied for in nine other countries. He is working on "another model solar home to be built on a lot adjacent to our own. With the exception of the collector panel itself, which will be the same for both houses, this new house will incorporate a passive system, in progress for patenting, that will create an inside-the-house space environment comparable to an entirely non-passive system." He is presently negotiating with prefab home manufacturers on this and hopes in the near future to market a complete two-story 1,500-sq.-ft. solar home with six rooms, 1¾ baths, and a fireplace for about $55,000, excluding land cost.

Looking east across the living room. The modified Rumford-style fireplace is capable of heating the living room, dining room, and kitchen.

Second-floor bedroom. The solar collector panels to the left are not completed.

Kitchen, with east-facing window.

Newport, Rhode Island
1,440 sq. ft. living area

CHURCH-COMMUNITY CORPORATION

The first solar house in Newport, Rhode Island, was sponsored by the Church-Community Corporation, a nonprofit housing group, in order to gain expertise for its low-income housing programs and to give the carpentry students of Newport County Vocational-Technical Facility at Rogers High School an opportunity to learn their trade by working on a real house and to become acquainted with the future of solar heating on an individual basis. The house was designed so that it would be fairly easy to build and could use off-the-shelf components. Ade Bethune, the corporation's vice-president, acted as the project manager. Gordon N. Preiss, P.E., from the Naval Underwater Systems Center, New London, Connecticut, was assigned to the project to design the solar system. Mr. Preiss was initially interested in designing a hydronic system, but the corporation wanted the house designed for a low-income family, which could mean perhaps a single mother and three children. In other words, they wanted a fail-safe system that did not require an engineering background to operate. Mr. Preiss understood this drawback of his more efficient but more complex hydronic system and thus became an advocate of the relatively simple air system that was agreed upon.

LOCATION AND ORIENTATION

The house is located at 50 Halsey Street in Newport, Rhode Island. The lot has a 50′ frontage on the street and is 100′ deep. The long axis of the building runs roughly east-west, so there is a wide southern exposure. The house is situated 10′ from the northern property line. Earth is banked higher against the north wall than the south in order to help insulate the former.

The prevailing winds come from the southwest in both summer and winter. The storm winds in summer come from the east and southeast, and in winter from the east and northeast. The house presents a relatively small surface area to winter storm winds and has only a small amount of glazing exposed to them.

ARCHITECTURAL FEATURES

This three-bedroom, two-story wood-frame home, measuring 20 x 36′, has 720 sq. ft. of floor area on each story. The full basement is unheated.

The house is designed as a heat- and energy-conserving comfortable family home. As can be seen from the floor plans, the living room, kitchen, and bedroom on the first floor are all oriented toward the sun. An overhang protects the interior from the hot summer sun while allowing the winter sun to provide a substantial amount of passive heat gain. The street entranceway, stairwells, pantry, and closets cover the entire north wall, providing an effective thermal buffer. Similarly, on the second floor, the stairwell, closets, and a dead-air space behind the tub provide insulation for the two bedrooms as well as the small study between them.

The full unheated basement accommodates the heating system and has a rock-storage bin at the east end. A produce-storage room was planned for the west end, near a bulkhead leading to the backyard and vegetable garden, but was never built because of budgeting priorities.

The 12″-wide poured-concrete foundation sits on footings 12″ high and 24″ wide. Two beams running the width of the basement permitted the 2 x 8 floor joists to run along the long axis of the house and thus made stairwell construction easier.

Flooring in the kitchen is a double layer of ⅝″ plywood topped with congoleum. The remainder of the house features wide 1″-thick knotty-pine boards.

The full double-flue masonry chimney is located near the center of the house to minimize heat losses.

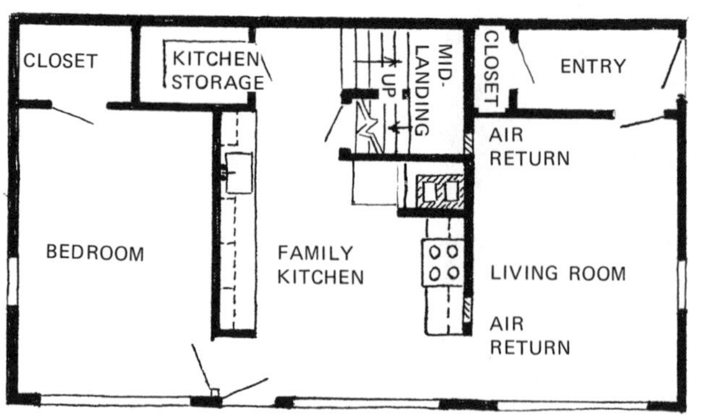

GROUND FLOOR

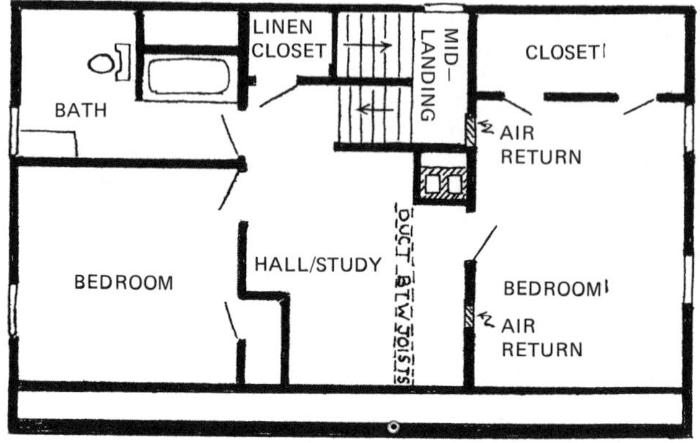

SECOND FLOOR

ternal skin on the roof's south slope. The rest of the roof has tarpaper and asphalt shingles.

Exterior Walls

The exterior walls are framed with 2 x 6 studs on 24″ centers. These have been sheathed with 4 x 8′ sheets of exterior-grade plywood. Plywood provides very good bracing against racking—that is, the distortion of a building under horizontal shearing forces, usually wind pressure against exterior walls. In addition, because of the small number of seams, infiltration losses are reduced. Tarpaper covers the plywood, and untreated white cedar shingles, 5″ to 6″ to the weather, form the exterior skin. These shingles weather to beautiful silver-gray with age. The cavities between the exterior plywood and interior gypsum board are filled with cellulose-fiber insulation.

Interior Walls and Ceilings

All interior walls are 2 x 4 studwalls; they and the ceilings are sheathed with ½″ gypsum board.

Roof

The roof rafters are 2 x 6s on 24″ centers. The site-built solar collector is built directly over the ⅝″ plywood roof sheathing and thus forms the weatherproof external skin on the roof's south slope. The rest of the roof has tarpaper and asphalt shingles.

Insulation Summary

Ceiling: R-36; 8″ cellulose fiber

Walls: R-27; 6″ cellulose fiber. The cellulose fiber was blown into the cavities between the 2 x 6 studs after the polyethylene vapor barrier was applied but before the gypsum board was installed. A plywood sheet was held against the studs to prevent bulging, but this proved to be an unsatisfactory way of insulating. It was thought that this method would permit easy inspection of the quality of the insulating; however, although the cellulose was relatively stable, it did tend to bulge somewhat after the plywood sheet was removed and thus made application of the sheetrock more difficult. In the future cellulose will be blown in through holes in the exterior plywood.

Basement: No insulation was applied either to the exterior or interior basement walls or floor. Because the engineer did not think it worth doing within the limited budget. However, the present owner may want to add insulation later.

A single skylight is the only fenestration on the north side of the house. The east airlock entranceway, stairwells, pantry, and closets are all located on the north wall to insulate the living spaces from the north winter winds.

Doors

The street entranceway, which faces the cold east and northeast winter storm winds, has an airlock vestibule measuring approximately 4 x 9′. The side entranceway from the driveway on the warm south side of the house enters directly into the family kitchen. Both entrance doors are the steel-insulated Pease doors with magnetic weatherstripping. The site-fabricated exterior basement door is of 4″-thick wood-frame construction with plywood facing and fiberglass insulation. All three bedrooms have well-fitted doors, permitting these rooms to be isolated when not in use and when heat is not required.

Windows

Each of the three rooms on the first floor has a large wood-sash double-glazed ¾″ thermopane fixed picture window. A double-hung window was installed immediately to the east of each of these to permit good ventilation in summer. The first-floor bedroom has another double-hung window on its west wall, and the living room has another on its east wall. Upstairs, the larger bedroom has two double-hung windows to the east, and the smaller bedroom and the bathroom each have one on the west wall. Ade stated, "We wanted wood storm windows but finally had to settle for combination storm and screen aluminum windows." As all the window sashes were of 4 -inch-wide wood-framing stock they had to be built up on the inside to the width of the 2 x 6 studwalls.

There are two cellar windows on the south side and one on the west for the produce-storage room. Each of these is fitted with an inside-mounted site-fabricated Kalwall Sun-Lite Premium double-glazed storm window.

The only glazing on the north wall is a site-built operable skylight above the stairwell leading to the second floor. In addition to being an effective light source, this skylight is a good ventilator in summer. It too is fitted with a double acrylic panel.

No shutters were installed. "The new owner started with only venetian blinds on the three picture windows on the south side. However, he plans to use curtains in addition, as we advised him to do."

View from kitchen to living room on the east.

Detail of the mechanical room of the air-type collector, rock-storage solar system.

LANDSCAPING

A hedge has been planted along the north and west sides of the house which, when it matures, will help to insulate the house from summer heat and winter cold.

A tulip tree, which grows fast and straight with thick foliage, has been planted 15′ to the west of the house to provide shade from the hot summer afternoon sun. Similarly, a linden tree has been planted to the east to provide protection from the low-angled early-morning summer sun.

A lawn provides an additional cooling effect in summer, and the loose-gravel driveway disperses the sun's rays, causing less glare than a flat, uniform surface.

SOLAR-HEATING SYSTEM

This house has two solar components. A substantial amount of passive heat gain is received directly through the large south-facing windows.

The active component is described next.

Collector

The 450-sq.-ft. collector, built by Peter F. de Bethune, Ade's nephew, is 12½ x 36′ long and has a tilt angle 67° from the horizontal. It consists of regular ⅝″ plywood roof sheathing, a 1½″ airspace for circulating air, a .032″ aluminum absorber plate painted with 3M Nextel selective flat black paint; a 1½″ dead-air space, and a ⅝″ sandwich of two layers of Kalwall Sun-Lite Premium. Each collector section is 2′ wide to fit the 24″ O.C. roof rafters.

The circulating airspace is created by nailing 1½″ x 1¾″ vertical wood fins onto the roof sheathing over the 2 x 6 roof rafters. The absorber plate, in 4 x 12½′ sheets, is then stretched across these fins. A second set of fins of the same dimensions is then nailed over the absorber plate on top of the first and running in the same direction. The Sun-Lite panels are each 2′ wide and 12′4″ long and have a 1 x ⅝″ wood frame around the perimeter. They rest on the outside fins, and each pair is secured to a wood fin with aluminum battens that are silicone-sealed and screwed. Strips of Sun-Lite, ⅝″ wide, arranged in S-curves, separate the two layers of fiberglass glazing.

The roof sheathing stops short of the ends of the rafters by about 6″ at both top and bottom to accommodate air passage to and from the collector from the supply and return manifolds. The collector supply manifold runs the entire length of the house behind the top of the roof. Air is blown down the collector to a hot-air manifold running the length of the house at the base of the roof.

Storage

The storage bin, containing 17 cu. yds. of rock, measures approximately 8 x 10 x 6′ high and is located at the east end of the basement. Its 6″-thick pad footing was poured at the same time as the foundation footing. The 6″ concrete basement floor was then poured over this. A 6″ layer of beadboard was placed against the inside of the east wall of the basement, and a concrete block wall was laid against that to form one wall of the storage reservoir. Concrete was then poured to form the other three walls which are 10″ thick. A 6″ layer of Styrofoam was then laid inside the bin on the basement floor and a 4″-thick concrete pad was poured over this.

Chain-link fencing on the north and south ends of the storage bin separates the rock chamber from about an 8″ airspace at either end. From one airspace, hot air flows across the bin to the other when the system is sending heat to storage. When the house demands heat from storage, the flow reverses direction. Gordon Preiss later realized that a better design would have been to have the two outlets one on top of the other at the same end. The crushed rocks vary in diameter from 2½″ to 5″, because that is what the builders were able to get at the last minute. Ade advises builders to "not start anything until you have your supply of two-and-a-half-inch round stones delivered and waiting on the site." The top of the bin is covered with a plastic vapor barrier and a concrete slab, and then it and the south, north, and west walls are insulated with 6″ of beadboard. The concrete pad at the bottom of the storage reservoir was sloped slightly to one corner and a tube was installed from that point to the outside of the storage in order to drain off any possible moisture accumulation.

Heat Distribution

Air distributed by the furnace blower is heated in order of priority: (1) by the sun striking "collectors" during hours of sunshine; (2) when the sun does not shine, by a "heat sink"—that is, the heat-storage bin of round stones in the basement; and (3) by the furnance oil burner, only when there is no heat and storage has been exhausted. The schematic diagram shows how the air is routed.

The heating system is divided into two zones—first floor and second floor—each equipped with its own thermostat. The Tro-a-Temp control system, designed by Gordon and manufactured by the Trolex Corporation of Kenilworth, New Jersey, automatically determines the mode of operation. It directs sun-heated air to the rooms, to storage, from storage to furnace, or to the attic to vent it during summer. The control system "ended up costing too much, as we had to interface this control with the work of an electrical contractor on one hand and a sheet-metal heating man on the other. Neither of them knew what it was all about. Thus backtracking and lost time. Today complete systems are available with dampers and control panel all built in—more efficient and more economical."

Control system located under the basement stairs.

Detail of rock bin construction.

Top: Ade Bethune, project manager for the construction of this home, relaxes in the kitchen. Note the large south window.

Above: The living-room doorway leads to the east airlock entry.

AUXILIARY HEATING

The 85,000-Btu forced-air oil-fired furnace is the smallest capacity that the corporation was able to procure at the time of construction. Though the engineer considered it too large for this small well-insulated house, it is the standard type of furnace used in this area. A wood stove can be hooked up to the spare flue if desired.

PERCENT SOLAR-HEATED

The solar system has not been monitored. However, the engineer has estimated that the active system provides about 55% of the house's heating needs. The total solar contribution may be higher because of the large south-facing windows and could be quite a bit higher if insulated shutters or curtains were added.

Oil consumption from August 1, 1977, to May 1, 1978, was 361 gallons.

COOLING SYSTEM

The double-hung windows on the first floor provide good cross-ventilation. The insulation, the south-roof overhang, and the vegetation mentioned earlier provide an additional cooling effect in summer. The basement bulkhead door can be opened to create a cool draft up the stairwell.

A ceiling grille above the second-floor study is opened during summer months. With the skylight and double-hung windows open on the second floor, drafts are created toward this grille. When the attic reaches a preset temperature a roof fan comes on automatically, increasing the draft and thus the cooling effect on both the attic and the second floor. The planned kitchen storm door will provide additional ventilation yet avoid insects.

WATER SUPPLY AND WASTE SYSTEM

City water, coming in at ground temperature, is piped into a copper coil buried in the stones near the hot end of the storage chamber, where it is preheated prior to going into a conventional oil-fired 30-gallon hot-water tank. The bathroom has a water-saver toilet and shower head. Waterborne wastes enter the city sewer system.

ELECTRICAL POWER SYSTEM

This house has a standard electrical utility grid hookup No fluorescent lighting is used, but a substantial amount of natural light enters the living spaces. Though the solar system includes three electrically operated blowers (one in the conventional furnace) and motorized dampers, most of this is on low voltage.

MAJOR HOUSEHOLD APPLIANCES

The electric range, refrigerator, washer, dryer, TV, and stereo are not particularly energy-conserving models, yet the electric bills have been very low, as the following monthly kilowatt-hour consumption figures for the 1977-78 heating season illustrate: August 29, 176 kwh; September 20 (bill date), 238 kwh; October 20, 230 kwh; November 18, 304 kwh; December 20, 310 kwh; January 19, 304 kwh; February 17, 320 kwh; and March 21, 212 kwh.

FOOD SYSTEM

A substantial amount of unshaded garden space exists to the west of the house. The corporation has planned a cold-storage room, which could easily be added there.

COSTS

The Church-Community Corporation had hoped that with the free services of Gordon Preiss (the solar engineer) and the carpentry students this house would cost considerably less than a conventional house; however, they discovered that it cost as much as it would have had they hired a contractor. The project took considerably longer than the three to six months a contractor would have taken and thus the carrying charges were greater. Because of their inexperience and in some cases lack of commitment or incentive to cut costs, the students wasted more material than a profit-conscious contractor would have. Between the first school year and the second school year a contractor had to be hired to close in the framing that the students had started. He redid some of the students' work, and when the new class of students started work in the fall there was similar duplication of work and thus a certain loss of time and materials. Another disadvantage of building in this manner was that the project was not able to save on materials purchased to the same degree that a contractor could.

Despite all of these problems a fine, energy-efficient, comfortable, and attractive house resulted. The final cost was $43,000, including $8,000 for the solar installation. The experience that the students gained is immeasurable.

Old Lyme, Connecticut
1,900 sq. ft. living area

Solar-Tec House

GEORGE C. FIELD CO.

The George C. Field Co. has been in the construction business on the Connecticut shoreline for 80 years. Its Solar-Tec division (Colton Road, P.O. Box 175, East Lyme, Conn.), managed by LeRoy R. Clark, has now built five solar-heated houses. Roy Clark has provided the motivation for the company's solar direction, as he is interested in "trying to do some good things for the environment and people in particular, and trying to give the company a start toward what may be the answer to the energy problem in the future." This house was built for speculation, monitored for one winter, and then placed on the market. It was bought by Alan and Mary Bradford in October 1977.

LOCATION AND ORIENTATION

The Solar-Tec house is located on a ¾-acre lot overlooking the wooded hills of Old Lyme, Connecticut, and is only half a mile from boat-launching and the saltwater beaches of Long Island Sound. The house faces due south and is built into an east-sloping hill. The basement is thus buried on the west side; and, because of excavation, also on the north side. A natural grove of cedars provides privacy, wind protection, and shade and reduces the visual impact of the large south-facing rooftop collectors without affecting the amount of incident solar radiation, even at the lowest solar angles.

ARCHITECTURAL FEATURES

This wood-frame traditional New England saltbox design has eight rooms on two floors whose total area is 1,900 sq. ft., plus an unfinished basement family/recreation room opening directly onto the yard. A two-car garage and a covered walkway provide thermal buffering for the main entrance on the north side of the house.

The foundation is poured concrete on three sides with a 2 x 4 studwall on the east side. Prefinished oak flooring was used over plywood subflooring and 2 x 10 floor joists.

Exterior Walls

Standard 2 x 4 studwall construction was used. Vertical cedar boards were chosen for siding because of their superior insulating and rot-resistant qualities. A gray-blue exterior stain was used rather than paint.

Interior Walls and Ceilings

Standard ½" gypsum board painted in light colors has been used for walls and ceilings throughout the house. A cathedral ceiling was used for the second floor, as the back of the collector had to be insulated along its entire length anyway.

Roof

Standard asphalt shingles were placed over exterior-grade plywood sheathing and 2 x 6 roof rafters.

Insulation Summary

Ceiling: R-25; 5½" fiberglass plus 1" Styrofoam-SM on both the north- and south-sloping roofs. No roof venting is used, as the George C. Field Co. has found that none is required if no dead-air space exists between the ceiling and roof (the cavity is completely filled with insulation) and if a good vapor barrier is used.

Walls: R-18; 4½" Totalwall system composed of 3½" fiberglass batts with an external sheathing of 2 x 8' sheets of 1"-thick tongue-and-groove Dow Styrofoam-SM.

Basement: Only the east wood-frame wall is insulated. It has 3½" fiberglass batts. As the basement is unfinished, the basement ceiling was insulated with 6" fiberglass batts so it could be kept cooler than the main part of the house.

Polyethylene vapor barrier has been used on the warm side of all insulation. Special care was taken to ensure that all windows and doors were properly caulked and weatherstripped.

Doors

The protected north entranceway has a windowless, insulated steel-clad door with magnetic weatherstripping. Doors leading from the second-floor master bedroom to a small east-facing balcony, those on the first floor exiting on to the large east-facing deck and the west-facing porch, and those from the family/recreation room are all aluminum-frame thermopane sliding doors. These doors are fitted with insulated shutters that slide on standard closet-door tracks. The shutters are of wood-frame construction with 1" of fiberglass insulation.

Windows

Pella windows are used throughout the house, as Roy feels that these are one of the tightest-fitting, lowest-heat-loss windows available. The double-glazed windows with a removable inner glazing were chosen over standard thermopane insulating windows for their slightly higher insulating value.

The window area is a relatively moderate 170 sq. ft. The bulk of the windows are on the east side because of the spectacular view. Windows were not placed on the south side because of the low-level shading from the cedar trees and to ensure privacy; however, the two small operable Ventarama skylights placed in the kitchen provide substantial amounts of daylight, passive heat gain, and ventilation.

Another skylight above the second-floor hall provides natural light through two stories of hallways and stairs. When this skylight is open during the summer, a chimney effect is created so that hot air is efficiently vented up and out.

LANDSCAPING

Existing cedar trees were left around the house perimeter for reasons mentioned earlier. A considerable amount of filling had to be done to raise the level of the land where the garage now sits in order to reduce the slope of the garage driveway. Grass was sown to reduce erosion of the existing and man-made slopes, as well as for cooling and aesthetic reasons.

SOLAR-HEATING SYSTEM

Roy believes strictly in using air systems, as they are less expensive and more readily built on site than liquid systems. They are also not subject to freezing, nor is a leak in the system as serious as in a liquid system. This system is basically the same as the one installed in House 24, with a few exceptions.

Collector

This site-built collector system is composed of an array of 36 3 x 6½' panels arranged three rows high and 12 columns wide. Their total area is 650 sq. ft. The system is identical in area and construction to that of

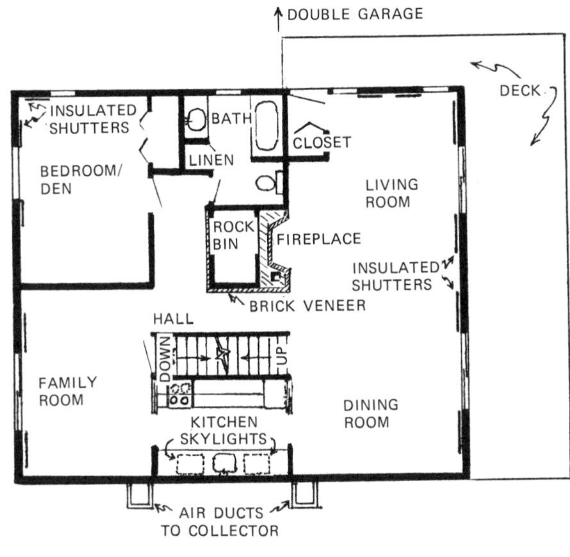

GROUND FLOOR

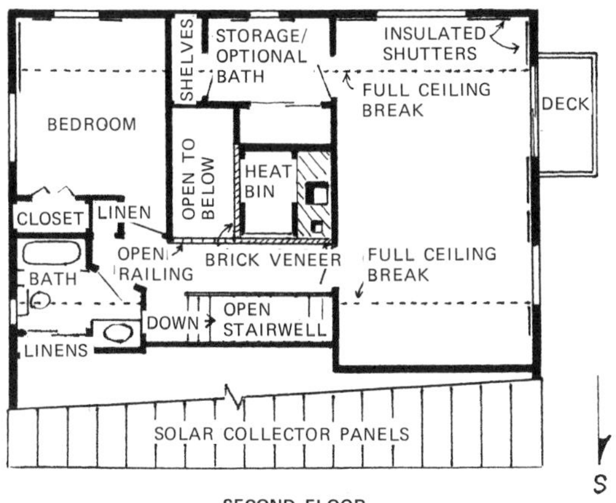

SECOND FLOOR

House 24 except that on the latter the panels are two rows high and 18 columns wide. See House 24 for construction details.

Storage

The 6 x 6 x 30′-high rock storage butts against the back of the centrally located east-facing fireplace and chimney and runs from the basement floor to near the ceiling of the second floor. The inside dimensions are 5 x 3 x 29′. The 1,080-cu.-ft. bin is filled with 30 tons of rock 4″ to 6″ in diameter. This large size was chosen to facilitate the best airflow by reducing the pressure drop through the storage bin. The structure is of steel frame with steel sheeting secured to the inside to contain the rocks. A 3½″ layer of fiberglass outside the steel sheeting minimizes heat losses from storage. An attractive 4″ red-brick veneer was used to face the chimney and rock storage so they appear as one unit. Since the structure is exposed to the living spaces and the stairwell, which wraps around it, any heat losses from either the chimney or rock storage are given off as usable heat. The other advantages of this type of storage are that it permits hot air to be immediately dumped into storage without any significant line losses, and that hot air from the adjacent Heatilator fireplace is easily ducted into storage rather than directly into living spaces. The massive structure serves as a constant but aesthetically pleasing reminder of how the house is heated. The main disadvantage to this type of storage system is that, because of its height, it is more costly than a typical basement storage system of comparable capacity.

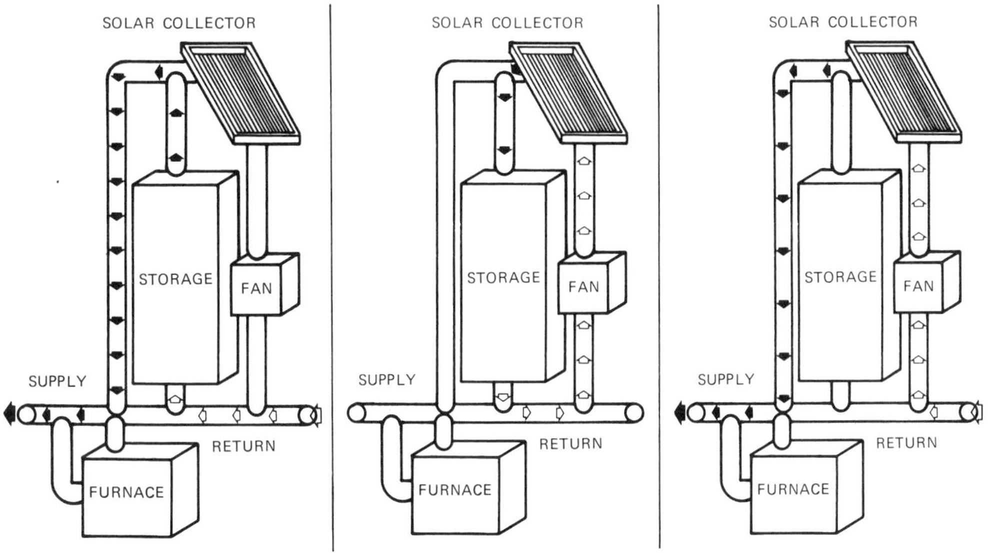

Heat Distribution

The air-handling system—an all-forced-air system—is similar to that of House 24 except the latter has no furnace and air direction is reversed by a damper. When heating from storage, if the collector is cool and the storage hot, air is drawn upward through the storage reservoir, heated, and then distributed throughout the house. When storing heat, with the collector temperature higher than the storage temperature, heat is ducted directly to the storage reservoir. When heating from the collector, the hot air is circulated directly from the collector to the house.

Two blowers are actually employed. The first, a ¼-hp blower, which is integral to the backup oil furnance, picks up hot air coming from the collector or storage (or if the solar system is not in operation, from the house return-air registers) and distributes it to the house. When the solar system is functioning the 1/3-hp second fan, or solar fan, becomes operational. Working in conjunction with the furnace fan, it blows air at 1,500 cu. ft. per minute through the collector and downward through the bin, where much thermal stratification occurs. The furnace blower draws air upward through the bin to pick up heat. Return registers are located near the peak of the second-floor ceiling, so that any warm air that does rise to that point during the heating cycle will be returned to storage.

The main feeder duct is 8 x 30", changing to square where it rises. The feeders to each collector row from the main manifold duct are 7"-diameter round duct. Some ducts are fiberglass; others are standard galvanized. Some are insulated with 1" rigid fiberglass aluminum-foil-faced insulation.

A Rho Sigma differential thermostat activates the blower and damper motors in order to switch the system from one mode of operation to another. Roy Clark's firm is working on a dampering system that doesn't rely on the relatively expensive and large commercial damper motors that they now use. Their main objective is to get the costs down without sacrificing efficiency.

As the lot is well treed, the solar collectors on the south sloping roof are barely visible from the street.

AUXILIARY HEATING

A Lennox oil furnace is the main backup heat source. If the house requires heat and it cannot be supplied either from storage or directly from the collector, the oil furnace is automatically turned on. There is also a manual control for the oil furnace so that a family that really wanted to conserve oil could switch this off and burn only wood in the fireplace instead.

Roy admits that his firm did not do much research as to which fireplaces are the most efficient. They chose not to install an outside air intake to the firebox, although Roy actually installed one in his own home. The Solar-Tec house Heatilator was fitted with a metal cover to reduce heat loss up the flue when there is no fire. An extra flue was installed in the chimney with a knockout in the basement in the event that the new homeowners want to install a wood stove in the family/recreation room.

PERCENT SOLAR-HEATED

The design calculations estimated a 65% solar-heating contribution. The company monitored the system during the winter of 1976 - 77 before selling the house and discovered that the actual performance matched the predicted performance. With thermostats set at 70° F. the Solar-Tec house cost $45 to heat in December, $55 to heat in frigid January, and $35 for the month of February. Fuel oil cost 47¢ per gallon. The fact that the winter of 1976-77 was colder than usual was offset by an unusual number of sunny days, but the overall fuel savings are typical of what can be expected over the years. The Bradfords monitored the system during the winter of 1977-78 and recorded very good results, similar to those recorded by Solar-Tec.

COOLING SYSTEM

No air conditioning or other mechanical cooling devices are used or needed. The skylight above the stairwell creates a chimney effect when open and thus very effectively exhausts unwanted hot air. Good insulation and operable windows also help to keep the house cooler in summer. The prevailing southeast summer breezes run along the deck and thus allow one to enjoy that space even during the hot summer.

There is a summer dump which allows hot air to be dumped to the outside after heating the domestic hot water. The system is designed to withstand heat buildup in the event of a power failure.

WATER SUPPLY AND WASTE SYSTEM

A community water system composed of drilled wells and a conventional underground supply system services this house and about 20 others in the area.

For the domestic hot-water supply, a pump takes water from an 80-gallon holding tank and circulates it through 100′ of ¾″ finned copper tubing whenever the solar blower runs. This tubing is located near the top of the storage reservoir and is accessible through a trap door in the side of the structure. The water is heated in the copper tubing and returns to the 80-gallon Ford tank. Hot water is then tapped off the top of this tank to a 52-gallon electric hot-water tank, which boosts the temperature if required. The factory-insulated electric tank was further insulated on site with 3″ of wrapped fiberglass insulation. The percent of the domestic hot water that is supplied by the solar system has not been determined, although it is known that in July the contribution is 100%. During that month, the electricity was turned off to the hot-water tank, as it was not required.

No special water-conserving fixtures were installed. A conventional septic system was installed.

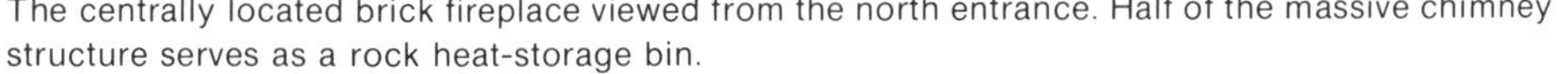

The centrally located brick fireplace viewed from the north entrance. Half of the massive chimney structure serves as a rock heat-storage bin.

The small but efficient galley kitchen is conveniently located midway between the family room and dining room. The two kitchen skylights are the only fenestration on the south side of the house.

ELECTRIC POWER SYSTEM

The house gets its power from the local utility grid. No fluorescent or other particularly energy-conserving lighting fixtures were installed; however, windows and skylights were located so as to minimize the need for artificial light during daylight hours.

COSTS

Roy Clark will not say how much it cost the George C. Field Co. to build this house; however, the company recently sold it for $77,000 including the ¾-acre lot. He said the land price was fairly low but the cost of the septic system and the landscaping was fairly high because of the steep slope. The installed cost of the complete solar system was approximately $8,000.

CONCLUDING THOUGHTS

Roy is very happy with the Solar-Tec system. "The company will continue toward providing the same type of system but at a lower price. We are now going more toward custom solar houses and can't envision putting up a subdivision of, say, ten solar houses until there is a wider acceptance of solar heat. We should push energy conservation first and really encourage the use of solar energy, but when we do a cost analysis for some people at current prices it often just doesn't work economically. If people have the financial resources now, it is a better investment than having your money in the bank; however, if one has to eliminate a substantial portion of the house to install the solar system and has to borrow mortgage money at current interest rates, solar becomes less attractive. It should be noted that our system provides more heat at a lower installation cost than any other system on the market that we know about. If there was a more cost-effective system, we would use it." As for the occupants, the Bradfords, they are enthusiastic about the system.

Left: The chimney/rock storage bin gives dramatic indication of the source of heat needed to maintain the house at comfort levels.

Near Osgoode, Ontario
1,850 sq. ft.
including basement

MARTIN and CAROLE STANLEY-JONES

The Stanley-Joneses started building their new home in the summer of 1975. They thought at first in terms of a well-insulated dwelling, but then they came across an article on solar panels and decided instead to build a solar-heated house. Carole and Martin designed the building and solar system themselves. As they are both electrical engineers some of the design aspects were not as difficult for them as they would be for others; however, they had never attempted a major building project before. They contracted the foundation work and hired a carpenter for six weeks to help with the framing. The rest of the work they did themselves. Martin describes Carole's contribution: "Whatever activity you can think of, my wife was there working at it—the installation of the septic tank and field, plastering, painting, wiring, plumbing, tile laying, doors, trim, brick and stone facing, hardwood flooring, carpeting, and on and on. She built half the house while I built the other half." Somehow during all this Carole found the time and energy to give birth to a healthy boy—their first child.

LOCATION AND ORIENTATION

The house is near Osgoode, Ontario. It faces due south and is located on the southwest corner of a relatively flat 25-acre parcel of land. The house is quite exposed on its windward side, as the cold northeast winter winds speed unimpeded across the treeless fields. One small poplar tree on the south side provides some summer shade. Future plans call for the planting of a good windbreak and more shade trees.

ARCHITECTURAL FEATURES

This one-and-a-half-story house in the French Canadian style has 1,850 sq. ft. of heated area, including a full basement. The poured-concrete foundation is insulated externally with polystyrene foam insulation varying in thickness from 1" at the bottom to 3" at the top. There is a ⅜" drainage space between the wall and the insulation. It has two second-story dormers on the south side and one on the north. A large overhang along the entire length of the south side provides shade to the first floor in summer but allows the lower winter sun to penetrate the large south-facing windows, providing a significant amount of solar-heat gain.

The large archways between living spaces on the first floor are all fitted with louvered or sliding doors. When opened they give a feeling of spaciousness and allow good air circulation. They can be closed to provide privacy or better zone temperature control. The second floor has a door at the top of the stairs permitting that floor to be sealed off, so the second floor can be kept at a lower temperature when desired. The chimney effect of warm air rising up a stairwell is thereby controlled.

The den on the southeast corner of the house with its high-efficiency fireplace and large south-facing window for effective daytime solar-heat gain could serve as a snug family retreat during severe cold snaps

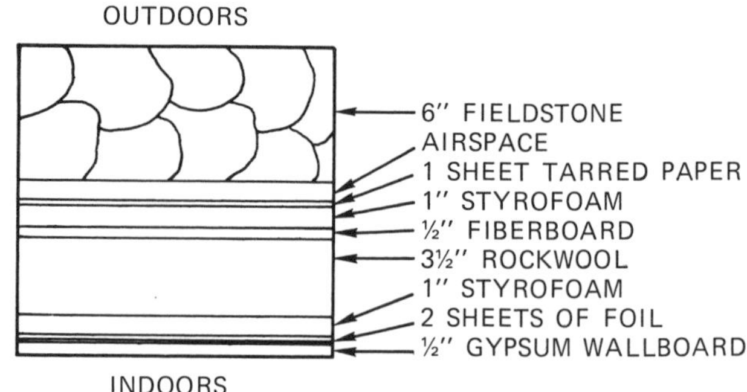

WALL CONSTRUCTION

Martin Stanley-Jones and his son, Andrew, discuss the future of solar heating in Canada. The water-storage tank is buried beneath them. Note the absence of windows on this west face of the building.

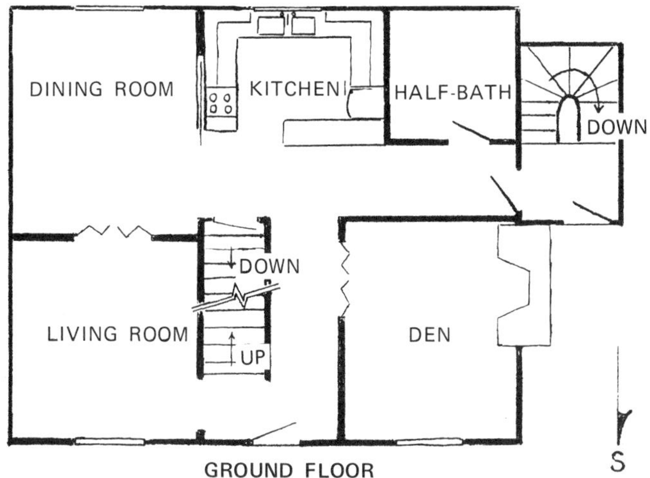

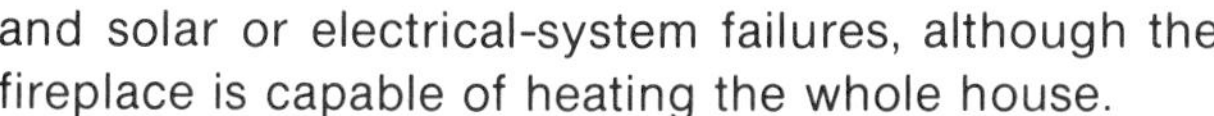

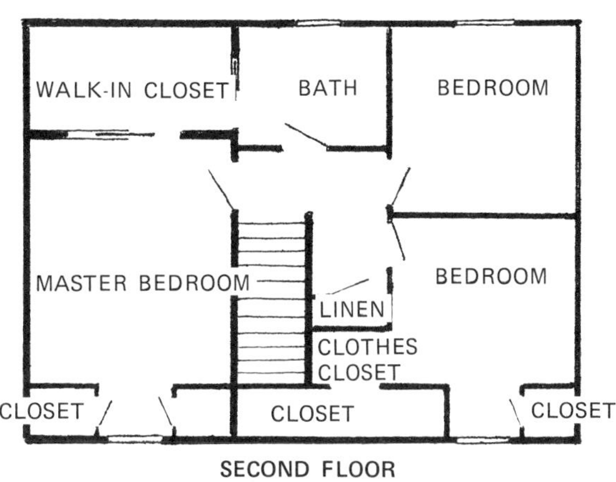

and solar or electrical-system failures, although the fireplace is capable of heating the whole house.

Exterior Walls

The exterior walls are of standard 2 x 4 wood studwall construction with 6″ exterior fieldstone facing. The diagram of the wall cross section illustrates how a high insulating value was achieved.

Interior Walls and Ceilings

All interior partition walls are also of 2 x 4 studding. All interior partition walls and ceilings are sheathed in ½″ gypsum board. It is painted light in color to compensate for the relatively small window area.

Roof

Standard exterior-grade plywood sheathing, building paper, and asphalt shingles were used over rafters spaced on 16″ centers.

Insulation Summary

Walls: R-27; various materials as shown in diagram

Ceilings: R-52; R-20 rock wool, first covered with R-20 fiberglass and then another layer of R-12 rock wool

Basement: Approximately R-14 near top of foundation (3″ polystyrene foam). The foam tapers off to about 1″ thickness near the bottom of the foundation.

The house is quite exposed to the strong northeast winter winds; however, it is so well insulated and weatherstripped that it requires only a sixth of the heat of a comparable house insulated to Canadian government (Central Mortgage and Housing Corporation) minimum standards in 1975 when it was built.

Doors

The front entrance is on the warmer south side of the house and is protected by the overhang. The entrance most used, especially in winter, is via an entrance hall on the east end of the house whose temperature is kept just above freezing. This two-door airlock system decreases the amount of air infiltration. This entrance is heated via a small heat exchanger controlled by the upstairs thermostat. The idea was to provide enough heat to stop freezing but not enough to maintain the first-floor temperature. Since the second-floor thermostat is always lower than that of the first floor and the heat exchanger is smaller than normal, it is possible to guarantee a low side-entrance temperature and thus low heat loss upon use. The outside door is solid wood and weatherstripped but will be exchanged for a better-insulated steel door like the one used for the front entrance.

Windows

Window area, except on the south side of the first floor, was kept to a minimum. There are no windows on the east and west sides of the house. Still, the total window area in living spaces is 12% of the floor area compared to CMHC's minimum requirement of 10%. All the windows on the first floor are double-glazed thermopane. They are made by Dashwood and are of cedar-sash construction. The second-story windows are Solaris 3″ double slider type with exposed cedar sash. All windows are now fitted with interior wooden louvered shutters.

The Dashwood windows were chosen for their low air penetration; however, 25% more heat is lost through the windows in this house than through all the walls. Martin has considered triple-glazing the windows, particularly those on the north side; however, he now feels that it will be best to add insulated shutters.

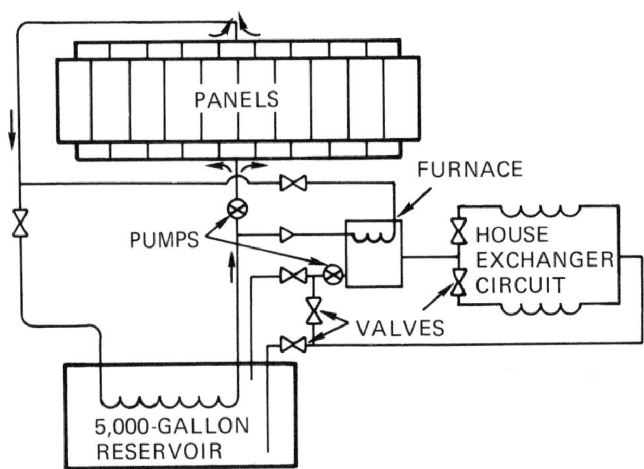

SOLAR-HEATING SYSTEM

The house has a liquid solar system. This type is more difficult to construct and install and requires more maintenance than an air system, but it is more efficient.

Collector

The collector system is composed of 10 Sunworks, water-type collectors each measuring 3 x 7′. The collector area is 210 sq. ft. gross and about 200 sq. ft. net.

Many solar-heated houses have a collector area roughly half that of the heated floor area. The Stanley-Joneses were able to get by with such a small collector area and thus a relatively small investment in solar equipment because of the superior insulation and weatherstripping. It is significantly cheaper to insulate than to insolate. In addition to the initial capital savings with a smaller collector area, maintenance costs will be reduced. The collector panels face due south and are tilted 45° from the horizontal. Each collector is glazed with a single sheet of tempered 3/16″ glass with a solar transmittance of 92%. The absorber plate is composed of selectively blackened 7-ounce (0.01″) copper sheet to which ¼″ m-type copper tubing has been silver-soldered. This is backed by 2½″ fiberglass insulation. Extruded-aluminum mullion and housing contain the various components.

Martin would not use these same panels again, as they are not Canadian-made and are not designed for the Canadian climate. He feels that in cold Ontario the efficiency has to be maximized and therefore what's needed is a collector with greater insulation and an absorber-plate design that allows greater exposure of the heat-transfer medium to the plate surface. Martin feels that Fibretech (5 Montée des Arsenaut, St. Paul l'Ermite, P.O. Box 100, Comte l'Assomption, Quebec S5Z 2N4) produces a panel that better meets his criteria. The Sunworks collectors cost $300 per panel, or more than $14 per sq. ft., delivered on site in 1974.

In order to prevent freezing in the collectors, 20 imperial gallons of a 50% ethylene glycol solution is used as the heat-transfer medium. A ¼-hp centrifugal pump circulates this fluid at 4 gallons per minute in a closed loop through the collector to a heat exchanger in the storage tank.

Temperature sensors are placed in the top of the storage tank and the collector. When the temperature in the collector is hotter than that in storage, a differential thermostat commands the pump to circulate the ethylene glycol.

Storage

The cylindrical storage tank is 8′ in diameter and 16′ long, of ¼″ plate steel. It holds 5,000 imperial gallons (6,000 U.S. gallons) and is buried underground just to the west of the house. The tank, salvaged from a wrecking yard, cost $500 delivered to the site. It was painted on the inside with lead paint. The outside was wrapped with polystyrene foam varying in thickness from 6″ at the bottom of the tank to 12″ at the top. The manhole was covered with a protective layer of wire mesh and the tank was then covered with earth. Because of the extremely low heat loss in the house and the tank, the system is too effective, and the storage liquid tends to overheat. In order to rectify this a second tank the same size will be added. This will reduce the temperatures in storage but not the quantity of heat stored. The extent of the overheating problem is unknown; however, when the final control system is installed it should be possible to determine. The present control system heats the tank to a preset maximum temperature of 60° C. (140° F.) by late June. Last summer from June 24 through September the system had to dump heat by running the heat-transfer fluid through the collectors at night and dissipating heat to the cooler night air. Ironically, some designers had recommended that the Stanley-Joneses use a storage tank only one-fifth the size.

Heat Distribution

The second loop in the heating system uses conventional hot-water baseboard radiators. When rooms need heat a thermostat activates a 1/12-hp centrifugal pump that circulates hot water from the top of the tank to the house.

Auxiliary Heating

An oil-fired water boiler is integrated with the solar system. Martin has taken steps to improve its efficiency. Normally, in-house air is used for combustion air and for draft control on the chimney. Martin adapted the vent system so outside air is used in both cases. One has to be careful when setting up this system that the flue-stack temperature doesn't drop too low and cause condensation in the stack. Before this furnace retrofit was done the flapper on the chimney would wobble excessively, particularly in strong winds. Wind blowing across the chimney would suck a considerable amount of air up the stack. There is a good description of this type of furnace adaption in an article in the February 1976 *Popular Science*, and a subsequent reader comment in the June 1976 issue.

A high-efficiency (manufacturer claims 80%) Northern Heatliner fireplace manufactured by Northern Fireplace Ltd. is capable of heating the whole house. An outside vent allows outdoor air to be heated and circulated into the house. Some of this air then becomes the air supply for combustion in the fireplace. The Stanley-Joneses are delighted with the Northern Heatliner, although they have encountered a few problems. A manually operated flap is installed in the ductwork near the fireplace; however, as this is not on the outside wall they have had a considerable amount of moisture and ice buildup in the ductwork. Because the flap is neither airtight nor insulated, infiltration and conductance heat losses occur. Martin added a bug screen on the outside duct and will later install an airtight, insulated exterior flap. Newer models of the Northern Heatliner have a fan in the outside air duct

The efficient Northern Heatliner fireplace with its glass doors and an outside air intake duct is capable of heating the entire house.

Martin displays the spare Sunworks water-type collector. Water flows through the parallel ¼" copper tubes.

The ¼-hp pump on the left circulates the heat-transfer medium in a closed loop through the collectors to a heat exchanger in the storage tank. The 1/12-hp pump on the right serves the hot-water baseboard radiators in the living spaces.

with an outside flap that automatically closes when the fan is off. If Carole and Martin built again they would place the fireplace chimney on an interior wall. Masonry fireplaces have a large heat capacity, but when they are constructed on an outside wall much of this heat is lost to the outside. Also, outside-wall chimneys are more apt to accumulate creosote buildup and are more influenced by the house stack effect—that is, as warm air rises in a house, cold outside air is sucked in through openings such as chimneys and cracks in doors and windows.

Martin, an electrical engineer, is building his own automatic-control panel for the solar-heating system.

PERCENT SOLAR-HEATED

During the first full heating season that the solar system operated, which was 1977-78, the oil-fired boiler consumed 175 imperial gallons (210 U.S. gallons) of oil with house temperatures maintained day and night at 21° C. (70° F.). Martin calculated that the heat loss for the building was 39 million Btu for that heating season. With 100,000 usable Btu per imperial gallon of fuel, he determined that the oil furnace therefore supplied 17.5 million Btu. This represents 45% of the house's heating needs. The remaining 55% is supplied by the solar system, direct solar gain, fireplace, and other sources of heat. No calculations have been done to determine the fractional contribution of each. The fireplace burned half to three-quarters of a cord of cedar and poplar. The electric usage is 32 kwh per day, of which 66% is considered to be used for hot-water generation. An average 2.5 gallons of propane is used every three months, and the three occupants—two adults and one infant—generate a certain amount of heat.

During the 1977-78 heating season, the stone facing for the exterior walls was not complete, nor were window shutters installed. Also the switchover from oil heat to solar heat and vice-versa is presently manually controlled. With the stone facing, window shuttering, and automatic control system complete and with the capacity of the storage system increased as discussed previously, Martin anticipates that the fuel-oil contribution will drop to 25%.

COOLING SYSTEM

No mechanical cooling system is used or needed. The large south overhang and the superb insulation keeps the house from overheating during hot summer periods. The operable windows allow good cross-ventilation from the cool north side of the house to the warm south side.

WATER SUPPLY AND WASTE SYSTEM

Water is supplied from a 12′-deep sand-point well. Domestic hot water is supplied by a standard 40-imperial-gallon (48 U.S. gallons) electrically heated hot-water tank. Eventually the spare solar collector will be fitted with fiberglass glazing and connected to a 200-imperial-gallon (240 U.S. gallons) storage tank to preheat hot water. No particular water- or energy-conserving fixtures were installed, although the cavity underneath and around the bathtub was insulated with rock wool. Water left in the tub will radiate heat to the house for up to two hours.

The Stanley-Joneses built a split septic system so that blackwater (toilet waste) is on one line and graywater is on another. This gives them the flexibility of later installing a heat exchanger in the graywater line to allow for the extraction of useful heat.

Kitchen waste is recycled where possible or composted with the manure from the animals the Stanley-Joneses raise.

ELECTRICAL POWER SYSTEM

A standard 200-amp electrical service feeding off the local utility grid was installed. Future plans call for a 1,500-watt gas-driven generator that will be able to power the two freezers so that frozen food does not spoil when external power is not available and to power the pumps for the solar system.

Energy-conserving warm-white, mostly dual-beam, fluorescent tubes of 40 watts each are used in the basement, kitchen, baths, and two smaller bedrooms.

The north side of the house presents a large surface area to the cold winter winds, but excellent insulation and insulated shutters on most windows minimize heat losses.

The kitchen is compact but has ample storage and is well organized for the preparation and preserving of the large amount of home-grown foods.

MAJOR HOUSEHOLD APPLIANCES

A propane-gas stove was selected over a less-energy-efficient electric one. An exhaust fan above the stove was selected to recycle heat into the house after filtration rather than exhaust it to the exterior. An electric refrigerator is used, as the only large gas models that they could find are made in Brazil. The initial cost is three times that of an electric refrigerator and parts are costly and difficult to obtain. The refrigerator now in use is not particularly efficient, as it is frost-free and is a stand-up model with a freezer compartment down one side. Some energy was saved by disconnecting the butter warmer.

Two well-insulated secondhand chest-type freezers were purchased—one to store meat, the other to store vegetables. As freezers are most efficient when filled to capacity, when both are only half full all the food is transferred to one freezer.

A General Electric automatic clothes washer with water-level and temperature control is used. The Inglis propane dryer is exhausted to the outside, but Martin is considering incorporating a heat exchanger in the exhaust.

FOOD SYSTEM

Carole and Martin are attempting to become self-sufficient in food production. Ducks and white New Zealand rabbits provide much of their meat. A side of beef is usually bought once every two years. Milk is provided by their goats. At the present time they can fulfill most of their vegetable needs year-round from a large organic garden. Apples are bought in bulk in the fall of the year, and chickens and eggs are bought direct from a neighboring farmer. Grains for animal feed are purchased, but eventually the Stanley-Joneses will grow their own.

Some of the harvest is stored in the freezers, but the bulk of it is stored in a 21 x 5 x 8′-high concrete cold-storage area centered on the south side of the house under the concrete-slab veranda. The inside walls and ceiling of the cold storage are lined with aluminum foil. The outside of its east and west walls is insulated with polyurethane foamboard tapering from 3″ at the top to 1″ at the bottom. The outside of the 21 x 8′-high south wall is insulated to a depth of 4′ with polyurethane, thus allowing the earth to moderate the temperature via the lower uninsulated portion. Two outside vents control humidity. Shelves allow produce to be stored at temperature and humidity levels most suitable to their needs. The space is unheated, yet the temperature never drops below 33° F. if the vent fan is not used.

COSTS

The total cost of materials and labor for the house and all its systems was $30,000. This includes a $4,000 contract fee for basement construction and $2,500 for a carpenter's wages for six weeks. Also included in this price is the $5,500 cost of the solar system. Each of the 11 solar panels cost $300 in 1974 delivered to the site. Carole and Martin were able to keep the costs relatively low by doing most of the work themselves.

CONCLUDING THOUGHTS

It seems obvious from talking to Carole and Martin and from seeing the results of their work that Ken Kern must have been thinking of people like them when he wrote, "In my judgment, a positive philosophical outlook and way of life must necessarily precede the achievement of a quality owner-built home."

Belmont
St. John, New Brunswick
1,600 sq. ft. living area

GLEN and GALE MURRAY

When Glen and Gale Murray were planning their new home, they decided that it would be designed to show people that there were alternatives to standard building practices and to total dependence on fossil fuels and electricity. They solicited the help of two equally enthusiastic professionals—Ray Bradburry, a local architect, and Ernie Adset, an engineer with New Brunswick Power who had worked on a company solar project. Glen applied for a Canadian government grant for the solar system, and to his surprise the application was accepted on the first round of demonstration-project grants.

The die was cast, but the Murrays' commitment resulted in more frustrations than they had anticipated. They had expected that local builders would be outbidding one another for the opportunity to construct the area's first solar-heated house, but, in fact, they had difficulty finding a contractor willing to face the challenge. They also had considerable difficulty securing a mortgage, solely because the traditional lending companies were reluctant to put up money for a solar residence. Both of these hurdles were eventually overcome. Bob Johnson, a local builder, acted as the contractor. His carpenters did have trouble, as they had never worked on a project like this one, and it took them a lot longer than anticipated—but they claim to have enjoyed the job anyway.

Compounding some of the Murrays' other problems was the need, because of time constraints associated with making the grant application, to make quick decisions which sometimes were costly in terms of time and money. Their perseverance was not without its rewards. There are still some bugs to be worked out in the solar system, but the end result of all their labor is a beautiful, energy-conserving house that is very comfortable to be in.

LOCATION AND ORIENTATION

The house sits on a hill overlooking a beautiful inlet running off the St. John River at Belmont, a suburb of St. John, New Brunswick. It is positioned near the front of the lot, with the long axis facing due south, and is well protected from the cold prevailing and storm winter winds by trees on the north and west sides of the property and by neighboring woodlots. The east side of the property is less densely wooded, and the south side has only one large deciduous tree, permitting the southeast summer breezes (as well as the winter sun) to reach the house.

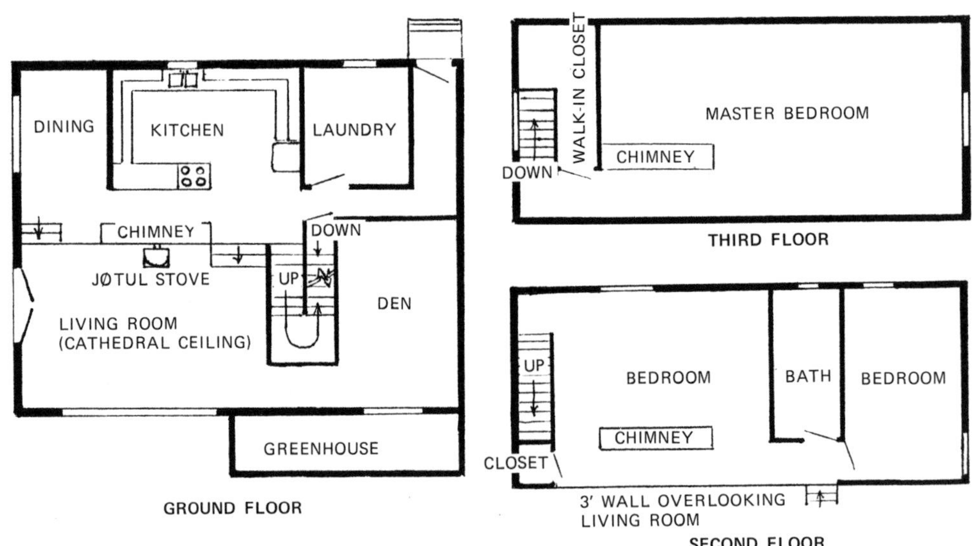

ARCHITECTURAL FEATURES

This Cape-style high-peak-roof house has roughly 1,600 sq. ft. of living space on three floors. The first floor measures 24 x 32′, and the second floor with its partial loft is about two-thirds as large. The third floor was initially designed as the attic, but Gale and Glen decided to use it for a quiet recreational and sleeping space for themselves.

In designing the layout of the rooms, the Murrays wanted to create an open living environment which would extend to the outdoors. Fortunately, principles of solar-heat gain and natural ventilation were compatible with their life-style and goals.

The living room and the den both face south and provide a spectacular view of the inlet. The open-plan kitchen and dining areas share the hearth with the sunken living room. The laundry room is located toward the cooler northwest corner of the house. On the second floor a loft bedroom looks down on the living room. The bathroom is conveniently located at the top of the stairs between this bedroom and their young son's room.

A cedar deck which will later be built around the southwest corner of the house will help to connect the interior with the outside environment.

The basement foundation proved to be quite expensive. Because of the southern slope and the 12-13′ tides which bring water almost up to the house, the 8″-thick poured reinforced concrete foundation wall is 16′ high. The perimeter of the foundation was tarred and then insulated with shiplap-edged 1½″ Dow Styrofoam-SM. Railroad ties will soon be sunk into the south slope to prevent soil erosion from tidal action. The basement floor is 4″ concrete, reinforced with steel wire mesh, over 1½″ Dow Styrofoam-SM and a gravel bed. The upper floors have 2 x 10 joists, 16″ on center, covered with plywood subflooring. The finish floor of the main level is ¾″ beveled oak, except for the kitchen area, which is quarry tile. The floors of the upper levels are carpeted, primarily for noise reduction, but also for aesthetics and for a feeling of warmth.

Exterior Walls

The 2 x 6 studs of the exterior walls were intended to be spaced on 24″ centers; however, someone made a mistake and placed them on 16″ centers, making the walls unnecessarily stronger and somewhat decreasing their insulation value because of the thermal bridging that takes place across studs. The contractor obtained a very good price on 1 x 6 shiplap boards, which he used initially for building the concrete forms and then recycled to sheath the exterior of the structure. Building paper was applied over this, followed by vertical unfinished tongue-and-groove cedar. For the gable ends which form the east and west walls of the second and third stories, the diagonal cedar siding complements the roof lines.

The exterior walls are insulated with 6″ of fiberglass. As well, a polyethylene vapor barrier was installed.

Interior Walls and Ceilings

All interior partition walls are of standard 2 x 4 studwall construction. Walls are sheathed in ½″ gypsum board, except some that for aesthetic reasons are covered with ¾″ tongue-and-groove cedar boards. All ceilings are ¾″ tongue-and-groove cedar.

Roof

The 2 x 12 rafters spaced on 24″ centers form the structural frame for the roof and the cathedral ceiling. The roof was sheathed with ⅝″ plywood and then covered with building paper and asphalt shingles. Glen and Gale had initially favored the use of cedar shakes; however, since the architect felt that they might get very damp on the cool, well-shaded north side of the house and thus deteriorate prematurely, their use was ruled out. The spaces between the rafters were insulated with 10″ of fiberglass and a 2″ airspace above that. The tiny attic space has two gable vents; however, when the decision to convert the large attic to a living space was reached, provisions were not made for soffit venting. Glen is now somewhat worried by possible moisture buildup within the airspaces and insulation.

Insulation Summary

Foundation (walls):	R-7.5; 1½″ Dow Styrofoam-SM with shiplap edges
Walls:	R-20; 6″ fiberglass batts, foil-faced
Ceiling:	R-35; 10″ fiberglass batts, foil-faced

View from the southeast corner of the living room. A Jøtul #4 Combifire connected to the massive central chimney and an oil-fired furnace integrated with the solar system provide auxiliary heat.

Doors

The main entrance to the house on the north side faces the street and the driveway and is well protected from winter winds by the woodlot. It was designed as a double-door airlock entrance, but the interior doorway has not been installed yet. The hall running along the east wall and the laundry room acts as a buffer from the north winter winds. The exterior door is a steel insulated type with magnetic weatherstripping. Steel insulated French doors with magnetic weatherstripping and insulated thermopane glass open out onto the deck on the west side of the house.

Windows

Lockwood pine-frame windows manufactured in Scoudouc, New Brunswick, were used on all the vertical walls. These are double-glazed thermopane windows with a large fixed glazing above and a smaller screened awning-type window vent below.

The loft bedroom, bathroom, and the child's bedroom each have a Danish-made Velux wood-frame insulated-glass roof window providing good-quality diffuse light with minimal window area. These operable Velux windows pivot on a center pin to permit good ventilation and to facilitate cleaning. The largest window area is on the south; that on the north side has been kept to a minimum.

The entire south face of the roof was asphalt-shingled before the 2x6′ modular water-type collector panels were secured to the roof.

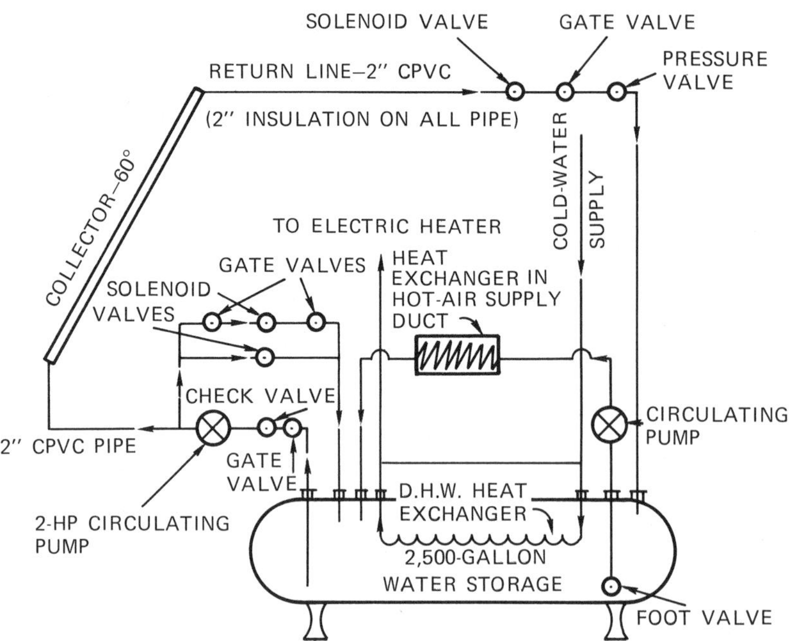

SOLAR-HEATING SYSTEM

The large amount of glazing on the south side of the house provides an uncalculated but apparently substantial amount of passive direct solar gain; however, the heart of the heating system is the active component.

Collectors

The 384 sq. ft. of water-type Solatherm Engineering Inc. collectors are mounted over the top of the shingles on the south slope of the roof and thus face south at a tilt angle of 60°. Each modular 6 x 2′ collector panel is composed of a sandwich-type absorber made by spot-welding two aluminum sheets together so that the flow of the heat-transfer medium is integral to the absorber and thus makes good contact with almost the entire surface. The exterior surface is electrolytically coated with a black chrome selective surface which has a minimum solar-radiation absorptance of 0.95 and a maximum heat emittance of 0.2. The coating is capable of withstanding temperatures up to 350° F. with no ill effects.

The glazing is one sheet of tempered glass having a value of solar-radiation transmittance of approximately 0.95. These two components are housed in a black anodized-aluminum box frame. The collectors are placed above the roof deck on 2 x 2 nominal wood strapping centered on 24″ and screw-secured to the latter by black anodized-aluminum mullions that overlap the edges of each panel and thus also serve to make the collector array a rain screen.

In order to prevent corrosion in the aluminum collectors, 20 imperial gallons (24 U.S. gallons) of NUTEK-876 supplied by Nuclear Technology Corporation (Amston, Conn.) were mixed with the water in the storage tank. As this is a drain-down system no antifreeze was used.

Storage

The 2,500-imperial-gallon (3,000 U.S. gallons) water-storage tank, 21′ long and 5′ in diameter, is located in the basement. It was designed by another engineer at New Brunswick Power whom Ernie Adset, the solar engineer for this project, knew. The fiberglass-reinforced polyester tank was made by Guilfords in Dartmouth, Nova Scotia, and cost about $3,000. The tank sits in two cradle supports, which in turn rest on 3′-high concrete plinths. The tank is insulated on all sides and ends with 6″ of fiberglass.

In addition to this active storage system, the mass of the building components, particularly the gypsum board, quarry-tile floor, and large centrally located brick chimney, stores heat.

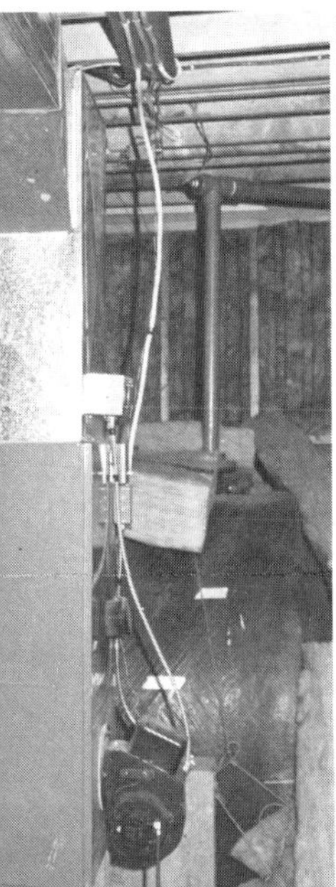

Left: Detail of the oil furnace. Note the protruding ends of the water-to-air heat exchanger in the hot-air-supply duct on the left-hand side of the furnace. The solar-heated water tank providing hot water to this heat exchanger is in the background.
Above: The 2,500-gallon fiberglass tank is wrapped with 6" of fiberglass insulation. The 2-hp Armstrong pump forces water through the collector panels.

Heat Distribution

A thermistor is mounted on the underside of one of the upper panels 2' below the top, and another such temperature sensor is mounted at the top of the storage tank. When the differential thermostat indicates that the collector surface temperature is greater than the water-tank temperature, the 2-hp Armstrong pump forces water upward through the collectors, where it is heated and returned to the storage tank. The system automatically drains when collector temperature drops below that of the water in the storage tank.

When the house thermostat demands heat, if the tank temperature is above 26° C. (78.8° F.) a 1/6-hp Armstrong pump pumps tank water through the York car-radiator-type water-to-air heat exchanger, which is located in the forced-air heating system's return-air plenum. The heat exchanger is capable of transferring 40,000 Btu per hour at a water temperature of 100° F. and an air temperature of 65° F.

The in-duct 1-hp Phillips Lau blower forces air through the heat exchanger, where it picks up heat and then transfers it to the living spaces through floor registers.

AUXILIARY HEATING

If the tank temperature is not 26° C. when the house demands heat or if, when the heat exchanger is operational, the room temperature drops below the desired temperature, the oil-fired hot-air furnace automatically comes on. Hot air is distributed by the in-duct blower linked to the solar system. The oil furnace is capable of supplying the complete house heat loss if necessary. It has a rated heat output at the bonnet of 105,000 Btu per hour with a fuel consumption no greater than 1 gallon per hour.

The second backup is a Jøtul #4 Combi-fire, a stand-up fireplace which converts to an efficient wood stove by simply closing the airtight door. It sits in front of the large brick chimney centrally located between the dining/kitchen area and the living room. Its mass and that of the chimney are capable of storing a substantial amount of heat. They face south and absorb heat from direct solar gain on sunny days.

Above: The well-organized kitchen was designed with the needs of two very busy working professionals in mind. Appliances were chosen more for their convenience than for their energy-conserving features.

Right: View from the dining room on the east to the living room and large south-facing windows.

Below: The central brick chimney extends through three floors of the house, radiating heat to all levels. Excellent Velux roof windows are featured in this loft bedroom and in the bath and child's bedroom to the east of it.

PERCENT SOLAR-HEATED

The solar system was calculated to provide 50% to 60% of the house's heating needs; however, the actual effectiveness of the solar system will not be known until after the 1978-79 heating season, the first season that the system has been fully operational. The previous winter, the National Research Council of Canada's Division of Building Research monitored the system, but Glen said that some of the monitoring equipment malfunctioned and they also had a great deal of trouble with leaks. He stated that half of the collectors leaked onto the roof because of the difficulty he had in tightening the soft aluminum fittings and, he suspects, because of the expansion and contraction of the fittings. He says he solved the leaks by "tightening the hell out of some fittings and replacing others with plastic."

Now that the system is functioning, NRC has taken out the monitoring equipment for reasons which Glen says haven't been explained to him.

Last winter, without the solar system functioning, the house consumed approximately 500 imperial gallons (600 U.S. gallons) of fuel oil and half a cord of maple firewood with the thermostat set at a constant 68° F. The degree-days for the site were about 8,450.

COOLING SYSTEM

No mechanical cooling system was designed into the building other than the operable vent windows. Any heat that would tend to stratify on the ceiling of the second floor because of the open concept and cathedral ceilings is readily exhausted by opening the Velux roof windows. Glen states that winter heat stratification is not a problem. The good insulation helps to keep the house warm in winter and cool in summer. As well, the deciduous trees are very effective in providing summer shade.

WATER SUPPLY AND WASTE SYSTEMS

Household water is supplied from a drilled deep well on the property. Domestic hot water is preheated by a heat exchanger consisting of 250′ of ¾″-diameter coiled copper (type K, soft) tubing hung from the top of the tank. Final heating, if required, is done by an electric immersion heater within the Cascade 40 hot-water tank. The electric heater was chosen because the Murrays wanted the domestic hot-water supply to be independent of the oil-fired furnace.

None of the plumbing fixtures is particularly water-, resource-, or energy-conserving, except for the shower, which was specifically chosen for its universal lifelong ball-bearing mechanism which eliminates the need to change washers. The Murrays practice conservation methods rather than using conserving fixtures. They had designed a Clivus Multrum composting toilet into the system but after reading an article in a Maine newspaper which gave a very negative assessment of the toilet, they decided not to purchase one. Instead, blackwater and graywater wastes are disposed of in a standard septic system. Organic solid wastes are composted. The family makes a conscientious effort to minimize the amount of waste by attempting to minimize consumption and by buying durable products that can be either reused or recycled in some form. There are no community facilities for recycling solid wastes.

ELECTRICAL SUPPLY

The Murray house receives its electricity from New Brunswick Hydro. There is no provision for an auxiliary electrical power supply because the Jøtul wood stove and a few candles can cope with a power failure.

The placement of windows as described earlier provides good illumination, thus minimizing the use of electric lighting during daylight hours.

FOOD SYSTEM

The Murrays have planted a small organic vegetable garden and later plan to build a greenhouse. The footings for the greenhouse have already been poured in front of and below the den, where there is a doorway to the basement.

COSTS

The Murray home was not inexpensive. Most of the work was contracted through the builder mentioned before, although Glen and Gale participated whenever their jobs and the ordinary business of running a household permitted. They were actively involved in all the design decisions and were very cost-conscious, but the uniqeness of the site and the house itself resulted in costs that were higher than they had initially anticipated. The foundation alone cost about $9,000 because of the high tides. The total cost of the solar system, including the backup oil-fired furnace, was about $15,000, of which approximately $3,000 went for the storage tank. Fortunately, the $12,500 government grant for the solar system was available. The total cost of the house was about $70,000.

CONCLUDING THOUGHTS

Glen occasionally speaks to various community groups about his family's experiences building and living in a solar-heated house. He encourages anyone before installing an active system to design the house right in the first place from an energy-conservation point of view, to make use of as much passive solar heat as is practical, and to attempt to do this economically.

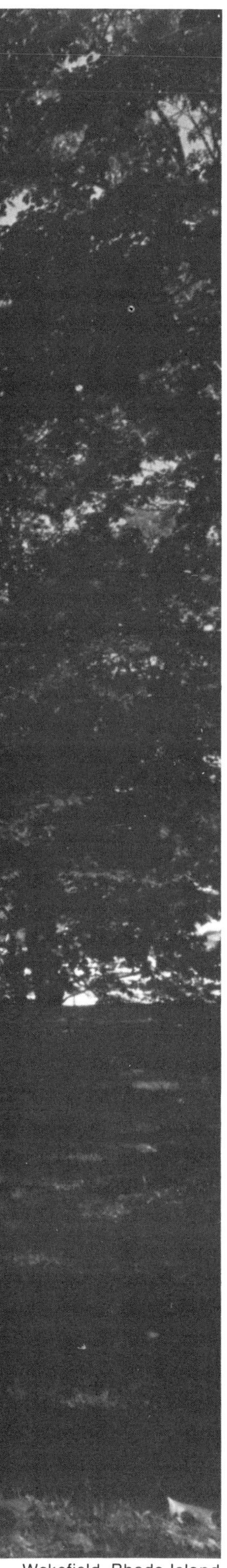

Wakefield, Rhode Island
1,200 sq. ft. living area
plus 800 sq. ft.
living space in basement

PHILIP and HELEN CARPENTER

Helen and Philip had bought their building lot many years ago anticipating that one day they would build their retirement home overlooking the waters of Point Judith Pond in Rhode Island. They had over the years refined their sketches so that every detail of their plans was carefully thought out and designed to meet their needs and the demands of the site. Then the Arab oil embargo hit in 1973. By the end of that year they decided that they should try solar heating. This decision was prompted by their concern about future fuel scarcities and escalating prices and also by a sense of patriotism. In Philip's words, "We have always been inclined to serve. In World War II, for example, when gasoline was scarce because it was needed for the war effort, we sold our car and went to bicycles." In March 1974 they visited the Providence Home Show and met one of the exhibitors, Spencer Dickinson, owner of Solar Homes Inc.

Dickinson is an experienced, well-respected local builder (and now state legislator) who was just completing his first solar-heated home in Jamestown, Rhode Island. The result of this chance encounter was the Carpenters' ideal retirement home—a well-engineered, functional, comfortable, and aesthetically pleasing home that is heated by the sun and costs very little to operate.

LOCATION AND ORIENTATION

The house is in Wakefield, Rhode Island. Because of the odd shape of the lot, the house is oriented 15° east of south rather than due south. If it had been oriented due south it would have adversely bisected the lot and had a less desirable view. The building is located on the brow of a hill sloping up from Point Judith Pond on the east to an elevation of 30 feet above the water. From the living-room deck, office, and workshop the Carpenters have a spectacular view of the saltwater "pond" and the boats that ply its waters on the way to and from the Atlantic.

Three-quarters of the main floor of the house is at ground level, and about a quarter of the basement is at ground level and thus exposed on the east side. The rest of the basement is windowless and completely underground.

Several oak and beech trees had to be removed before construction, but many still remain as well as some maple trees. These deciduous trees, which surround the house on all sides, provide some windbreak against the winter prevailing east winds and the northwest storm winds. They provide welcome shade during the hot summer but still cast some shadow on the collectors in winter, so gradually the trees on the south edge of the lot are being trimmed or removed.

ARCHITECTURAL FEATURES

This one-story, two-bedroom home measures 28 x 64′ including the one-car attached garage. The living-floor area is 1,200 sq. ft., but 800 sq. ft. of the basement is also used as living or utility space; it requires little heat.

The attached garage on the west end of the house is set back slightly from the south edge of the house for aesthetic reasons as well as to provide a west window in the kitchen for better natural lighting, ventilation, and view. The garage acts as a buffer against the cold northwest winter storm winds and acts as an effective airlock, as the entrance to the house through the garage is the one most often used, especially in winter.

The baths, bedrooms and their closets, and the stairwell to the basement insulate the main living area from the cooler side of the house. The guest bedroom, when not in use, is usually kept at a temperature of 50° F. in winter. The kitchen, dining area, and living room receive a substantial amount of passive heat in winter through the south-facing windows. A 2′ overhang shades the windows in summer.

Although the kitchen is on the west end of the house, it still receives considerable morning light because of the orientation of the house 15° east of south. Close to the garage and on the same level, it is efficient for bringing in groceries and other supplies. It is also convenient to the garden, which is located immediately to the south and west of the garage.

The living room has a spectacular view of Point Judith Pond. There are sliding glass patio doors to a 10′-wide deck that runs the depth of the house and extends around the corner to the front door on the south. In the basement, Philip's workshop is in the northeast corner, under the master bedroom. A door from the workshop opens to a patio under the deck; he likes to work outdoors when the weather is suitable. The solar storage system, heat pump, and controls are to the west of the workshop area. Under the kitchen Philip has designed a small, compact, efficient laboratory where he conducts microbiological experiments. (Before retirement he was a professor of microbiology at the University of Rhode Island.) Out of curiosity he occasionally analyzes water samples from the solar storage. So far he has not found anything abnormal or alarming.

There is an office/meeting area/den beneath the living room with a door to the patio.

The unheated attic accommodates the piping to and from the collectors and is large enough to supply substantial storage space of seasonal clothing, camping gear, and other infrequently used possessions. The foundation walls are reinforced concrete 1′ thick. The basement floor is a 4½″ concrete slab poured over 2″ Dow Styrofoam-SM insulation board, under which is an additional 5½″ of concrete and a gravel base. The floor in the office-den area is carpeted over a rubber pad. The laboratory and lavatory floors are covered with linoleum. Main-level flooring is ½″ plywood and particle board with rubber-backed wall-to-wall carpeting in living room, hall, and bedrooms and linoleum in the kitchen and bathrooms.

Exterior Walls

The outside walls are 2 x 6 stud construction spaced 16″ on centers. The exterior is sheathed with ½″ exterior-grade plywood and covered with untreated cedar shingles, which are being allowed to age naturally.

Interior Walls and Ceilings

All interior walls are of standard 2 x 4 studwall construction. They and the 2 x 6 ceiling joists are sheathed with ½″ gypsum board painted off-white in order to better reflect light. In the den a 2 x 4 studwall is set back from the exterior concrete wall to accommodate 6″ fiberglass batts. The wall is covered with ⅜″ gypsum board and wood paneling.

Room

The roof trusses are composed of 2 x 4 rafters, and the 2 x 6 ceiling joists are on 16″ centers. The sheathing is ½″ plywood, and the roofing is black asphalt shingles over felt paper. The collector on the south slope forms part of the weather skin.

Insulation Summary

Ceiling: R-40; fiberglass batts
Walls: R-20; fiberglass batts
Basement: R-20; fiberglass batts (in 2 x 4 studwall set back from concrete wall)

Special care was taken to ensure that all doors and windows were properly weatherstripped and caulked. Before the door and window trim was applied, Philip made sure that fiberglass insulation was forced into any spaces between the jambs and the framing.

Doors

The front entrance on the warmer south side does not have an airlock but it is rarely used in winter. The door is of conventional wood-panel construction with four glass panes at the top. It and the aluminum storm door

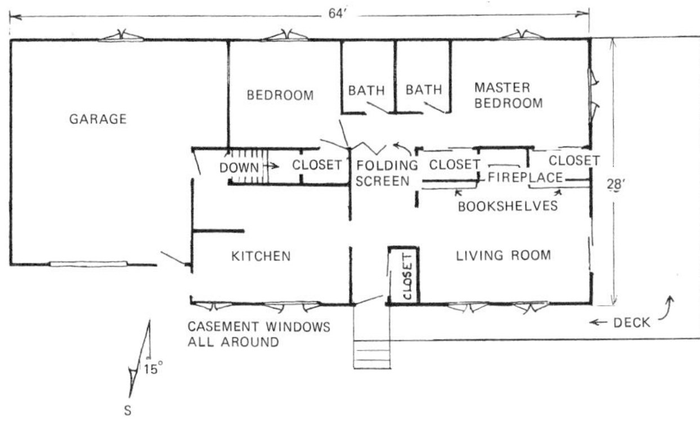

are well weatherstripped. It is possible that with the south-facing glazing in the door and the good weatherstripping there could be a net heat gain. There is a similar entrance into the garage. The original wooden door between garage and kitchen was replaced with a steel insulated door. It has an operable thermopane window and a screen to provide good summer ventilation. The garage door for the car is electrically operated so that it can be opened by remote control from the driver's seat. Glass windows permit some passive solar-heat gain in the winter when sunlight enters under the overhang. This is very useful if one wants to work in an otherwise unheated garage in winter. The outside doors from the basement workshop are of the same type as the front door. Both patio doors are the Andersen wood-frame thermopane type and have thermal-insulated drapes. No doors are on the windward and cold north and west sides of the house except for the kitchen entrance, which is protected by the garage.

Windows

High-quality operable fixed and casement Andersen wood-sash thermopane windows are used throughout the house. They have been placed for best view as well as natural light and ventilation. A large amount of glazing on the south wall provides a substantial amount of solar gain in winter. The open concept of the living area and the placement of doors and operable windows along three sides permit excellent ventilation. The house has only two windows along the north wall—one in each bedroom. The bathrooms have no windows. The master bedroom has a large east-facing window so that the Carpenters can experience the sunrise from this room and do away with an alarm clock. Light from a north window in the garage balances that from the glazing in the garage door and thus good-quality light is provided for working in this space. All windows are equipped with thermal-insulated drapes.

LANDSCAPING

As mentioned earlier, care was taken during construction to preserve as many of the existing trees as possible to provide summer shade. A grass lawn has been planted to provide additional cooling during the hot summer. Mrs. Carpenter planted the hillside to the east with indigenous vegetation and allows it to grow wild. This provides a no-maintenance, aesthetically pleasing landscape that also controls erosion.

The low-profile north side of the house has only three windows—one for each bedroom and one for the garage. A patio under the east deck provides a sheltered outdoor work area adjoining the basement workshop.

SOLAR-HEATING SYSTEM

This active solar-heating system was designed and built by Spencer Dickinson of Solar Homes Inc.

Collector

Fifteen 4 x 6′ water-type solar collector panels are mounted side by side along the roof at a tilt angle of 57° and orientation of 15° east of south. The gross area is 360 sq. ft. The glazing is two layers of 0.040″ Kalwall Sun-Lite Regular and the absorber plate is 16-ounce copper sheet to which ½″ copper tubes have been soldered. The tubes run in a serpentine pattern from bottom to top with a 6″ spacing between parallel runs. In order to reduce stresses between the absorber plate and tubes when temperature differentials occur, each panel is composed of four small absorber sheets that are slightly and loosely overlapped, rather than one large sheet. The absorber is painted with nonselective black Rustoleum. The absorber plates were laid on top of the tar roofing paper and then covered with the two layers of Kalwall glazing within an aluminum frame. These frames were bolted to the roof and then joined at their edges with aluminum cleats over rubber gaskets. At the roof peak, the top of the panels sit under a 4″ overhang. The roofing shingles start two courses up from the bottom edge of the panels.

There are 6″ of fiberglass batt insulation between the rafters immediately behind the collector. This is a draindown system; therefore, no antifreeze is required to prevent freezing in the collector. Each panel feeds off the same ½″ copper delivery pipe running inside the attic along the bottom of the panels. Each panel has its own feeder shutoff valve, enabling the flow rate to be adjusted or an individual panel to be shut down for repairs without affecting the operation of the other panels. A 1″ copper return pipe at the top of each collector panel runs down the panel and connects to a 1″ copper return header again running the length of the attic along the bottom of the panels. The total capacity of all the piping in the system is only 9 gallons.

When thermal sensors in the collectors and the storage tank indicate a 5° differential, the ⅛-hp panel pump in the basement pumps water through the panels. When the pump is off, the 1″ return line is drained by gravity. Water tends to stay in the ½″ feeder lines, so an adjustable thermosensor in the center panel activates one of two solenoids in the control room to drain this line. There is also a manual drain.

Storage

The 5,000-cu.-ft. storage tank, measuring 22 x 8 x 6′ high (outside measurements) and containing 4,500 gallons of water, is located on the north side of the basement just west of the workshop. Its walls are constructed of 1″-thick reinforced concrete, the floor slab is 4″-thick reinforced concrete, and the top is 5″-thick reinforced concrete poured over Filon, a fiberglass material that acts as a vapor barrier. The walls and floor of the storage tank are painted with five layers of PPG epoxy. Access to the tank for maintenance is via two manhole covers in the top slab. They have been sealed to prevent moisture from escaping. The bottom of the tank is insulated with 4″ load-bearing Dow Styrofoam-SM board. The builder, Spencer Dickinson, enclosed the tank in an insulated room with a 2′ walkway. There is 6″ of fiberglass between the storage-room ceiling joists. A 2′ crawl space between the top of the tank and the ceiling permits access to the manhole covers. Philip describes some improvements that he made to the storage reservoir. "The room got quite hot, which told me that I was losing heat from the tank that could be conserved by additional insulation. Hence I covered the top with six inches of fiberglass and taped an inch of beadboard to the two walls of the tank, then covered that with gypsum board. The room temperature dropped 15° F. overnight."

Heat Distribution

The heart of the heating system is a Vaughan (Wescorp) Solargy EC-44, 44,000-Btu-per-hour water-to-air heat pump which heats the house with forced air. The heat pump extracts heat from the top of the tank, where temperatures usually are around 70° to 100° F. The output temperature of the heat pump is typically about 180° F., and a typical value for the C.O.P. (coefficient of performance) is 2.7.

The heat pump was bought as part of a package with an 80-gallon electrically heated domestic hot-water tank plus a 20-gallon 10,000-watt water heater that acts as a backup when the temperature of the water from storage is such that the water might freeze going into the heat pump. The thermostat in this backup heater is set at 45° F., but since the tank temperature never dropped below 53° F. the heater has never been used.

The heat pump takes heat from the storage water and produces hot air, which is delivered to the house at 105-110° F. via standard ductwork and diffusers on the outside walls placed under windows and the sliding glass doors. The ducts have 2″ of fiberglass insulation with a black plastic covering taped with duct tape.

AUXILIARY HEATING

As mentioned earlier, the backup hot-water heater has never been used. A fireplace located on the inside wall between the living room and the master bedroom is the principal source of auxiliary heat. It is built of firebrick, but the back of the firebox is made from a sheet of ½" steel plate on the exterior of which the boiler pipe has been welded. On demand from a manually operated switch near the fireplace, a 1/12-hp pump circulates water from the solar-system storage tank through the boiler pipe. The circulation is so rapid that the temperature increment through the pipes is only 4° or 5° F.; however, the amount of heat stored is substantial. During some winter months almost as much heat was transferred to storage from the fireplace as from the solar collector panels. Philip estimates that they burn two cords of wood (mostly oak) during the heating season.

The fireplace has folding glass doors and air intake made from an 8"-diameter flue pipe leading to the basement workshop. This pipe also serves as an ash clean-out and could be easily adapted to outside venting if desired. Behind the steel plate and boiler pipes, there is a cavity that has been filled with fiberglass and rubble in order to reduce unwanted heat loss. The back wall of the large brick chimney is exposed in the master bedroom to provide texture, color, and radiant heat to that space.

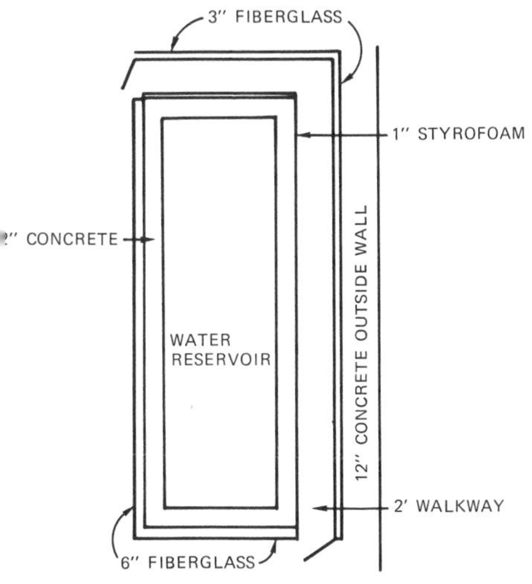

Above: Helen Carpenter relaxes in the living room. The back of the massive centrally located fireplace is exposed to the master bedroom. In addition to supplying radiant heat through glass doors the fireplace helps to heat hot water circulating from the solar water-storage reservoir.

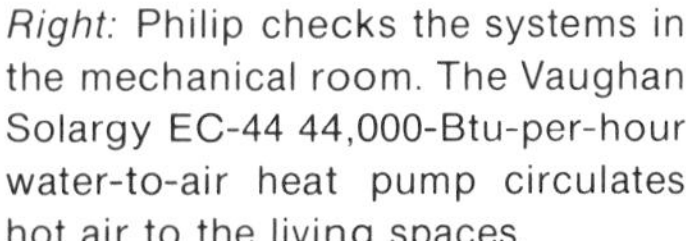

Right: Philip checks the systems in the mechanical room. The Vaughan Solargy EC-44 44,000-Btu-per-hour water-to-air heat pump circulates hot air to the living spaces.

The mechanical room takes up a small amount of space behind the two pairs of white louver doors.

PERCENT SOLAR-HEATED

Regarding the passive contribution from the south-facing windows, Philip commented, "In the fall and spring, we get a significant amount of passive heating. This morning [October 5, 1978], for example, the outdoor temperature is fifty-six degrees, but with doors and windows closed the hall temperature is seventy-six. The tank temperature is a hundred and two degrees today. This situation is likely to obtain until well into November. In winter, after the heat pump has warmed the house from its overnight sixty-two degrees to the daytime sixty-eight, sun through the windows keeps the indoor temperature at sixty-eight to seventy-five until three or four in the afternoon, when the sun gets too far to the west. The heat pump starts again at four or five."

The Carpenters arranged with the University of Rhode Island to have monitoring equipment installed to determine how much heat is derived from various sources. Philip now has three electric meters that he monitors daily (total house current, heat pump plus associated water pumps, and electric hot-water heater), together with three clocks (heat pump, solar panel pump, and fireplace pump) as well as numerous thermometers both conventional and electronic. The results of Philip's data collection recorded here are for the 1977-78 heating season, when he logged 6,296 degree-days against the average of 5,900.

Philip says, "I was amazed at these results, which reinforce the conclusion I have been approaching anyway that insulation is the most important factor in household energy independence. It looks as though we actually get only about thirty-two percent of our heat from the sun. The remaining sixty-eight percent is derived from us as warm bodies, but principally from the fireplace and from the electricity that we use for various nonheating purposes."

1977-78 HEATING DATA

Source	Btu (millions)	Percentage of heating requirement
1. People (2) (calc. from dietary intake, minus allowance for outside activities)	2.9	3.8
2. Lights, cooking, refrigeration (calc. by difference from measured electric usage)	12.6	16.6
3. Water heating (67% solar preheating plus 33% measured electric heating)	10.8	14.3
4. Sun, active (measured)	12.0	15.8
passive (convection from storage during Sept., Oct., and May, calc. from degree-day data—3.4×10^6, plus calc. sun through south windows during Oct.-Apr.)	4.5	5.9
5. Electric heat (heat pump, measured electric usage)	10.5	13.9
6. Wood, fireplace (2 cords oak and beech); est. 50% up the chimney; of the remaining 50% stored (measured)	7.3	9.6
to room	15.2	20.1
Totals	75.8	100.0

COOLING SYSTEM

The heat pump can be operated as an air conditioner by simply activating a switch on the house thermostat. The air conditioner, however, is never used, as the house is so well insulated and so well designed for natural ventilation that it never becomes uncomfortably warm.

If the air conditioner was required in summer and if it was to run effectively the storage-tank temperature should be lower than it is. This could be accomplished by turning off the panels during the summer, thus sacrificing solar domestic hot-water heating. They did run the air conditioner two and a half days during a hot spell with the solar panels operating. The tank temperature rose 5.5° F. per day, and then the air-conditioning system shut off halfway through the third day. When Philip contacted Vaughan, the heat-pump manufacturer, he was informed that ideally the temperature of the water entering the heat pump (from storage) should not be more than 88° F. and that the system would shut off if the temperature reached 120-130° F. In Philip's case the air conditioner actually shut off when the temperature reached 131° F. He has come to the conclusion that if an air conditioner was required, he would "probably have an auxiliary thousand-gallon uninsulated tank outside the house with a couple of valves so that it could switch the heat-pump water intake to the outside and use that as a reservoir, or I would put in an outdoor fin system, or pump storage water to the solar panels at night to dissipate some of the heat."

WATER SUPPLY AND WASTE SYSTEM

The Carpenter house is hooked up to the local town water supply but has a septic system for waste disposal. The two bathrooms on the first floor (one off the master bedroom, the other for guest and general use) are placed back to back in order to reduce piping. The fixtures are mostly conventional except for one bath shower, which has a water-conserving shower head. This not only conserves water but saves energy required for domestic hot-water heating. There is a McPherson basement toilet that uses half the water that a conventional toilet uses.

ELECTRICAL POWER SYSTEM

The Carpenter home is connected to the local electrical grid. Although there is no auxiliary power source the Carpenters are not overly vulnerable in the event of a power blackout, because the house is well designed for passive heating of the living areas and the fireplace can supply a substantial portion of their heating needs, particularly when the north part of the house is isolated from the south-facing living room and kitchen/dining area.

As mentioned earlier, windows and doors are placed to provide excellent natural lighting. Much of the artificial lighting is provided by fluorescent tubes. All the basement is lit by fluorescents.

MAJOR HOUSEHOLD APPLIANCES

The Carpenters' appliances are not especially energy-conserving. They have a standard Sears, Roebuck electric stove and refrigerator purchased new in 1976. They have had the same chest-type freezer since 1945. A standard automatic washer and dryer has been installed. The latter exhausts air 6′ to 8′ into the garage. They do not have a dishwasher.

FOOD SYSTEM

A prolific 900-sq.-ft. essentially organic garden provides all the summer vegetable needs as well as food for the freezer. A hothouse is used to extend the growing season for lettuce and radishes. Black polyethylene film is used as a mulch. It has the advantage of warming up the soil for an early crop, preserving moisture, and keeping down weeds. Its main disadvantages are that it adds no organic matter to the soil the way organic mulches do and that it is manufactured from a nonrenewable resource—oil.

COSTS

The Carpenter house cost between $60,000 and $70,000 (excluding the land, which was purchased many years ago), and the solar system cost about 10% of this. These figures do not take into account any work that Philip has done. The heat-pump package, which included one 20-gallon and one 80-gallon hot-water tank, cost $2,700. The operating costs during the entire 1976-77 heating season were $146 compared to neighbors who paid from $100 to $300 per winter month. The value of the two cords of wood that was burned was about $100. Operating cost in 1977-78 was $100 plus two full cords at $35 each.

CONCLUDING THOUGHTS

I asked Philip if he had any criticisms of the design. He replied, "I haven't thought of a thing to change yet. Both of us are very enthusiastic, as we've never lived in as comfortable a house. It's been an enjoyable experience. I feel missionary about it and thus don't hesitate to share what we have learned when people come along."

Jamestown, Rhode Island
960 sq. ft. living area

TOBEY and CAROL RICHARDS

Tobey and Carol Richards had lived in Jamestown, Rhode Island, a number of years back and wanted to return to the gentle pace of life and the tranquil environment of this community. They began looking for a house to buy and accidentally discovered this 100% solar-heated home built by Spencer Dickinson of Solar Homes Inc. In Tobey's words, "When we were looking for a house we weren't very concerned about the cosmetics. What really concerned us was the quality of construction and the operating costs. We saw the 'For Sale' sign, liked the house, and bought it—it was as simple as that. In many ways it is no different from anyone else's house. Buying this house and living in it didn't require any great change in our life-style."

LOCATION AND ORIENTATION

The Richards house is located at 46 Lawn Avenue, Jamestown, Rhode Island. Its long axis is oriented 5° west of south. The prevailing winds are from the southwest in summer and northwest in winter. The summer storm winds usually come from the southeast. The winter storm winds often come from the southwest, but the worst winds usually come from the north.

A line of deciduous trees runs along the road parallel to the western property line, providing privacy plus some wind protection and shade from the summer late-afternoon sun. Pine trees along the east side of the building provide additional protection.

ARCHITECTURAL FEATURES

Spencer Dickinson designed the building to take best advantage of the topography and climate and to minimize their disadvantages. Tobey describes how this was done.

"The house is shaped and acts somewhat like an airfoil. It is low on the north windward side and high on the south side. Earth berms were constructed very high on the north, east, and west walls. These provide insulation and along with the shape of the house deflect the wind upward and over the front of the house, leaving a warm dead-air space on this south side. Even on a cold winter day if you don't go too far from the south face of the house it seems very warm because of this large insulation blanket of relatively stable air."

The compact 960-sq. ft. single-story house measures 24 x 64, including the attached two-car garage. It has an attic but no basement. It is built on a 6" concrete-slab foundation. The open-concept kitchen, dining, and living-room areas are oriented toward the warm south side of the house. The master bedroom and another bedroom that Tobey has converted into a den also face south. The spare bedroom, bathroom, utility room, and kitchen cupboards on the north wall act as thermal buffers. The garage acts as an extremely effective thermal buffer, as prevailing winter winds and the worst winter storm winds hit that side of the house. The floors are constructed of ⅝" particle board over 2 x 6 floor joists and are carpeted throughout the house. There is a large deck on the south side of the house. A roof overhang shades the interior of the house in summer while permitting the low-angled winter sun to penetrate through the south-facing glazing to the living spaces.

Exterior Walls

The exterior walls are of 12" poured concrete over the 6" concrete slab and footings. The 2 x 6 studwalls were constructed within this shell and insulated with 6" of fiberglass. The south wall is constructed of 2 x 6 studs over the short concrete foundation wall. The studwall is sheathed with ⅝" plywood, reflective aluminum foil, and cedar shingles and insulated with 6" fiberglass batts.

Interior Walls and Ceilings

All interior partition walls are constructed of 2 x 6 studs and insulated with 6" of fiberglass so that each room can be isolated from the rest of the house when desired. All interior walls and the ceiling are sheathed with ½" gypsum board and painted light colors for good illumination.

Roof

The truss roof is covered with ⅝" plywood, building paper, and asphalt shingles. The solar panels, in addition to their primary function of collecting solar energy, serve as a substantial portion of the south-facing roof skin. The gable ends are sheathed with the same type of cedar shingles that are used on the south wall of the house.

There are 12" of fiberglass insulation on the attic floor. Soffit vents and two louvered vents near the ridge of the gable ends ventilate the attic.

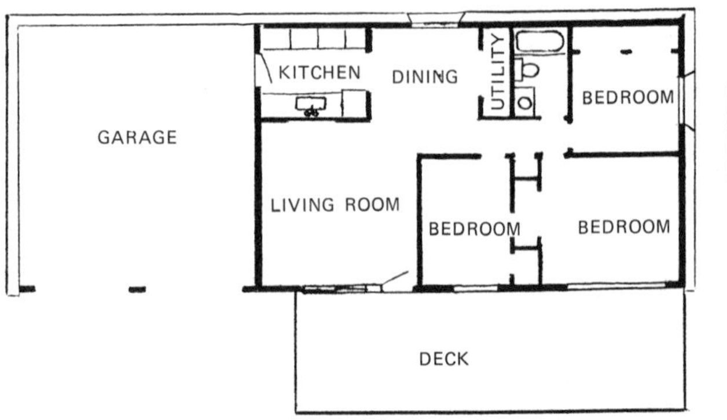

Insulation Summary

Ceiling: R-40; 12" fiberglass batts
Walls: R-20; 6" fiberglass batts in both exterior and interior walls
Foundation: Refer to storage description

Doors

The south entranceway opens directly into the living room. Because of the generally stable air mass on the south face of the house the infiltration losses are not as great as they would be if the door were on another wall. The door is solid-core wood construction with six panes of single glass.

The west door, which conveniently opens from the garage directly into the kitchen, is the one most often used in winter. It is a standard hollow-core door with plywood skins. Both doors are well weatherstripped.

Windows

Triple-glazed thermopane Andersen wood-frame casement windows are used throughout. Most of the glazing is on the south wall of the house, although there is one window in the north wall of the dining room and one in the east wall of the spare bedroom. The inner glazing is polarized gray glass to reduce thermal losses.

East and north aspects. Earth is bermed up high on the east, west, and north walls. Note the few windows and small amount of window area.

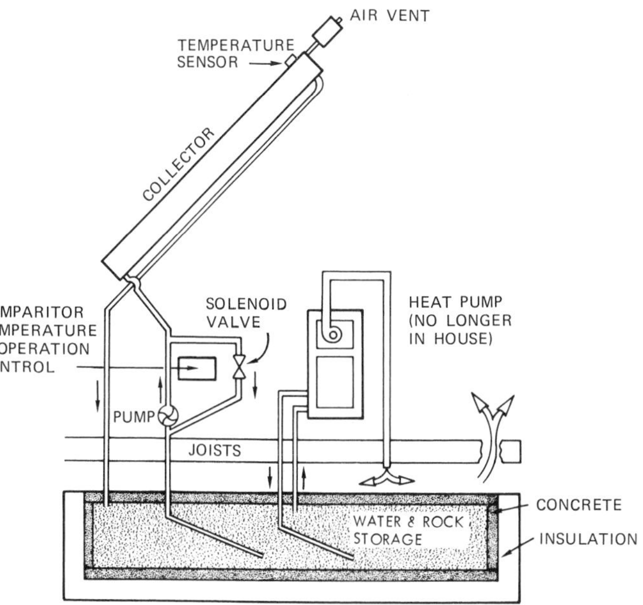

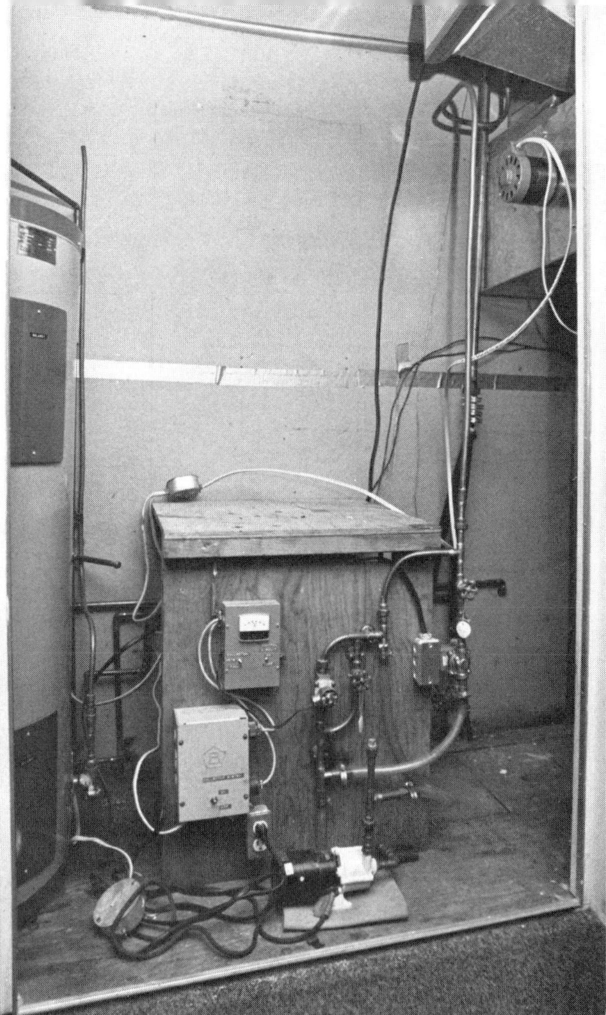

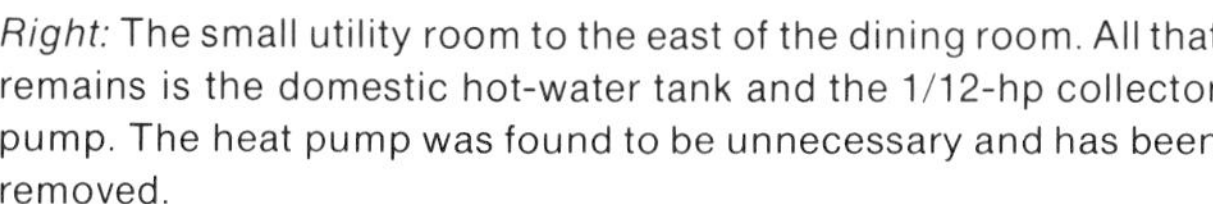

Right: The small utility room to the east of the dining room. All that remains is the domestic hot-water tank and the 1/12-hp collector pump. The heat pump was found to be unnecessary and has been removed.

SOLAR-HEATING SYSTEM

A substantial but unmeasured amount of solar-heat gain is received through the large area of south-facing windows, but the really unusual feature of this home is its active solar system, particularly the storage reservoir.

Collector

The 360 sq. ft. of water-type collector is composed of 15 4 x 6′ panels arranged side by side along the south-facing roof. They are oriented 10° west of south and tilted at 56° from the horizontal. The panels, manufactured by Dickinson's Solar Homes Inc., are double-glazed with 0.040″ Kalwall Sun-Lite Regular. The absorber plate, located about 1″ below the inner glazing, is made of 16-ounce sheet copper. Corrosion-resistant ½″ marine copper tubes spaced 6″ apart are soldered to the copper sheet. To minimize strain caused by expansion and contraction, the absorber plate actually has four sheets of copper that are slightly and loosely overlapped. All the copper is painted with flat black nonselective heat-resistant Rustoleum. The panels are framed with aluminum and are joined together by an aluminum clamping bar that is sealed with GE silicone and bolted to the roof. The 6″ of fiberglass insulation is integral to the roof rafters. During a good snowstorm, the panels will be covered with snow, but on a sunny day solar energy passes through, heats up the collector, and melts the snow enough so that it slides off the slippery glazing.

Inside the attic along the bottom of the collector runs a double copper pipe manifold with one part for the water input and one for the gravity return. Water flows to and from the center point of each manifold. There are air vents or valves at each end of the collector array, similar to the type used for ball-type swimming snorkels. As water is pumped up through the collector's copper tubing, air is forced ahead of it and out the vent. When the water reaches this point, it forces the ball against the vent, thus closing the system. When the collector drains at night, water pressure is taken off the ball, permitting the vent to open, thus venting the system to atmospheric pressure and allowing it to drain much quicker. Otherwise the system would drain more slowly and lose more heat in the process.

Storage

The storage reservoir, measuring 22 x 38′ in area and 16″ high (inside measurements), is contained within the 6″ poured-concrete slab and the 12″-thick concrete foundation walls and underlies the entire living space. There are 4″ of Dow Styrofoam-SM alternately layered with asphalt and polyethylene to insulate the storage bin's 6″ slab floor and concrete-block walls from the foundation walls and floor. The concrete reservoir itself was carefully sealed with two layers of coal tar and then filled with 65 tons of 1″-diameter round stone and capped with polyethylene sheeting and a 4″ concrete-slab top. The stones, at $50 for the lot, provided an inexpensive practical structural support for the concrete-slab top. The cavities were then filled with 13 tons of rainwater and tap water.

No reinforcing steel was used for the reservoir top, as the metal tends to act like a screen, thus reducing the amount of heat transfer to the crawl space. Between the top of the bin and the uninsulated floor of the living areas, there is a 2′ crawl space.

Heat Distribution

A 1/12-hp pump circulates water from the storage to the collector.

When the living space needs heat, the system was designed to provide forced air, using a Vaughan EC-15 water-to-air heat pump rated at 15,000 Btu per hour. It is capable of extracting heat from the storage reservoir even when the storage is as cold as 40° F. and delivering it to the living spaces with air at a temperature of 180° F. The heat pump, located in the utility room near the center of the main floor, has a coefficient of performance of 2.7 (or about 4.0 if the heat from the heat-pump motor is taken into account).

In practice, the heat pump turned out to be superfluous and was removed. At all times during the winter, some heat migrates up through the carpeted wooden floor to the rooms; however, when additional heat is required, perimeter hot-air floor registers are opened and hot air from the 2′ airspace is allowed to circulate into the living spaces by natural convection. A thermostatically controlled blower can be used to speed circulation but is rarely required.

AUXILIARY HEATING

The only auxiliary heating that was installed was an electrical immersion heater with the heat pump that ensures that the input-water temperature to the heat pump does not drop below 40° F. This too proved to be superfluous.

PERCENT SOLAR-HEATED

All of the heat used in the Richards home is supplied by the sun, household appliances, and the occupants themselves. This is a fortunate accident; Spencer Dickinson had expected the heat pump to be necessary.

During the heating season, December to March, the average interior temperature is 72-74° F., while the daytime, clear outside temperature ranges from 30-42° F. and the night temperature ranges from 10-25° F. The pre-dawn coldest average temperature is around 6-8° F. Tobey stated that when they have company during the winter, the increased heat output will raise the temperature to between 75° and 80° F., at which point they usually open windows to vent the excess. Tobey and Carole calculated that the portion of their utility bill related to the operation of the heating system was $15 for the 1977-78 heating season.

COOLING SYSTEM

Tobey and Carol say that there is no problem with excess heat. A certain amount of heat is conducted through the uninsulated floor and carpet, but not enough to be uncomfortable. In the summer, the roof overhang prevents excessive direct solar gain through the south-facing windows. The superior insulation and the cross-ventilation from the north-south windows provides additional cooling. Being near the ocean, the house receives cool offshore breezes in the evening. The heating system is shut down early in summer, the floor hot-air registers are closed, and the temperature of the storage medium drops. Summer interior temperatures average 2° to 3° F. warmer than in winter.

East and south aspects. The roof overhang blocks summer sun but permits entry of the low-angled winter sun.

WATER SUPPLY AND WASTE SYSTEM

The house is linked to the town water supply. The water is preheated by 55′ of flexible copper coil located in the storage reservoir before it reaches the well-insulated Vaughan hot-water tank. None of the other water fixtures are particularly energy- or resource-conserving. Graywater and blackwater are disposed of via the town sewer system.

ELECTRICAL POWER SYSTEM

The house is linked to the local electricity grid. There is nothing particularly unusual or energy-conserving about it except that substantial fenestration, the open concept, and light-painted walls optimize good illumination.

MAJOR HOUSEHOLD APPLIANCES

The electric stove, refrigerator, clothes washer, dryer, and dishwasher are all from Sears, mainly because Carol's parents have always used Sears and have been very satisfied with their performance and durability. The clothes washer is an apartment-size water-conserving type. The outside clothesline is used in the summer for drying clothes. The drying cycle is usually turned off on the dishwasher in order to conserve energy. The purchase of a freezer is planned in order to preserve more garden produce and also because food supplies often run short in the winter due to the shutdown of the island bridge during storms.

FOOD SYSTEM

A garden provides the Richardses with fresh corn, beans, radishes, peppers, cucumbers, melons, tomatoes, and cherries. "The whole island is loaded with wild blueberries, cherries, and grapes," Carol reports. They delight in foraging for these wild edibles, and Carol is adept at preserving them and their garden produce.

COSTS

The complete solar system, installed, cost almost $8,000; however, Dickinson can with the knowledge gained duplicate the system for $5,000 to $6,000. Tobey was reluctant to say how much he paid for the house but did say that the asking price was $42,000.

CONCLUDING THOUGHTS

During their first winter in the house (1976-77), the temperature of the storage medium was not initially up to the required temperature, so that the heat pump had to be used for a while. Even then the cost for space heating was only $70 for the whole year. The following winter it cost less than $40 for space heating, as the temperature in storage was up and the heat pump was off. During the first winter the total electrical bill went constantly downward. After the heat pump was shut off, the total electrical costs dropped to less than $30 per month. Needless to say, Tobey and Carol are delighted.

Near Guilford, Connecticut
1,300 sq. ft. living area

HOUSE **10**

VIRGINIA and EVERETT M. BARBER, JR.

In December 1972 and January 1973, Everett Barber, then president of Sunworks Inc., a firm specializing in the design, manufacturing, and distribution of solar-energy equipment, conceived plans for an energy-conserving ecological home that would be heated by the sun and powered by the wind. The architectural firm of Charles W. Moore Associates, Essex, Connecticut, with Richard Oliver, was hired to do the architectural detailing, while Everett designed the mechanical and environmental systems. The initial design was completed in June 1973 and construction bids were tendered. Bids came in at $60,000 and above, well above what the Barbers were prepared to spend. So the designs were reworked and the bids retendered. This time, bids came in around $37,000 (exclusive of land costs, solar system, well, and septic system). The house was not completed until December 1975, and in Everett's words, "We almost went bankrupt." The house cost closer to $75,000. A substantial portion of this escalated cost is attributed to the $20,000 spent on the septic system, which normally should have cost about $1,700. The fragile nature of the local landscape required the installation of an extensive curtain drain—a drainage ditch that surrounds the septic tank and leaching field. The bottom of the curtain drain is well below the bottom of the leaching field; thus groundwater is kept out of the leaching field. The delays caused by this problem ran up rental accommodation and mortgage costs much in excess of what had been anticipated. "We never would have bought the land or built the house had we known about the septic problems." Nevertheless, Virginia, Everett, and their two young children are now comfortable in their solar-heated home.

LOCATION AND ORIENTATION

The Barber home is located near Guilford, Connecticut, within easy commuting distance of Everett's new business, Sunsearch Inc. It is quietly nestled into a gently south-sloping hillside surrounded by deciduous trees and looks down over a protected marsh area to the south—an area rife with the sounds of songbirds, bullfrogs, and crickets.

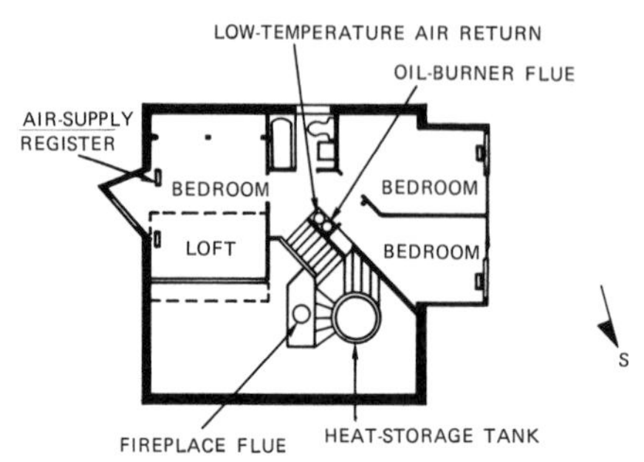

SECOND FLOOR

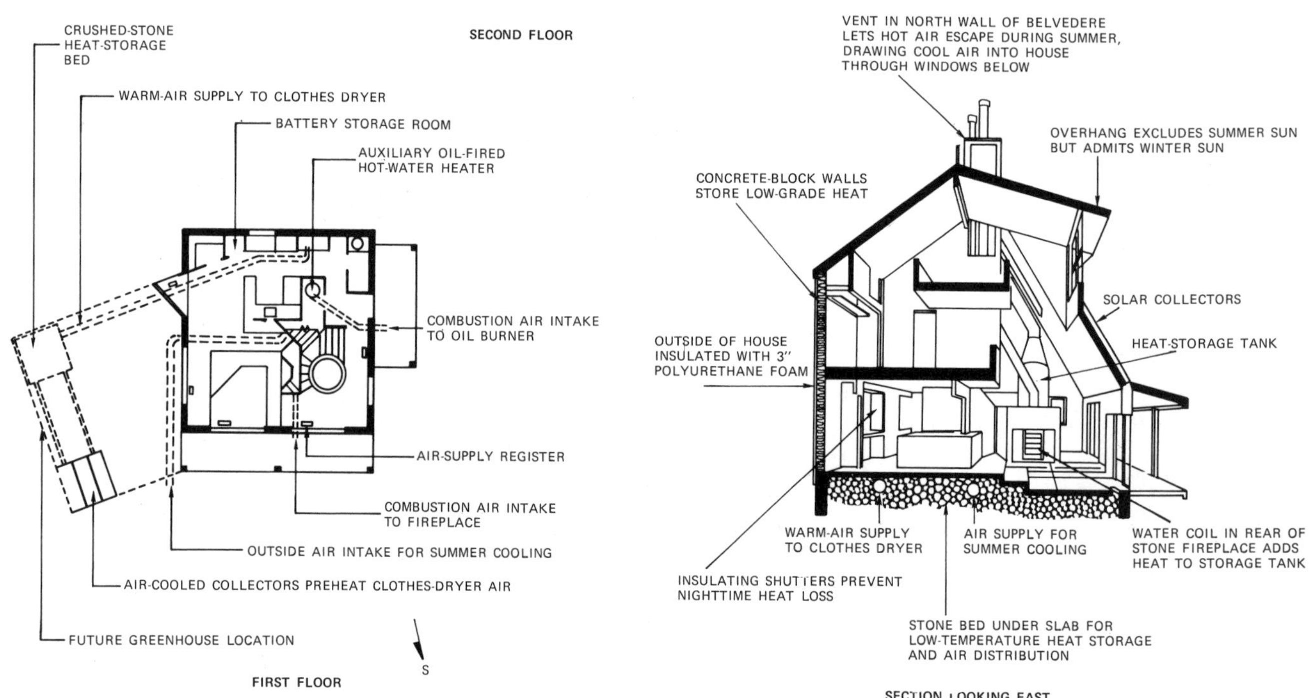

FIRST FLOOR

SECTION LOOKING EAST

ARCHITECTURAL FEATURES

This two-story 1,300-sq.-ft. house was designed for a "typical" middle-income family of five. An effort has been made to meet all the basic needs of the family within this relatively small, compact space. The house measures 28 x 28′ and approximates a cube—a shape with a high volume-to-enclosed-surface-area ratio and thus relatively low heat-loss characteristics.

The house faces southwesterly and has most of its window glazing on this south facade. The layout is open concept to facilitate heat and ventilation airflows as well as to suggest spaciousness.

The kitchen is small and compact but very well organized. The sunken living room has little furniture, as the floor itself was designed as a lounge around the central fireplace. Large cushions serve as a variation of the easy chair. A bathroom, the cupboards, and storage areas on the north wall help to insulate the living spaces. The master bedroom has a loft/study area above and a full-length closet along the north wall to act as a thermal buffer. These two spaces have an attractive open view of the living room below, but despite the aesthetic advantages Everett plans to install sliding glass windows between the bedroom and space below in order to control noise.

The two children share one bedroom, and the other is normally used as their play area. A raised platform at one end of the room, which is strong enough for children to walk and jump on, stores a spare mattress and bedding. When guests stay overnight the mattress is pulled out and placed on top of the platform.

The house has no basement but has a 4″-thick concrete slab floor poured over the 2′-deep rock storage bed. The floor slab was not isolated from the foundation walls, as Everett felt that the exterior walls were well enough insulated so that this would not be necessary; however, he has discovered that there is still a substantial heat transfer occurring from the slab to the wall and then down the foundation wall to the ground. The floors of the second level and the loft are 2 x 10 joists surfaced with plywood and oak.

Exterior Walls

Outside walls are 8″-thick concrete blocks laid on top of a poured-concrete foundation wall. At the time of construction the costs for this type of wall were two-thirds that of a comparable frame wall (including the insulation mentioned below). Everett stated that they neglected to seal off the tops of the concrete blocks and as a result, the convection currents that form in the block cavities lead to moderate heat losses at the top of the walls. The exterior surface of the concrete-block walls was sprayed with 3″ of polyurethane foam insulation. The north wall received 4″. The foam, if untreated, will degrade over time and become porous; therefore, Thoroseal, a paint normally used to seal concrete walls, was applied over the foam. The Thoroseal was initially applied incorrectly by the contractor. The polyurethane should be allowed to age a certain amount before the finish coat is applied. The Thoroseal adheres perfectly if the outer surface of the foam is somewhat porous. Because the sealant was applied too early, the smooth surface and trapped moisture in the foam led to blistering of the sealant, necessitating resealing later. Another unexpected and continual problem is the delight that woodpeckers seem to take in hammering holes in the foam, particularly in high places that are difficult to reach. The problem is not yet a serious one and the holes can be patched, but it is a nuisance. One solution that Everett has suggested is to put screen mesh over an initial application of foam and then spray a second thinner layer over that. In spite of these problems, Everett still feels that it is a good idea to use this type of wall structure and insulation.

Interior Walls and Ceilings

The concrete-block walls are exposed on the inside and painted light in color. Interior partition walls are of standard 2 x 4 studwall construction. They and the ceilings are covered with ½″ gypsum board painted a light color for good illumination.

Roof

Standard framing techniques were used for the roof. Dormers were built largely for aesthetic reasons. A belvedere was constructed at the roof peak for natural lighting and ventilation. Asphalt shingles were applied over the entire roof, even under the collectors. The initial specifications called for the collector panels to be installed between the rafters; however, the builder, Richard Riggio, was concerned about the difficulty of preventing leaks with such an installation and thus encouraged Barber and the architects to finish the roof in the ordinary fashion and later install the collectors over the shingles, as described later in the text. The asphalt shingles should last longer, but when they do need to be replaced it will be a difficult job, as the collectors will have to be removed.

East entrance. Walls are concrete block, insulated on the outside with polyurethene foam. Greek wrestlers in bas-relief adorn the south wall.

The central Rumford-design fireplace provides radiant heat to the living room and provides additional hot water to the large solar-heated reservoir behind.

Insulation Summary

Foundation, north side:	R-26; 4″ polyurethane foam
Foundation, other sides:	R-19.5; 3″ polyurethane foam
Walls:	Same as foundation. The sprayed-on foam provides an excellent seal around windows and other construction joints to minimize infiltration losses.
Ceiling:	R-30; 10″ fiberglass batts

Doors

The sliding glass Acadia aluminum patio doors on the south face of the house provide access to the deck and also allow significant solar-heat gain during the winter. The deck roof prevents summer overheating of the building interior. The high-conductivity aluminum frames are cold in the winter, but condensation problems have not been significant. A third patio door on the west side of the house opens out onto what will eventually be a patio area on the rock ledge.

A regular-size entranceway, with a steel insulated door with magnetic weatherstripping, near the driveway on the sheltered east side of the house is the one most frequently used. An overhang from the second-floor bedroom provides shelter from the elements. From this doorway one can enter directly to the kitchen or the living room. The Barbers eventually plan to build a porch/airlock from this east entranceway to the south deck.

Windows

All of the windows are operable Andersen wood-frame double-glazed thermopane. Most of the windows face southwesterly, and most have overhangs to prevent direct solar-heat gain during the summer and to permit them to be opened for ventilation when it's raining. The overhangs have been designed to let in the winter sun. The north side has only two small windows. R-10 multilayer shades made by the Insulating Shade Company Inc. (Box 689, Durham, Conn. 06422) will make the south-facing windows very effective collectors.

View from kitchen looking south to living room.

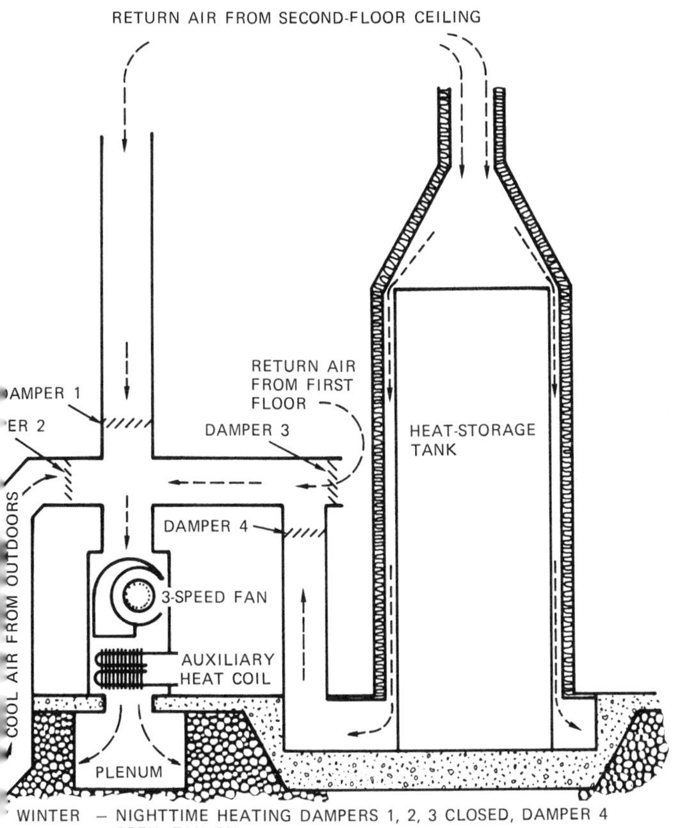

WINTER – NIGHTTIME HEATING DAMPERS 1, 2, 3 CLOSED, DAMPER 4 OPEN, FAN ON.
– DAYTIME STORAGE OF OCCUPANT AND SOLAR GAIN THROUGH WINDOWS INTO STONE UNDER FLOOR. DAMPERS 2, 3, 4 CLOSED, DAMPER 1 OPEN, FAN ON.

SUMMER – NIGHTTIME COOLING FROM OUTSIDE AIR INTO STONE, WINDOWS OPEN, DAMPERS 1, 3, 4 CLOSED, DAMPER 2 OPEN, FAN ON.
– DAYTIME COOLING OF HOUSE FROM COOLNESS STORED IN STONE, DAMPERS 2, 1, 4 CLOSED, DAMPER 3 OPEN, FAN ON.

AIR ROUTING

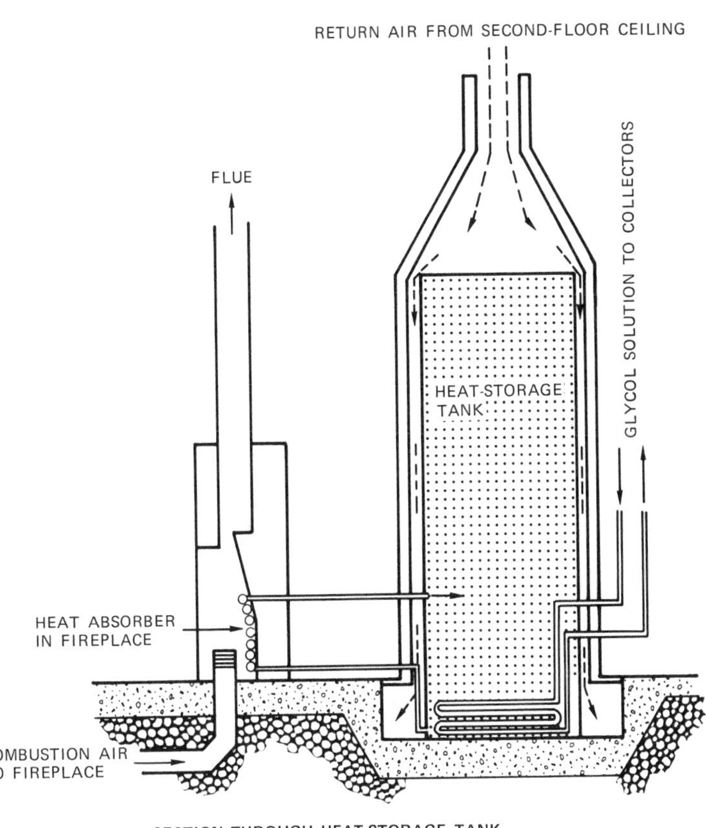

SECTION THROUGH HEAT-STORAGE TANK

SOLAR-HEATING SYSTEM

The passive aspects of the solar collection system have already been mentioned. Everett has very cleverly integrated this with an efficient active system.

Collector

The 400 sq. ft. of flat-plate water-type collector, built by Sunworks Inc., was installed on the southwesterly facing roof, which is tilted at 57° to the vertical. The 19 panels of different, nonstandard sizes were placed over the asphalt shingles with sufficient space between each collector to permit a worker to move about between them without the use of ladders, thus facilitating installation and maintenance. A J-shaped metal bracket with a redwood 2 x 4 secured at the bottom of the J was nailed to the roof over the top of the shingles. A 3/16″-thick strip of Miracle Seal, made by Revere Chemical Co., placed under the bracket extrudes up and around the nails, making a perfectly watertight seal. The collector panels are screwed to the bracket and the redwood 2 x 4. The single glazing for these panels is 3/16″ glass. The 0.010″ copper sheet absorber plate has copper tubes ⅜″ in diameter soldered to it, 6″ apart, in a grid pattern running the length of the panel. The absorber plate and tubes are finished with a selective black coating with an absorptance-to-emission ratio of 10. Everett claims that on a clear day the collector has an efficiency of 60% when the absorber temperature is 100° F. above the outside temperature. The underside of the absorber is insulated with 2½″ of fiberglass, and the whole is encased in an aluminum frame. The coolant, water with 40% ethylene glycol added, is circulated by a ½-hp centrifugal pump.

Storage

Heat is stored in several ways. The masonry walls provide useful storage of heat generated from normal operation of the heating system and from direct solar gain through the windows. The walls will heat the house air whenever the latter is at a lower temperature, as when the heating system is off, and will also radiate heat to the living spaces.

The concrete-slab floor was designed to store heat in a similar way. It is carpeted only in the living room, where the Barbers sit on the floor around the fireplace.

A 5′-diameter, 12′-high cylindrical steel storage tank filled with 2,000 gallons of water stands conspicuously near the entranceway, and guests must pass it to enter the living space. Everett explains why he designed the system this way: "I did it to make people realize that a certain amount of the volume of your house must be given up to store the amount of heat to allow you to sustain this type of life-style. I attempted to give some visual scale to the quantity of energy used." The water in the tank is heated by a heat-exchange coil in the bottom of the tank that is connected to the solar panels. The original 20-sq.-ft. heat exchanger was found to be too small and was replaced with a 70-sq.-ft. unit. Air used to heat the house is warmed as it is passed over the outside of the tank. A sleeve surrounding the outside of the tank provides a passageway for this air. The sleeve is insulated on the outside with 3″ of fiberglass, and the whole is covered with a skin of galvanized metal sheeting. During the heating season, the temperature in the tank will vary from 80° F. to 140° F. The tank can store approximately 1 million Btu when operating over a 60° F. range. (The steel inner wall of this main storage tank showed signs of corrosion at the air-water interface when the tank was not full. The problem was solved by draining the tank, sandblasting the inner surface, and coating it with epoxy.)

A third way of storing heat is in the rock-storage reservoir under the floor slab. This 2′-high storage reservoir of the same dimensions as the house is filled with 4″-diameter stones. A vapor barrier and a 1″-thick layer of rigid extruded polystyrene insulates the stones from the ledgerock below and the foundation wall at the sides. Temperatures in the rock storage during the heating season vary from 65° F. to 90° F., and the usable heat-storage capacity is about 0.4 x 10^6 Btu.

West aspect.

Heat Distribution

A return-air duct draws in warm air at the uppermost part of the house. On sunny days the single 1/3-hp blower drives this air into a plenum in the center of and under the floor slab, from where it is forced outward through the rock storage. The warm air near the ceiling is generally at a lower temperature than the water in the 2,000-gallon tank and therefore cannot be stored there but can be stored in the relatively cooler rock storage. At night the blower drives hot air within the storage-tank jacket through the auxiliary heater, through the rock storage, and thence to the living space via registers around the perimeter of the first floor.

The uninsulated fireplace chimney, the return-air duct leading to a jacket around the water-storage reservoir, and the reservoir itself give some scale to the quantity of heat used.

AUXILIARY HEATING

There are several auxiliary-heating systems. A Rumford-design stone fireplace stands in the living room. It has an outside air-intake vent which at first sometimes resulted in ashes being blown all over. With some modifications the fireplace now works quite well. The installation of Pyrex doors is planned in the future. The fireplace chimney stack, made of galvanized metal, is exposed and uninsulated until it reaches the upper-level ceiling. The stack therefore radiates a substantial amount of heat. A grid of boiler pipe is placed in the back of the fireplace, above the fire. Water leaves the bottom of the 2,000-gallon storage tank, passes through the boiler pipe, becomes heated, and by natural convection returns to the upper part of the tank.

The third source of auxiliary space heat is from a 50-gallon oil-fired water heater that also serves as the auxiliary domestic hot-water heater. This heater has an output capacity of 110,000 Btu per hour and accomplishes space heating by circulating heated water through a water coil located downstream from the heat-storage tank in the main air duct. Everett made some refinements to the oil-fired heater. He raised it from the floor slab to a pedestal 6" above and connected a positive outside air supply to the combustion air intake as well as one to the flue draft.

PERCENT SOLAR-HEATED

The contribution of the solar system to space heating has not yet been thoroughly evaluated. In the winter of 1976-77, when there were 6,500 degree-days, the house used 900 gallons of fuel oil. In the winter of 1977-78, the house used 600 gallons with the solar system active since mid-January 1978. The winter of 1978-79 was the first time that the solar system functioned for a full winter. Everett calculates that the active component supplied 60% of the heating requirement while the passive component provided 20%. The fireplace is capable of supplying the remaining 20%.

COOLING SYSTEM

Artificial cooling of the house is not used. The natural chimney effect draws air from the house out through a vent in the belvedere at the top of the house. The exhausted air is replaced by cooler air entering the windows at the first-floor level. The air movement set up by this effect helps to keep air velocities fairly high in the house, which helps to maintain a comfortable environment, even during hot weather. Finned coils are located outside the vent in the belvedere. During hot weather excess solar heat is passed through the finned coils, which further stimulates the chimney effect. The excess solar heat circulates by gravity flow from the collectors below.

The use of insulation on the outside of the thermally massive walls significantly reduces the cooling requirement.

Provisions have been made to draw cool outside air into the house at night and store it in the rocks, concrete slab, and masonry wall. During the day, warm house air can be blown through the rocks to cool it, and the massive walls give up their "coolness" to the warm air.

In warmer climates, it would be appropriate to similarly integrate the cooling potential of the 2,000-gallon water storage.

WATER SUPPLY AND WASTE SYSTEM

Water is supplied from an on-site drilled well. After drilling the well it was discovered that the iron content was very high. The town required that an iron filter and a water softener be installed before the Barbers could assume occupancy. This additional unexpected expenditure resulted in the cancellation of plans for a filtered graywater system that would have been used to furnish water for flushing toilets. There are 40 sq. ft. of collector to heat domestic hot water for a 65-gallon tank in the mechanical room. A heat-exchange coil within the tank is connected to the oil-fired water heater. The 10-sq.-ft. heat exchanger in the hot-water tank was found to be too small and was replaced by a 24-sq.-ft. unit.

ELECTRICAL POWER SYSTEM

At the present time the Barber home is linked to the local utility grid, but Everett plans to install two 10′-diameter wind generators to augment the utility-company power. The first to be installed will be a 2-kilowatt Australian Dunlite generator. The second will be designed and built by Everett Barber. In the future, Everett envisions using the wind system to charge the batteries of a small electric car that would probably have a range of about 30 miles on one charge.

The substantial amount of natural light coming from many directions minimizes the need for artificial lighting during the day. On a clear night enough light is provided from the skylight in the belvedere that one does not even require the use of hall lights to go from the bedrooms to the washroom. Rheostats are used for incandescent lights, and task lighting is used to conserve electrical-power consumption.

MAJOR HOUSEHOLD APPLIANCES

The Barbers had planned to buy one of the new Amana energy-conserving refrigerators at the time that they made their appliance purchases. However, Virginia felt that it was too small for their needs, so they opted for one of the standard models. Everett had considered a heat-recovery device for the refrigerator, but the costs proved to be prohibitive. A commerical unit is made by Halstead & Mitchell that could be used to preheat domestic hot water, but it costs about $1,000.

The electric cookstove and clothes washer have no particular energy-conserving features. Eventually Everett plans to preheat air coming into the electric clothes dryer and dishwasher with two Sunworks air-type collectors linked to a 3-cu.-yd. rock heat-storage reservoir. A manual switch will be used on each appliance to supply electricity to the heating elements when the solar system cannot supply enough useful heat.

COSTS

Refer back to the introductory paragraph for information regarding costs. Operating costs have been reasonable considering that the solar system has not been operational a full winter. In 1977-78, the 600 gallons at 50 cents per gallon cost $300. The winter electric bills for that same period averaged $27 per month; during the following summer months the costs averaged $18 per month.

CONCLUDING THOUGHTS

As an extra energy-conserving measure, Everett plans to build an insulated cover to be placed over the belvedere in winter to minimize the stack-effect heat losses. After this and some of the other modifications mentioned previously, the house will be performing pretty well as predicted. The only major problem that the Barbers had was the financial constraint referred to earlier. To quote Everett, "We wouldn't build on so small a budget again. It puts too much of a strain on the family." One small but significant feature of the house is a flat-roof area off the belvedere where Everett could escape for a moment from the worries and problems that always confront a pioneer.

Right: Pressure and temperature gauges located on the stairwell allow the homeowner to monitor the operation of the solar system.

Far Right: View from living room to kitchen and master bedroom above.

socket, Rhode Island
sq. ft. including basement

HOUSE **11**

'76 Sunhouse

ROBERT E. GRENIER

Robert E. Grenier is a builder and realtor in Woonsocket, Rhode Island. "With the high cost of fuels, particularly since 1973, I started to think of solar and then stumbled across Dr. Harry E. Thomason's patented trickle-flow-collector solar system. I subsequently became a licensee. I never intended to get into the conventional heating business, but often they are interrelated with the solar and I seem to be getting carried in that direction. You install one system and people want you to do another. I do the building design and then subcontract most of the work. As I need the physical as well as the mental exercise, I do the heating-system installations myself with the help of one man."

The '76 Sunhouse that Grenier built on speculation and subsequently sold to a client is one of more than a dozen Thomason-type systems that he has installed in his own buildings or installed for other builders.

LOCATION AND ORIENTATION

This house is located on a 100 x 100′ corner lot of a suburban community in Woonsocket, Rhode Island. The house is oriented with its short axis 10° west of south. The long south side of the house faces the intersecting street and looks out at two other solar-heated houses that Grenier has built.

ARCHITECTURAL FEATURES

This one-and-a-half-story Cape-style high-peak wood-frame structure is 26′ wide by 44′ long and has about 2,800 sq. ft. of heated space, including the part of the unfinished basement not taken up by the solar-storage reservoir. The room layout is well designed for efficiency and energy conservation. The top floor has two bedrooms separated by the central staircase and the bathroom. A 4′-wide insulated but unheated storage area runs the entire length of the south side of the upstairs. A similar 6′-wide storage area runs the entire length of the north side. Clothes closets cover the north wall of each bedroom except for the 6′-wide vanity in the master bedroom. These closets and storage areas provide good thermal buffering for the bedrooms. In addition, the bathroom is on the north wall and can be used as an additional thermal buffer if the occupants wish to keep it at a lower

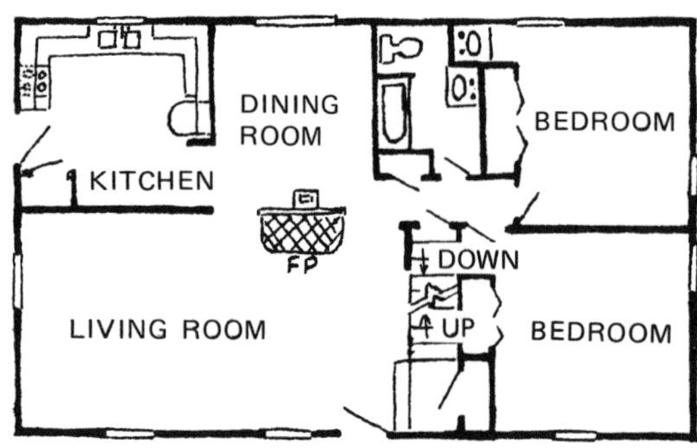

GROUND FLOOR

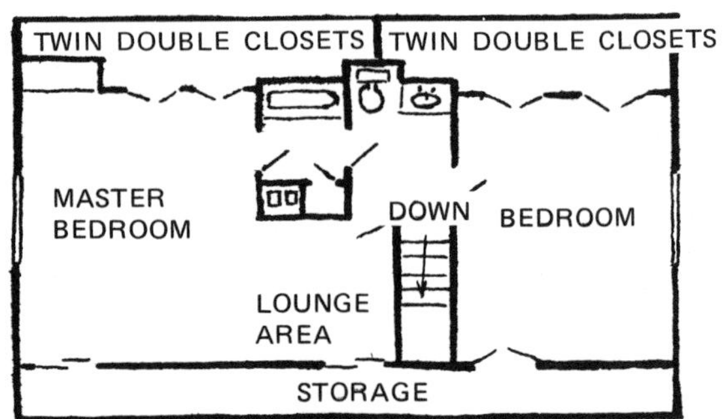

SECOND FLOOR

temperature. The bathroom layout is the European style, in which the tub can be isolated from the water closet and sink. A door at the top of the stairs allows the upstairs to be isolated from the downstairs, a feature especially useful during emergency power or fuel shortages.

Both downstairs bedrooms are on the sunrise side of the house. Closets on the interior west wall of each bedroom act as buffers for noise from the living areas, open staircase, and bathroom. In addition, they provide a certain amount of thermal buffering should the family desire to isolate the bedrooms from the rest of the house. The downstairs bathroom is very conveniently located in the hallway linking the living/dining room, bedrooms, and basement stairs. The living room on the warm south side of the house has substantial window area on the south and west. The central hearth and chimney is common to the living and the dining room, which is in turn linked to the compact, well-organized kitchen. In an emergency heating situation, these three rooms could be battened down and isolated from the rest of the house. With the more or less open-plan concept the three would serve as a "warm room" or "survival room" that could be heated very adequately with just the wood stove.

The foundation walls are of 12″-thick poured reinforced concrete over 9″ of crushed gravel. The basement floors are 4″ reinforced concrete except under the solar-storage reservoir, which has 6″. The upstairs floors are 2 x 8 joists on 12″ centers. They were first sheathed with ⅝″ plywood and then covered with the paper-based, sound-deadening Homasote sheathing prior to being carpeted.

Exterior Walls

Standard 2 x 4 studwall construction was used. The cavities were insulated with 3½″ fiberglass batts and the exterior sheathed with 2 x 8′ sheets of tongue-and-groove extruded polystyrene 1″ thick. The exterior skin on the north, east, and west walls is 4 x 8′ sheets of Select Siding, a Masonite pressboard product designed to look like vertical boards. The exterior skin of the south wall is brick veneer. Clapboard was used for the gable ends.

Interior Walls and Ceilings

Interior partition walls on the first floor are of 2 x 4 studwall construction. The kneewalls on the second floor are 2 x 3 studs. The ceiling of the second floor is formed by the 2 x 6 collar ties—the horizontal members used to provide intermediate support for opposite roof rafters. All walls and ceilings are sheathed with ½″ gypsum board.

Roof

The standard gable roof with its 2 x 6 rafters on 16″ centers is covered with ½″ plywood. Asphalt shingles clad the north part of the roof; roll roofing was applied to the south side before the collector was installed. The collector, which covers all of the south slope except a small area around the edges and the bottom of the roof, also acts as a weatherproof skin.

Insulation Summary

Basement: No insulation except 2″ of rigid extruded polystyrene on those walls contiguous with the storage reservoir

Walls: R-17; 3½″ fiberglass batts with integral vapor barrier plus 1″ extruded polystyrene tongue-and-groove sheathing. A polyethylene vapor barrier was also added in the kitchen and bathroom.

Kneewalls: R-12; 3½″ fiberglass batts

Ceiling: R-40; 12″ fiberglass above the collar ties (equivalent to two-thirds of ceiling area)

Attic floor: R-20; 6″ fiberglass on the floor of the attic storage space

The builder, Robert Grenier, stands on the west side of '76 Sunhouse. His own home immediately opposite and another that he built on the adjoining lot to the east also use the trickle-flow solar system.

The long hot-air register running above the doorway between living room and dining room is typical of that found in all of Grenier's solar houses.

Doors

The doors on the south and west leading to the living room and kitchen respectively are insulated steel with magnetic weatherstripping. Infiltration losses could be substantially reduced with porch/airlocks, especially for the west door, which receives the prevailing and storm northwest winter winds. The kitchen door is conveniently located next to the driveway and the garden area.

Windows

The house has a generous amount of window area on the first floor, although not as much as a typical Cape-style house. In order to make the windows appear larger at the front (south) of the house, the frames were extended downward and the area between them filled with wood sheathing that makes a subtle contrast with the brick veneer. Two windows in each of the downstairs bedrooms provide good ventilation and illumination. The open-concept kitchen, dining, and living areas optimize the illumination and ventilation capacities of windows and doors in those areas.

All the windows are double-hung, wood-sash, insulated thermopane windows. As well, each has an aluminum storm window. The windows are fitted with curtains or drapes, but they were not chosen for superior insulating qualities.

SOLAR-HEATING SYSTEM

The house receives a fair amount of direct-gain solar heat into the southeast bedroom and into the living room, some of which is subsequently convected and radiated into the dining room area; however, the heart of the heating system is the active Thomason-designed trickle-flow solar collectors.

Collector

The collectors fit flush against the south slope of the roof and are thus oriented 10° west of south and tilted at 52° from the horizontal. In the future, Robert plans to install the collectors at 45° to facilitate construction and maintenance. He feels that the slight loss in efficiency is outweighed by some of the other advantages of a lower pitch. The outside dimensions of the collector array are 43 x 19½' high for a gross area of 838 sq. ft. Subtracting mullions and edge trim leaves about 760 sq. ft. of net collector area. There are 20 collector panels measuring 2' wide and 19½' long. Each is framed with 2½"-deep aluminum storm door stock. The glazing is composed of 4 x 2' panes of single-weight glass that are sealed at their edges with U-shaped strips of neoprene. The absorber plate is 0.026" corrugated aluminum roofing. The corrugations are flat on the hills and flat in the valleys, and the surface of the aluminum is embossed so that the pores or pockets create a larger surface area for the water to trickle over. The absorber was coated with a nonselective black paint manufactured by the Farboil Paint Co. The absorber rests on 1″-thick rigid extruded polystyrene insulation. Water is pumped from storage to a ½″-inside-diameter copper header pipe at the top of the collector. This header pipe has one 1/16″-diameter hole per valley, which permits water to trickle down the absorber, gathering heat as it passes over the warm surface. The heated water is collected in a 0.032″ enclosed aluminum gutter at the base of the collector and subsequently flows by gravity to storage.

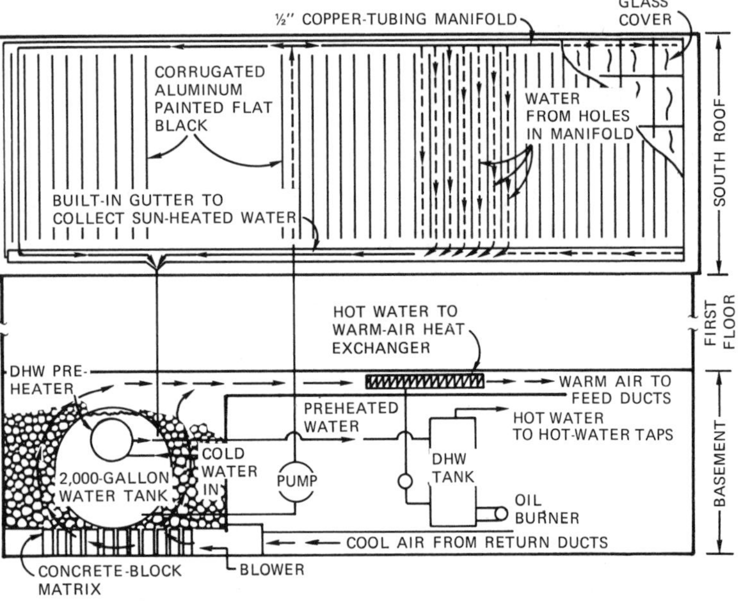

SOLARIS SOLAR-HEATING CYCLE (patented)

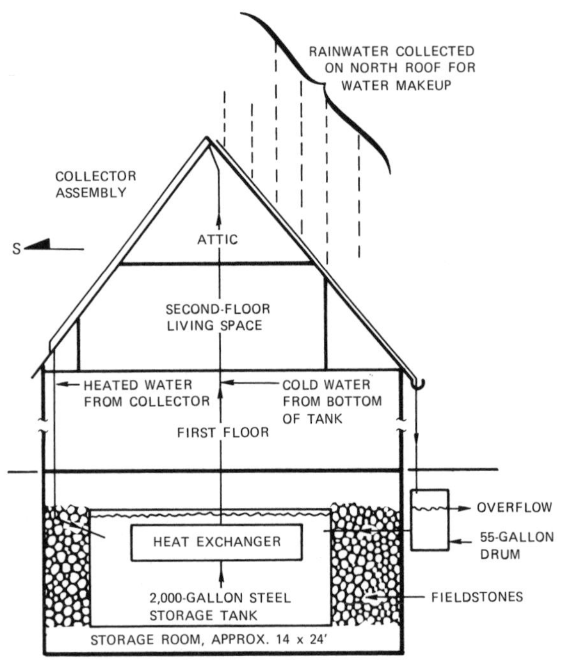

Grenier has been very satisfied with the collector. In nearly four years of operation it has worked as well as expected and has suffered no substantial damage. There has been about a 5% paint loss, but with the subsequent oxidation of the aluminum to a flat gray color, the loss in efficiency is probably insignificant. He feels that the absence of a corrosion inhibitor might partially account for the durability of the paint surface. The glazing is not completely watertight, so a certain amount of condensation escapes and a certain amount of rainwater enters the collector, but it is felt that this does not significantly affect the collector efficiency either. The vent holes at the top of each panel near the header to relieve condensation pressures are probably redundant, and Bob fears that the heat loss through them could be substantial.

Storage

The storage reservoir, measuring 12′5″ x 23′6″ x 7′ high (interior measurements), is located in the northwest corner of the basement. Two of its walls are formed by the outside foundation walls; the other two are of 10″-thick reinforced concrete. The interior surface of the walls and the 6″ poured-concrete floor are

Detail of typical hot-air register.

lined with 2" of rigid extruded polystyrene insulation. An uninsulated 2,000-gallon cylindrical steel water tank, 5' in diameter and 17' long, runs the length of the concrete bin. It was red-leaded and was brushed inside and out with a cement-and-water mixture. The tank rests on an air-distributing manifold of concrete blocks and is completely surrounded by 50 tons of stones 1" to 8" in diameter. The larger stones are closest to the heat source (steel tank) to allow larger voids for air circulation and consequently heat transfer to living-space air. The smaller stones near the outside edges of the bin reduce airflow and add to the insulating quality of the exterior (foundation) walls. In new installations Grenier has used fist-sized stones throughout the entire bin. A 1 x 3 wood-frame drop ceiling from the basement ceiling joists was built to facilitate insulating the top of the tank with 2" of Styrofoam-SM and 3½" of fiberglass. An insulated access port high on one of the interior concrete walls and a manifold cover on the steel tank permit inspection of the storage system.

Heat Distribution

When thermistors located in the collector and the storage indicate to the differential thermostat that the former is 10° warmer than the latter, a 1/3-hp centrifugal pump pumps water from the bottom of the steel storage tank to the header pipes, from where it trickles down the collector, picks up heat, and continues its gravity flow to the inlet at the top of the storage tank. When the collector cools down, the differential thermostat turns the pump off and both the feeder pipe and the return line completely drain, thus negating the need for antifreeze. Bob states that the pump does not work to capacity and that a 1/10-hp would probably be quite adequate and would save electricity.

The heat distribution to the living spaces is by a forced-air system. When the house thermostat demands heat, a ¼-hp blower comes on, draws cool air from the house, filters it, and forces it through the rock bed, where it picks up heat which is subsequently delivered to the living spaces. This is a low-temperature, high-volume, low-static-pressure system that is designed to work with the laws of gravity and not against them. Both the hot-air and cold-air registers are long and linear. In each room the cold-air-return registers are along the floor near and running parallel to the outside wall. As soon as the outside wall skin becomes cold, the air near it becomes cold and thus denser. It therefore flows downward to the cold-air register assisted by the negative pressure created by the fan. The warm-air-delivery registers are located high on the wall opposite the cold-air registers and within the center wall of the house. With this type of system the house often gets adequate circulation without the use of the fan. This happens most frequently in the spring and the fall.

Typical hot-air supply ports from basement to between-stud cavities leading to hot-air-supply registers in living spaces.

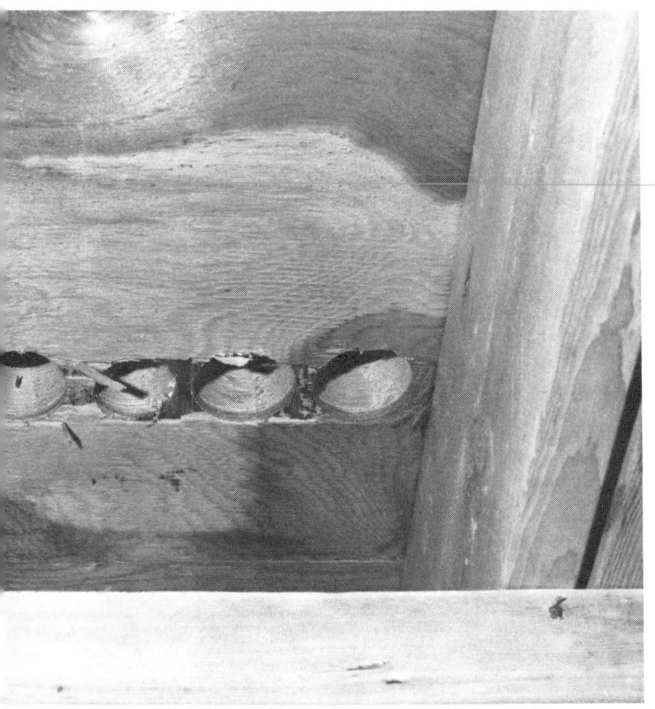

Cold-air-return registers are also linear and are located on the exterior wall opposite the hot-air-supply registers.

AUXILIARY HEATING

The small oil burner, which is primarily used to heat the domestic hot water, will on demand from the house thermostat circulate heated water from the domestic hot-water tank through a finned-copper-pipe heat exchanger located in the main warm-air-delivery line coming from the solar heat-storage reservoir, thus supplementing the heat from the latter, on an as-required basis.

A Franklin stove/fireplace sits on the hearth that is centrally located between the dining room and the living room. In this position the Franklin will heat a large area of the house—a feature which is especially important during emergency situations. The central chimney containing the flue for the wood stove and that for the oil burner runs up through a closet in the master bedroom, and thus any heat loss from the chimney before it reaches the attic is confined to living spaces.

PERCENT SOLAR-HEATED

Grenier has calculated that about 75% of this home's heating needs are provided by the solar system. This figure is arrived at using figures for oil consumption based upon past experience with similar dwellings. The table here gives data for two years of operation for which Grenier kept a record of oil consumption. No wood was used to supplement the space heating during this period. "And in all fairness," says Grenier, "the owners of '76 Sunhouse during the 1976–77 period were conservative."

Time period	Conditions	Average oil consumption expected without solar heat	Actual oil consumed	Percent heat by solar
Sept. 1975 to Aug. 1976	House vacant; heating first floor (1,144 sq. ft.) and 700 sq. ft. in basement. Holding 50 gallons of domestic hot water at usable temperature; average living-space temperature 70° F. during heating season.	1157 gallons	405 gallons	65
Sept. 1976 to Aug. 1977	House occupied; heating first floor (1,144 sq. ft.) second floor (1,000 sq. ft.), and 700 sq. ft. in basement. Providing domestic hot water; average living-space temperature during heating season 70° F.	1800 gallons	450 gallons	75

Grenier claims that on a "typical" cold cloudy winter day if the storage bin has a large charge of heat and if the demand is not too intense, he has a three- or four-day carryover of heat; that is, he can count on drawing usable heat from storage for this period of time to answer a reasonable heat order. If the heat demand is fairly intense, the auxiliary oil burner will come on to supplement the solar heat.

COOLING SYSTEM

According to Grenier, the demand for air conditioners is low in this area. In the '76 Sunhouse the perimeter lawn, good insulation, and the placement of windows for cross-ventilation keep the house comfortable even during the hottest summer days. Each bedroom downstairs has windows on two walls, permitting cross-ventilation. Similarly, the kitchen, dining room, and living room have windows and doors on three walls, thus providing excellent cross-ventilation and thus natural cooling. The upstairs bedrooms each have only one double window; however, with the door at the top of the stairs open, a chimney effect is created, bringing air up the stairs and out the windows. The excellent insulation upstairs makes the need for cross-ventilation less important. During clear, sunny summer days, the collector has a cooling effect on the south-facing roof. As the collector is used to provide domestic hot water in summer, the water trickling down the collector keeps the roof cooler than it would be without the collector. The net result is an air-conditioning effect on the second floor.

Inspection and entry port to rock storage. A ¼-hp blower forces air through the rock bed and to the hot-air-supply registers.

Detail of cold-air-return register looking up from basement.

WASTE AND WATER SYSTEM

The house is hooked up to the city water supply. Domestic hot water, as mentioned previously, is heated in a 40-gallon tank by an oil burner. It is first preheated in a 40-gallon galvanized tank that is immersed within the solar-heated water. During the summer months nearly 100% of the domestic hot water is heated by the solar system. On a year-round basis 75% of the domestic hot water is heated by solar.

Water-saving shower heads were installed as well as anti-scald shower/tub mixing valves.

Blackwater and graywater are disposed of through the city sewer system.

ELECTRICAL POWER SUPPLY

A standard 200-amp service linked to the local utility grid supplies the home's electrical needs. Good window placement optimizes illumination from natural lighting. Rheostats are used for general lighting in the living room and dining room.

COSTS

Bob was reluctant to discuss the total cost to build the house. He sold the house to the first owners for about $50,000. The material costs for the entire solar system was less than $3,000 when it was built in 1975.

CONCLUDING THOUGHTS

I talked briefly with the first owner of the house after meeting with Bob Grenier. The family was absolutely delighted with the house—its architectural features and the mechanical system. They were particularly pleased that it costs so little to heat their home and that they were among the pioneers in the utilization of renewable energy resources. The house is by outward appearances very conventional, but the many energy-conserving features and the relatively simple resource-conserving solar system make it exceptional. Bob Grenier is a fine example of a professional builder who can build cost-effective, aesthetically pleasing solar houses.

WILLIAM E. S. BIRD

William Bird is a well-established architect in Princeton, Massachusetts. Bill describes why he decided to build a solar house: "For several years I have been thinking about building a small house for the average family which would be a departure from the ordinary builder's house. About the time of the energy crisis I read an article in a local paper about the work of Dr. Harry E. Thomason in Washington, D.C., the developer and patent holder of a water-trickling solar collector. I then wrote to him and subsequently attended a two-day seminar at his home in Washington. I liked his system, incorporated it into the design of this house, and started construction in October 1975. We had no trouble getting financing from a local bank—in fact, we had offers from a couple of different banks. They seemed to like the idea of having their names connected with a solar house."

Bill did all the design work and then worked side by side with a very experienced and skilled professional carpenter. Separate contractors were hired for the heating, plumbing, and electrical work. The result is a well-engineered, energy-efficient, moderate-cost, comfortable, and attractive home. Bill has rented the home to a young family who are delighted to be experiencing a solar-heated house.

LOCATION AND ORIENTATION

The house is oriented 10° west of south and sits high on an open parcel of land in Princeton, Massachusetts. A mixed deciduous and coniferous woodlot is to the west of the house and does afford some protection from the prevailing westerlies; however, the back of the house is completely exposed to the northeast winter storm winds. Bill admits that he did not really take the wind into account, as he was more concerned with the solar aspect.

ARCHITECTURAL FEATURES

This 1,500-sq.-ft. one-and-half-story wood-frame home measures 40 x 24′. It has a kitchen, dining/living area, bedroom, and bath on the first floor, and two bedrooms, a large storage room, and another bath on the second floor.

Bill kept the house as compact as possible and oriented the living areas toward

Princeton, Massachusetts
1,500 sq. ft. living area

the warm south side of the house. The first-floor living area is buffered by the entranceway, stairs, bathroom, and bedroom. A cathedral ceiling over the living room makes the home appear larger than it really is.

The west third of the unfinished poured-concrete basement houses the solar system's storage reservoir. Floor joists are 2 x 8 fir on 16″ centers. Standard wood-frame construction techniques were employed.

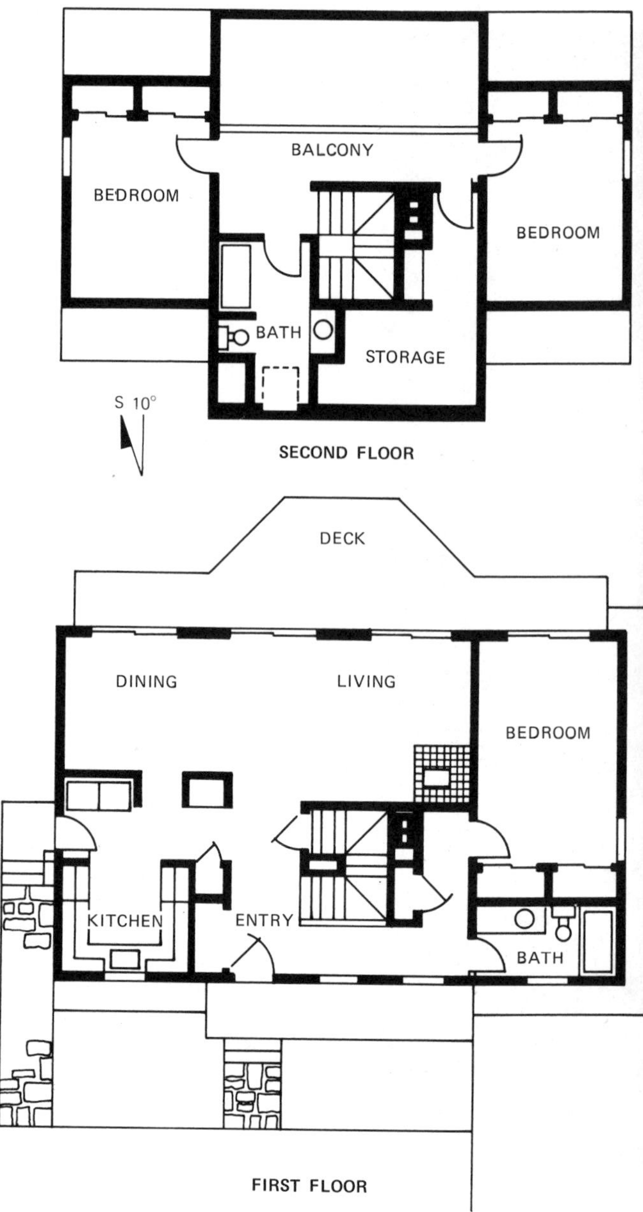

Exterior Walls

Standard 2 x 4 studwall framing techniques (16″ O.C.) were used. The wall cavities were insulated with 3½″ fiberglass batts with foil vapor-barrier backing. Exterior sheathing is ⅝″ Texture 1-11 plywood treated with white Olympic brand stain.

Interior Walls and Ceilings

All interior walls are of 2 x 4 studwall construction. They and the 2 x 6 ceiling rafters are sheathed in ½″ gypsum board, the most economical material for interior wall surfacing. Walls and ceilings are painted white for better illumination.

Roof

Exterior-grade plywood over 2 x 8 rafters is covered with building paper and then economical black asphalt shingles on the north roof. On the south roof the collector array forms the weatherproof skin.

Insulation Summary

Ceiling: R-20; 6″ fiberglass batts with foil backing

Walls: R-12; 3½″ fiberglass batts with foil backing

Basement: No insulation. Bill stated that the outside perimeter of homes in his area were generally not insulated at the time he built, but the new energy code now requires that basement walls be insulated.

Doors

Four pairs of insulated double-glazed sliding glass aluminum patio doors grace most of the south facade of the first floor. These permit the entry of a substantial amount of passive solar heat in winter. Insulated draperies on transverse rods were furnished and installed for the patio doors by Eames Interiors of Templeton, Massachusetts. They consist of a heavy synthetic fabric on a fire-resistant foam backing. A roof overhang blocks the high summer sun.

The two main entrances both have 1¾″ solid-wood-core birch-veneer doors. They are weatherstripped, but neither has a storm door or an entrance vestibule. The doorway to the kitchen is next to the driveway, convenient for unloading groceries. Both entrances are also conveniently located near the stairways to the basement and the second floor.

Windows

The only glazing on the south side is the patio doors mentioned above. Windows on the north, east, and west sides of the house have been kept to a minimum. These Hope steel casement windows have sealed double glazing. "In severely cold weather condensation forms and freezes on the inside of aluminum doors and steel sash. Better units are available which incorporate a thermal break to overcome this problem," Bill says. A Velux roof window provides diffuse light to the north entranceway.

A Thomason-type trickle-flow collector and south-facing patio doors provide solar heat to this 1,500-sq.-ft. home. Insulated drapes are used to control unwanted heat gain and heat loss.

Builder and architect William Bird relaxes on the patio of his first solar-heated house. In the beginning, paint peeling from the corrugated-aluminum absorber partially clogged the drains. The hinged mullions near the bottom of the array facilitated cleaning the drain gutter.

View looking east from the living room.

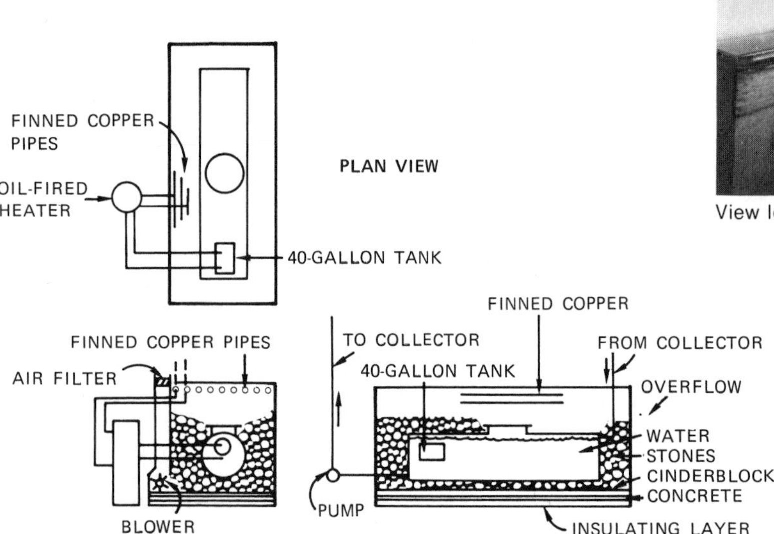

SOLAR-HEATING SYSTEM

Collector

The solar system is based on the Dr. Harry Thomason trickle-type water collector. The site-built collector is an integral part of the south-facing roof structure. It therefore faces 10° west of south and tilts at an angle of 50° from the horizontal. The house and collectors were oriented west of south to take advantage of afternoon solar-heat-collecting conditions; afternoons are generally warmer and often clearer than mornings. "Because of warmer afternoon air temperatures around the heat collector and in the attic behind the collector, less heat is lost and more is captured and transferred to the heat-storage apparatus," Bill explains. The nine collector panels each measure 4′ wide by 23′ high and have a total area of approximately 800 sq. ft. They were constructed in a barn near the site and raised into place and secured over two layers of weathertight 15-pound felt building paper.

The collectors were constructed in the following way. A framework of 2 x 4s was nailed flat and then surrounded by a perimeter frame of 2 x 4s nailed on their edges. Fiberglass insulation was placed in the spaces between the flat 2 x 4s and then covered with 0.021″ 2′-wide sheets of corrugated-aluminum standard barn roofing. The aluminum was selected because it lasts longer than steel and because it is cheaper than copper. Bill spray-painted this absorber plate first with an etching primer and then with Sherwin-Williams Polane, a nonselective flat black paint specifically recommended for this purpose by the manufacturer. More than 50% of the paint has peeled off and the exposed aluminum has oxidized to a dull, flat gray color. There has been no apparent significant decrease in efficiency as a result of this peeling; however, it did present some problems with drain blockage.

Aluminum U-channel supports measuring ¾ x ¾″ were secured horizontally 2½′ apart and thus provide a ¾″ spacing between the absorber plate and the glazing. The glazing material is a single layer of 0.040″ Kalwall Sun-Lite Premium. Bill feels the main advantage of the Kalwall glazing is that the lightweight, easy-to-install material can cover a whole panel, thus reducing labor costs and leakage problems. In addition, breakage is less likely than with glass. Aluminum flashing is used around the perimeter. The joints between panels are caulked with GE silicone and covered with 1 x 3 cedar battens.

A considerable amount of water was lost from the collector initially, as water that tended to condense on the underside of the glazing leaked out from the lower end of the panel. Since modifications have been made to stop the loss, Bill is quite satisfied with the collector; however, he points out that in the future, for aesthetic

Auxiliary heat is supplied by heat exchangers in the top of the rock storage. Note the inspection cover for the steel tank.

The oil-fired heater supplies domestic hot water and hot water for the heat exchangers in the top of the rock storage.

The low-tech aspect of trickle-flow collector systems appeals to many builders. Water is pumped to the top of the collector and gravity flows down over the absorber plate, where it absorbs heat, and then returns to the storage tank.

reasons, he would use more channel supports on the interior of the panels as the glazing tends to sag with the 2½′ spacing.

The feeder pipe to the collector is 1″-diameter copper tubing. It dispenses water to a ⅜″-diameter manifold at the top of each panel. The manifolds have 1/16″-diameter holes feeding each valley of the corrugated sheet. Water trickles down the corrugations to an insulated gutter, running the entire width of the collector array, from where the heated water is drained to the storage tank.

Storage

The uninsulated 1,600-gallon water-storage tank is 7-gauge steel and measures 17′ long and 4′ in diameter. It is surrounded by 30 tons of 2″-diameter stones contained within a concrete bin whose interior dimensions are 9 x 22 x 7′ high. The tank rests on an air-distributing ductwork of concrete blocks. The interior of the steel tank was red-leaded and then three coats of a water-and-cement mixture were brushed on. The concrete bin was waterproofed, made airtight, and insulated on its interior with 3½″ fiberglass within a 2 x 4 studwall framework. The studs were covered with plywood before the stones were dumped into the bin. A 1″ slab of extruded polystyrene foamboard insulation was placed under the storage-reservoir floor. The storage reservoir is located under the master bedroom and bathroom at the west end of the house. The top of the bin was formed by the floor joists of these rooms, and the spaces between the joists were insulated with 6″ of fiberglass. In retrospect, Bill feels that it would have been better to have the storage under the living-room area rather than the bedroom, which requires less heat. In spite of the 6″ of insulation, a certain amount of heat penetrates upward through the floor.

Heat Distribution

When the collector temperature exceeds the storage temperature by 10° F. a 1/3-hp centrifugal pump is automatically turned on to pump relatively cold water from the storage tank to the manifolds at the top of the collector. The water trickles down the corrugations, is heated, and returns to the storage tank. Whenever the temperature of the collector falls below that of the water in the storage tank, the pump automatically shuts off and the collector is drained, thus avoiding any problems with freezing. Plain washing soda was put in the water to act as a rust inhibitor. The hot water in the storage tank warms the stones surrounding it.

Whenever the home becomes cool a thermostat activates a ½-hp electric blower. The blower draws cool air from the living space, filters it, and then blows it through the concrete-block ductwork at the bottom of the storage reservoir. The air migrates upward via spaces between the blocks to the stones and tank, where it becomes heated and then is ducted to the living spaces.

When I asked Bill about possible damage to the collector because of overheating when the system was not functioning, he replied, "During the summer of 1977 the collector was not operating for a month because the solar sensing device had malfunctioned and was being repaired. During the summer of 1978 the tenants elected to forego solar water heating for several weeks. In neither case has there been any apparent damage to the collector."

AUXILIARY HEATING

Auxiliary heat is supplied by passing air over a finned copper radiator piping suspended near the top of the rock storage. This radiator is heated by water from the oil-fired heater that also supplies domestic hot water.

A Jøtul #4 Combi-fire which serves as either an open fireplace or an airtight stove provides additional backup heat.

PERCENT SOLAR-HEATED

Bill says, "I estimate that approximately two-thirds of the heating required for interior space and for hot water has been supplied by the sun. I also estimate that hot-water-heating requirements were about twenty percent of the total." In the winter of 1976-77 when the hot-water radiator coil was not installed in the rock storage it cost $200 for fuel oil at 47¢ per gallon to heat the house. Bill calculated that heating a comparable nonsolar house in the same area would have cost about $600. "During that winter the wood stove was rarely used and temperatures were maintained at about sixty-five degrees. During the winter of 1977-78, with a baby in the house, the stove was used regularly. A full cord of wood was burned and the temperatures were maintained at about seventy degrees."

COOLING SYSTEM

The house is very well ventilated in summer because of the open, windy site. With the sliding glass doors and windows on the north side of the house open, very good cross-ventilation occurs from north to south. On the second floor a straight line can be drawn by connecting points in the center of the west bedroom window, the bedroom door, hallway, and the east bedroom door and window. The summer prevailing westerlies create a cross-ventilation from west to east along this line, pulling with it hot air that is convected upward from the first floor along the cathedral ceiling. This and good insulation keep the house cool even on the warmest of days.

WATER SUPPLY AND WASTE SYSTEM

Water is supplied from a drilled well. Domestic hot water is heated in an oil-fired, glass-lined, 40-gallon hot-water tank. All water on its way to this tank from the well passes through an uninsulated preheater tank that is suspended at the top of the 1,600-gallon tank. The only water-conserving fixture is an American Standard Water Saving Cadet toilet, which uses one-third less water than a conventional model.

A standard septic system handles waterborne wastes.

ELECTRICAL POWER SYSTEM

This house receives its power from the local utility. Fluorescent lighting is used in the kitchen and bathrooms. On the first floor the open concept, white paint, and judicious window placement provide a well-balanced natural lighting scheme. The second-floor hallway with its open railing overlooking the living room is bathed in diffuse light reflected upward from the first floor. The white walls of the two upstairs bedrooms maximize the illumination from the small window areas. In addition, when the bedroom doors are open a certain amount of light penetrates to and from the hallway.

FOOD SYSTEM

A vegetable garden measuring 40 x 20′ was planted in 1978; the results were very satisfactory.

COSTS

The solar collectors cost $2,500, including installation. The whole solar system cost about $4,500, including materials and labor. The complete project cost $55,000, including $7,500 for the land, $1,500 for the well and pump, and $1,000 for the septic system. These costs do not include a considerable amount of time that Bill spent on the project—time which he did not keep a record of. Still, considering that this is a prototype house for Bill's firm, the Mountain Co., the costs are not far out of line with a conventionally heated house of comparable design.

CONCLUDING THOUGHTS

Bill is very happy with this type of solar system and has incorporated it into two other solar-heated houses for clients. These homes are even more energy-efficient than Sunhouse 1. The walls are constructed of 2 x 6 studs with 6″ of fiberglass insulation and the roof rafters are 2 x 12s with 12″ of fiberglass insulation. The exterior walls have plywood sheathing, building paper, and then the Texture 1-11 siding. One of these has been completed in Grafton, Massachusetts. This house is much larger—2,700 sq.ft. The solar-collector area is 1,100 sq. ft. The storage tank holds 3,000 gallons and is equipped to be used by the fire department in case of fire. Another house has been started in Hardwick, Massachusetts, and should be completed in 1979. This house is essentially Sunhouse 1 with modifications.

Since building the Mountain Co.'s first solar home, Bill has received many inquiries. In addition to building the two new houses he has been conducting related seminars and doing consulting work. He offered this opinion on the future of solar energy: "I think there is little hope for a widespread application of active solar-heating systems unless fuel costs rise considerably or the federal government offers subsidies. House buyers are very reluctant to make an additional outlay of five thousand dollars or more even though the cost could be amortized over the years."

Warren, Vermont
Multiple-family dwelling

Dimetrodon

JAMES SANFORD, RICHARD TRAVERS, BILL MACLAY

Space limitations and the magnitude and relative complexity of Dimetrodon preclude a detailed analysis of the type applied to the other houses. Rather I have chosen to highlight just a few of the many outstanding features of this project.

Dimetrodon is a unique experiment in autonomous living by a group of dynamic young people, who are attempting to apply environmentally appropriate technology on a community scale.

James Sanford, Richard (Dick) Travers, and Bill Maclay, the designers who conceived Dimetrodon, thought it made sense for a group of people to share the initial heavy investment in a natural energy system. As members of such a community they anticipated that they would enjoy more freedom than an individual or nuclear family attempting to live a self-sufficient life-style, and they have found this to be true. Each member can travel away from the community knowing he can count on others to carry out the duties required to maintain Dimetrodon. In addition, the spatial concentration of living spaces meant that construction costs per unit would be lower and that common walls would result in lower heat losses than for single-family detached units.

Dimetrodon was initially designed as ten distinct apartments plus communal space grouped around a central courtyard. Each apartment owner has a share in and benefits from a number of communal facilities and services such as space heating, power supply, water supply, waste disposal, agricultural production, and common game room, laundry room, kitchen/dining room, root cellar, and workshops. The proprietors of each apartment are provided with the architectural structure and connections to the various utilities and then finish the apartment interior in accordance with their own needs and wants.

The communal building and four of these apartments are now constructed, occupied, and in various stages of completion. When the entire project is completed, the building will still be about the same size and shape as the original design, but because the communal aspect of the development has worked so successfully Bill, James, and Dick feel that two, three, or possibly even four units may be used for community space and only two or three new units may be used as apartment space. They anticipate possibly having some rental units so people can come to Dimetrodon without having to make the long-term commitment of common ownership. In this way there will be a larger number of people sharing the Dimetrodon experience as well as a constant influx of new ideas.

Dimetrodon is located on Route 1, Warren, Vermont, and is built on a slope of Prickly Mountain. The building is oriented so that each living space has a spectacular view of the valley below and to the north and so that the solar collectors integral to the building face due south.

HEATING SYSTEM

When the initial planning was being done for the project, Sanford and Maclay traveled to Washington, D.C., to consult with Harry Thomason, one of the few people at that time who had developed a successful solar system. The plans for Dimetrodon's heating system evolved from that visit. Also while in Washington, they visited the Museum of Natural History, and it was here that they chose the name Dimetrodon—the dinosaur with large dorsal plates through which the cold-blooded creature could absorb solar radiaton or dissipate body heat.

Like its namesake, the Dimetrodon building has a large dorsal plate, but one fashioned after the Thomason trickle-flow collector. Significant direct solar gain is received through windows on the south side of the building complex, but the trickle-flow collector is designed to be the main source of solar heat. About 300 sq. ft. of collector have now been installed; when the project is complete, there will be about 2,500 sq. ft. net. The collectors face due south and are tilted at 60° to the horizontal. They have black-painted galvanized corrugated-iron sheeting and a double glazing of Kalwall Sun-Lite Regular fiberglass-reinforced plastic. The glazings are 1½" apart and 1" above the absorber plate. The collector is presently vented in summer. It has stood up well in the four years since its installation. The storage system is composed of three 4,000-gallon steel tanks located in the basement under the two southwest apartments. The storage was initially designed according to Thomason's patented system using fist-sized rocks, placed around the tanks, through which air would be blown and then distributed to the living spaces. However, the hot-air heat-distribution system was never installed. Until the summer of 1978 the large mass of stone and water simply radiated heat through the floors to the apartments above the storage bin. On a sunny cold winter day at this approximately 8,000-degree-day site, with this heat from storage and passive direct solar gain and no other source of heat, the temperature within the south-facing units would never drop below 45° F. before the owners got home from work.

Recently the stones were removed and the three tanks were placed side by side and sprayed on the exterior with insulating foam. The heat-distribution system will now be a hot-water hydronic one rather than forced-air. Dick Travers explains these changes: "A lot of the reason for the changeover had to do with some oversights when we first started. The rocks we put in were supposed to be about fist-sized, but we ended up with everything from fist-sized rocks all the way down to sand, so the spacing for the air to circulate through was not adequate. In addition, the heating-duct trunk line to get to the other side of the building would have to be about four square feet, and we really didn't allow too much room for that. A two-inch water pipe will carry about the same amount of heat." They have come to prefer radiant heat over the fairly dry heat of forced air and wanted to experiment with an interesting wood-burning furnace-and-boiler combination. The new wood-burning furnace, which will become operational during the winter of 1978-79, is a catenary arch built of firebrick and composed of two identical chambers that are separated by a vertical firebrick-checkerboard wall through which flue gases pass from the primary combustion chamber to the secondary combustion chamber. Flue gases swirl around inside the secondary chamber, where nearly complete combustion of the flue gases is supposed to take place. This chamber has a door that allows the furnace to be used for firing pottery, glassblowing, or other crafts. There is a small 5'-long tunnel from the furnace over to the triple-pass-fire-tube boiler—a commercial unit without the oil burner, manufactured by the Federal Boiler Co. Inc., Elmwood Park, N.J. 07407. It is a 38-hp boiler, which means the boiler is way oversize for the building if it were to run continuously. For that type of operation it is about four times as large as required for the present structure and about twice as large as required for the completed structure. This size was chosen because they are going to burn as hot and as efficient fires as they can in order to get the most Btu out of the wood. They hope the boiler is oversize enough so that the temperature of the flue gases, as they pass through all these tubes and meet the relatively cold water circulating around the outside of the tubes within the boiler, will sink below the condensation point of the water vapor

The south-sloping roof was designed to accommodate Thomason-type trickle-flow solar collectors. Only the right-hand side of the collector is glazed and operational at the present. The communal building below this completed collector and Dick Travers and Connie Colman's apartment to the left receive substantial solar heat through the south windows in winter.

Looking north from the south windows of Dick and Connie's apartment to the kitchen and dining area. The Elm woodburning stove is manufactured by Dick's firm, Vermont Iron Stove Works.

within the flue gases. The water vapor will then condense out, giving up heat, which will be collected. This potential energy in water vapor which is converted into (sensible) heat when the vapor condenses is known as latent heat. A pound of water vapor at room temperature has about 1,050 Btu of latent heat.

A draft inducer will be installed to bring all the flue gases through the system in order to get the rapid fire and also because there won't be any reason for the gases to rise anymore because they will be so cold. The draft inducer is simply a fan right in the line which takes the flue gases over to the chimney. When asked about the problems of creosote buildup on the inducer and in the chimney, Dick Travers replied, "What we have heard is that we might get a smoky start-up when the fire doesn't burn quite as efficiently for the first two or three minutes of firing, but after that you get such good combustion that all this water that will have condensed off should be just slightly discolored with just a little bit of ash in it. We hope the creosote will be totally avoided." A cylindical-shaped tube brush is used to clean all the tube surfaces to ensure a good heat exchange.

From the boiler they will have the option of pumping water to all three storage tanks, but Dick says they will probably use two tanks at a time and use the third tank just for the solar hot water. The boiler will be good for maintaining any temperature they want from around 120°F. to 200°F. and what works best with the solar system. There is no automatic dampering system for the furnace. Dicks says, "We will just get a feel for how much wood is required to raise the temperature of the water in storage a certain amount. We figure it is going to take about three loads of wood to raise it from well-water temperature to one hundred and eighty degrees, so if we just do one load at a time it will raise the water temperature forty to fifty degrees. In the coldest part of winter we may have to have two fires a day. I am not sure how long they will last—maybe three or four hours—although in the spring and fall we might go a week." The boiler system is not under pressure. Water is just pumped through the boiler, to the tank, and back to the boiler, and the tanks are at atmospheric pressure. There is a heat exchanger in each tank which will exchange the heat to a pressurized-hot-water hydronic system.

The apartment owners will be responsible for doing their own plumbing within their apartments—be it radiant floor heaters, a large central hot-water radiant sculpture, or whatever.

There is no doubt that this system will work, as some precedents have been set. For example, Professor R. C. Hill of the University of Maine, with whom the Dimetrodon people consulted, designed a successful furnace to operate under similar combustion conditions (but with a forced-air system) and to work in conjunction with the solar-heating system of the Maine Audubon Society Headquarters Building. It remains to be seen excactly how effective the Dimetrodon furnace will be.

Each apartment unit now has a wood-burning stove. There is a central propane-fired furnace, but this is rarely used. Last year it was used only over Christmas when most people were away. This furnace will be sold when the wood-burning furnace becomes operational.

DOMESTIC HOT WATER

For the domestic hot water another system of heat exchangers will be installed in the large storage tanks. A separate heat exchanger in the solar storage tank will allow the solar system to provide hot water in summer. There will be a series of water-holding tanks totaling about 500 gallons of storage. The domestic hot water will be pumped and have automatic valves switching it over from the boiler to the solar system. Until this system is completed the hot water will continue to be supplied by propane heaters.

ELECTRICAL POWER SYSTEM

A 1,800-watt Jacobs wind generator supplies some of Dimetrodon's power needs. The 32-volt system is hooked up to 16 very large storage batteries of the type used for hospitals and other large facilities where a source of auxiliary power is essential. They were donated to a school that was conducting alternate energy experiments, and subsequently purchased by Dimetrodon at a fraction of the new cost when they were found to be unneeded by the school.

The Dimetrodon plans to use 32-volt pumps and motors for all the mechanical systems, and the wind generator will provide the power for these. They also have a direct-drive downwind generator which is in the process of being repaired. It will also be connected to the power system. The Jacobs provides from 150 to 250 kwh per month in the winter and quite a bit less in the summer. At the present time the winter demand of Dimetrodon is about 400 kwh per month. Bill doesn't expect that they will ever be completely self-sufficient in terms of power consumption, especially considering the mild winds during the summer, but the wind generators should provide enough power during the winter months to run the essential systems.

Connie and Dick have a spectacular view of the valley to the north from their study/bedroom and sleeping loft.

Detail of a heavily insulated owner-built door.

North aspect.

The large firebrick woodburning furnace and commercial triple-pass fire-tube boiler heat water which is stored in large steel storage tanks for distribution on demand to hot-water radiant heaters throughout the building.

FOOD SYSTEM

A prime objective of Dimetrodon is the provision of high-quality, organically grown produce. Toward this end Dimetrodon now supplies a substantial portion of its own vegetables and fruit. A common root cellar provides low-cost storage. Usually they raise one or two pigs every year and may in the future raise some cattle on their pasture. Bill reports that since the beginning of the project they have managed to keep their food costs down to $10 per person per week.

CONCLUDING THOUGHTS

Another unique feature of Dimetrodon is that each of the members has designed a career for himself that fits into that broad category of things that are defined as being environmentally appropriate. Bill Maclay and Jim Sanford have established their own architectural and consulting firm in nearby Warren and specialize in the application of natural energy systems to building design. Dick Travers heads Vermont Iron Stove Works, a firm also in Warren, which manufactures the Elm, an attractive high-quality cast-iron wood-burning parlor stove. Connie Colman, Dick's wife, does massage and also teaches classes in yoga and nutrition. She is considering going to medical school as a continuation of her studies into a holistic approach to health. John Norton, who was one of the moving forces at Vermont Castings Inc., manufacturer of the Defiant and Vigilant wood-burning parlor stoves, now works for Northwind Power Company, a firm in Warren that specializes in the repair, distribution, design, and manufacture of wind generators. Alex Smith works in the neighboring town of Waitsfield, where she is one of the editors of the *Green Mountain Independent*, a newspaper which has a policy of featuring stories about environmental concerns, the development and application of natural energy systems, and other related topics. Steve Nikitas, the most recent person to join the Dimetrodon group, works as a reporter for the same newspaper.

The members of Dimetrodon are among a new wave of people who are deeply concerned about the quality of life—a concern which extends from the hearth to the workplace and, indeed, to all aspects of their lives. As Bill Maclay points out, none of them earns a great deal of money but they firmly believe in what they are doing, and they enjoy it.

Looking to the south-facing windows of the open-plan kitchen, dining, and living area of the Travers home.

Observation tower.

Bill Maclay.

Right: The communal kitchen. Floors, counters, sink, and cupboards were built from scrap plywood.

Opposite page: Southeast aspect.

Princeton, New Jersey
1,900 sq. ft. living space

DOUG and MEG KELBAUGH

Doug Kelbaugh is one of the leaders of the solar movement in the United States. Doug and his wife, Meg, own and run the Environmint Partnership, which is a combined horticultural and architectural practice. Doug and two other architects work out of the Kelbaugh residence, where they are presently designing a half-dozen passive solar projects. He teaches part-time at the New Jersey School of Architecture and consults frequently with the New Jersey and U.S. Department of Environment and HUD. He has consulted on over 20 solar buildings and is a frequent speaker at solar meetings and conferences. He was one of the directors of the Second National Passive Solar Conference held in Philadelphia in March 1978. Meg runs the horticultural practice and is studying at the New York Botanical Garden. She also studies ballet with the regional ballet company. They have a four-year-old son, Casey.

LOCATION AND ORIENTATION

The Kelbaughs' passively heated Trombe-wall solar home was built in 1974-75 on a 60 x 100′ lot at 70 Pine Street—in an older, densely populated district—near downtown Princeton, New Jersey. A zoning variance was granted to build 5′ from the northern boundary and 13′ from the sidewalk on the eastern boundary. This made it possible to save one of the largest deciduous trees on the street, provided one large outdoor area rather than four small ones, and minimized the amount of shadow on the south-facing solar collector. The long axis of the house runs east-west and the collector thus faces due south. The long axis does not run quite parallel to the other houses on the street, as when Doug first designed the house, he didn't realize how insignificant the decrease in solar gain is when a collector is oriented a few degrees from due south. The nearness of the neighboring house to the north tempers the effect of the cold north winds. Deciduous trees provide effective summer shade.

ARCHITECTURAL FEATURES

This 2,100-sq.-ft. (1,900 sq. ft. of living space) two-story wood-frame structure is a fine example of a tightly constructed, energy-efficient solar home. The open first-floor plan favors natural ventilation and efficient heat distribution. From the kitchen one can easily observe what is going on in the street. A large archway in the south wall connects the handsome greenhouse with the kitchen and dining/living areas. A half-bath, pantry, closets, and a storage shed on the north wall act as an effective thermal buffer. Bookshelves covering most of the west wall provide additional insulation.

There is a small basement under the greenhouse which accommodates the backup gas furnace and domestic hot-water heater and a small workshop. Access is via a space-saving trap door in the greenhouse floor. On the second floor, the two bedrooms and a study are strung along the warm southern concrete wall. Closets, the bathroom, and the hallway on the north wall insulate the living spaces. The child's room has a sleeping loft.

The European-style bathroom, with the water closet separate from the bath, permits more than one person to use the bathroom at one time without an excessive number of fixtures. The utility room next to the bath with its linen closet, ironing board, hamper, and laundry facilities is conveniently located on the same level as the bedrooms. A loft area above the utility room provides storage.

The foundation is of 8″ Way-lite concrete blocks treated on the outside with stucco and tar. Rigid extruded polystyrene insulation 1″ thick runs to a depth of 2′, although Doug now feels it would have been better to use 2″ or 3″ polystyrene.

The first-level floor is a 5″-thick concrete slab painted gray-blue and partially covered with area rugs. It experiences some passive solar-heat gain in winter, but remains cooler than the room temperature. It is also cool in summer, which is an advantage. The concrete was used mainly because it was the cheapest type of flooring. Future plans call for a quarry-tile or slate floor. The second-level floor is 2 x 8 tongue-and-groove roof decking, treated with Watco oil and paste wax, over exposed beams. This floor doubles as the ceiling for the first level, thus economizing on labor costs and material use. The beams and ceiling are finished with urethane varnish.

Exterior Walls

Standard 2 x 4 studs on 16″ centers are used for the east, west, and north walls. The outside sheathing is ⅝″ plywood, recycled from the forms used for the concrete wall, covered with ⅜″ rough-sawn 4 x 8′ sheets of unfinished cedar plywood. The large-dimension sheathing minimizes the number of seams and the amount of air infiltration. The south-facing wall is a solid-concrete Trombe-type passive collector. This will be described later.

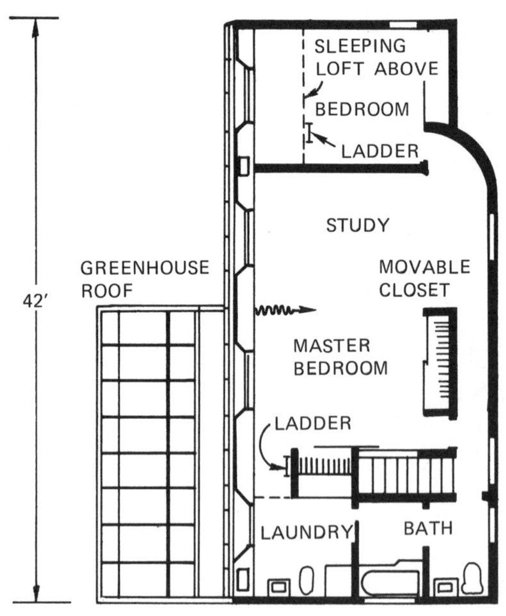

SECOND FLOOR

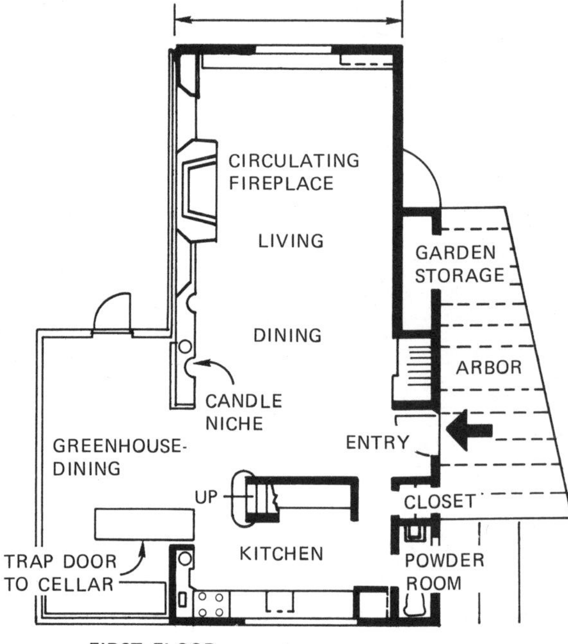

FIRST FLOOR

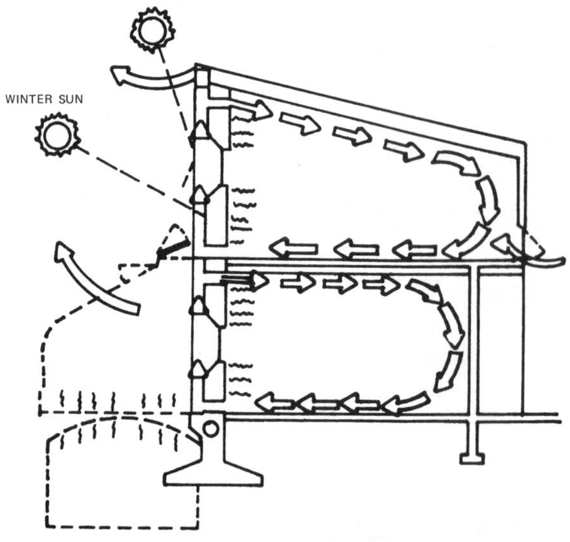

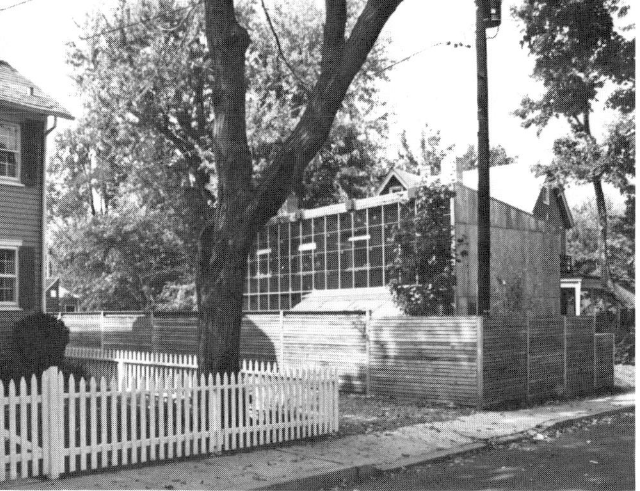

The two-story Trombe wall provides 75% of the heating needs. Windows within the concrete wall are behind the glass wall. Note the vents high on the south wall to exhaust summer heat from the collector and the living spaces.

North entrance. Durable, weathertight cedar plywood paneling is accentuated with bright-colored window and door trim.

Interior Walls and Ceiling

Standard 2 x 4 studwall construction clad with ½″ sheetrock, painted light in color for good light reflection, is used for interior walls. Ceilings on the second floor are also of ½″ sheetrock.

Roof

The shed roof with a slope of 3′ in 20′ is constructed of 2 x 10 joists on 16″ centers covered with ⅝″ plywood roof decking, tarpaper, and 36″ roll roofing with an 18″ overlap. This is not the most attractive roofing material but it cannot be seen from the street. The shed roof with roll roofing is one of the least expensive roofs one can construct. It is also easy and quick to build, durable, and easy to maintain.

Insulation Summary

Ceiling: R-40; 9½″ of blown cellulose fiber (recycled newspapers)

Walls: R-18; cellulose fiber, 3½″ in second-floor walls and 4½″ in first-floor walls

Foundation: R-5; 1″ Styrofoam-SM slab insulation

Doors

The front door on the north side of the house is a 1¾″ urethane-core steel door. The foam weatherstripping ensures a good seal against air infiltration. It would be ideal to have a vestibule; however, the neighboring house provides considerable wind protection. Some sort of arbor will be built in the future to provide additional protection. The doorway most used is that through the greenhouse on the warm wind-protected side of the house, as that entrance is closest to the driveway. Andersen wood-sash sliding glass patio doors are used on the west wall of the first floor. Lined curtains of cotton and milium insulate the door on winter nights. A horizontal valance and ½″ foam-tape weatherstripping between the valance and the curtain rod reduce airflow over the window glass. The bookshelves on either side of the doorway act as side valances.

Windows

Most of the windows are Andersen thermopane wood sash. Doug added a third layer of glass (available in kit form from Andersen) to most east, west, and north windows. Two of the windows are owner-built of double-glazed acrylic. The kitchen windows were primarily designed to allow the cook to see what is going on in the street. The bathroom windows are small but provide adequate light and ventilation. Doug and Meg indulged in a skylight over the bathtub, mostly for aesthetic reasons. Windows in the Trombe wall provide light as well as direct-gain solar heat in early morning, when the Trombe wall is the coolest. The heat gain in the bedrooms, where the south windows are larger than downstairs ones, is quite substantial.

Two low windows on the north wall light the second-floor hall. At night, fabric-covered extruded polystyrene insulation board is slid down aluminum channels on either side of the windows.

LANDSCAPING

As mentioned earlier, the house was partially designed and oriented to preserve one very fine old silver maple tree. This huge majestic tree, the garden, and the lawn on the south and west sides of the house have a considerable cooling effect on the house during hot summer days.

SOLAR-HEATING SYSTEM

The passive solar system is patterned after that developed by Felix Trombe and Jacques Michel in Odeillo, France. The collector and storage are one and the same and circulation is by natural convection.

The 15″-thick poured-concrete structural south wall, measuring approximately 20′ high and 40′ long and having a net area of 600 sq. ft., serves as a Trombe-wall solar collector and storage. The exterior of the wall is painted with 3M Nextel, a selective black coating. There is a 6″ airspace between the black concrete wall and a double-glazed wall. Sunlight penetrates the glass and is absorbed in the wall, heating both concrete and the air between the glazing and the concrete. The heated air expands, becomes lighter, and rises. Ventholes in the concrete wall near the ceiling of each floor allow the hot air to enter the living spaces, while vent holes at floor level allow cool room air to replace it. This process of gravity convection or thermosiphoning carries most of the absorbed solar energy into the house during the day. Heat also migrates through the concrete in eight to ten hours and then radiates this stored heat to the living spaces at night.

The Kelbaughs initially had a problem with reverse thermosiphoning. At night, warm air would exit at the ceiling and wash down between the glazing and the concrete wall and then reenter via the bottom vent, losing considerable heat through the glass in the process. Doug found that by simply covering the top vent at the inside of the wall with a ½″ mesh screen and a 1-mil polyethylene flap, of the type used for dry-cleaning bags, hinged at the top edge with tape, he was able to eliminate the reverse thermosiphoning.

Another problem encountered was heat migration to the second floor. Because there was an open stairwell to the second floor and the backup forced-air furnace seldom cycled, warm air tended to migrate upward from the first floor and collect on the second floor, resulting in winter temperatures 4° to 5° F. higher than those on the first floor. Doug attempted to solve the problem by putting a doorway at the top of the stairs and by glazing the window that opens from the master bedroom into the stairwell. He describes the result: "There has been no subsequent decrease in heat stratification, leading me to believe that, first, the second-floor Trombe wall, which is of slightly larger area than the first floor, is oversize; second, significant air infiltration to the second floor occurs between cracks and crevices; and third, only a small fan and duct can significantly reduce or eliminate heat stratification in a two-story passive solar building."

The standard Lord and Burnham greenhouse was initially a source of considerable heat loss and temperature fluctuations. An extra layer of glazing nearly halved the heat loss. Hourly heat loss from the single-glazed unit at a design temperature of 0° F. was 30,000 Btu compared to 79,000 Btu/hr from the entire house. The double glazing and other conservation measures have cut the total heat loss to about 60,000 Btu/hr. Painting the concrete floor black for better absorption and adding eight black-painted 55-gallon water-filled steel drums, which serve as plant benches, has leveled off the diurnal temperature fluctuations. A lined cotton curtain will be installed in the archway to the greenhouse to reduce heat loss from the main part of the house during winter nights.

AUXILIARY HEATING

The main backup to the solar system is a Sears gas-fired furnace located in the small basement below the greenhouse. The hot-air-distribution ducts were poured within the Trombe wall. The furnace is rated at 85,000 Btu with a net delivery of 58,000 Btu/hr, which is somewhat less than the 60,000 Btu hourly rated heat loss of the house when the outside design temperature is 0° F. Their fuel bill was $78 in the winter of 1976-77; they calculated it would have cost $500 without the solar system. That winter was cold but clear—5,500 degree-days and an average of 60.5% of possible sunshine, 5.5% above the norm.

Upstairs air temperatures ranged from 60° to 75° F., downstairs from 54° to 69° F., and the greenhouse from 52° to 79° F.

As extra backup, a Heatilator wood-burning fireplace, exposed on three sides for better radiant heat, was installed on the south wall of the living room. Doug feels that the heat gain from the fireplace is offset by the increased air infiltration that it causes. He

Looking west to the living room from the dining area. Note the hot-air-supply vents high on the inside of the Trombe wall. Plastic film prevents reverse thermosiphoning.

From the dining area to the greenhouse. Large black-painted water drums serve for passive solar storage and as plant stands.

recommends an outside air intake to the firebox in order to avoid this problem.

Doug and Meg were given a heat-saving tube grate as a Christmas present. It is made of U-shaped tubes that draw in cool air at the bottom and shoot heated air into the room at the top. Some of the hot air goes up the flue if the tube grate is too low. The hot end of the tubes should be designed or placed so that hot air is

Left: Detail of one of the Trombe-wall hot-air vents. The 1-mil polyethylene flap hinged at the top with tape and the ½″ mesh screen prevent reverse thermosiphoning.

Below: Note one of the cold-air-return vents to Meg's left.

Left: The two north windows of the upstairs hall have fabric-covered Styrofoam sliding shutters.

exhausted no more than 2″ or 3″ below the fireplace lintel.

The hot-air vents from the furnace to the upstairs bathrooms have been left closed. Instantaneous heat is supplied as needed when the bathrooms are in use by means of 250-watt infrared heat lamps. Used sparingly, these are a highly efficient way of heating.

PERCENT SOLAR-HEATED

Doug Balcomb of Los Alamos Scientific Laboratories installed monitoring equipment which enabled the Kelbaughs to determine the outdoor temperatures, indoor temperatures, and storage temperatures. From this information Doug was able to measure empirically the house's hourly heat loss. At a design temperature of 0°F. it worked out to be 56,300 Btu/hr for the entire building, including the greenhouse, compared to the ASHRAE theoretical heat loss of about 66,000 Btu/hr with two-thirds of the air changed per hour and about 61,000 Btu/hr with half the air changed per hour. The accompanying table shows that the solar contribution is in the neighborhood of 75%.

Doug Kelbaugh, owner and architect.

1976-77 WINTER PERFORMANCE

		Theoretical	Empirical
HEAT LOSS			
5,556 degree-days; design temp. 65°F. inside, 0°F. outside			
Based on storage temp. degradation field studies[1]			115,500,000 Btu
Based on ASHRAE methods[2]		136,675,000 Btu	
HEAT GAIN			
Miscellaneous:			
occupants	3,250,000 Btu		
electrical[3]	4,800,000		
gas appliances[4]	4,750,000		
	12,800,000		
gas furnace[5]	18,450,000 ($78)		
SUB TOTAL	31,250,000 Btu		
Solar[6]		105,425,000	84,250,000
Solar/SF glass[7]		124,000	99,000
Fuel savings[8]		1,405 ccf natural gas	1,123 ccf
Dollar savings[9]		$450	$360

[1] Comparison of decrease over 12 hours in temperature of the Trombe wall, greenhouse water drums, greenhouse concrete floor,and house floor slab with the hourly difference between indoor and outdoor temperatures. Hourly heat loss at design temperature is 56,300 Btu.
[2] Standard calculation using U-factors, slab perimeter loss, and 2/3 air change per hour. Hourly heat loss at design temp. is 65,600 Btu.
[3] 1,406 kwh.
[4] 105 ccf natural gas burned @75% efficiency with 100% capture on cookstove, 60% capture on gas dryer and domestic hot-water heater.
[5] 246 ccf natural gas @75% efficiency.
[6] Percentage of possible sunshine 60.6% vs. norm for region of 55%.
[7] 850 SF glass.
[8] @75% efficiency.
[9] @32% per ccf.

COOLING SYSTEM

The exhaust vents high on the south wall were designed to create a chimney effect in summer and draw cool air through windows on the north side of the second floor. However, the Kelbaughs found the upstairs was too warm at night after hot summer days. Doug recommends larger eave vents or operable windows through the Trombe wall to increase natural ventilation. Because of the high summer sun much of the solar radiation is reflected off the glazing. This factor plus good insulation and shading from deciduous trees keeps the house cooler than it would otherwise be.

The greenhouse is cooled in summer by having air-inlet vents low on the south foundation wall and air-exhaust vents at the peak of the greenhouse. A bright-red roll-up shade helps to keep the greenhouse cool and also adds a bit more flair to the house.

WATER SUPPLY AND WASTE SYSTEM

The Kelbaugh house is on city water and sewer. The bathrooms were described above. Doug has wrapped his domestic hot-water heater with 3″ additional fiberglass. In the near future, he plans to take advantage of the HUD $400 grant for the installation of solar preheating for the hot water. Two active collectors will be installed on the roof of a backyard shed which doubles as a toolshed and playhouse. This solar preheater should provide two-thirds to three-quarters of the hot water.

ELECTRICAL POWER SYSTEM

A standard 100-amp electrical service was installed. There is a minimum amount of window area, particularly on the north wall; however, the greenhouse on the first floor floods the living space with natural light during the day. Task lighting helps to conserve energy. Doug wired the house himself with standard concealed wiring. For a typical 12-month period their electrical consumption is about 2,306 kwh.

MAJOR HOUSEHOLD APPLIANCES

The only real energy-conserving appliance that the Kelbaughs invested in is a natural-gas-fired automatic dryer without a pilot light. It is not used very much, as they prefer to hang the clothes outside on a clothesline if it is not too cold or raining.

FOOD SYSTEM

The greenhouse has the potential to supply a substantial portion of the Kelbaughs' vegetable needs during the winter months; however, Meg presently uses it to grow plants for her ornamental horticultural business. Winter temperatures in the greenhouse seldom drop below 50° F. at night; however, Doug feels that this temperature is unnecessarily high and that he should let this temperature drop to 40° F. by installing a curtain in the archway and thus reduce heat losses from the living spaces to the greenhouse.

They have been planting a small garden in front of the Trombe wall. Vegetables thrive next to the warm south wall. They get considerably more sunlight than in a normal garden because of reflection of the high summer sun off the glazing; thus, Doug and Meg are usually munching on succulent fresh vegetables two or three weeks before their neighbors. They also get noticeably higher yields than their neighbors—a bounty which is much appreciated, as Meg is a vegetarian and Doug eats very little meat. They have been so busy with building the house to this point that they haven't bothered to preserve any produce.

The large archway provides a visual link between the greenhouse and the small, well-organized kitchen and the remainder of the main floor.

COSTS

Total construction costs were $55,000 excluding Doug's labor. He acted as the general contractor and did all his own wiring, plus the greenhouse construction and all the glazing on the south wall. He and Meg did all the finishing of the floors and the painting. It was mainly the concrete and construction work that was contracted. It is difficult to assess the cost of the solar system, as it is an integral part of the house structure; however, Doug estimates it to be between $8,000 and $10,000. With an added cost of $8,000, a discount rate of 2% (that is, 9% interest minus 7% inflation) and a 5% annual escalation of the real cost of natural gas, the system will pay for itself in 17 years. If the real cost of natural gas escalates at a 15% rate, the system will pay for itself in 10 years. When one considers that the Trombe wall can reasonably be expected to last the life of the building compared to 20 years for a typical active water-type solar collector, the economic advantages are multiplied.

CONCLUDING THOUGHTS

In addition to those improvements mentioned earlier, Doug recommends enlarging the eave vents and/or installing operable windows in the south wall to increase cross-ventilation. With larger eave vents the electric fans would be unnecessary. The upper and lower vents in the Trombe wall should be slightly more frequent or larger so that the combined area of the openings is about one-half that of the cross-sectional area of the solar chamber they vent.

This type of solar home has many advantages. The solar system is extremely durable; initial, maintenance, and operating costs are lower than those of most active systems; it functions very efficiently as both a heating and a cooling system; it has no moving parts and is simple to build, maintain, operate, and understand. On top of all this it is a very attractive house.

ɔrthwood, New Hampshire
ɔ96 sq. ft.
cluding basement

HOUSE **15**

RICHARD and BARBARA RECKARD

Barbara and Richard Reckard are part of the new wave of back-to-the-landers. They have the energy, common sense, and resourcefulness of many of the earlier pioneers, yet they have the advantage of access to more tools and how-to literature and of knowing how to keep abreast of developments in environmentally appropriate technology.

They are pursuing a path of self-reliance while working to help make their community a better place for all to live. Richard has been elected to the local planning board and thus now has a more direct influence on community development. Their home, which is partially solar-heated by a Trombe wall, is described below.

LOCATION AND ORIENTATION

The Reckard home is located on the outskirts of the town of Northwood, New Hampshire. It is built into the south slope of a hill and is oriented due south. It is partially buried on the north and west sides and is well protected on these cold sides by a thick mixed forest. On the south and east, the pine trees were cut out, but the deciduous trees remain to provide summer shade. A two-car garage to the north provides further protection from the winter winds or what is locally known as the "Montreal Express."

ARCHITECTURAL FEATURES

The house was built in two stages. The first part is a central two-story structure which Richard and Barbara built themselves with some help from their children. Here they lived while the rest of the house was being completed. The first, or basement, level, measuring 24 x 24′, has the north and west walls buried into the hill. This first level was designed to accommodate a guest room, utility room, and wood storage; however, it served as a master bedroom and kitchen/dining room while the extensions to the core structure were being built. On the second level, the living room was placed at the warm south end of the structure. The children's two bedrooms were built outside the basement foundation at the cooler north end of the house.

Local tradesmen were hired to carry out most of the second stage of construc-

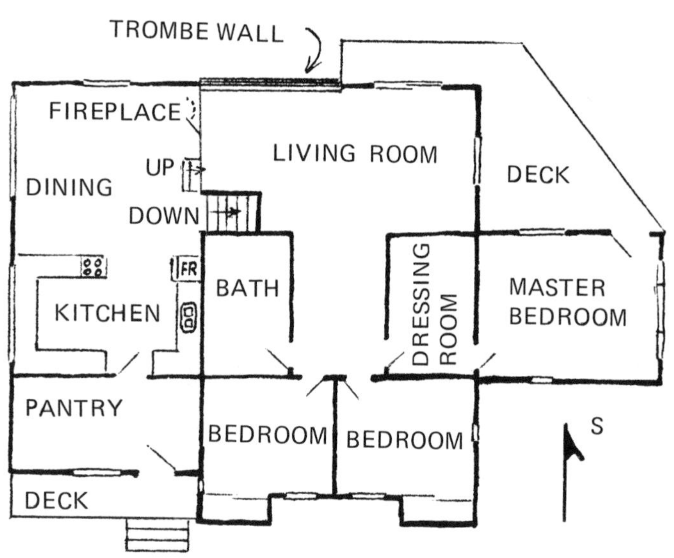

The partially completed Trombe wall on the south face of the house is barely visible through the deciduous trees. Glass blocks in the center of the wall permit light entry.

tion, which involved the addition of two wings or extensions on the same level as the upper level of the house core structure. A master bedroom was built onto the cooler (winter) side of the house, while an open-concept kitchen/dining room was built onto the east side of the house. The absence of a wall between the living room of the main part of the house and this east extension accounts for much of the good illumination and air circulation. The low cathedral ceilings of both these extensions permit the easy addition of loft space if it is desired.

The basement floor is 4" of poured concrete over a gravel base, while the main level has 2 x 6 tongue-and-groove floorboards. The floors in the new wing are new 2 x 6 tongue-and-groove boards that were properly dried. Those in the original part of the house were milled from pine cut on the Reckard property and laid while still green. As a result, a certain amount of warpage occurred. Carpeting was laid in the children's bedrooms to cover this warpage, reduce the noise level, and give a feeling of warmth and coziness. Both pine and hemlock were used for the floor joists, but the latter has experienced checking and splitting since it was installed—a characteristic common to hemlock which results in no significant strength reduction. Closets and the kitchen pantry were built on the north wall to serve as thermal buffers.

Exterior Walls

The south and east exterior walls of the first floor of the core structure are made of concrete blocks, whereas the stronger poured-concrete walls were erected on the north and west to also act as a retaining wall. Both types of walls were built on concrete footings, and both were properly waterproofed with tar sealer. A drain pipe was installed at the base of the north and west walls to further reduce possibilities of water seepage. The basement has always stayed dry.

A post-and-beam type of framing was used for the rest of the structure, including the foundations for the extensions. Most of the hand-hewn timbers came from a local barn which was more than 250 years old. The post-and-beam walls were infilled with full 1 x 4 rough-sawn studs which are not load-bearing. Initially, random-width rough-sawed green pine boards cut from timber taken off their own woodlot was used for exterior and some interior sheathing; however, Richard and Barbara subsequently replaced the exterior boards with ½" plywood and used the boards to sheath the garage. They found the house to be much tighter, warmer, and more resistant to racking. Later, properly dried 1 x 6 vertical shiplap pine boards were used as siding on the entire house. The walls are insulated with 3½" fiberglass batts and have a polyethylene vapor barrier stapled under the interior sheathing.

Interior Walls and Ceilings

Interior walls are of standard 2 x 4 studwall construction. Some walls are sheathed with gyproc; others are sheathed with pine boards. All ceilings are of the exposed-beam type and thus form the floor or roof for

Northwest corner. As the house is built into the side of a south-facing hill, the north side of the basement is completely buried. Bedrooms are located on this cooler north and west side of the house.

Vents below the north windows of the children's rooms. Other vents high on the south side of the house were designed to create effective natural ventilation in summer. Insulated covers seal these vents in winter.

the next level. The ceiling of the basement level is the 2 x 6 pine tongue-and-groove floorboards of the upper level. The ceiling of the upper level of the core section is 2 x 6 tongue-and-groove boards that the Reckards purchased from a salvage yard in Boston. The children did all the nail pulling, and Richard planed the boards on a machine borrowed from a neighbor.

New, well-dried 2 x 6 tongue-and-groove boards were used for the ceiling/roof of the extensions.

Roof

The shed roof of the core section has a 1/12 pitch with the high side to the south. Closed-cell 2″ polyurethane foamboard with felt paper on both sides was laid directly over the 2 x 6 tongue-and-groove roof decking of the core section. Double-coverage roll roofing was then laid over this.

The shed roofs of the wings have a 4′ rise in a 16′ run, sloping downward from the central core of the house. Clerestories were created in both cases as the peak of each extension roof rises well above the other roof. The only green lumber used in the extensions was the inexpensive, rough-sawn, locally milled 4 x 8 roof rafters. The extension roofs have 2″-thick closed-cell polyurethane foamboard with aluminum foil on both sides laid directly over the 2 x 6 tongue-and-groove roof decking. Asphalt shingles were laid immediately on top of the insulation and nailed with long, narrow box nails that penetrated through the insulation to the wood roof decking.

Insulation Summary

Basement:	None
Walls (main floor):	R-15; 3½″ fiberglass batts
Ceiling (central core):	R-21; 2″ closed-cell polyurethane foamboard
Ceiling (extensions):	R-21; 2″ closed-cell polyurethane foamboard

Doors

The entranceway most frequently used, especially in winter, enters the kitchen from the north side of the house via a porch/pantry/airlock. It is somewhat protected by the bedroom walls, which extend farther north, and by a slight overhang. The single site-built wood door is of Z-brace construction with tongue-and-groove boards on either side. The cavity is insulated with fiberglass.

South-facing entrances to the basement level and to the living room from the deck are thermopane aluminum-frame patio doors. They also serve to provide direct-gain passive solar heat when unshaded by the deciduous trees in winter. Aluminum was chosen over the less conductive wood frame because of the much higher cost of the wood. The Reckards have experienced no frost problem. The doors are covered with heavy curtains during cold evenings.

Windows

Initially, Barbara and Richard installed used windows salvaged from old buildings and other sources. They discovered after installation that many of them were of poor quality. They also made the mistake of using green lumber for the window frames. As a result, many windows rattled and leaked, and were subsequently replaced with better-quality ones. All the operable windows are new Andersen wood-frame windows. Some of the fixed thermopane windows were salvaged from a building that had to be demolished because of the widening of the highway, and the remainder were purchased from a glass company at relatively low cost as they were custom-built for clients who never picked them up.

The largest window area is on the south side. The north side has a small window area. The windows of the north bedrooms are in an alcove, and thus protected to a considerable degree from the elements. Where the roofs of the two wings extend above the roof of the main part of the house, clerestories were created to provide indirect lighting to the kitchen/dining area on the east and to the master bedroom on the west.

Richard and Barbara are in the process of designing suitable insulated shutters or curtains. They have considered using "space blankets" that roll up like Roman blinds or purchasing Mylar and fabricating their own. Richard is also researching the possibility of a photocell-operated insulated curtain or shutter.

Other Architectural Features

It is worth describing the detached garage/workshop because of its unique, attractive design features and the materials and method of construction used. The one-and-a-half story structure has a loft, presently used for storage, that receives good illumination through clerestory windows. The superstructure was made of "scrounged" telephone poles that were pressure-treated with preservative. Each pole was set on a concrete pad placed below the frostline and then further treated below ground level with used crankcase oil before the hole was backfilled. The square-edged random-width boards that were originally used for vertical siding on the house now serve the garage. Battens will complete the siding. The roof is sheathed with aluminum barn roofing. The floor is presently dirt but eventually a concrete slab will be poured.

Looking toward the living room from the kitchen and dining room. The open fireplace was installed largely for aesthetic reasons.

A Riteway wood-burning stove centrally located in the living room is the main backup to the solar system.

SOLAR-HEATING SYSTEM

The solar-heating system is a very simple low-cost one. As mentioned earlier, a substantial amount of direct solar gain is provided by the large south-facing window area. Deciduous trees and the shed-roof overhang provide shade and thus prevent overheating during the summer.

Because of financial constraints the Trombe wall is not yet completed, but as the characteristics of these walls are now well known its performance can be predicted with a fair degree of accuracy. (Refer to House 14.) We elected to include the Reckard house in this study to illustrate an aesthetic and functional application of combined mass-wall and direct-gain passive solar and wood heating.

At least as much solar heat will be provided by the 144 sq. ft. of Trombe wall which forms an integral part of the south wall of the core section of the house as is provided by direct gain. The Trombe wall section, measuring 12 x 12′, extends from the footings to midway up the living-room wall. It is constructed of sand-filled 8″ concrete blocks which will have 4″ of brick on each side. The exterior surface of the outside brick will be painted flat black. A 4″ airspace and then a double glazing of Kalwall Sun-lite is proposed. Slots at the top and bottom of the Trombe wall permit convected air to flow to and from the living spaces. The wall will be vented to the outside to further guard against summer overheating problems. The Trombe wall was relatively inexpensive, as Richard bartered two cords of wood for the mason's labor to lay the blocks.

AUXILIARY HEATING

The main backup initially was a Riteway wood-fuel space heater. This had been replaced by a Danish-made H.S. Kedlar • Tarm combination wood/oil boiler located in the basement that provides space heating and domestic hot water. The space heating is accomplished by high-performance hot-water baseboard heaters in the various rooms. The hydronic system operates on two zones, each controlled by a separate thermostat. The thermostat for the three bedrooms is kept day and night at 63° F., but since it is located in the master bedroom, the coolest part of the house, the children's bedrooms are comfortably warm. The rest of the house, which is on another zone, has its thermostat kept at a constant 65° F.

The Reckards state that the boiler has not lived up to their expectations. It runs very efficiently on oil but is not a good wood burner. If the unit is dampered down during the day when no one is home, creosote problems develop. During the winter of 1977-78 they had two chimney fires. When the damper was opened enough to avoid this problem, the firebox would not hold a full charge of wood for the day. They have received similar reports from other users of this boiler. The Riteway, which is centrally located on the main floor, on the other hand, performed admirably. It can heat a large area and hold a full charge of wood all day without serious creosote buildup. During the 1977-78 heating season, which had 7,383 degree-days, the Reckards burned about 400 gallons of fuel oil and about eight full cords of hardwood, which was purchased in 4′ lengths for $30 per cord.

The combination wood/oil boiler will in the future, or until modifications can be made to improve its wood-burning performance, be used only to burn oil. The combination of the high-efficiency oil burner and the exclusive use of the efficient Riteway for burning wood will, the Reckards hope, result in lower fuel consumption.

A Rumford-style masonry fireplace between the dining room and living room was built largely for aesthetic reasons. Richard did specify outside venting to improve its efficiency; however, as communications broke down between the carpenter and the mason, the vent was never installed. Although the fireplace's chimney is against an outside wall it does not penetrate the wall's insulation barrier.

PERCENT SOLAR-HEATED

The completed system has not been operational a full heating season; however, it is anticipated that the combined direct-gain and Trombe-wall elements of the design should provide about 50% of the heating needs.

COOLING SYSTEM

No mechanical cooling devices are used or needed, as natural cooling is achieved in a number of ways. Deciduous trees provide good shade. Further shading is achieved by the shed-roof overhang above the living-room windows on the south side of the house. Small screened vents on the cool north wall near the floor of the children's rooms in conjunction with the high operable windows in the living room at the warmer south end of the house provide good cross-ventilation. These north vents are sealed with insulated covers in the winter.

Cooling is also achieved with the aid of the Trombe wall. In the summer, when it is vented to the outside, a chimney effect is created which draws room air into the space between the Trombe wall and the glazing and subsequently exhausts it to the outside. Both the air movement within the living spaces and the replacement of warm house air with cooler air from the cooler north side of the house keeps the occupants cool. The insulation, closets, and pantry that help to keep the house warm during the heating season also serve to buffer the interior spaces from summer heat. Barbara summarized their feelings about the comfort of the house during the hot season thus: "We have found that the house cools very effectively. The circulating patterns created by the house design are among the most successful features of the house."

WATER SUPPLY AND WASTE SYSTEM

A 250-foot drilled artesian well supplies all the family's water needs. Domestic hot water is integral to the wood boiler. Optional electric heating elements in the boiler provide hot water during the warm season. The only water-conserving fixture is a water-saver shower head. The women are not too happy with it, however, as it takes longer to wash their hair than it did with a regular shower head and thus probably does not save water in these particular cases. Overall, though, it does save water and the energy required to heat it.

A standard septic system handles blackwater and graywater wastes. Other organic waste is composted to be used in the Reckard garden. Other waste that is not reusable is separated at home and then taken to the local dump, where the town requires citizens to place different waste in appropriate containers. There are separate bins for various colors of glass, metal, cardboard, newsprint, plastic paper, miscellaneous, and a separate area for large items such as furniture or appliances. A colorful, eccentric woman whom everyone called Sunshine graced the town dump until recently with her presence. She would salvage waste, sell it at a modest price, and turn the money over to the town. Her cheerful presence is sorely missed by the townsfolk.

ELECTRICAL POWER SYSTEM

The Reckards obtain electrical power from the local utility company. There is not enough wind near their house to make wind power feasible.

Multidirectional natural lighting minimizes the need for artificial lighting. Many windows are at high levels to optimize the amount of daylight that they allow in. The clerestories on the two wings are particularly effective in this regard. Many of the lighting fixtures use fluorescent tubes.

Left: The H.S. Kedlar·Tarm combination wood/oil burner located in the basement supplies hot water to baseboard radiators throughout the house. It was intended to replace the Riteway, but the latter has proved to be a much superior wood heater and thus will remain. *Right:* Looking south from the deck into the living room and to the master bedroom on the left-hand side.

MAJOR HOUSEHOLD APPLIANCES

A propane cookstove was chosen largely because it was recommended by the home-economics teacher at the local high school. The pilot lights are not used in order to conserve energy. The refrigerator, according to Richard, "has been around for years and years. It grew up with a friend of mine whom I've known since we were small children, and that refrigerator was always at their house until we received it." The new chest-type freezer was purchased at a discount from the building-supply store where Barbara works while the electric washer and dryer were purchased secondhand. A clothesline is used in the summer.

FOOD SYSTEM

Normally the Reckards have a large organic garden; however, because the whole family helped build the house, the size of the garden was substantially reduced during the construction phase. A greenhouse is planned for the future. Richard built a direct-gain solar-heated chicken coop in the backyard, where a dozen chickens usually roost. Direct gain is received through a relatively large (compared to the roof) skylight on the south-facing roof. The chickens supply all the eggs the family needs, plus some meat and fertilizer. They have no plans to acquire other animals, except perhaps a goat.

COSTS

Building costs were kept to a reasonable amount because the family did a great deal of work themselves and because they were able to do some bartering. Doug worked in a lumber yard when they first started building, and then Barbara obtained work at a building-supply center, so they were able to buy materials at discount prices. In addition, as mentioned earlier in the text, much of the lumber was milled from timber that was taken from their own woodlot.

CONCLUDING THOUGHTS

Richard and Barbara Reckard are very happy with the design of their home. Richard says, "I only wish we had had a better knowledge of structural things, especially where the carpenters had to add on the extensions. Our lack of knowledge cost us a lot of money." There was a substantial amount of labor involved in tying in the extensions to the core section of the house.

In spite of some of the difficulties, what has emerged is an aesthetically pleasing, energy-efficient home that radiates the warmth of a labor of love.

Master bedroom with door opening onto deck.

ar New Milford, Connecticut
60 sq. ft. including
enhouse and basement

STEPHEN and NANCY LASAR

Stephen and Nancy Lasar began looking for alternatives to the conventional way of life in the early 1970s. They began to practice organic gardening, raised a couple of goats and a few laying hens, and became vegetarians. They were learning self-reliance and how to live inexpensively. Their decision to build a passively heated solar home was a logical extension of their life-style.

Stephen was working as an architect for the architectural firm of McHugh and Associates in Farmington, Connecticut, and was involved in the designing of a government-funded solar-heated housing project for the elderly. The more he studied solar heating, the more he became interested in passive systems.

In the fall of 1974, they found a suitable country property of seven acres—800′ above sea level, 42° N. latitude, 6,700 degree-days. They analyzed the site all winter, started work in May 1975, and moved into the house in November.

The main goals in designing this home were to provide living accommodations for themselves, suitable work spaces where Stephen and Nancy could practice their respective vocations of architecture and painting, and space for the raising and preserving of foodstuffs—and to do all this with minimal environmental impact. This meant that, wherever possible, locally available, renewable resources would be used, and that passive solar energy would be the main source of heat, with wood heat their only backup. It meant also being content to allow the microclimate within the house to swing somewhat with the diurnal and annual climatic changes. The occupants would then become the active components in the system, opening and closing shutters, donning or taking off clothing, or stoking the wood stove as required. These goals called for some radical architectural design features by conventional standards.

LOCATION AND ORIENTATION

The Lasar home is located near New Milford, Connecticut. It is in a valley on the west side of a 15° hill. The house is oriented 5° west of south, and the long axis runs east to west. It has a spectacular view to the south and west of majestic tree-covered hill country. The northwest winter winds blow consistently and strongly, so the rear of the building was partially buried into the hill in order to minimize their impact.

The hay field surrounding the house and the low deciduous trees that Steven and Nancy planted on the west side provide summer cooling and shade. A row of fir trees planted along the north side is designed as a windbreak. Shade trees are planned for the south side of the house.

This house incorporates several passive-solar design features to collect solar heat: direct gain, isolated gain through greenhouse attached to the lower level, and indirect gain through the Trombe wall located behind the glazing opposite the deck.

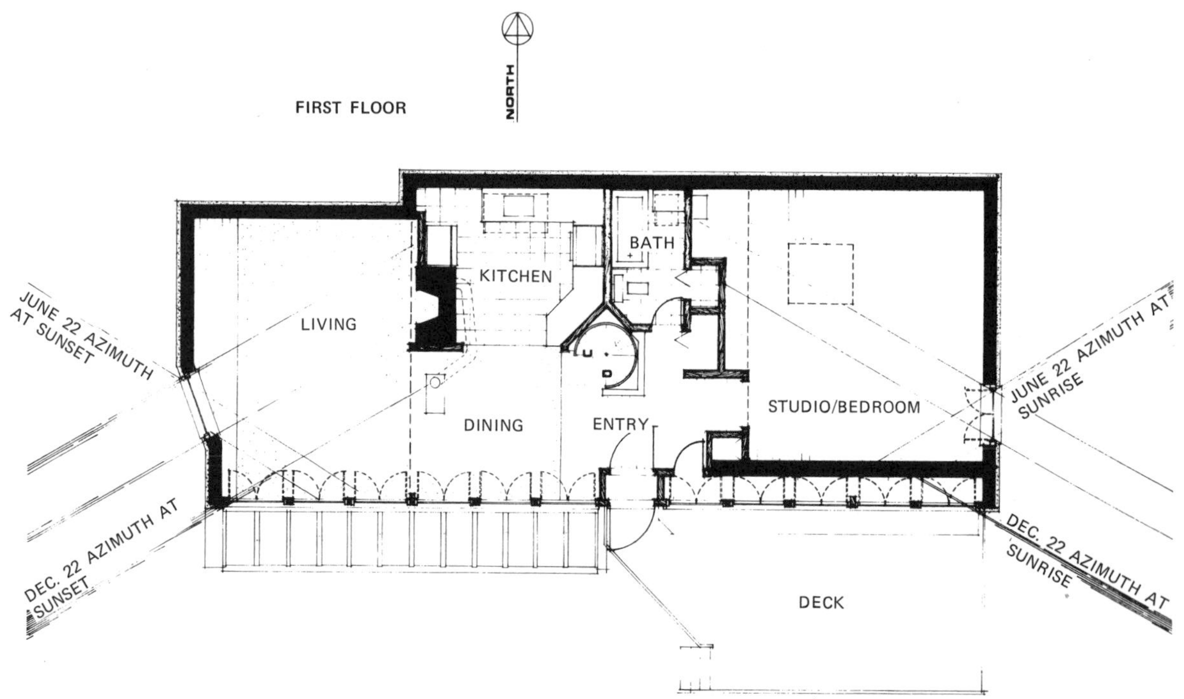

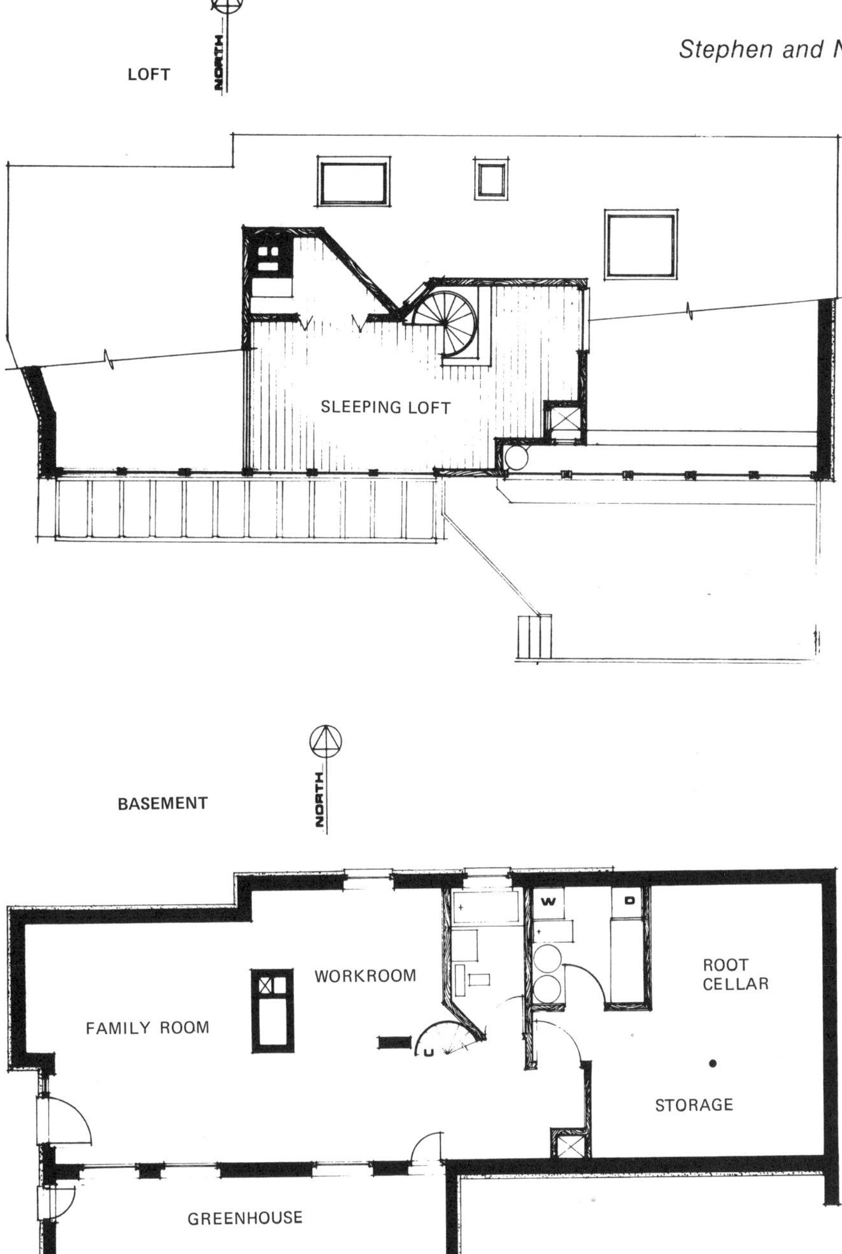

ARCHITECTURAL FEATURES

This two-and-a-half-story house measures 22 x 55′ and has a total area of 2,460 sq. ft. The second-floor living room, kitchen, dining room, and studio/bedroom occupy 1,200 sq. ft., the dormer loft 250 sq. ft., the greenhouse 125 sq. ft., and the full basement the remainder. The layout was designed to capture some of the character of their old New York City loft "with free-flowing flexible work spaces and minimal formal living spaces." The open concept also facilitates heat flow and cross-ventilation for summer cooling.

The basement floor, which is an integral part of the solar design, was constructed in the following manner. Crushed gravel was first carefully leveled in between the poured-concrete footings and then covered with two layers of 1″ extruded polystyrene rigid insulation with the joints staggered. On top of the polystyrene, 10″ concrete blocks were carefully laid on their sides and aligned so that air ducts were created running in a north-south direction. This array is served by a feeder duct running from east to west. The blocks were then covered with poured concrete. How this floor functions for heat storage will be explained later. The massive second-story floors are composed of 8″-thick precast concrete panels covered with a 2″ poured-concrete slab. A spiral staircase from the basement through to the loft conserves space.

Exterior Walls

The exterior north, east, and west walls consist of 10″ concrete blocks. The south side is glass and wood post-and-beam construction. The massive concrete-block walls have been finished using the "Dryvit" method, a system of insulating and finishing exterior walls that has been used in Europe for more than 20 years. Rigid moulded polystyrene insulation (beadboard) is cemented to the wall with Dryvit Primus/adhesive. A Primus coat is then trowelled onto the outside of the insulation, which is then covered with a fiberglass reinforcing mesh. A waterproof finish coat that can be pigmented to any desired color is finally added. Stephen applied the materials himself but discovered that it would have been just as cheap to hire a plasterer, as what they saved on labor they spent on extra materials by applying the primus and finish coats too thickly. In Stephen's words, "I was not crazy about using the 'Dryvit' method but it's the best available as far as I am concerned. 'Dryvit' Primus and finish are made up of a mixture of cement and plastic. Although it is a waterproof surface from the outside it does breathe, thereby requiring no control or expansion joints, and in that sense it is completely satisfactory. My objection to the material is its plastic component. We use too many plastic elements in our lives and I try to reduce dependence on plastics." Standard 2 x 6 wood-frame construction was used for the loft wall, and post-and-beam construction was used for the main south wall. Stained vertical Canadian spruce boards are used for exterior siding.

Interior Walls and Ceilings

The interior of the east, west, and north poured-concrete and concrete-block walls has been left unfinished. The fireplace is integral to the concrete-block wall dividing the kitchen/living areas. Other interior walls are of standard 2 x 4 studwall construction. These and the ceiling are sheathed with ½″ gypsum board painted white to contrast with the gray walls and the dark concrete floors. The ceiling joists are 2 x 10s.

Roof

The simple, easy-to-construct, low-cost, low-maintenance shed roof presents a low profile to the cold northwest winter winds. Standard ½″ exterior plywood roof sheathing and tarpaper were covered with roll roofing for the flatter loft roof; asphalt shingles were used for the steeper roof. These materials were less expensive than some of the more aesthetic alternatives.

Insulation Summary

Ceiling: R-24; fiberglass batt insulation in both loft and main ceiling. Airspace between the top of the insulation and the roof's decking and soffit vents at both the north and south eaves ensure good ventilation.

Walls, south side: R-19; fiberglass batt insulation

Walls, concrete: R-16; beadboard, extending down to the footings except around the storage/root cellar, where it extends to 4′ below grade

Where wood framing is used the vapor barrier is attached to the warm side of the fiberglass insulation and is either paper or aluminum. All windows and doors are carefully caulked and weatherstripped. Treated wood was used for sills sitting on concrete. Cracks around window frames were chinked with loose fiberglass insulation.

Doors

The main and most-used entrance is in the center of the south wall on the second floor running off a large deck. One enters through an outside storm door, a small vestibule, and a solid-wood door—in other words, through an airlock. Another entrance is through a metal-clad insulated door on the west side of the basement. A similar door provides access to the greenhouse.

Windows

The south wall is composed of 376 sq. ft. of vertical thermopane windows. All the operable awning windows and the large fixed windows are manufactured by Caradco. Although Andersen manufactures the most popular wood-sash window, Stephen feels that the Caradco window is superior. The 125′ of greenhouse glazing is sloped 60° to the horizontal. Vertical operable windows are installed between the greenhouse and basement to prevent overheating of the former and to provide winter heat to the latter.

The fixed west living-room window is angled so as to be perpendicular to the solar azimuth on December 22, when the heat gain is most needed. By June 22, the solar azimuth is such that much of the solar radiation is reflected. The main reason for placement of this window on the western wall, however, is to afford a spectacular view of the countryside and the sunsets.

A small east-facing window in the studio and one in the loft provide natural dawn lighting and direct solar gain in the cooler mornings.

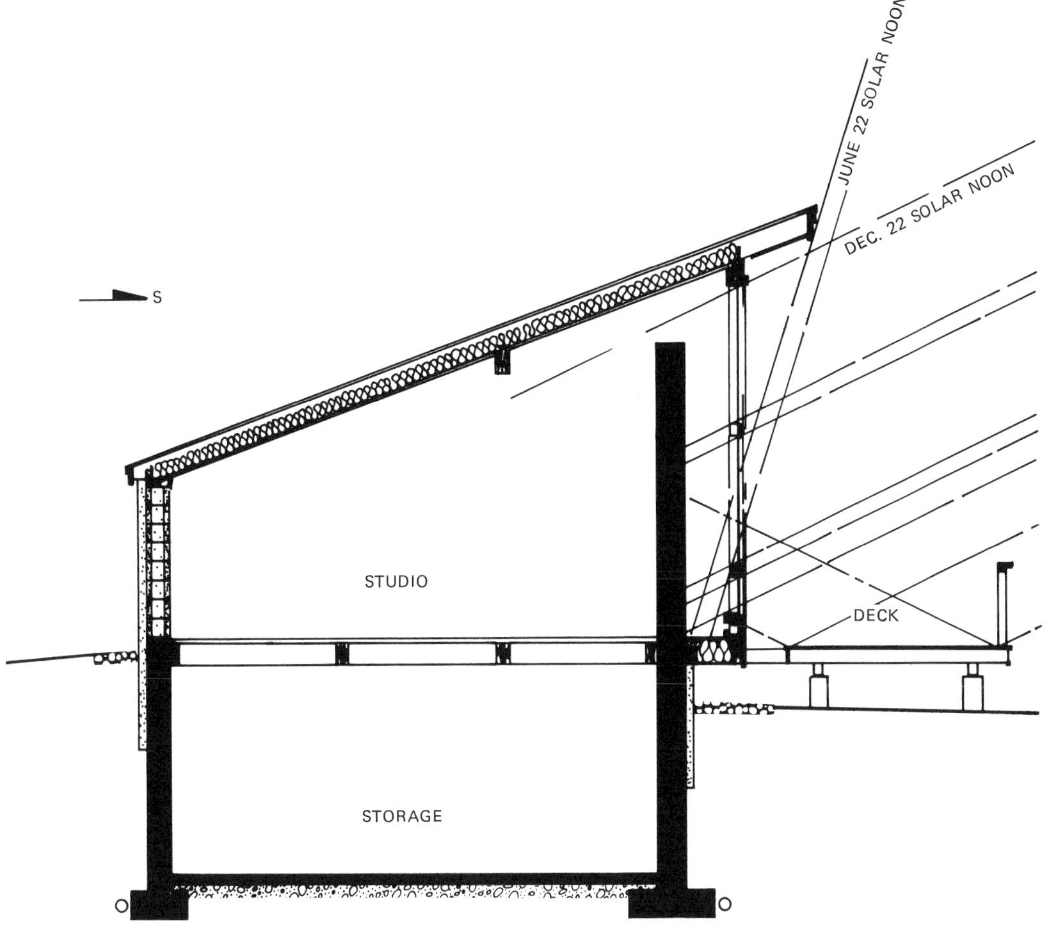

SECTION LOOKING EAST

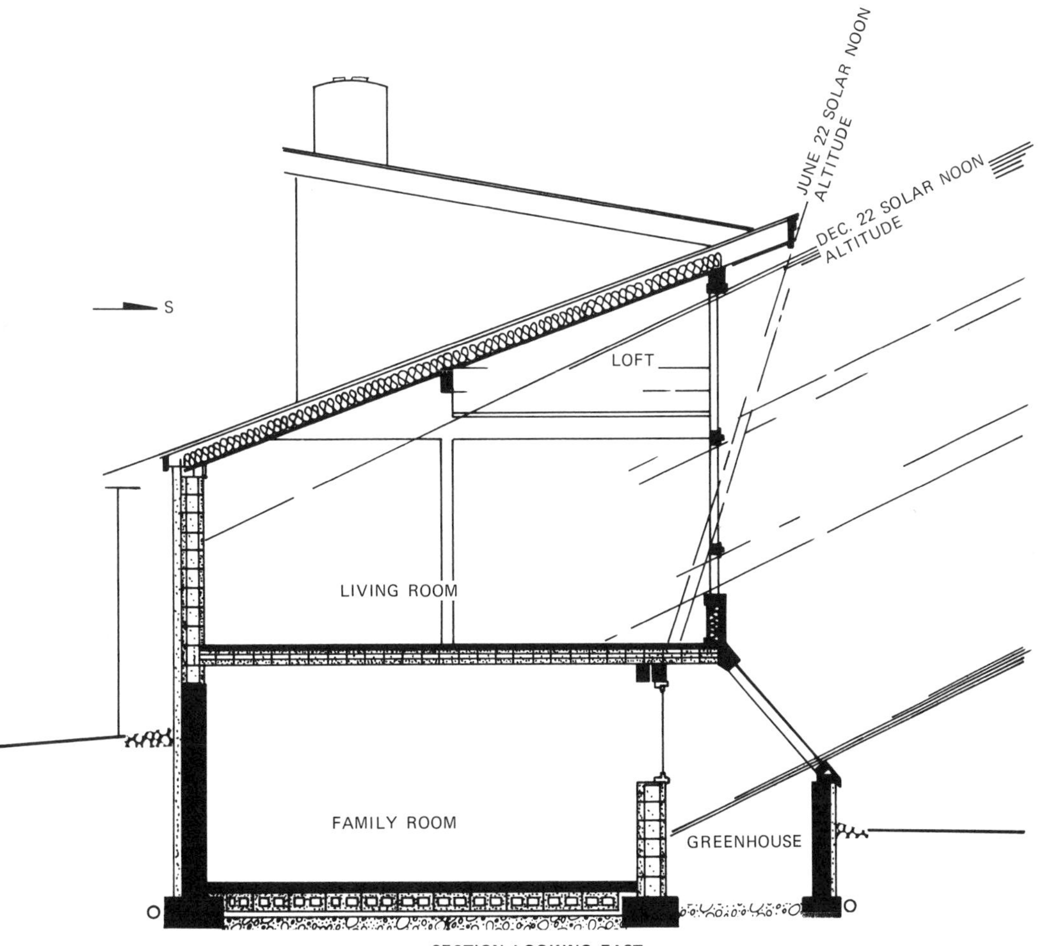

SECTION LOOKING EAST

There are no windows on the north wall except for one small operable window in the loft, which is shuttered in winter and used for cross-ventilation in summer. The second-floor bath, studio, and kitchen each have a Velux thermopane wood-sash roof window which admits substantially more light than a vertical window. The diffuse radiation that the roof window admits is essential for the painting/architectural studio. The Velux windows can rotate a full 180° for maximum ventilation as well as simplified cleaning of the outside pane. Stephen has been experimenting with different shutter designs and had thought of adopting a manually operated wood-frame fiberfill shutter, but he has not been able to solve the condensation problem typically associated with interior shutters. Instead, he plans to install triple glazing on north and east windows and on one roof window.

SOLAR-HEATING SYSTEM

In this remarkably simple passive heating system the house itself acts as both the collector and storer of solar heat. Solar-heat gain occurs in three ways. The large south-facing vertical windows facing the kitchen/dining area and the living room permit direct solar gain. Solar radiation strikes the massive concrete walls and floor, where it is stored as heat until the rooms start to cool, when this thermal energy is then radiated back to the living spaces. Some direct gain occurs through the east and west windows, but the result may only be a net gain in winter when shutters are used.

The studio uses a 1′-thick, 16′-high, 16′-long Trombe wall to collect solar energy. The concrete wall, which is an extension of the foundation wall, rises to about five-sixths the height of the studio ceiling. There is a distance of 2′ between the wall and the south-facing glazing, which allows room for shutters to swing and facilitates cleaning of the interior glass. Solar energy passes through the glass and strikes the black-painted Trombe wall. Air is heated and rises by natural convection and spills over the top of the Trombe wall to heat the studio space. As it cools it circulates down the north wall and along the floor to reenter via an open doorway to the base of the Trombe wall. Thermal energy is also conducted through to the inside of the Trombe wall and then radiates to the studio at night.

Stopping the Trombe wall short of the ceiling creates a clerestory effect which permits the entry of southern light to complement that from the east window and the northern roof window. This creates ideal lighting conditions for the Lasars' architectural work and painting.

The cedar deck serves as a pleasant recreational area. In winter its flat snow-covered surface reflects sunlight toward the glazing, resulting in considerably higher efficiencies. The southern overhang of the shed roof is designed to effectively shade the south-facing glazing in summer while permitting the passage of the winter sun.

The solar greenhouse absorbs solar energy. The mutual uninsulated black-painted (nonselective) concrete-block partial wall between it and the basement acts as a small Trombe wall. Operable windows in this wall can be opened to allow convected hot air to spill over into the basement. Radiation occurs as described for the studio Trombe wall. Overheating in summer is prevented by vents on the east and west walls and by covering the greenhouse glazing with a canvas awning.

With most passively heated open-concept dwellings there is a tendency for hot air to stratify. In this case it would occur in the loft area. In the summer this is no problem, as any excess heat can be vented out the loft windows. Stephen solved the problems of winter stratification by installing ductwork in a vertical shaft extending from the loft to the basement and connecting this ductwork to the east-west header of the supplemental storage—the block plenum array under the basement floor slab. A ¾″-hp fan pulls hot air down through this system and pushes cool air under the slab back upstairs to be heated again. The first winter the house tended to overheat on sunny days, as the switch to supplemental storage was not made soon enough. The fan has to be set to come on before the house overheats.

AUXILIARY HEATING

The only backup that Nancy and Stephen use is wood heating. A tiny concrete-block fireplace on the inside wall between the kitchen and the living room serves mostly an aesthetic function. A Lange airtight stove with a capacity to heat 7 to 9,000 cu. ft. is centrally located between the dining and living rooms. Although the stove is in an ideal location for heat distribution, the stovepipe length to the flue is too long for this type of stove, resulting in a serious creosote buildup. The stove will therefore have to be moved into the kitchen closer to the flue.

The first winter they tried to economize on burning wood, and sometimes the fire went out because they had adjusted the air damper too tightly. If the outside temperature was 0° F. the interior temperature would be 52° F. by morning. By the second winter they had learned how to operate the stove efficiently.

Northwest corner. Note how the house is built into the south-facing hill and the small amount of window glazing on the north side.

Dining room, living room, looking west. Concrete-block walls, insulated on the exterior with polystyrene foamboard, and masonry floors store solar heat.

The black-painted poured-concrete Trombe wall has inset copper pipes connected to domestic hot-water preheater tank. Experimental insulated shutters are stacked below the water tank.

PERCENT SOLAR-HEATED

Stephen estimates that solar energy supplies between 65% and 75% of their heating requirement. For each of the first three winters, which have been as harsh and cold as any on record, the Lasars burned less than two cords of wood (mostly seasoned ash and maples but also some fruitwood and rotting elm), which is equivalent to about 300 gallons of fuel oil. In February, March, and April of 1976 they collected data using a "dynamaster record" with thermocouple points. These were average temperature months and the wood stove was burning only 14% of the time. In January, which was an extremely cold month, the wood stove provided a substantial portion of the backup heat. It is anticipated that the solar contribution will reach 85-90% when suitable insulated shutters are devised and installed.

Due to the radiant-heating nature of the thermal mass, the winter comfort range is between 60° and 68°F. Average fluctuations are from 58° to 75°F. and isolated extremes (with no backup heat) from 52° to about 80°F. in the living room.

COOLING SYSTEM

As mentioned earlier, the southern overhang effectively blocks out the high summer sun. The roof windows on the cooler north side and the operable windows on the warm south have been carefully placed to provide good cross-ventilation. The good insulation provides an effective thermal barrier to the hot summer sun and canvas awnings are placed over the greenhouse and some of the windows.

WATER SUPPLY AND WASTE SYSTEM

Water is supplied from a drilled well. The domestic hot water is preheated by passing it along several black-painted parallel ¾" copper pipes which are recessed in a horizontal 1½"-deep by 9½"-wide depression in the south face of the Trombe wall. This 100′ of pipe forms a closed loop with a black-painted uninsulated water tank to the west of the Trombe wall. This is connected in series to an insulated 40-gallon tank where the water temperature is boosted to 125°F. by an electric coil. This system does not work too effectively because in summer the sun does not directly strike the pipes, and during winter nights the tank, which is near the unshuttered south windows, loses too much heat to the outside. Stephen describes a different domestic system that he is using for Solar Merryall, a planned community of three solar-heated residences that he and a partner are building near Stephen's own home. "Solar Merryall features a thermosiphon domestic hot-water system that has proved to be a great success. Two or three Sunworks absorber plates were installed under south-sloping roof skylights with water tanks located above. Water flows to the tank by thermosiphon action when sunlight warms it. No flow occurs when water is cold. (Cold water does not rise.) Water is kept from overheating and freezing because it is located within the living space."

The plumbing fixtures have no particular water-conserving features. One of the luxuries that the Lasars afforded themselves was an extra bathroom; however, they did economize by obtaining a salvaged bathtub and bathroom sink.

A standard septic system was installed. Stephen had considered a composting toilet; however, the town wouldn't allow it at the time. Properly installed, a good septic system is a nonpolluting waste system and a good alternative to a composting toilet.

The Lasars compost other organic wastes and use this on their garden. They attempt to minimize the use of nonrenewable resources, which is compatible with their overall desire to live lightly on the earth.

ELECTRICAL POWER SYSTEM

While Nancy and Stephen were analyzing their site during the latter part of 1974 and the early part of 1975, they investigated the possibility of installing a wind generator, as they certainly had the winds that winter. However, the costs proved to be prohibitive. The following summer they discovered that there are hardly any winds during the warm season.

They opted to hook up to the local utility grid and attempted to minimize their consumption. Window placement was designed to make the best use of natural light. Fluorescents are used in the studio and baths. Vita-Lite, made by Duro-Test Corp., are used in the studio and baths. Stephen had read reports stating that Vita-Lite tubes more closely approximate daylight than other types of fluorescent lights.

Studio side of the Trombe wall. During the day when the sun shines on the wall, hot air is convected over the top of the wall. In the evening, heat radiates from the wall to the studio.

Looking southeast from the living room to the dining room and loft bedroom above.

Stephen describes the design of his home to a group of visitors.

Carrie Lasar in a moment of quiet contemplation in the loft bedroom.

MAJOR HOUSEHOLD APPLIANCES

The Lasars' appliances are not particularly energy-conserving in themselves; however, they have few of them, and those that they do have are used wisely. They feel that their Caloric propane cookstove is the best on the market. "We have turned off their pilot lights and operate with matches or flints." A 12-cu.-ft. Frigidaire preserves food, but no freezer is used as the root cellar is adequate for storing foodstuffs for their vegetarian diet. They repaired an old Sears automatic washing machine and use either an outside clothesline or the greenhouse for drying clothes, depending on the weather.

FOOD SYSTEM

There is no problem procuring organically grown grains in this area of Connecticut, but as organically grown vegetables are very expensive in winter, Stephen and Nancy designed an outside herb and vegetable garden, greenhouse, and a cold-storage area at the east end of the basement to supply and store a great portion of their foods. They are somewhat torn between some of the more intensive methods of gardening and more natural ways. Presently the garden location is rotated from year to year. Although kitchen wastes are composted, this is not done intensively either.

With the land that they have and the system that they have designed, Stephen and Nancy could be nearly self-sufficient in food if they desired and if the need arose.

COSTS

Stephen had estimated that construction costs would be in the neighborhood of $40,000. The final cost amounted to $42,000. In a passively heated house where the solar "system" is integral to the house itself, it is often difficult to determine the costs attributed to the solar component. Stephen estimates, however, that in his case about $3,300 was spent on energy-conserving and solar elements.

CONCLUDING THOUGHTS

Stephen and Nancy, after having lived in the house for three years, have only two criticisms. First, although the Trombe wall works well, Stephen feels it would have been better if it had been built lower and longer, or lower and deeper, so that it would still have the same capacity but convected air would enter the room at about shoulder level rather than near the ceiling.

They wish now that they had used more of an open concept in their planning; however, that was something they had compromised on from the beginning, as they felt there was a possibility that they would sell the house and that it would be much more marketable with its existing layout.

Stephen has built a similar home of 3,000 sq. ft. for an older couple in Washington, Connecticut. It is not quite as dependent on the sun as his own home and it has more north skylights and windows and more operable windows. They use a combination gas/wood/oil furnace with a baseboard hot-water system to supplement the solar heating.

The planned community mentioned earlier is on 12 acres of land which include a trout stream, the West Aspetuk River, a woodlot, and a hay field. Stephen designed the project with its three passively heated houses for maximum privacy and careful preservation of the beautiful landscape. Solar Merryall 1 is sold and occupied, Solar Merryall 3 is nearly completed, and Solar Merryall 2 will be built in 1979. Stephen and his partner are building these homes on speculation. They have been approached by many people who have had the desire to build passively heated solar houses but could not find available or affordable land. Most of the land in their region is in large blocks. In Stephen's words, "I can't get a lot of commissions to build passively heated residences because people don't have the land. Then I see all these ranch houses—forty- and fifty-lot subdivisions—and it drives me crazy. We're offering this as an alternative." Because of these difficulties in securing land Stephen plans to move more into the design and construction of commercial buildings. He sees a tremendous possibility for energy conservation through the use of passive solar heating particularly in schools, offices, and other buildings that don't require much heating at night.

Stephen is now working in Litchfield, Connecticut, with Clifford Cooper, A.I.A., Architects, a firm which is designing many solar-gain house additions, new solar-oriented houses, and one completely passively heated and cooled 140-unit condominium.

HOUSE **17**

yvale, Prince Edward Island
50 sq. ft. living area
luding solarium

JOHN and DONNA RAMSEY

We have included John and Donna Ramsey's home in this book because of its many examples of environmentally appropriate technology applications. Their home was built by themselves almost entirely out of salvaged materials. It is heated by wood stoves and passive solar heat. They are not connected to the local utility but instead have powered their home for the past seven years with only a wind generator. Their water is heated by wood stoves and a Grumman Sunstream solar hot-water heater. John and Donna are passionately committed to an energy- and resource-conserving life-style.

LOCATION AND ORIENTATION

The Ramsey home is situated on a 40-acre farmsite in the district of Emyvale, Prince Edward Island. Ten acres are cleared and there are 15 acres of spruce and 15 acres of hardwood trees. It is built on a south-facing slope and designed to present a low profile to the cold northwest winds. Coniferous trees on the north and an attached garage and woodhouse on the northwest end of the house provide additional protection. The south view is a completely unobstructed panorama of the countryside. The long axis runs east to west so that the large expanse of glass at the front of the house faces due south. A modest-sized barn/workshop was erected about 50 yards to the east of the house, and it was here that the milling and prefabricating was done and where building materials were stored while the house was being constructed.

The house was built on the south side of a spruce-lined clay secondary road (which is more like a lane), an eighth of a mile from the paved main road. "Although some people have questioned our sanity for having such a long lane," says John, "the level road is easy to walk during the usual two-week spring breakup and the few days in winter when it fills up with snow after a storm. The majority of island residents do not seem to feel privacy is important, because the trend is to build as close to the road as possible." Spring breakup used to affect the road for about six weeks until, with the urging of the Ramseys, the provincial Department of Highways put in culverts and shale in the low spots where water tended to collect. Donna and John several years ago successfully fought the department to retain the spruce trees lining the road. The department engineers felt that snow would be trapped between the rows; however, the trees have actually kept the snow off the road, as the Ramseys predicted. "Islanders traditionally have a low regard for trees," commented John, "although this is slowly changing. The new minister of Highways has stated that trees are a valuable resource."

In the view on page 172, Donna Ramsey's father prepares the field to the south of the house. The house is heated entirely by the solarium/greenhouse, south-facing windows, and wood-burning stoves. The two Grumman Sunstream solar collectors on the roof preheat domestic hot water. The picture above, taken from the east, shows the 200-watt Wincharger mounted on the roof of the wood shed.

ARCHITECTURAL FEATURES

This one-and-a-half story, three-bedroom house has 2,150 sq. ft. of living space. The layout is basically open concept to facilitate air circulation—cooling cross-ventilation in summer and warming radiant and convected heat from the wood stoves and a solarium in winter. Many of the rooms can be closed off, however, so that the kitchen, dining room, and living room can be isolated from the rest of the house if desired.

The south-facing rooms—the office/den and parlor on the first floor and the master bedroom on the second floor—require no heat other than the passive solar on a sunny day. The one substantial error that Donna and John felt they made in the initial design was to have located the rooms that are most used in winter—the kitchen, dining room, and living room—on the cooler north side of the house. They could have made more effective use of passive solar heating had these living spaces been located on the south side of the house. This situation has been improved with the recent addition of the solarium, which acts both as a thermal buffer and as a source of passive solar gain. The unusually shaped glass for the solarium was recycled from a newly constructed office building. When winds blew one of the windows out of the new building the contractor, for safety reasons, replaced them all. John purchased them for a fraction of their new cost.

The basic dimensions of the house are 28 x 40′. A quarter basement measuring 14 x 20′ and made of concrete blocks is located under the kitchen-bathroom utility area. The rest of the house is supported by concrete piles. John would use the stronger poured concrete in another basement, as the damp clay soil typical of Prince Edward Island is more subject to frost heaving than some other soils; there are hairline cracks along some of the seams between the concrete blocks.

Both post-and-beam as well as standard wood-frame construction techniques were employed, but nearly all the material used was either salvaged, milled on the site, or recycled. Most was obtained from a nearby barn and house, and from another house that the Ramseys were living in during the construction phase of their new home. John went into partnership with two others and bought a portable sawmill/planer, milled all his own lumber, and did some custom sawing for several neighbors and then sold his share of the sawmill at a slight profit. Although he saved a substantial amount of money this way, it was a great deal of hard work. If he were doing it again, John says, he would use lumber from his own woodlot instead.

The province has recenlty passed a dilapidated buildings act which, according to John, "effectively allows them to put the torch to any building that is left lying around neglected." This act has reduced the number of vacant buildings on the island. As well, the influx of newcomers interested in living a conserver life-style has created a demand for houses worthy of renovation. It is therefore now more difficult to salvage used building materials.

The first-floor 2 x 10 rough-sawn floor joists were Pentox-pressure-treated. Above the board subfloors there is a moistureproof-paper vapor barrier. Finish floors of either pine or hardwood were installed, depending on what materials were available. A 4" air-space exists between the bottom of the subfloor and the 4" fiberglass floor insulation.

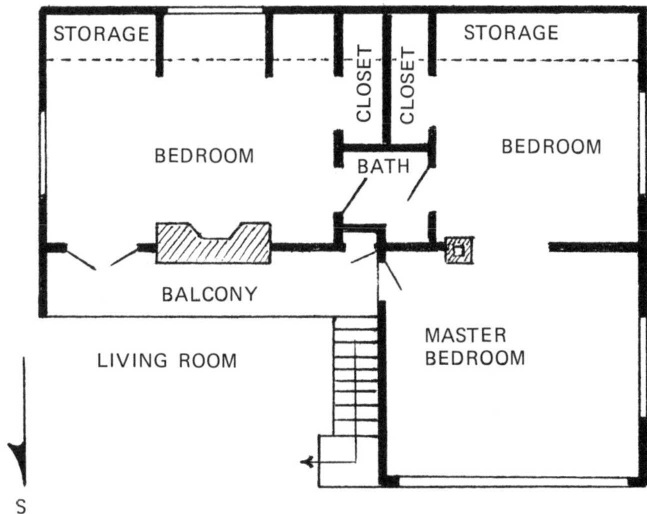

SECOND FLOOR

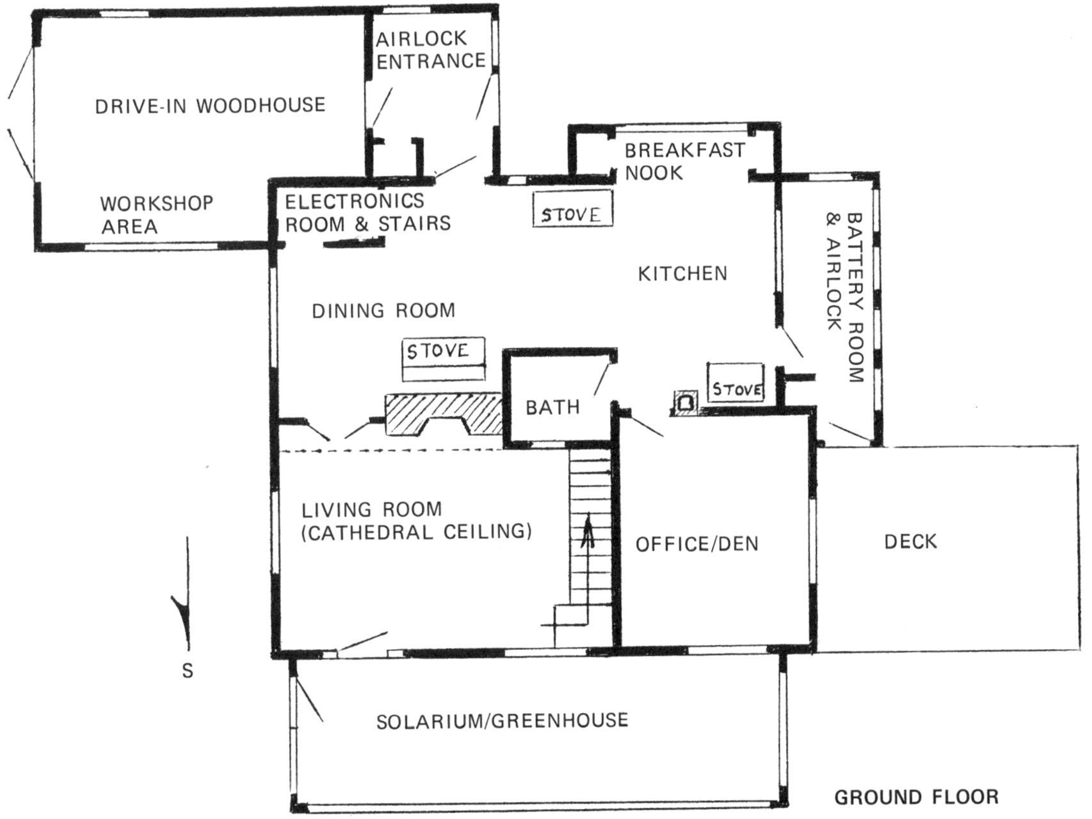

GROUND FLOOR

Exterior Walls

Full-size 2 x 4 studs which John milled himself are used for the exterior walls, although he says that he would use 2 x 6 studding for any future houses. The weather skin is salvaged rough-sawn spruce boards treated with a homemade water-repellent preservative made from a 10:1 solution of Penta concentrate (2 quarts); boiled linseed oil (1.75 quarts); paraffin wax (¼ to ½ pound) and fuel oil (4 gallons). Behind these boards is building paper and 4″ of fiberglass insulation and a polyethylene vapor barrier; and, in some cases, aluminum foil with the reflective surface facing inward. Where aluminum foil was stapled to the studs, 1″ furring strips were nailed horizontally to the studs to give the airspace required to make the foil effective. Wood boards of various dimensions and applied in various patterns finish the wall interior. Below the finished exterior walls, a skirting of Pentox-pressure-treated lumber was installed to further insulate the house from the winter cold.

Interior Walls and Ceilings

Interior walls are of standard 2 x 4 studwall construction. They are finished similarily to the interior of the outside walls. The first-floor ceiling has aluminum foil, an airspace, and a 1 x 4 board finish ceiling. Heat is thus reflected back down into the living space.

The second-floor ceiling is supported by 4 x 6 roof rafters sheathed with 1″-thick tongue-and-groove roof boards.

Roof

On top of the tongue-and-groove roof boards John secured 2 x 4s on edge horizontally across the length of the roof. The cavity between this strapping was then filled with 4 x 8′ sheets of beadboard layered with staggered seams to a depth of 4″. Tongue-and-groove boards milled on John's portable mill were laid perpendicular to the strapping and then covered with building paper and black asphalt shingles. The latter were chosen because of their low cost and because they blended aesthetically with the weathered gray siding.

Insulation Summary

Ceiling:	R-18; 4″ beadboard and 2″ wood
Walls:	R-16-17; 4″ fiberglass, wood inside and out
Crawl space:	R-19; 4″ fiberglass, 4″ airspace, and 3″ to 4″ wood

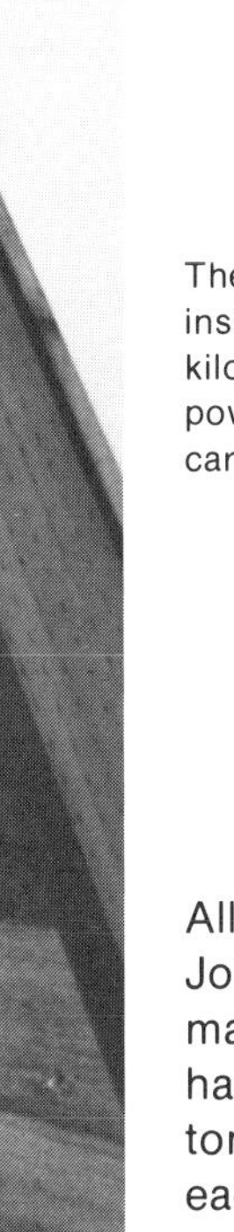

The new solarium addition will also function as a greenhouse once insulated curtains are installed. The garage/workshop, the 3-kilowatt Dunlite wind generator (which supplies the total electrical power needs for the home), and one of the Ramsey's recycled cars are in the background.

Doors

All of the doors were recycled from other buildings. John found an easy, inexpensive way of stripping the many layers of old paint off the doors without even having to remove the hardware. He took them to a tombstone maker, where they were sandblasted for $5 each. The house has three entrances. The one on the east end of the house with its exterior door facing south features a small, bright, unheated vestibule/airlock. It also serves as a storage space for the wind generator's batteries. The second entrance is through a smaller vestibule/airlock on the north side of the house. The doorway faces east, and the back of the vestibule is sheltered from the northwest winds by the garage. The icebox is located in this space. The third door is on the south wall entering the solarium from the parlor. An outside door on the solarium's west wall is also sheltered from the northwest by the woodhouse.

Windows

The numerous windows in the east vestibule are the small-pane, old-fashioned double-hung type. John salvaged them from the demolished houses. All the other windows in the house are thermopane insulated glass, for which John made his own frames. These windows were purchased from a manufacturer at half the retail price, as they had been custom-ordered by customers who neglected to take delivery. None of the windows has insulated curtains or shutters, although John and Donna are looking at the possibility of installing insulated curtains that open and close with small motors activated by a photovoltaic cell.

The Dunlite's 56 2-volt lead-acid storage batteries are located in the porch on the east side of the house.

The wood-burning stove, recycled building materials, and furniture shown here in the north-facing kitchen are typical of the materials used throughout this home.

HEATING SYSTEM

As mentioned before, the rooms on the south side of the house receive a substantial amount of passive solar heat. The south-oriented master bedroom has an Ashley wood stove but it is often only used two or three times in a winter because of the passive heat gain, plus that from a small hot-water radiator that is connected to a wood stove on the first floor. A south-roof overhang provides summer shade while permitting the entry of winter sun.

The main source of heat for the Ramseys' home is the decentralized wood-fueled space-heating system. Every room has its own wood space heater or cookstove, and each stove on the first floor is equipped with copper hot-water coils feeding a radiator in another room on the second floor. John and Donna plan to replace this system with a centralized wood-fired system, with oil or gas backup, but still using the existing hot-water radiators for heat distribution. The existing stoves are quite beautiful. At first they were inefficient, but this is no longer the case. "I made them airtight," says John, "by completely going over them and sealing all holes with stove cement. Even the deck lids are sealed except for over the firebox. For a five-dollar investment we are amazed at the increase of heat, and the long burning time of wood in the firebox. The draft also improved, which means vents can be kept closed, or nearly so, prolonging burning time and allowing all the heat to circulate around the oven and hot-water box before entering the flue."

At any one time, three different fires may be going, although most of the time only one or two is in use. Still, the house never drops below 45°F. even on a cloudy winter day when the Ramseys are both at work in Charlottestown. It usually takes about an hour to get the temperature up to 70°F. when they return home.

PERCENT SOLAR-HEATED

The winter of 1978-79 will be the first winter that the solarium has been operational. When the insulated curtains that are planned for the solarium are installed, it and direct solar gain to the second floor could account for as much as 40% of the house's heating needs.

COOLING SYSTEM

The south-roof overhang, superior insulation, the lawn, and the solarium with its summer venting all help to keep the house cool during the summer. In addition, ventilating slots, separate from the windows, were installed. On the north side of the house the screened vents with hinged wooden doors are close to the floor. Larger vents were placed high on the south side, thus creating good cross-ventilation from the cool north side to the warm south side of the house. In winter insulated panels are installed and the vents are sealed.

WATER SUPPLY AND WASTE SYSTEM

Water is obtained from a drilled well with a deep-well pump run by a DC motor run off the wind generator with a belt-driven system that John designed.

At the present time domestic hot water is heated by coils in one of the wood stoves, by a propane heater, by the Grumman Sunstream solar heater, and by the wind generator. When the generator produces more electricity than it can store, which occurs 30 to 60 days out of a year, the excess is used to heat water. Eventually a relay valve will be installed, so that heat produced from the wind generator and solar system which is in excess of that required for the domestic hot-water supply will be shunted into the space-heating system. The Ramseys' Flushomatic toilet uses 1 pint of water per flush. They had considered installing a Clivus Multrum composting toilet but concluded that the price was prohibitive and that they had no need for the compost, as they had plenty from other sources. A standard septic system and a dry well handle the waterborne waste.

Organic solid wastes are composted for the garden. As there is no tin-can or glass recycling facility on Prince Edward Island, John and Donna try to minimize the purchase of products using these containers. Pop bottles are returnable, but the manufacturers have now mostly switched to nonreturnable cans. John has the barn "half full of glass bottles. I won't throw them out but there is no place to put them. I was thinking of perhaps hiding them in the woods until glass becomes valuable." They are conscientious about returning egg cartons, paper bags, boxes, and other reusable containers to the stores and have been active in trying to get the government to adopt waste-recycling programs.

West and south aspect.

ELECTRICAL POWER SYSTEM

In 1971, the local electrical utility company wanted $3,700 to bring power to the building site. Instead, John and Donna opted to install a 110-volt Dunlite wind generator. The complete system, including the wind generator, 60′ tower, 56 2-volt lead-acid storage batteries, and automatic controls, cost $4,300. Today a similar setup would cost $8,500.

The 13′ diameter, 3,000-watt, 30-amp generator begins charging in an 8-mph wind and reaches its maximum output at 25 mph, at which point a governor prevents a further increase in speed and output. The 112-volt battery system has a capacity of 300 to 500 amp hours, the equivalent of about three weeks to a month storage reserve. The system supplies an average of about 400 kwh per month. During the summer this may drop as low as 300 kwh per month, while in the winter it may supply as much as 450-500 kwh.

The system is fully automated with the aid of transistorized control circuitry. Whenever the winds blow, it charges the batteries, and the house then takes its power directly from the batteries. The house is double-wired. All the brown electrical outlet covers are direct current (DC), whereas all the white ones are alternating current (AC). All the lights and nearly all the appliances are run off DC. An electronic, transistorized 250-watt sine wave inverter which is about 95% efficient converts DC into AC. Their small portable color television set and the stereo run off this system. A small, low-power square-wave converter is used for smaller, less sensitive AC appliances.

John had a gasoline generator as a backup for a year or so but he sold it as it was never required. "I calculated what my power consumption would be relative to my intake pretty accurately and as a result have almost a perfectly balanced system. The amount of volume stored never varies more than one week, so that under our present standard of living we would never run out of power."

MAJOR HOUSEHOLD APPLIANCES

John and Donna don't do without many of the conveniences of a typical modern household. They have the TV and stereo, power tools, a vacuum cleaner, mixers, toaster, blender, iron, and more.

Two of the most beautiful old wood cookstoves that I have ever seen still function as cookstoves, direct radiant heaters, and water heaters for hot-water radiators on the second floor. A more modern propane cookstove is used for summer cooking, although John is considering installing countertop propane burners, thereby eliminating an extra stove. One thing they like about propane appliances is that they are easily convertible to methane use, simply by changing the size of the gas jets.

The Ramseys had a kerosene refrigerator for a long time but became concerned about escalating fuel costs and the heavy demand of the refrigerator along with the problem of having an additional fuel to store and handle. They opted for a 110-volt AC-DC heat absorption refrigerator (no motor) which draws less than an amp when operating. It was made in Poland and imported into Canada mainly for the recreational-vehicle industry. For an induction motor such as that in a refrigerator or freezer, the starting load is three times the operating load. For example, a freezer running on 300 watts requires 900 watts to start it. Therefore one has to have a large capacity and thus a very expensive inverter. The only way to do it is to buy one of the old refrigerators that is belt-driven (not one of the new ones that is hermatically sealed), and convert it to DC, or convert an icebox to DC, or locate a heat-absorption cooling unit.

Donna and John wash some clothes by hand and others at a laundromat near work. They soon plan to purchase a low-power-consumption Hoovermatic washer. Clothes are dried at home on a clothesline.

FOOD SYSTEM

Most years an organic garden provides a beautiful harvest of fresh produce, but some years because of travel and work pressures the seeds have not been planted. John and Donna plan to build a cold-storage cellar, and once the insulated curtains are installed in the solarium they will begin to use it as a greenhouse. Membership in a Charlottetown food cooperative helps them to economize on food purchases.

Opposite: The cathedral-ceilinged parlor with stairs leading to the second-floor bedroom.

COSTS

The cost of the wind-generating system was discussed earlier. It is difficult to estimate the cost of the whole project, as the home slowly evolved over a period of five years; however, John feels that they didn't spend more than $15,000 for materials *including* the wind-generator system. This does not include the innumerable hours of labor that this ambitious couple poured into their home.

CONCLUDING THOUGHTS

This is one of the most beautiful and comfortable homes that we visited. It is a labor of love and a commitment to an environmentally appropriate, self-reliant way of life. But, John explains, "We couldn't expect the average person to move into a house like this. Everything works perfectly well but there are too many extraneous components, too many things going on at once, and everything is way overbuilt. The house is efficient, but it just evolved over a period of time and we built according to what materials we could scrounge. We certainly couldn't mass-market something like this. If we expect the average person to cope it has to be a standardized system while at the same time tailored to specific needs.

"I'm working on a design for a new house now that will have everything planned out to the last detail before we start. We will take more advantage of passive solar heating and use a solar-tempered heat pump with automatic climate control as the core of the system. It will be operated by energy produced from a wind generator and draw much of its heat from the solar system." John would like to use a water-to-water heat pump so that it can be efficiently integrated with his domestic hot-water and refigeration systems; however, he feels that water-to-water heat-pump technology is not very well developed yet. John and Donna are in no hurry—they can afford to wait. It doesn't cost much to run a wind generator, a solar system, or wood stoves when the wood comes from your own woodlot.

In the meantime, John and Donna will continue developing their business, Alternatech Associates Ltd. (Emyvale, P.E.I.), one of the leading Canadian renewable-energy companies. They presently distribute wind equipment and solar domestic hot-water heaters and offer a renewable-energy consulting service.

Before concluding this chapter on the Ramsey home it is worthwhile to mention some of the institutional barriers that John and Donna had to overcome. Initially they were not able to secure a mortgage because the lending institutions, always concerned about resale value, felt their plans were too "far out." The Ramseys therefore paid cash as they went along, which posed some difficulties. At one point John was working at three different occupations.

They also had difficulty securing fire insurance because their primary source of heat is wood. As well, they were initially bothered by the provincial electrical inspector because of their unorthodox design and power source. John informed the Department of Municipal Affairs that there was not much they could do to him as he planned to be independent of the utility company. As a result they stopped bothering him.

Many of the early pioneers in renewable-energy use ran into similar problems. However, as more and more people become interested in using the sun, the wind, and wood to power and heat their homes, the institutional barriers are becoming fewer.

Right: The classic wood-burning cookstove, antique furniture, and natural building materials provide warmth.

Below: Carryover from direct passive solar gain through these south-facing windows and a hot-water radiator connected to the cookstove in the kitchen mean that the Ashley wood stove in the master bedroom rarely has to be used.

Experimental Manor

NORMAN B. and JEANNE SAUNDERS

Norman Saunders is a professional engineer, inventor, designer, and builder who specializes in solar technology and circuit engineering. He has applied these to the control of solar and air-conditioning systems. He regularly conducts related seminars and classes for architects, builders, and others interested in these fields. He is the author of *Solar Heating Basics* and numerous papers, and serves as director of the Massachusetts Bay Chapter of the New England Solar Energy Association and chairman of its Solar Economics Committee. He has been responsible for the design and installation of solar systems in a number of different buildings, as well as conducting experiments on an ongoing basis for the past 18 years on his own passively heated home, which we describe in this chapter. The house with its present solar system has been performing excellently, but Norman feels this type of house should not be built again. In the course of his experiments, he says, he has made many mistakes (as have many inventors) and is anxious to have these mistakes, as well as his successes, broadcast for the benefit of others.

LOCATION AND ORIENTATION

Experimental Manor, as Norman named his home, is located at 15 Ellis Road, Weston, Massachusetts—43° 22′49″ N. Lat. The house is located on the north end of a 2¾-acre plot of land with a meadow in the middle and specimen food-bearing trees along the edges. The house sits in a frost pocket with a large hill about 20 yards from the house. The building is shaded by the hill and trees until 8:30 sun time in the winter and 10:00 a.m. in the spring and fall. It is oriented due south.

ARCHITECTURAL FEATURES

Experimental Manor is a two-story, 2,625-sq.-ft. house. Its long axis, running north-south, measures 46′, and its short axis measures 32′. As the foundation had to be constructed below the frostline, Norman decided to excavate to a depth of 4′ and use the earth to backfill up to the house to a level just below the windowsills on the north. The east, west, and north walls therefore are partially buried. A sand bed was laid within the perimeter formed by the poured-concrete footings and exterior walls, and then a grid of concrete blocks was laid on their sides to form 19 major air channels and a larger number of minor ones. This grid, which was

Weston, Massachusetts
2,625 sq. ft. living area
including balcony

designed to encompass the major solar-heat-storage reservoir, was then topped with inexpensive metal sheeting and a 6″ poured-concrete slab. This also serves as the floor for the first story. The floor of the second story would have been poured concrete, except for the architect's objections.

The room layout is designed to work with nature. The kitchen, dining room, and living room are open concept to facilitate air circulation and the effects of radiation from the massive building components. The kitchen is located on the east side of the house, so it is warmed by direct solar gain from the morning sun. The dining/living area, located on the south side of the house, is similarly heated by direct solar gain. Bedrooms are located on both floors on the cooler north end of the house. Norman's office is located on the north end and the workshop on the south end of the first floor.

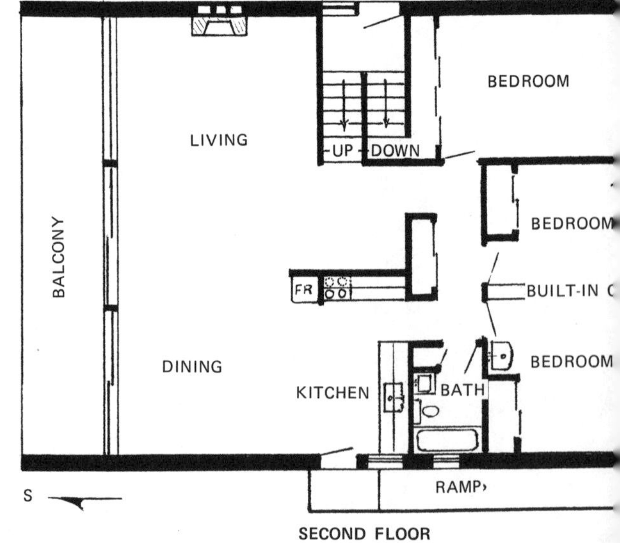

SECOND FLOOR

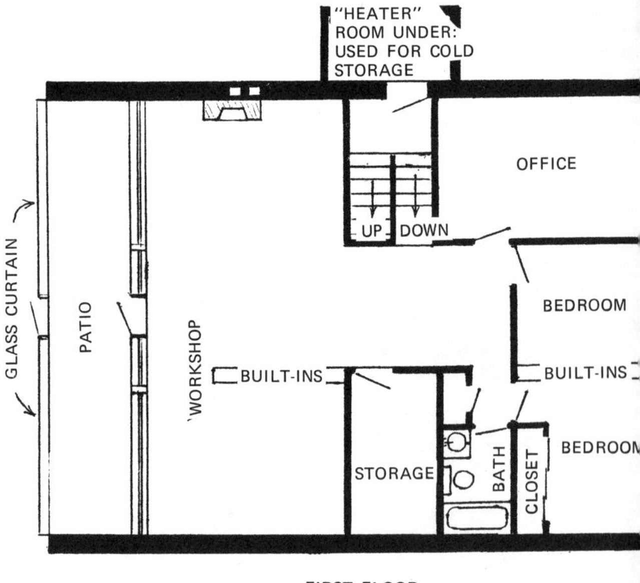

FIRST FLOOR

Exterior Walls

The east and west walls were built of 12″-thick pumice aggregate concrete block, for its heat-storage capability, insulating qualities, appearance, and ease of maintenance. The east and west walls extend 1′ beyond the north and 6′ beyond the south wall. The roof overhang and floors create a balcony and patio area between the south-wing extensions. The block cavities of all extensions were supposed to be filled with poured concrete, and cavities adjacent to the house interior were supposed to be filled with exploded mica insulation. The insulation was meant to be continuous, but it is not, as the contractor evidently poured concrete where he felt there should be concrete. Steel ties were not used in the walls in order to minimize thermal short-circuiting. These walls, whose exterior surfaces were left unfinished, are equivalent in insulation value to a 4″ studwall with fiberglass. Norman advises anyone building today not to use pumice but rather a 2 x 6 studwall insulated with 6″ of fiberglass or a solid block wall, which would have a greater heat-storage capacity than pumice, with insulation on the outside. For outside insulation, he recommends either 2″ of foam or 4″ of fiberglass or cellulose.

"The pumice makes a beautiful, dull inside surface and I like it very much this way," says Jeanne, "but it was hard to get the plasterers, painters, and other people who worked on the house to leave it alone."

The south walls are largely glass with the exception of the lower 18″ (½ meter), which allow for some privacy and furniture display. A glass curtain wall was recently added extending from the bottom of the balcony's south edge to the patio. The north walls are also extensively glazed for the very desirable light that north windows afford and also because, based on the data available in 1959, when construction on Experimental Manor began, the heating-season loss after solar gains were taken into account was calculated to be less than the heat loss through a 2 x 4 studwall with full fiberglass insulation. The exterior vertical siding on the north wall is cypress—one of the best siding materials because it is naturally resistant to rot and termites and because it requires no finish. As in this case, it weathers to a silver gray.

Interior Walls and Ceilings

Interior partitions are standard 2 x 4 studwalls. They were finished with 18 tons of plaster, which add to the thermal and heat-storage capability of the house. Al-

Earth is bermed up to just below the lower-level windows on the north side of the house.

most all are plastered only on one side with storage built into the other side.

Roof

The roof has a slight slope of 3° downward to the north. There are 19 layers of various materials, some of which were applied to cover roof-surface damage caused during rooftop collector experiments by collector mounts. The insulating value is calculated to be equivalent to about 13″ of insulation, or R-45.

Insulation Summary

Foundation:	None other than the insulating value of the earth. Norman recommends, however, that one use 2″ of foam under-slab construction and up to 8″ of foam with an under-slab heat store
Walls:	R-19; pumice block and exploded mica fill
Ceiling:	R-45; various materials

Doors

The west entry, which is closest to the driveway on the northwest corner of the lot, has a doorway opening to a landing midway between floors. Short flights of stairs lead to the first and second floors. The east entry is direct to the kitchen. A long gently sloping hung wooden ramp was installed in anticipation of old age. A third entry is located in the lower south window wall. Norman says, "The doors themselves are nothing special regarding their insulation value, but they are well sealed with metal tongue-and-groove weatherstripping."

Windows

The east and west glazing is about normal or small, relative to the north and south window area, to restrict excessive summer heat gain. Even then, the effects of the sun entering these windows were quite dramatic when the house was first built. In the morning, especially in the spring and fall, the bathroom, kitchen, and dining room were flooded with light and warmth. In the afternoon the heat from the low sun was often insufferable. With the growth of vegetation near the building the conditions are less extreme.

On the north wall there are identical windows on the lower and upper stories composed of large fixed windows and 19 metal casement windows. There are a total of 38 sash windows on the house. These large fixed single-glazed windows here and everywhere except on the upstairs south windows were fitted with a second pane 4 centimeters from the first, resulting in 20% less heat loss than commercial double glazing would have permitted. Half of this difference is due to the larger spacing between panes and half to the fact that wooden spacers are used rather than a continuous metal frame. When the house was initially built the architect could not be persuaded to use wood frames throughout because he feared that the glass could not be made to adhere to the wood. As a result the casement windows are still single-glazed. The resulting condensation has led to severe rotting of the wood windowsill in the northwest corner. The south wall has a total of about 400 sq. ft. of glazing on two floors composed of six panels per floor each measuring 5 x 6½′ high, plus the glass curtain in front of the first-floor patio. Both the fixed windows and the casement windows of the south window wall are commercial thermopane insulating glass in metal frames. The glass for the glass curtain is composed of numerous panes of 24 x 16 x 1/16″ glass salvaged from one of the experimental rooftop collectors. Milium-coated curtains were used at north windows. After monitoring, Norman calculated that the heat-loss reduction in the upper south windows was about 10 kwh over a winter night, or about 10¢ a night per curtain pulled.

SOLAR-HEATING SYSTEM

Over the years Norman has experimented with a dozen different types of collectors on Experimental Manor. The present passive system, as described here, is the most successful. He will not install another rooftop collector and risk further roof damange until such time as he is absolutely convinced that it is better than the present system.

Collector

The south-facing glazing of this direct-gain passive system provides the majority of the solar heat. The upper-floor glazing has a gross area of 28.4m^2 (305 sq. ft.) and a net area of 19.5 m^2 (210 sq. ft.) when framing is considered. The lower-floor glazing gross area is 25.5m^2 (274 sq. ft.), but the net area is only about 10.7m^2 (115 sq. ft.). The shadows from the balcony railing, roof overhang, balcony, and wall extensions further reduce the net areas at different times of the day and year. The addition of the glass curtain significantly improved collector performance. The curtain is composed of columns of single-glazed sheets (each 0.4m x 0.6m) in a 2 x 4 frame extending downward from the edge of the balcony at an angle of 80° from the horizontal. The net area of this curtain is 94% of the gross area, which means that a greater proportion of the sunlight striking the glazing enters the interior space than for the upstairs window wall.

Heat is transferred to the downstairs living spaces simply by opening the interior door or the operable windows in the downstairs window wall and turning on a fan to pull the cold air from under the slab out through the heater room (original furnace room now used to store garden produce). Norman states that this collector works excellently; however, there are some disadvantages to the collector design. The main one is the roof overhang. In December, the sun strikes nearly all of the upper collector; however, the shadow from the overhang increases as the angle of the sun increases from the horizontal after the winter solstice. Between April 11 and September 1, the only direct sunlight entering the house is from the east, west, and north windows. Conventional wisdom at the time his house was built recommended an overhang of this size. Another disadvantage of his system is that the glass is not as good for solar-radiation transmission as it should have been. The contractor tried to help by putting in heat-absorbing glass. The following figures compare the design data to Norman's observed data: absorption, 5% vs. 5% observed for visible light but 30% for sunpower; reflection, 18% vs. 20% observed; masking (mullions and muntins), 10% vs. 30% observed. On a cold winter day the outside of the glass is sometimes warmer than the inside of the room. Another problem that Norman has observed is that a line of 10′-high trees, 50′ to the south, blocks 20% of the diffuse insolation and much of the remainder strikes the glass at such an acute angle as to be deflected away.

Storage

The concrete slab and foundation walls that were intended as the major solar-heat store have been of little use because of the large heat loss to the earth. The soil loss is much greater than anticipated. Water from surface drainage and the hill 20 meters to the east, despite attempts to stop it, still moves under the house close enough to the footings to bleed off nearly all the heat blown to the storage.

The pumice walls, masonry portion of the second-story floor, and the 18 tons of plaster effectively store heat; however, in order to do this the Saunderses allow the room temperature to rise to 25° C. (77° F.) when Mrs. Saunders is out. During a winter day when only Norman is home the interior temperature often rises to 30° C. (86° F.). These temperatures are not as uncomfortable as one would think, as at 25° C. a fan is turned on to move air to the north side of the house. The air movement tends to make one feel about 5° C. cooler. The practical amount of storage is a full day at the beginning and end of the heating season and a half-day in midwinter.

Heat Distribution

The lower floor is heated by direct radiation through the south-facing glazing and by natural convection of heated air from behind the glass curtain. When heat is stored in the lower slab, the "stack effect" draws heat up the stairwell to the second floor. Upstairs, in the morning, the sun comes in the east window and warms the bathroom, kitchen, and west wall of the living room. As the sun swings around to the south, sunlight shines directly into the dining and living rooms and heats up the masonry floor. Some is reflected onto the mantel and ceiling. In the afternoon and early evening, sun shines in the west window, striking the massive building components on the east side of the house. At night, as the living spaces cool, the massive elements re-radiate the stored heat into the rooms. When needed, any of four 20″-diameter fans and duct systems may be brought into play, manually, to increase general room air circulation, move hot air to the cooler north end of the house, or, if temperatures become excessive, to dump hot air into the under-slab storage. The north rooms of the lower floor, which are bermed to the windowsill, are heated year-round in order to keep the relative humidity down and thus minimize mold problems.

AUXILIARY HEATING

The major source of nonsolar heat is from electrical resistance wires imbedded in the plaster ceilings. Norman chose electric heat because it permitted easy evaluation of the amount of auxiliary heat used. A separate furnace room designed to accommodate an oil furnace was designed into the building to satisfy the building inspector; however, the Saunderses use it to store fruit and vegetables. The space could be used to house an air-to-air heat pump in the future.

A west-wall masonry fireplace was installed on each floor—one serving the dining/living area and the other serving the south office/workroom. Norman conducted experiments on the lower-floor fireplace, which is similar in design to the upper-floor one, and discovered that it comfortably burned 15 kilograms of dry wood per hour, producing an 80-kilowatt fuel rate. However, 90 kilowatts escaped up the chimney because of the preheating of the air used for combustion and the excessive fireplace draft. The fireplace masons installed flue dampers that only operate in the fully open or fully closed position.

PERCENT SOLAR-HEATED

During the heating season, the mean inside temperature for a 12-year period was 22° C. (72° F.) ±° C., while the mean outside temperature was 7° C. (45° F.) ±1° C. The means and uncertainties (expressed as standard deviations) for the heat inputs and outflows during this same 12-year period are listed below.

Heat input		Heat outflow	
People	0.3 kw±0.1	Roof	0.3 kw±0.1
Lights and cooking	1.0 kw±0.3	Earth	1.0 kw±0.1
Water heating	1.7 kw±0.2	Ventilation	1.5 kw±0.5
Sun	3.0 kw±1.0	Glazing	3.8 kw±1.4
Electrical heat	3.3 kw±1.2	Pumice blocks	1.4 kw±0.4
		Wood wall panels	0.5 kw±0.1
		Miscellaneous (sewage & unaccounted-for losses)	0.8 kw±0.5
Total	9.3 kw±1.6	Total	9.3 kw±1.6

About half of the electrical heat input was used to operate electrical devices needed to carry out research. Norman emphasizes that the above figures are for the "heating season"; however, his house needs some heat (solar) practically every week in the summer as well. Norman says, "At night it would get cool enough in the summer to be uncomfortable if we didn't have the solar heat from the day stored in the house. The thermal masses in the building prevent it from getting too hot during the day as well as giving it the necessary heat in the evening." Considering the whole year, the percentage of solar heat during the 12-year period was 55%; but since the 1974-75 heating season, when the glass curtain was first installed, the sun has consistently supplied 65% of the heating needs. Mean inside and outside temperatures have remained about the same.

When asked about how comfortable the house is, Jeanne replied, "I can't remember being uncomfortably cold more than once or twice, and I can't remember being uncomfortably hot in the summer more than three times."

COOLING SYSTEM

The Saunders home gets two-thirds of its heat from the sun, but since this is accomplished by letting the inside temperatures sometimes get up into the 80s in winter in order to effectively store the heat, the large 20″-diameter fans are needed to create the air movement which allows one to feel cool at these higher-than-normal room temperatures. Overheating is not a problem in summer because of the roof insulation and thermal mass helped by the large roof overhang and wall extensions on the south and the deciduous trees protecting the east and west windows. If necessary, cool air from beneath the floor slab can be circulated to the rooms.

A ramp was built for the east entrance in anticipation of old age. Deciduous trees and shrubs protect the east windows from the hot morning sun in summer.

Massive pumice-block walls, masonry floors, and plastered partition walls and ceilings store passive-solar-heat gain and help to modulate temperature swings.

Norman B. Saunders, engineer, inventor, designer, builder, and solar pioneer.

WATER SUPPLY AND WASTE SYSTEM

As water supplied from the town mains is metered, the Saunderses try to conserve it. During the first ten years since Experimental Manor was built, water consumption averaged 283m^3 (about 75,560 gallons) per year. Tapwater had to be used for the flower and vegetable gardens and the lawn as most of the 30-odd inches of rain that this area of Massachusetts receives falls during the wrong time of year. In the 11th and 12th years consumption of city water dropped to 206 m^3 as a pump was installed to continually pump groundwater from under and around the house to keep the water table at an acceptable level. In 1973, a new perimeter drainage system was installed which obviated the need for continual pumping. Groundwater is now intermittently pumped to maintain an economic balance between heat conservation, energy use (i.e., for pump operation), and plant growth. Plants benefit from the nutrients in the groundwater that are leached out of the soil.

Domestic hot water is supplied by an 80-gallon electric water heater. The points of hot-water use are about 40′ from the tank so that heat radiated from the tanks and copper delivery pipes warms the house. "At the time of building a special low rate was available. I made the most of it."

Blackwater and graywater run into a septic tank and a leaching field composed of over 100 m^3 (130 cu. yds.) of rock. Solid wastes such as paper, metal, and glass are sorted and delivered to a recycling center. A 4 x 4 x 8′-high concrete-block compost stack emptied yearly takes care of organic wastes suitable for garden use.

ELECTRICAL POWER SYSTEM

Electric power is supplied by Boston Edison. Norman had considered a wind generator and other power alternatives, but their use made no sense for his locale. Natural lighting, which Norman describes as the best and most practical use for the sun, is supplemented with fluorescent lights and some incandescents.

MAJOR HOUSEHOLD APPLIANCES

Norman and Jeanne state that they bought their appliances before there was general awareness or concern about the amount of power that appliances consume. In fact, there are no figures for power consumption in their appliance pamphlets. Jeanne occasionally schedules the baking of bread in her pre-Korean War electric stove for when she thinks it is going to add to the comfort of the house. They have no freezer. An automatic dryer is seldom used as Jeanne chooses to dry clothes on racks on the balcony.

FOOD SYSTEM

A 200 m^2 (2,160-sq.-ft.) garden provides all of the Saunderses' vegetable needs for six months and half of their needs for another three months. In addition, they have six varieties of apple trees as well as pear, peach, cherry, quince, plum, black walnut, filbert, chestnut, and hickory.

They preserve little of the garden produce, preferring instead to grow it in such a way as to meet day-by-day needs. Hay cut from the meadow is added as mulch in the summer and then dug in in the spring.

COSTS

Of the original construction of Experimental Manor, 90% was done by a general contractor, 6% was later contracted out, and some of their four children and Norman did the rest. The house was built to a modification of a stock plan from which houses had been built a half-dozen times before. Norman states that Experimental Manor cost less to build than the conventional version. Changes to enhance solar heating were primarily changes in building materials and methods rather than additions. The total costs of change were therefore small and were outweighed by the saving in the installation of the electric-resistance heating in place of a furnace and distribution system.

Subsequent costs for solar modifications were kept low, as labor was inexpensive. For the first ten years of solar changes, 10% of the work was contracted out while the Saunderses' son Laurence did about 40% and Norman did 50%. The present changes (solar curtain) were accomplished with Norman contributing half the labor and his students the other half. As mentioned, the glazing was recovered from recycled rooftop collectors.

CONCLUDING THOUGHTS

Jeanne is most enthusiastic about describing the fun and excitement of living in Experimental Manor. She says, "It was even really exciting listening to the funny little clicking that went on all the time—the clicking of the stepping switch as it brought temperatures down to the chart recorder in the basement. It has been just a joy living in this house!"

The experience gained from Experimental Manor and other experiments has led Norman to believe that 100% solar-heated houses are economically feasible in Massachusetts. His continuing goal is to design buildings that are 100% solar-heated and whose first costs are no more than that of conventionally heated buildings. Norman thinks that he will achieve this goal in the very near future.

HOUSE **19**

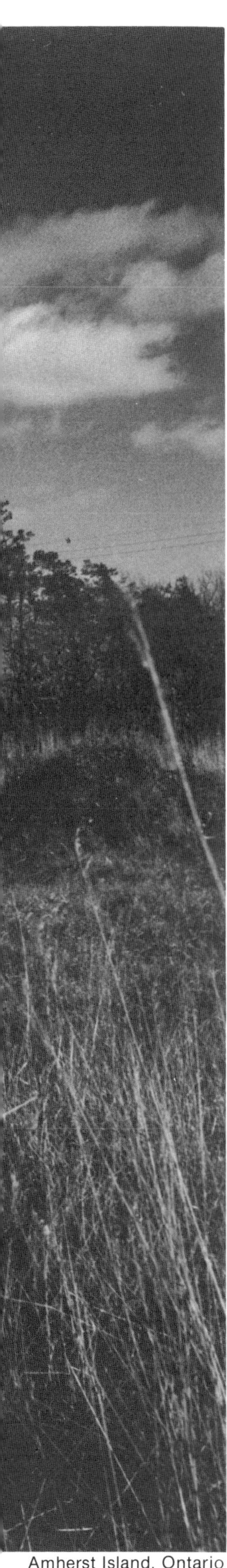

Amherst Island, Ontario
1,445 sq. ft. living area

Prospect House

DEBORAH, LOUISE, and LORNA SEAMAN

In 1976 Lorna Seaman and her young daughter Deborah were part of a farm community of young back-to-the-landers on the north shore of Amherst Island, Ontario. Lorna and her mother, Louise, who was living alone 1,000 miles to the east, decided that rather than living so far apart and running two separate establishments, they would pool their resources and build a house together. Lorna states, "The reason for choosing solar was not that I had become an avid conservationist and then decided to build a solar-heated house—rather it was the other way around." She was introduced to a young architect and builder named Greg Allen, who had already built a couple of solar-heated houses and was keen to build another. Greg introduced her to the idea of building an ecological home—one designed to minimize its impact on the environment and to use the sun as its primary source of heat. Lorna and Louise had only $25,000 for the construction, but Greg estimated that he could build it for this amount. The sod was turned that summer, and work began on Prospect House, one of this country's most innovative experiments in residential building.

LOCATION AND ORIENTATION

Lorna wanted to retain a close association with the farm, which is on Amherst Island, near Kingston, Ontario. So they had a lot severed off one of the pastures with road frontage next door to the farm. It has been a real advantage for this female family having the men next door. A friendly cooperative relationship involving barter of labor exists between them. For example, Lorna helps the farm with haying during the summer, while the men gather her wood and do odd jobs for her in the winter. Also Lorna buys meat, honey, and other produce from the farm.

Their 1½-acre lot is located on a part of Amherst Island from which they can look north across a relatively narrow stretch of Lake Ontario to the mainland and from which they can look across pasture to the south and across the "Gap" (water) between Amherst Island and Prince Edward County. The proximity to these two bodies of water results in very pleasant summer breezes.

The house itself faces due south and is built into land sloping gently southward, so that the north side of the house is buried about 3′ into the insulating earth. Parking was designed on the crest of the hill on the north side of the house so that winds would keep this space clear of snow.

At this 7,500-degree-day location, where winter winds can be severe, the swamp surrounded by trees to the northwest of the house, as Greg anticipated, has proved to be an excellent weather barrier. Greg's design called for conifers to the north and west as an additional windbreak, but these have not been planted yet. This fall the women are concentrating on putting in honeysuckle, lilac, and other flowering shrubs to soften the lines of the house and complement its colors. Also, a large-leafed hardy deciduous tree—probably a Norway maple—will be planted to the south of the house to provide shade in summer, yet allow the sun to warm the house in winter.

ARCHITECTURAL FEATURES

There were many criteria which dictated the design of the house. It had to be an energy-efficient, low-cost, low-environmental-impact structure which met the needs of the three generations of women who were to occupy it.

Most of the south face of this 1,445-sq.-ft. one-and-a-half-story three-bedroom house was designed to integrate with the slab floor, massive central fireplace, and the mechanical systems to provide most of the heating needs. I'll describe how this works later.

The house is relatively small for three bedrooms, yet it feels very spacious. On the first floor the open-concept living areas are on the warm south side of the house and integrated with a large greenhouse area. The fact that the living room is split by the fireplace yet semi-open on either side makes the use of the space more flexible. Louise has her own private space by the hearth outside her east-wing bedroom/studio, yet when they are having a party the downstairs living area can be used as a single large space. Because Louise is the eldest, her bedroom was built on the first floor. She has a private entrance to the bath on the north and one to a patio area on the south.

The kitchen on the northwest corner of the house is well organized and compact. It is small but is open to the dining room. The kitchen is buffered on the north by a pantry and by a wood-storage area. The wood

Built into a gentle south-sloping hill, Prospect House presents a low profile to the cold north winds. The woodshed, on the right side, and the carport act as thermal buffers.

storage is convenient to the wood cookstove and the fireplace, and it has a hatch for loading from the outside.

The small double-entrance vestibule, stairwell, pump room, and bathroom, all on the north side of the house, plus the carport and woodshed to the north of it, provide additional buffering. Debbie's and Lorna's bedrooms on the second floor are separated by the fireplace. Each has a balcony looking out the south-sloping glazing and down into the greenhouse. Aesthetically this design feature is marvelous, but noise was a problem at times. Heavy curtains made of upholstery felt have been installed; they can be pulled across the complete south side of each bedroom to reduce noise levels and to provide additional insulation during winter nights. Carpeting over the plywood floors further reduces noise levels and makes the rooms feel cozier. Deep closets on the north side of each bedroom are an effective insulation barrier.

In terms of floor-plan organization, space utilization, and sense of space, the design worked very well. Lorna, Louise, and Debbie are delighted with it. Lorna says, "People who come into the house voice almost unanimous pleasure about the aesthetics of the main room. Greg has created a beautiful house, and there is something about the way he has designed it that is conducive to conversation, conviviality, and restfulness."

Exterior Walls

The west wall of the kitchen, east wall of the bathroom, and north wall are constructed of concrete block to a height of 4′; above that, 2 x 6 studwall construction is used. There are 4″ of rigid polyurethane insulation secured to the outside of the concrete block.

Post-and-beam construction, using totally salvaged barn timbers, was adopted for the east and west walls of the remainder of the house. The spaces between posts and beams were filled with 18″ aged, dry, well-packed hay bales, stacked like bricks. Interior and exterior surfaces of the hay-bale walls have 1″ to 1½″ of concrete, then stucco troweled on, a rather good fire barrier. These walls have an R-value of about 35 and have proved to be very satisfactory. Local authorities and the building inspector did not approve of this and some of the other unorthodox construction, but having been assured by an engineer and the National Research Council that the design was acceptable, Greg carried on anyway. He says, "I think when they finally saw it assembled they didn't think it was a bad idea after all."

Exterior walls on the second level are also of 2 x 6 studwall construction. Some of the stud cavities were insulated with 6″ fiberglass batts, while others were insulated with a polyester fiber, normally used for sleeping bags and clothing, that was recycled waste from a local mill on the mainland.

Lorna states that the experiment with this polyester fiber has been unsuccessful because the fiber has either settled in the wall or its R-value is so low as to be ineffective. Last winter the west wall of her bedroom where the fiber was used was extremely cold. Greg is of the opinion that its R-value should be about the same as fiberglass and that it should not deteriorate if it is not exposed to sunlight. However, the gypsum wallboard will soon be removed to examine the insulation and determine the reason for its failure. Barnboard, salvaged locally, is used for vertical exterior siding.

Interior Walls and Ceilings

The few interior walls were built using standard 2 x 4 studwall construction. They and the ceilings of the second floor were sheathed with ½″ gypsum board. The ceiling of the first floor was covered with rough-sawn oak boards that Greg purchased very inexpensively and then planed.

Roof

Lorna wanted to use cedar shingles on the roof but they were too expensive. A tin roof was chosen for its proven durability, and when labor is taken into account, it is the least expensive. The tin was nailed directly onto the laterally running 2 x 6 roof joists, thus saving on sheathing or strapping. The roof insulation therefore is directly below the tin.

Insulation Summary

Slab:	R-18; 4″ of polyurethane foamboard placed vertically around slab perimeter to a depth of 8′ or to bedrock (which was not always at 8′)
Walls, concrete block:	R-18; 4″ of polyurethane foamboard
Walls, east & west, first floor:	R-35; 18″ of hay bale
Walls, east & west, second floor:	R-20; 6″ polyester fiber
Ceiling (also forms north wall of upper bedroom):	R-20; 6″ fiberglass, some polyester fiber

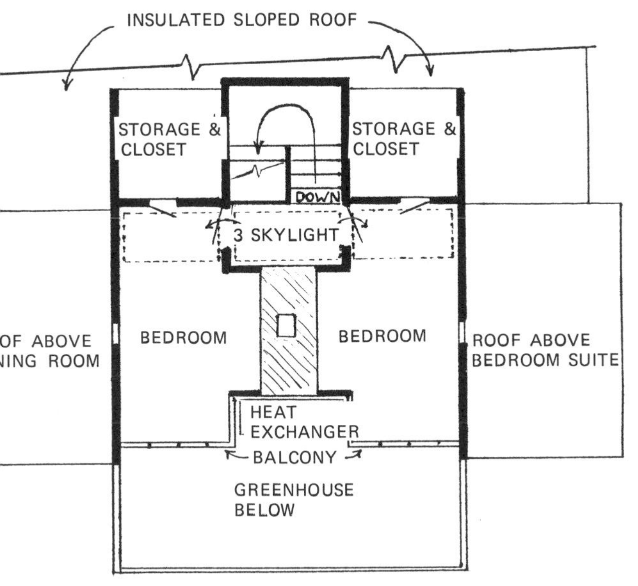

SECOND FLOOR

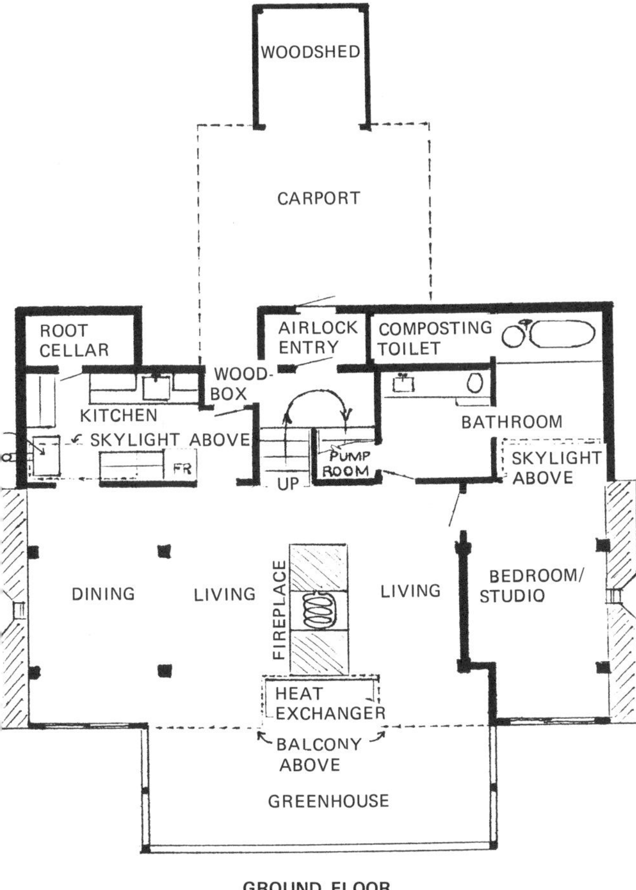

GROUND FLOOR

Looking east from the dining area to the massive central fireplace and the greenhouse. Note the use of recycled barn beams and ceiling boards.

Doors

The double entrance on the north side of the house is protected by the carport. It has a heavy site-built exterior door with barnboard on the outside and oak on the inside, between which are two airspaces separated by aluminum foil. It has an R-value of about 8.

The interior door of this small airlock entrance is a glass French door. Both doors are well weatherstripped.

In summer the exterior door is replaced with a screen door which permits good cross-ventilation.

Aluminum-frame thermopane patio doors were installed on the south side of the dining room and Louise's bedroom. Wood-frame or metal doors with a thermal break would have been preferable, but these were obtained through barter.

Windows

The large expanse of south glazing through which most of the passive solar gain is received is sloped at 45°. The exterior glazing is tempered glass separated from the interior glazing by a 5″ airspace. Some of the interior glazing is Plexiglas (acrylic) and some is Mylar. These materials were chosen because Greg got a bargain on them. He would have preferred double-glazed glass. Greg says, "The acrylic is not a very nice material to work with as it had to be bowed in order to give it sufficient structural rigidity. The dimensional accuracy required for that and the provision for expansion and contraction was a bit of a nightmare. In addition, if there is any stress concentration anywhere in the sheet it will start fracturing. For these reasons we switched to Mylar." The Mylar has stood up very well.

Although it does degrade under ultraviolet light, it will last a lot longer under glass; Greg thinks about 15 years.

Greg states that he would minimize the use of sloped glazing in future designs. For sloped surfaces, installation of glazing and curtain or shutters is much more difficult than for vertical surfaces. No effective economical overhang can be constructed for a sloped surface. As well, Greg estimates that there may be a 10% improvement in R-value of vertical glazing over sloped glazing. In the latter, convection currents in the airspace between glazing are more turbulent. In the airspace between vertical glazings the convective currents are more laminar so there is less heat transfer.

Another advantage of vertical glazing is that it absorbs more reflective radiation off snow than sloped glazing.

The sloped glazing has a full curtain of inexpensive white cotton muslin with ½-mil heavily aluminized Mylar secured to the side of the muslin facing the glazing. Rather than puncturing the Mylar by sewing, two other methods of attachment were used: spray-on urethane glue and iron-on tape. With the curtains closed running parallel to the slope of the glazing, Greg calculates that combined R-value is about 7.5.

Lorna reports that this curtain has stood up very well and has proved most successful as an insulating curtain.

I was concerned about the cost of having these curtains commercially cleaned or the difficulty in cleaning them oneself, but Lorna assured me this was no problem. She and a friend simply took them out on the snow in the middle of winter and brushed both the Mylar and cotton, using snow as the cleaning agent. "It did a beautiful job," says Lorna.

No thermopane windows are used in the house. All are double-glazed site-built units. By perfectly sealing the inner glazing with silicone and providing vent drain holes through the sill between the glazings, most of the condensation problem has been eliminated at a fraction of the cost of thermopane units.

All glazing is fixed, mostly for cost reasons, except for the patio doors and two vents at the top of the south-sloping glazing.

There is only one window on the north side of the house—an 18 x 15″ window placed at standing eye level in the kitchen, which gives a subtle but spectacular view of Lake Ontario.

One very narrow, tall window was placed on the west wall of the dining room and another in Lorna's bedroom. Similar windows are on the east walls of Debbie's room and Louise's room. Hay bales were cut back at an angle of 45° from the windows to give a wider angle of vision. These small windows minimize excess summer heat gain from the east and west.

Left: Detail of the greenhouse. Cotton muslin and aluminized Mylar curtains can be closed to reduce heat loss or prevent excessive heat gain through the south-sloped glazing.

The skylight in Lorna's bedroom.

A south-facing clerestory brings light and warmth into the kitchen at the north side of the house. An aluminized Mylar-covered urethane foamboard shutter with an R-value of 8 to 10 pivots on a center pin. When it is open, sunlight is reflected downward into the work space; when it is closed, it insulates the clerestory. An identical clerestory serves the bathroom.

"I wouldn't use the urethane foamboard again," stated Greg, "as it is not dimensionally stable if it heats up—it warps. I would look at another foam or a light fiberglass-filled panel."

Other clerestories bring light into the north side of the bedrooms, but Lorna has found that this extra fenestration was not necessary, as enough light enters the sloped glazing and the endwall windows.

SOLAR-HEATING SYSTEM

Prospect House was designed basically as a passively heated house. The system was meant to collect solar energy through the large amounts of south-facing glazing and store it in the massive building components—the gypsum board, block walls, fireplace, and slab floor. The slab floor was poured and allowed to cure and settle for several months and then a second pouring was done with ½" copper pipe installed 1" below the surface. The runs are serpentine shape, mostly east and west, 6" on center around the perimeter, and 12" on center in the middle of the floor. The idea was that if the floors got uncomfortably warm a pump would send cold water from a 2,000-imperial-gallon (2,400 U.S. gallons) storage reservoir located beneath the stairwell landing through the slab to absorb the excess heat and store it in the tank, from where the heated water could be recirculated through the slab at night to warm it if necessary.

There is perimeter insulation, as mentioned previously, but no insulation under the slab, as the intent was to use the earth as a thermal reservoir. Greg's calculations indicated that as long as you don't have water running through the soil, 6' to 8' of heat transferrred through soil is equivalent to 8" of good insulation.

Greg and Lorna are quick to point out that the dark-brown-painted slab floor has still not been proved effective. Because of furnishings and low winter sun angles the slab does not heat up appreciably. It is not yet known how well it will function as a radiant-heat source with water from the tank heated by alternate means.

Last winter (1977-78) the slab radiant heating system did not operate at all as the custom-seamed vinyl liner for the reinforced-concrete storage tank was not installed. The winter of 1978-79 will be the first real test of the system.

While the slab did not heat up appreciably, the air within the house did and tended to stratify on the second level. Greg stated that in the initial design he had really only considered getting rid of this heat in the summer and hadn't appreciated how great a problem it could be in winter. The solution he came up with in 1978 was to install an air-to-water heat exchanger to extract heat from this air and use it to heat storage-tank water.

The 2 x 8' heat exchanger was salvaged from a rooftop air conditioner. It is mounted on a 45° angle against the south side of the 4'-wide chimney and extends 2' on either side of it. It is enclosed with a chimneylike structure which extends to the peak of the greenhouse. A couple of standard Simpson Sears fans mounted below the heat exchanger pull hot air from the top of the structure down through the exchanger and send that air, which is cooled somewhat, into the room below. At the same time water from the 2,000-gallon storage tank is pumped through the heat exchanger's complex network of copper piping and then back to the tank. Lorna reports that warm air flowing down to the heat exchanger is 90° to 100° F. on any sunny day winter or summer. All during the summer of 1978, water coming out of the storage tank was 50° to 60° F. With the heat exchanger operational they were able to get the tank water temperature up to 77° F. and maintain it at that level.

A salvaged cast-iron radiator in the bottom of the fireplace served as a log grate and as another heat exchanger. It was very successfully dumping heat into the storage tank during the winter of 1977-78, until it developed a leak. This winter, a heat-exchange grille probably made of steel or copper will be installed over the flames, as it was found that the ashes formed an insulating barrier above the cast-iron heat exchanger.

Heat Distribution

The passive system has already been described. The pump room under the stairs houses four low-hp pumps. One is for the domestic water supply, one is for the floor radiant heating system, one is for the air-to-water heat exchanger, and the last is for the fireplace heat exchanger. Lorna reports that they are very economical to run.

Heat, which tends to stratify on the second floor, is pulled down through an air-to-water heat exchanger on the south side of the chimney. Note the two horizontal fans in the middle of the picture.

AUXILIARY HEATING

The central fireplace, in addition to helping to charge the water storage tank with heat, serves as a primary source of radiant heat. It was built of 22 tons of local beach stone. The firebox is open on both the west and east sides, and each opening has tempered-glass doors that Greg installed for $50 versus $150-300 for commercial units. Outside air from the south side of the house is ducted to the firebox. A manual control on the side of the fireplace opens and closes a damper on the outside edge of the floor slab.

The only other source of auxiliary heat in Prospect House is from a Fawcett combination oil/wood cooking range. Lorna says, "It took a little skill learning how to maintain the proper combination of draft and fuel to get the maximum amount of heat, but we have found that it is a good source of radiant heat for the cooler northwest corner of the house. We love having this radiant heat and the whole surface to cook on. If I were doing it all over again I think I might try to use wood entirely and get away from using oil altogether."

The kitchen is small, compact, and well organized. The doorway leads to the pantry/cold-storage room. A Fawcett combination wood/oil cookstove also functions as a space heater. Note the skylight above with its insulated shutter.

PERCENT SOLAR-HEATED

One cannot yet say what percent of the house's heat needs will be supplied by the solar system. "This winter will tell the tale,"says Lorna. "We have been pumping water through the floor just to make sure there are no leaks, but we are still not sure what is going to happen to the heat we are going to pump in during the cold winter. What we are hoping is that between the heat exchanger on sunny days and the fireplace on cloudy days we'll be able to keep the storage temperature up to about ninety-five degrees and send that through the floor slab. Although it probably won't give us a hot floor, we won't have the awful cold we had last winter. We are optimistic that this, in combination with radiant heat from the sun, fireplace, and cookstove, and the improvements in insulation that we are going to make, will result in a warmer home than last winter with less fuel consumption."

COOLING SYSTEM

With the exterior north door replaced with the screen door in summer, the sliding glass doors open, and the two vents at the top of the greenhouse open, the house gets very good cross-ventilation. Offshore breezes across the land help this process. On hot summer days with the curtain closed to prevent overheating, air is convected upward in a chimney effect between the glazing and the curtain to the open vent windows, thus increasing the ventilation.

Lorna reports, "Downstairs the house remains delightfully cool all summer long. During *very* hot summer days it is not feasible to stay in the upstairs, but I don't consider this a problem because who wants to stay in an upstairs bedroom, in the country, in the middle of a hot summer day? I have never been unable to sleep in my bedroom at night because it was too hot, because, even after the hottest of days with the vents open and the breezes, the upstairs cools down to a very comfortable seventy to seventy-five degrees."

The fans from the heat exchanger can be used to stir the air up to make it feel cooler. During an extremely hot spell, water from the storage tank could be pumped out to the garden and replaced with cold lake water. In the process of heating this fresh water the house would be kept cool. By using the tank as part of the air-conditioning system in summer, the water temperature in the tank can be maintained at such a level that it can be easily charged up in the winter.

WATER SUPPLY AND WASTE SYSTEM

Domestic water is pumped underground from Lake Ontario. The women boil their drinking water, as do many islanders, but Lorna admits that they are worried about the chemicals in the water that are not destroyed by boiling. For this reason they are looking into water distillers, including solar stills.

Domestic hot water is temporarily supplied by a 40-imperial-gallon (48 U.S. gallons) electrically heated hot-water tank. A friend of the family is working on a design for a solar/wood domestic hot-water system. They might put a heat-exchange coil in the firebox of a Fawcett cookstove and have the heated water thermosiphon to a tank in Lorna's bedroom closet, which is located above the stove. Since the upper-bedroom skylight is somewhat redundant, they are very excited about the possibility of using the space to accommodate solar collector panels for domestic hot water or for additional space heating.

Greg and his crew built the sink/bathtub out of ferrocement. They simply dug a hole in the ground to the shape they wanted, stamped in the chicken wire, and troweled on the cement. It was designed to permit complete immersion with only a low volume of water. The user sits in the tub and can use armrests on either side. It has worked very well. One set of drain connectors and one faucet serve both the tub and sink. A recycled second sink is located next to the composting toilet.

One of the many innovative experiments that Greg attempted on Prospect House was a graywater recycling system. Three filter tanks—one filled with charcoal, one with sand, and one with plants (largely cattails)—were built under the glazing in front of the greenhouse. The system worked for about a week and then started degrading. The space was designed to be easily converted into additional greenhouse space, which was recently done.

The composting toilet was site-built to the commercial Clivus Multrum composting toilet dimensions, using concrete blocks waterproofed on the inside with an asphaltlike plastic sealer. Pentox-treated plywood and irrigation pipe were used for the interior components. Lorna says it works well and they are very happy with it, but it does take a lot of attention. Usually the addition of peat moss is adequate, but when her nose indicates that special treatment is required, the balance is restored by the addition of a combination of wood ash, kitchen compost, and greenhouse earth.

Garbage is separated at home, and most is reused or recycled. Kitchen compost goes on the garden or into the toilet. Waste paper is used for kindling for the stove or fireplace. Very little garbage goes to the dump.

ELECTRICAL POWER SYSTEM

Prospect House has 100-amp service with power supplied by Ontario Hydro. Lorna would like to have a wind generator some time in the future but right now the costs are prohibitive.

Emphasis was placed on day lighting for every room in the house. Greg chose not to install fluorescent lighting, as he finds the frequency irritating to his eyes and points out that incandescent lights are not as inefficient as some people presume, as it can be a significant supplement to the heating load. In Prospect House, lights are used mostly in the winter when the house is demanding heat anyway.

MAJOR HOUSEHOLD APPLIANCES

In the summer when the Fawcett combination oil/wood cookstove is not being used, the women generally use an electric frying pan and a single-burner electric hotplate. They have a small, portable electric oven and an electric deep-well cooker, but these are seldom used. These smaller appliances are generally more energy-efficient than larger cookstoves and ovens.

"Our one big expender of energy is our refrigerator," says Lorna. "Since I'm working and mother is doing most of the housekeeping, she wanted to have a nice refrigerator. It was chosen strictly for convenience and is the one inconsistency in the house." They have no freezer, but there is a walk-in cold-storage pantry conveniently located on the same level as and to the north of the kitchen. As well as storing produce, it acts as a thermal buffer for the kitchen. Root crops can be stored there fall, winter, and spring, but during the summer, although it is well insulated down to 4′ (it has access to the cooler soil temperature below that) and insulated from the kitchen, there is enough of a summer heat gain to render it ineffective for root-crop storage. This is not too important as Lorna, Louise, and Debbie usually eat fresh produce during that period anyway.

An efficient space-conserving apartment-size Bendix washer/spin dryer is used in the bathroom for washing clothes. The balconies double as solar clothes dryers.

FOOD SYSTEM

As Lorna is a nutritionist, she is especially concerned about the quality of food that she, Louise, and Debbie consume. By being associated with the farm next door and producing a large amount of fresh vegetables themselves, they are assured of a good supply of high-quality foods.

The inner wall has been removed between the greenhouse and what was the graywater treatment area. A row of flatbeds running the whole width of the southern edge of the enlarged greenhouse is planted to winter vegetables—swiss chard, lettuce, radishes, and tomatoes.

Other plants will be started early in the spring to transplant into the fairly large outside garden.

COSTS

As mentioned previously, the contract to Greg Allen was for $25,000. He estimates that about 70% of this amount was for materials and subcontract work such as excavation. He stated that considering all the labor involved, $35,000 would have been a more reasonable contract amount.

So far, Lorna and Louise have spent an additional $5,000 for such things as the heat exchanger, kitchen cupboards, landscaping, and other work above and beyond the contract or from which she had released Greg from responsibility.

By the time all their plans for the house are realized they estimate that they will probably spend another $5,000—still a very reasonable total cost when compared to other dwellings, dwellings that in most cases are built with little regard for the environment.

CONCLUDING THOUGHTS

"I was very much concerned about the human element of changing our life-styles," says Lorna, "but Greg designed the house so well that it has made it easy for the three of us to live together. We each have our privacy, and the open space is such a good open space. Mother has made the transition from a very traditional life-style in terms of housing and everything else very nicely. She is very happy and now very much interested in the whole environmental movement."

Lorna states that since they love the house so much and believe so strongly in what they are doing, they have been able to tolerate the technical problems and are prepared to invest time and money to solve them. She points out that pioneers should be prepared to encounter all sorts of problems, to accept the failure of certain experiments, to readapt, and in some cases make major financial sacrifices. When one believes as strongly as these women do in a certain way of life, often a problem comes to be viewed not so much as a problem, but rather as a new opportunity.

Since Prospect House, Greg Allen has designed several other passive solar houses, and with Amherst Renewable Energies Ltd., of which he was a partner until recently, he designed collectors and solar systems for a number of projects, including the Bata Shoe Factory in Picton, Ontario; a domestic hot-water installation in a Toronto high school; a fish hatchery in Manitoba; the Rideau Falls Renewable Energy Demonstration Building in Ottawa; and the Ontario Science Center Solar Demonstration Building. He has also done a number of energy-conservation reports for various firms, including Dominion Stores.

Recently Greg teamed up with two other innovative designer/builders—Oliver Drerup and Elizabeth White—to form the firm of Allen, Drerup and White. They are located at 334 King Street East (Room 505), Toronto, Ontario.

Louise relaxes by playing the piano in the living area to the east of the fireplace.

HOUSE **20**

Stoverstown, Pennsylvania
1,450 sq. ft. living area

Sonnewald Homestead

TIM and GRACE LEFEVER

Tim Lefever was one of the original establishment dropouts. He earned a bachelors degree in electrical engineering from Penn State in 1940 and then went to MIT for a year, ending up at the Westinghouse Research Laboratory. The laboratory started to do war work, so Tim quit. He was subsequently sent to prison as a conscientious objector.

Previous to and during prison he was inspired by the writing of Dr. Ralph Borsodi about self-sufficient living and decentralist patterns of life. Tim later established his 60-acre homestead, where five Lefever children were raised. He named it Sonnewald, from the Pennsylvania Dutch for "sunny woods." Presently, Tim, his wife, Grace, and his son Dan run the nearly self-sufficient organic farm with the assistance of various people for various amounts of time—people who come to Sonnewald to learn about modern homesteading.

The Lefevers operate a health-food store at the farm, from which they sell much of their own produce. They also sell environmentally appropriate hardware such as wood stoves, wood furnaces, and flue heat exchangers, and they plan to sell solar collectors.

Tim does plumbing and related work in the local area as well. The Lefevers run an annual homesteading seminar at Sonnewald, participate in many natural-food and alternate-energy fairs, and now among many other things are very much involved in the Community Land Trust and other methods, mainly tax reform, that aim to implement the principles of Henry George to ensure equal rights of all individuals to the land. (Land under trust is land that is unlikely to revert to the speculative market, especially if the trust's charter explicitly forbids its sale.)

LOCATION AND ORIENTATION

The 60-acre Sonnewald Homestead is located at the southwest end of Stoverstown, an unincorporated village in York County, Pennsylvania. The house is generally exposed to the winds, but a deciduous woods to the northwest in a shallow ravine gives some protection. Its long axis runs east and west. On the north side the floor is at ground level; on the south side the floor averages about 2′ above grade.

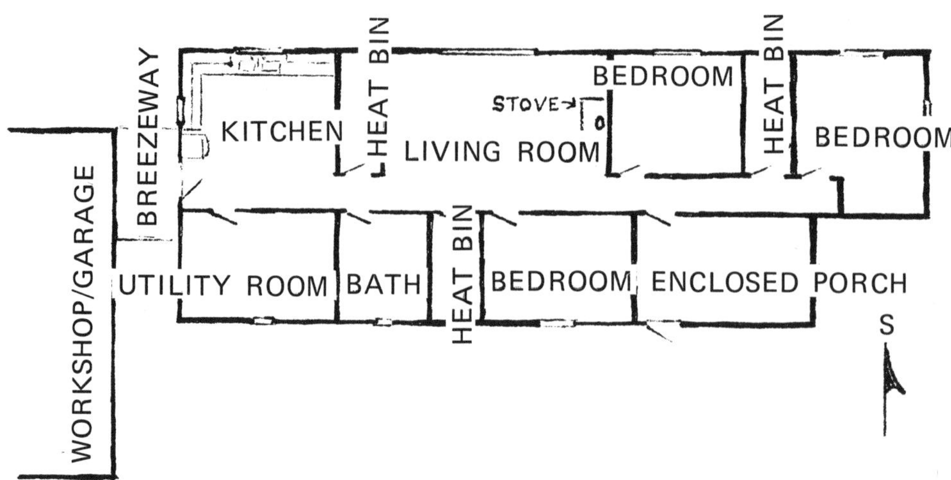

ARCHITECTURAL FEATURES

The Lefever house, built over a period of about four years and completed in 1958, is much the same design and to some extent a copy of the Dover, Massachusetts, solar-heated house built by Telkes, Raymond and Peabody in 1949. The east-west axis is much longer than the north-south axis. The south wall of the shed-roof structure is much higher than the north wall, thus minimizing wall area on the cold side of the house (though this feature is not too important in this case as little of the north side of the house is heated). An uninsulated enclosed porch on the northwest corner of the house insulates it from the winter north and northwest winds. Similarly, the large unheated workshop/garage adjoining the east side of the house and extending to the north of it provides a good thermal buffer for that side of the house.

The first story of this three-bedroom home measures 65 x 23′ average depth and has an area of approximately 1,450 sq. ft. It has a slab-on-grade foundation and no basement. The floor consists of about 2′ of quarry waste, 2″ of sand, one covering of lapped second-quality tarred roofing, 4″ of Zonelite insulating concrete, 3″ finish concrete, and "resilient" floor covering. Asphalt-coated 2″ fiberglass boards (the type used for refrigerated-room insulation) were installed completely around the inside perimeter of the foundation wall. The half-story unheated attic supports the collector and serves as storage space. The large country-style kitchen/dining area is on the southeast side of the house in order to catch the morning sun. The living room and two bedrooms are also on the warm south side of the house, and the unheated utility room, one bedroom, the bath, and the enclosed porch are on the colder north side of the house. The three large closets separating the various living areas were originally designed for solar storage. This will be discussed later.

Exterior Walls

The exterior walls were constructed of 8″ cinderblock to the ceiling level and of 2 x 4 studs to block-wall height. The concrete-block outer surface was simply painted white, and the studwall was rock-lathed and plastered. The vertical south face of the attic level supports the solar collectors. An accordion-type expanding aluminum-foil insulation was originally installed in the 3⅝″ stud space. In November 1976, Rapco ureaformaldehyde foam insulation was installed, compressing the foil. Tim says they are extremely well satisfied with the new insulation.

Interior Walls and Ceilings

All interior partition walls are of standard 2 x 4 studwall construction and rock lath and plaster or Weltex textured plywood. The 2 x 8 ceiling joists are similarly sheathed with rock lath and plaster. The ceiling was insulated more than 20 years ago with the same aluminum-foil insulation as the walls. Years later, 4″ of fiberglass batts were added, but Tim feels that several more inches should still be added. This squashed down the foil configuration.

Roof

The low-cost, low-maintenance shed roof is constructed with 2 x 6 rafters on 16″ centers covered with sheathing, building paper, and the original shingles. The 325-pounds-to-the-square asphalt shingles with asbestos fibers were the only shingles on the market at that time that had a class A fire rating. (A new class A fire shingle with glass fibers is now on the market.) Their life expectancy is up to 40 years but Tim feels theirs may last somewhat longer because the roof has no southern exposure. Tim tried to get white shingles to help reduce summer heat buildup in the attic, but as they were unavailable he settled for brown. There is a small roof overhang all around the perimeter of the house, which protects the building materials from the elements. The large overhang to the south protects the collectors in summer. The shop and garage overhangs provide protected areas for working outside during inclement weather and for storing things more or less out of the rain.

Insulation Summary

Foundation perimeter:	R-8; 2″ asphalted fiberglass boards
Exterior walls:	R-16; 3⅝″ Rapco foam plus original aluminum foil (accordion-type but now compressed)
Attic:	R-20; 4″ fiberglass batts over original accordion-type aluminum foil

Doors

The entranceway most often used is on the east of the house through an unheated porch area which joins the workshop/garage to the house. The doorway leading into the kitchen from the porch is therefore well protected; however, Tim feels the heat loss is substantial through it, as the door is opened and closed many times a day because of the large number of visitors and the high level of activity at Sonnewald. The other entranceway is through a second unheated porch on the northwest corner of the house.

Windows

Aluminum-frame windows with aluminum storm windows are used throughout the house. Pressure-treated cypress window frames (bucks) provide a thermal break between the two window frames and thus reduce conduction losses and eliminate condensation problems on the interior aluminum frame. The majority of the window area is on the south side of the building. The 80-sq.-ft. south-facing windows are shaded by an 18″-wide horizontal visor that is sized almost perfectly for keeping out the hot summer sun while allowing the winter sun to penetrate. The ratio of visor width (horizontal distance) to the distance from the bottom of the visor to the bottom of the window glass (vertical distance) is 1:3 or slightly more.

There is only one window on the east side of the house and only one on the west in order to minimize both summer heat gain and heat losses during the cold season. There are three small windows on the north face of the house—one for each of the rooms on that side.

Ordinary white window roller blinds are used on the south windows to reduce unwanted heat gain *and* heat loss in winter. Tim says, "For spring and fall the blinds should have been designed to pull from the bottom up and not from the top down, as during really hot days in these seasons we were getting sun in the bottom quarter of the window." Drapes were also installed in the living room about five years ago. Shutters of 2″ beadboard with protective duct tape around the edges were made for all the east, west, and north windows. Those for the north windows stay in place day and night all winter. Those in the east and west windows can be removed and reinserted for passive heat gain in winter and heat rejection in summer. The shutter on the west window is hinged at the top and has a magnetic cabinet catch at the bottom to hold it against the ceiling. At a cost of 15¢ per board foot they are very cost-effective shutters. The polystyrene, although a poor conductor of heat, still allows a fair amount of light penetration. "For the east and west windows," Tim points out, "we could have some outside vertical louvers or some deciduous shade trees, but the present use of the window 'plugs,' as we call them, is quite satisfactory. They require manual manipulation, of course."

SOLAR-HEATING SYSTEM

A significant amount of passive solar gain is realized through the south-wall glazing, but the main part of the heating need is supplied by the site-built, owner-built, active air-type solar system. Tim gives the following explanation for choosing an air system: "The advantage of air over water for the heat transfer medium is that you can keep the collector temperature so much lower and bounce heat directly into the room. At seventy-five degrees collector temperature you can get usable heat. It takes about ninety-five degrees with water. It is also much cheaper, much less likely to give trouble, and can be installed by any handyman."

Collector

The 520-sq.-ft. (450-sq.-ft. net) vertical collector array measuring 8 x 65′ is located just under the roof overhang on the south side of the house. The glazing is composed of 15 double-glazed 4 x 8′ panels of 7/32″ glass. Partly out of concern for their neighbors, an

Tim Lefever demonstrates a model of a typical solar panel showing the wood-frame construction and the double glazing.

industrial-grade glass with a matte finish was used in order to diffuse reflected light and thus reduce glare. This type of glass was also less expensive than clear flat glass and the transmission is about the same—about 85% to 95%. Radiation passing through the glass strikes a flat steel absorber plate that was sprayed with a rust-resistant primer and then a non-selective flat black paint. The air in contact with the back surface of the absorber plate is then heated. "I never thought," says Tim, "of putting fins on the back of the absorber when we built the collector. It could reduce the collector temperature, and of course the more you reduce the collector temperature the more heat you are getting out." The static airspaces between the two glazings and the inner glazing and the absorber help to insulate the collector. There is a dynamic airspace between the back of the absorber plate and ⅜" plasterboard (drywall). The back of the plasterboard is insulated with 1" fiberglass ductboard to minimize collector heat losses to the attic. Hot-air manifolds and ducts are insulated in the attic space but not in the living space.

Storage

At present there is no heat storage other than the general thermal capacity of the house. Three 4'-wide ceiling-height storage bins—one between each two rooms—were intended to house heat-storage material such as the eutectic salts that Dr. Maria Telkes experimented with and for a time utilized in the Dover House in Dover, Massachusetts. Telkes, one of the early solar pioneers, and architect Eleanor Raymond completed Dover House in 1948. It was designed to supply 100% solar heating using eutectic salts as the storage medium; however, the salt deteriorated and the house was only fully solar-heated for one winter. It was later converted to standard heating. As the problems with the deterioration of these salts in storage have never been fully resolved to Tim's satisfaction, a storage medium was never installed. He is thinking of one day putting in a number of 1-gallon plastic water jugs or some other system of partial storage such as concrete blocks.

Heat Distribution

The collector array is divided into three sections, with five of the 15 panels connected via ducts to each of the three storage bins. One squirrel-cage 1/6-hp blower, and one 20"-diameter 800-rpm fan, and one 16"-diameter 1,000-rpm fan circulate air up through the collector and back to the storage bins. Each of the bins has hot-air vents near the top of the bin and cold-air returns near the bottom, corresponding to the adjacent rooms to which the warm air circulates. The door on the bin between the living room and the kitchen is usually left open when the system is operational in order to provide additional circulation. The damper for the hot-air collector is closed at night manually to prevent reverse thermosiphoning from the kitchen/living room, which has auxiliary heating from wood and/or LP gas.

The north side of the house is largely unheated, has few windows, and presents a low profile to the cold winter winds. The garage/workshop is on the left-hand side.

A 300′ coil of 1″-diameter black butylene provides solar-heated domestic hot water in summer.

AUXILIARY HEATING

A propane upflow warm-air furnace is turned on early in the morning just to take the chill out of the air until the wood fire is burning well or the sun starts to warm the house. A medium-sized (approximately 50,000 Btu) airtight wood-burning stove, located in front of an interior chimney which forms part of the wall between the west living room and the middle bedroom, warms the living area very quickly. It is an efficient stove and takes minimal attention.

PERCENT SOLAR-HEATED

No sophisticated monitoring devices have been installed in the Lefever home but Tim calculates that about 50% of their space-heating needs are supplied by the solar system—40% from the active system and 10% from direct solar gain through the windows. He estimates that wood supplies another 40% of the heating needs. They burn one and a half cords of wood a year, which is mostly mixed top wood and waste from the woodlot and wood boxes and other wastes from the business. LP gas supplies about 5%, while the remainder is supplied by lights, cooking, appliances, electric blankets, and people.

A substantial portion of the success of their system can be attributed to the Lefever life-style. If they wanted to maintain a constant 70° F. temperature over the whole house 24 hours a day, the solar contribution would probably drop to about one-third of the total heat supplied. Instead, they allow the temperature of the house to fluctuate. They usually allow the nighttime temperature to drop as low as 50° F. if need be. They then use electric blankets on the beds—a very efficient way to heat. During a sunny winter day, the house tends to overheat somewhat, but rather than exhausting this hot air to the outside, they allow the house to continue to heat, thus giving it a greater carryover capacity into the evening. The Lefevers simply wear lighter clothing. Similarly, during cloudy winter days when the solar system provides considerably less heat, they don warmer clothing. When it gets too cool the auxiliary heaters are activated.

COOLING SYSTEM

Summer cooling is not a problem in the Lefever home. The roof overhang shades the collector, while the horizontal visor shades the south windows. The insulation, window "plugs," storage shed, and garage/workshop provide additional barriers to unwanted solar-heat gain. Good cross-ventilation can be achieved by opening windows on the cool north side and warm south side of the house.

WATER SUPPLY AND WASTE SYSTEM

A drilled well on the property provides potable water. A propane heater serves as the primary source of domestic hot water; however, a 300′ pancake roll of 1″-diameter black butylene pipe lying flat on the shop roof is used as a preheater during the summer. Without any glazing on it, water temperature sometimes reaches 120° F. The coil is left in place all winter after much of the water is drained. The black butylene is approximately the same price as polyethylene; however, the latter is not nearly as strong at high temperatures. The National Sanitation Foundation classes the butylene as satisfactory for piping drinking water.

The septic-type waste system is used to dispose of blackwater and graywater. A Clivus Multrum composting toilet is being installed in the new warehouse as part of the Sonnewald educational programs and as advertising for sale of the toilet. Human waste, grass clippings, weeds, and garden wastes will be composted here.

ELECTRICAL POWER SYSTEM

Sonnewald gets its power from the local utility grid, but it is not absolutely dependent on it for survival. The various backup systems, and the fact that the Lefevers could in a short period of time become totally self-sufficient, gives them the security that one could never get in a totally electric urban dwelling.

The house is designed to require only natural lighting during daylight hours, and the Lefevers tend to be frugal about electricity use at any time. Some fluorescent fixtures have been installed. The ones used for any great percentage of the time are Vita-Lites, which have the full sunlight spectrum.

MAJOR HOUSEHOLD APPLIANCES

The Lefevers eat mostly raw foods, so the cookstove is not used very much. Their refrigerator is not frost-free, and the chest-type freezer is more efficient than the upright alternative. There is nothing particularly energy-conserving about their automatic washer or dryer except that the latter is used only about 15 times per year. A clothesline is used the rest of the time.

FOOD SYSTEM

Sonnewald is not self-sufficient in food production but is close to it. According to Tim, "We could make the jump very easily in an emergency situation. We're pretty close to vegetarians, so that makes it relatively easy as we don't have to worry about any animals except chickens. We sell most of the eggs when the chickens are laying, as people come a long way for eggs when chickens are running out on the green. We have been raising grains such as wheat, oats, triticale, buckwheat, and soy beans and we now grow more grains than we need for ourselves. We have a dozen beehives, and the buckwheat helps the bees winter over a little better as there are not many wildflowers around in the fall. We have a large organic garden—much of the produce is sold from the health-food store built at the south end of the shop—and have built a sunken greenhouse in front of the store which will be going through its first winter in 1978-79. Much of the compost for the garden and the fields comes from leaves that I have been getting from the city every fall for at least the last ten years. Fruits are harder to raise than vegetables, but Dan has become an expert on organic fruit growing." While we were visiting the Lefevers, Dan demonstrated an old hand-operated cider press that he had purchased and subsequently refurbished. The cider running from the good old press was absolutely delicious. Dan has also been making some maple syrup and now has two years' experience making sorghum syrup.

Three cold-storage pits for farm produce are located under various farm buildings. All of the entrances to the pits are from inside the buildings, so there is no problem with snow clearance.

COSTS

Since the Lefevers did most of the work themselves and the structure is fairly simple and modest in size, the cost was quite reasonable when it was built. Tim estimates that a comparable solar system today would cost in the neighborhood of $3,000 plus labor.

CONCLUDING THOUGHTS

Tim, Grace, and Dan are proud of their accomplishments but are always striving to improve in any possible way. Tim feels there is not much one could do to improve the house except perhaps to lean the glazing back 20° to 30° to optimize solar gain in winter and to use more insulation.

My family and I had the joy of feasting on some of the fruits of the Lefevers' labor at a luncheon brilliantly orchestrated by Grace with the assistance of three young women who were apprenticing at the homestead. We ate, supped, and talked with them, Tim, Dan, and Mildred Loomis. Mildred, along with Ralph Borsodi, was one of the original founders of the decentralist movement in the U.S. She ran the School of Living for many years and founded *The Green Revolution*, a magazine devoted to the decentralist theme. It was an incomparable banquet.

HOUSE **21**

Lincoln, Massachusetts
2,500 sq. ft. living area
including shop

RANULF W. and ANNETTE GRAS

In the 1950s, Annette and Ranulf W. Gras devoted a considerable amount of time and effort to visiting "international communities" throughout the United States in order to better equip themselves to participate in the development of a planned community within commuting distance of MIT in Boston, where Ranny taught and conducted research. They had already gathered a number of families interested in joining them in developing such a community.

The end result was that the founding group of some 20 families, most of whom are still with the community today, purchased a large block of land in Lincoln, Massachusetts, and designed and developed their whole community, including roads, utility corridors, and building sites. A later project preserved 50 adjoining acres, including a large recreation pond where the families could skate in winter and boat, swim, and fish in summer. Each family was responsible for building its own home, but all were bound by agreed-upon regulations that were designed to minimize any detrimental environmental impact. Ann and Ranny appropriately decided to construct a solar-heated home—one of the first to be built in the country. Ranny designed the structure and subcontracted the construction out, although he helped the builders with a considerable amount of the physical work. The Gras family moved in in 1956.

LOCATION AND ORIENTATION

The Gras house is located on Laurel Drive in Lincoln, Massachusetts. It sits on the southeast brow of a steep hill overlooking beautiful woodland and the community pond below.

The house was designed and built to accommodate the site. The two-story south side of the house drops down the hill, and the single-story north side presents a low profile to the north and west winds. Due to the cut of the hill or cliff the house was oriented 3° east of south rather than due south. The lot and surrounding area is heavily wooded with deciduous trees. Some trees were cleared from in front of the south-facing vertical collector area to avoid too much winter shading. Enough deciduous trees remain to provide summer shade for the collector array and windows.

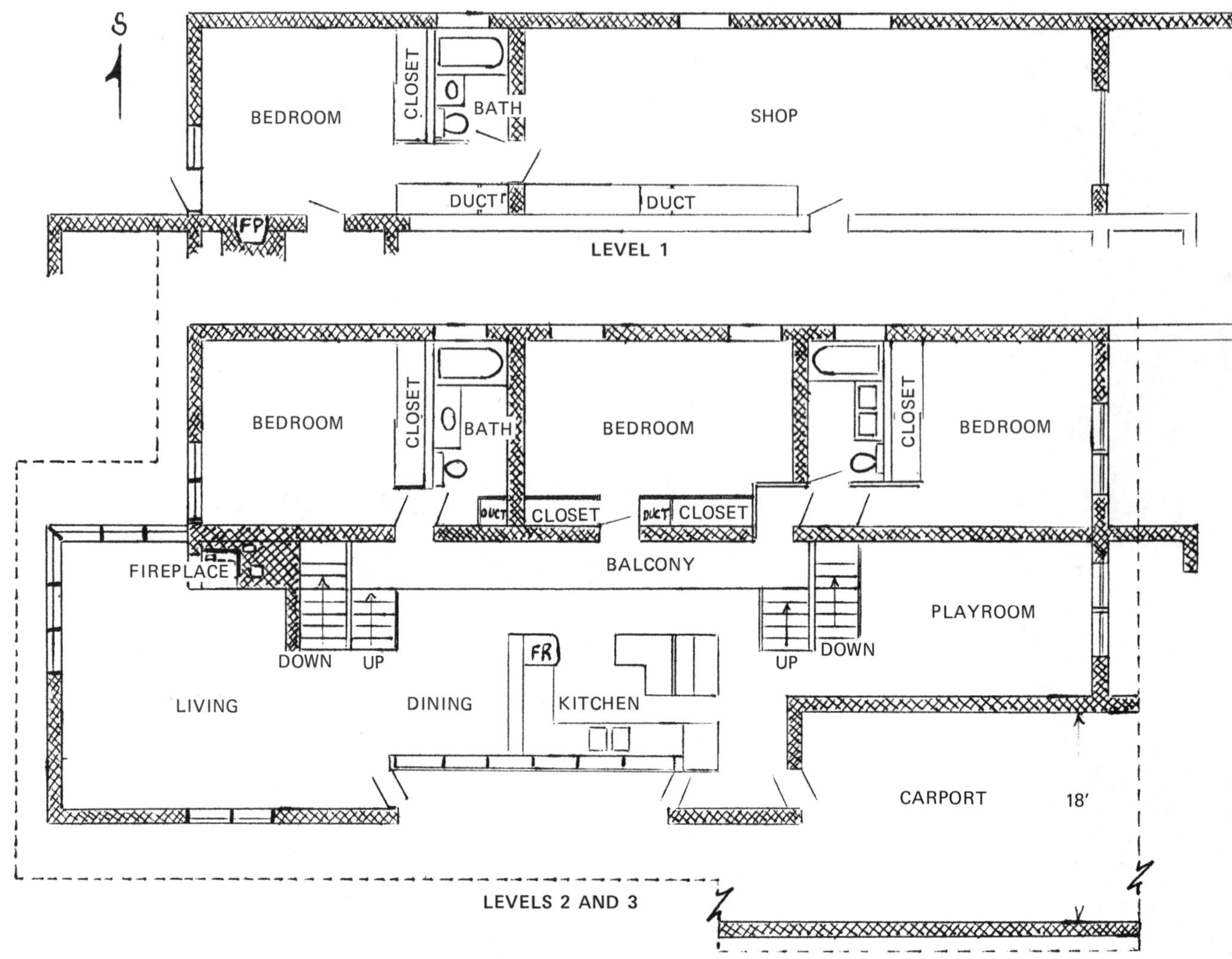

ARCHITECTURAL FEATURES

The long axis of this 28 x 70′, 2,500-sq.-ft. split-level dwelling runs roughly in an east-west direction. The main-level living area is an open-concept design running the entire length of the north half of the house. The playroom, kitchen, and dining/living area are arranged in that order from west to east. Mr. Gras states, "We felt the kitchen should look at the entrance and the street as in a lot of farmhouses there is usually someone in the kitchen."

The upstairs bedrooms and two baths, which are located side by side along the south wall of the house, are off a long open-rail balcony which overlooks the living area and is about 3½′ above the first-floor level. These bedrooms are elevated above a fourth bedroom and the large shop where Ranny had at one time planned to build a sailboat. A patio deck overhanging the cliff on the southeast corner of the house has a spectacular view through the woods to the pond. There is access to the patio from the bedroom at the east end of the lower level, and from the living room. A carport on the northwest side of the house provides some buffering from the elements. As it is on the same level as the kitchen it is easy to bring in groceries and other supplies. The gullwing roof seems appropriate to this home perched on the edge of a rocky cliff.

Continuous concrete footings 18″ to 24″ thick were cast directly on the ledge rock. Where the hill was too steep, holes were drilled in the rock and 1″-diameter reinforcing rod was leaded in. Horizontal reinforcing rods were then tied to these. The massive floors of all three levels are prestressed concrete slabs 6″ deep and 16″ wide running north to south. These slabs have three integral 4″-diameter air ducts.

The south side of the house was built just over the brow of the south-sloping hill. The north side presents a low profile to the cold winter winds and is protected by the carport.

Exterior Walls

The exterior walls are made of 6,000 pumice blocks bearing the trade name Lavacrete. Every other course of the 12″-wide blocks has H-sections of steel reinforcement to strengthen the wall and to prevent the accumulation of mortar shrinkage cracks. There is no wall insulation but the block itself, and there is no finish on the inside. The outside of the blocks is finished with a clear waterproofing called Thoroclear. The main purpose in using this type of wall was to provide thermal mass and a low-maintenance weatherproof skin that could breathe instead of having intentional fresh-air-intake ports or suffering infiltration losses around windows, doors, and other cracks. Other advantages of using this block are that it has nail-holding qualities comparable to oak, and is half the weight of concrete blocks.

Interior Walls and Ceilings

Standard studwall construction with ¾″ plywood was used for the interior nonbearing partitions. The interior load-bearing block wall running east to west between the bedrooms and the balcony provides additional thermal mass. The ceiling is Armstrong cement asbestos "Cushiontone" tile that Ranny selected for its good acoustic qualities. The ceiling is insulated with 6″ of foil-backed fiberglass.

Roof

The 2 x 12 rafters of the gullwing roof are spaced on 12″ centers in the living room and 16″ centers elsewhere and sheathed with ⅝″ plywood. Four-ply asphalt-paper roofing with a surface of asphalt and white marble chips forms the weatherproof skin.

Doors

The north entrance to the kitchen is well protected by the carport, so that even during hot and muggy rainy days the inner door can be left open to permit the entry of cooling breezes through the screen door. This is generally the only exterior door that is used during the winter. The carport buffer, storm door, and good weatherstripping then minimize infiltration losses. The doors to the patio deck from the bedroom and living room have a low R-value for insulation, because of the large glass area, but they are seldom used during the winter and are also well weatherstripped to minimize infiltration losses. The workshop has large doors which were designed to accommodate the building of the sailboat.

Windows

All of the windows are double-glazed, Twindo/insulated glass in redwood frames which are painted on the outside and varnished on the inside. Most are well-sealed fixed windows, though there are some smaller vent windows under fixed glazing. The redwood makes superb window sash because of its excellent weathering qualities. (At the time the Gras house was built, people generally were not aware of the extent to which the redwood forests are endangered.)

A large area of window wall is located on the southeast corner of the house, which provides a view of the woods and the pond below. This wall, plus the bedroom windows located in the collector wall and large west windows, also provides some passive solar collection, particularly in the winter, when leaves are off the deciduous trees. The Grases use no drapes or shutters, as the house is very private and the views are spectacular. Recent research indicates that, in some areas, there may be a net heat gain through double-glazed south windows, even when they are not insulated at night; but energy savings could certainly be made by using some form of insulated window covers.

SOLAR-HEATING SYSTEM

As mentioned previously there is a certain but unmeasured amount of passive solar-heat gain; however, the active system provides the majority of the solar heat.

Collector

The two-story 1,300-sq -ft. vertical air-type collector was site-built and constructed on the south wall of the building by Ann and Ranny in the summer of 1959. Five rows and 15 columns of double glass with a 1″ space between the panes form the collector glazing and the weatherproof skin for the building's south face. The glazing is contained within a wood frame which in turn is mounted on a 2 x 8 vertical studwall-like framing that is secured to the pumice-block south wall. Corrugated-aluminum sheeting secured to the outer edges of the 2 x 8s and immediately behind the glazing framework (1½″ behind inner glazing) was painted with a nonselective black paint. A fan drives air upward between adjacent 2 x 8s and behind the absorber plate, where it is heated prior to being distributed to the living spaces.

South- and east-facing windows provide direct solar gain as well as a spectacular view of the woods and pond.

The open-concept playroom, kitchen, dining room, and living room facilitate efficient circulation.

Storage

A Glauber salt storage system had been considered by Ranny, but it never was installed. The massive components of the house itself serve as the storage. These massive elements store both passive solar-heat gain and heat absorbed from the air convected through the building by the fans associated with the active solar system and the gas-fired backup furnace. The massive south wall acts somewhat like a Trombe wall, in that air passing between it and the back of the absorber plate absorbs some heat which during the course of a day will migrate through the wall and radiate to the bedrooms on the opposite side in the evening. The efficiency of the storage system could have been improved, as will be described.

Heat Distribution

A fan blows air up through the collector to a 60′ horizontal plenum at the top of the collector array, from where it is blown down directly to the rooms on the south side of the house, or down to a plenum beneath the first-story floor. The base of this latter plenum is the exposed ledge rock. In order for the system to work effectively, doors in the bathrooms and cellar have to be open in order to allow solar-heated air delivered to these areas to convect to the living spaces on the north side of the house. The floor slabs, as mentioned earlier, have 4″-diameter integral ducts running their length from north to south. Ranny states that he should have had vertical holes precast in either end of the slabs to link up with the ducts. In this way, he could now blow hot air from south to north through the ducts and exhaust it along the north wall or any chosen spot along the slab's length. "Ideally each room would have its own thermostat controlling a fan which would blow air through the floor, exhausting it into the room and then back to the collector through a return duct located in the closets. This can still be done without too much difficulty, but there is no pressure of malfunction forcing me to finish it."

AUXILIARY HEATING

The backup natural-gas-fired furnace, rated at 120-125,000 Btu, is the smallest furnace that Ranny could purchase at the time the house was built. The masonry fireplace on the south wall of the living room with its corner-type firebox is a real heat waster, but it is aesthetically marvelous. A second, smaller fireplace, in the lower-level master bedroom, is an efficient heater. The flues from the gas furnace and these fireplaces share the same chimney.

PERCENT SOLAR-HEATED

The Gras house has never been monitored with instruments. "I was not doing an experiment when I designed my house—it was to be a living 'machine.' If anyone were to supply the measuring and recording systems I might be persuaded to take data," says Ranny.

At the present time Ranny calculates that he gets about 50% of his space-heating requirements from the solar system with inside temperatures maintained at 67° to 68° F. It would be more efficient if the ducts were used for heat distribution. If the phase-change storage systems are developed to his satisfaction he might acquire one. He feels that were one installed in his house he could get up to 90% solar heating. With the large collector area that he has, this is possible.

Ranny offers the following advice to designers and future users of solar space-heating systems. "Designing a solar-heating system to provide a hundred percent of heating load involves providing for maximum heat load usually in December, with minimum sunshine input and lowest ambient temperature. For all other months, however, such a system will provide more heat than can be used or stored, which must be thrown away, at least until some practical means of energy conversion is developed. A solar-heating system that provides only sixty percent of December's load might actually provide ninety percent of the total year's load. Since cost is dependent on collector area, the incremental investment yields diminished returns even to the point of loss."

COOLING SYSTEM

No mechanical cooling is required. The large number of deciduous trees and the mainly indigenous ground cover near the house are the main factors contributing to the pleasantly cool interior atmosphere in the hot season. Vent windows and the shaded screen-door entrance help provide good cross-ventilation.

The upper horizontal plenum from the collector is vented to the roof venting channels to prevent the collector from overheating during the summer.

Ranny Gras demonstrates a model of the collector. Air moves through the large channel behind the black-painted corrugated aluminum sheeting.

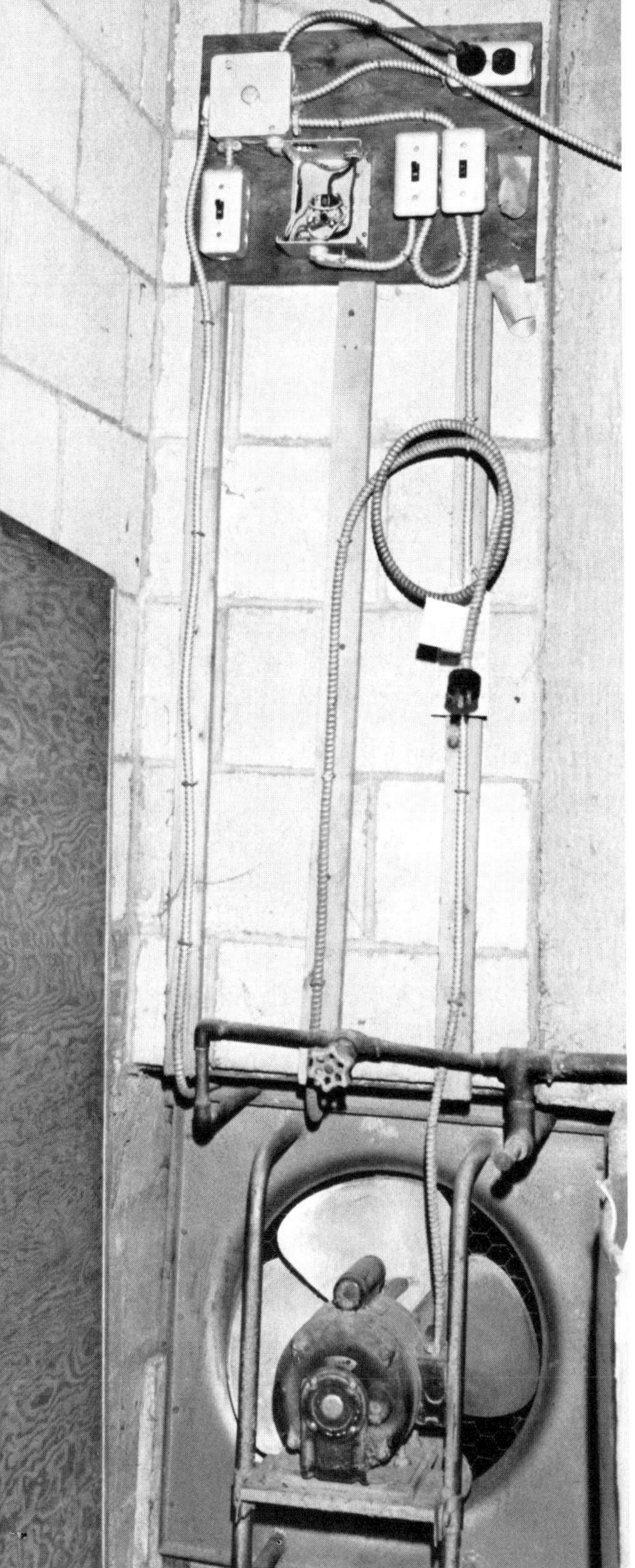
A large fan blows air up through the collector.

WATER SUPPLY AND WASTE SYSTEM

The Gras home receives its water from the local town system. Blackwater and graywater are disposed of in a cesspool.

The family attempts to be conservative in its use of water. Single-handle faucets allow one to instantly get the desired water temperature without getting frozen or scalded. Less water is wasted with this type of fixture. Bricks have been placed in the toilet tanks to reduce the amount of water used in flushing.

Three separate electric domestic hot-water heaters were installed. By placing them near the point of use, plumbing-line heat losses are reduced.

ELECTRICAL POWER SYSTEM

Electrical power is supplied by the local utility company. Lighting is provided by natural and fluorescent lighting. Fluorescent was chosen because Ranny prefers its quality of illumination and energy-conserving features. He installed the wiring himself, some of which is quite sophisticated. At several points in the house remote-control switching permits many different lights throughout the house to be switched on or off.

COSTS

The total cost of the lot, house, and solar system in 1956 was $42,000. The solar system itself cost about one-tenth of this total. Ranny hired contractors to do the foundation, walls, floor slabs, and roof on an hourly basis and also assisted in each phase of the construction. He did much of the exacting interior finishing work himself—labor which is not included in the cost mentioned above and which could not be easily duplicated in mass-production houses. He cautions others about trying to duplicate his design without a thorough grounding in the principles of thermodynamics and heat transfer. "My system works simply because I know what I am doing. If someone else tried to do it he could get into trouble, because the whole integrated design is critical to its function."

CONCLUDING THOUGHTS

I was not surprised to learn that in 1969 Ann, Ranny, and three of their teenage children embarked on what became a five-and-a-half-year round-the-world Odyssey aboard their sailing vessel *Merry Maiden*. They returned in 1975 "flat broke, but it was worth it."

This journey seemed only another logical expression of their thirst for adventure and knowledge and of their desire to march to their own drum—the same forces that prompted them to build one of the nation's first solar-heated houses.

Marlboro, Massachusetts
1,500 sq. ft. living area

FELIX RAPP

Felix Rapp first became interested in solar energy in 1973 while he was waiting in line for gasoline during the first initial shock waves of the energy crisis. "I soon after came across an article in *Technological Review* about solar, the amount of energy that was reaching the ground and how it could be utilized. I talked with Jim Barron, a fellow electrical engineer, and we concluded that it would be something interesting to get into. I went to MIT, where I took my degree, and scoured their architectural, engineering, and physics libraries and came across *Introduction to the Utilization of Solar Energy*, written in 1964 and published by McGraw-Hill [now out of print], a book which we still feel is one of the best on the subject. We started from there and by the spring of 1974 we built our first test collector."

Felix and Jim formed DIY-Sol, Inc., a company to manufacture and distribute do-it-yourself cost-effective solar-heating equipment. They self-published *DIY-Sol Heating System, Design and Construction Manual, Do-It-Yourself Solar Heating for Home, Industrial and Commercial Application,* a manual which in my opinion is one of the best. The sale of the manual financed the initial growth of their company.

A retrofit to Felix's own home using the DIY-Sol system is described here.

LOCATION AND ORIENTATION

The Rapp home is located in a quiet residential section of Marlboro, Massachusetts. The long axis of the house runs roughly in a north-south direction, not generally the best orientation for a solar retrofit, and sits on a west-sloping hill exposed to the winds. Prevailing winds are from the southwest, but storm winds come from all directions. There are some deciduous trees on the east side of the house which provide some protection from northeasters and from stray golf balls from the neighboring golf course. This tree row, 40′ high and 40′ from the house, has the disadvantage of slowing the wind down, causing it to drop great quantities of snow on and around the house during winter storms.

ARCHITECTURAL FEATURES

The 1,500-sq.-ft. one-and-a-half-story wood-frame split-level house was constructed in 1958, long before people generally became interested in energy conservation. It has three bedrooms, one and a half baths, a shallow attic, and a half-basement that accommodates the family recreation room and Felix's office. The built-in garage on the south end of the house provides some thermal buffering. If the temperature is 20°F. outside, the garage temperature will generally be around 35°F.

Neither the 10" poured-concrete basement wall nor the concrete basement floor have insulation.

Standard wood-frame construction techniques were used. Floor joists are 2 x 8s on 16" centers with plywood subflooring and oak finish floors.

Exterior Walls

Standard 2 x 4 studwall construction was used with plywood, foil-backed composition sheathing, and cedar shakes on the outside surface and gypsum board on the inside. There is no insulation in the exterior walls, but Felix plans to have the cavities filled with 3½" of cellulose fiber.

Interior Walls and Ceilings

Interior walls also are of standard 2 x 4 studwall construction. They and the 2 x 8 ceiling joists are finished with gypsum board. In 1973, 6" of cellulose insulation was poured into the attic.

Roof

Again standard procedures were used. The gable roof was covered with plywood sheathing, building paper, and asphalt shingles.

Insulation Summary

Basement: R-12; 3½" fiberglass on endwalls only
Exterior walls: No insulation; R-15, 3½" cellulose planned
Ceiling: R-27; 6" poured cellulose

Windows

Aluminum casement windows with aluminum storms were used. The Rapps experienced considerable ice buildup on the interior window in winter, which was leading to wood rot. The addition of a ¼" wood strip between the aluminum components acts as a thermal break and has eliminated the condensation problem.

Doors

All the doors are hollow-core wood-frame doors with aluminum screen/storm doors. Felix has weather-stripped all exterior doors to reduce infiltration losses. Neither front nor back door has an airlock; however, an entranceway through the garage provides a good thermal break, particularly in winter.

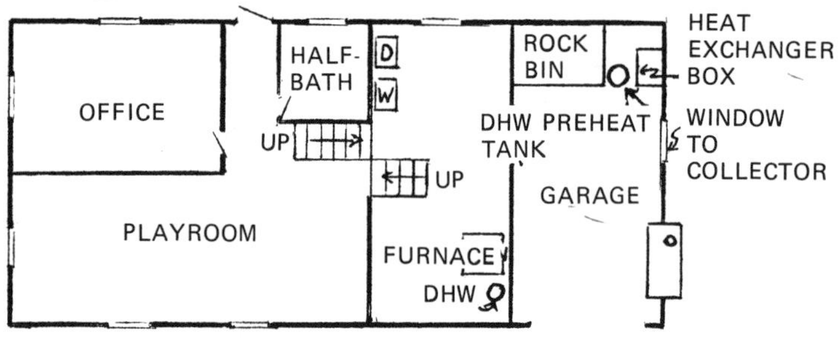

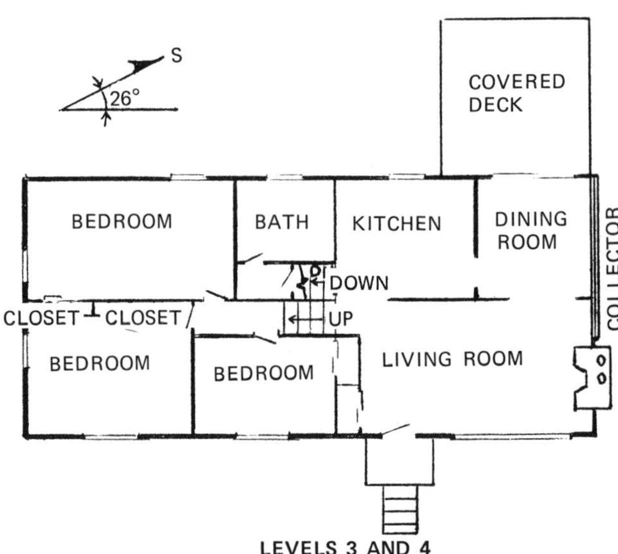

This home is typical of thousands of suburban houses built in the 1950s—before the energy crisis.

SOLAR-HEATING SYSTEM

This active solar system retrofitted to the Rapp home is one of the several do-it-yourself solar systems that DIY-Sol manufactures. The collector design is basically the same for all systems, but purchasers of their system have a choice of different sizes and of either a rock or water storage system for space heating. DIY-Sol also markets a separate solar domestic hot-water heating system.

Collector

The 200 sq. ft. (190 sq. ft. net) of built-in-place air-type collector is located on the vertical wall on the garage end of the house and thus is oriented 26° west of south. The overall dimensions of the collector array, composed of seven vertical panels, is roughly 14 x 14′, although individual panels vary in height from 12′ to 16′. The Xsoltherm absorber is the heart of the collector. Each absorber panel is 24″ wide, 36⅝″ long, 1¼″ thick, deeply corrugated, black selectively coated 5-mil aluminum foil. Absorptivity is 0.9 to 1.0 and emissivity is 0.2. Because the absorber is very light (less than 1 pound) it responds very quickly to temperature changes. Thin galvanized wire 4″ from the end of each absorber and strung above and below the absorber secure it in place and minimize undesired heat transfer to the back and sides of the collector. The insulation underneath the absorber is Celotex Technifoam, TF-400, a rigid lightweight insulation board with an isocyanurate foam core and reflective aluminum faces on both sides. It is an industrial roofing product with an insulating value of R-9 per inch. The Technifoam TF-400 has recently been discontinued and replaced with TF-610, similar in composition but with glass fibers in the core for additonal strength. The TF-610 is rated at R-8 per inch.

The panels are double-glazed Dupont Tedlar 400 BG 20TR Poly Vinyl Fluoride film. The inner glazing is 1 mil thick, and the outer is 4 mil. It has a life expectancy of about seven years. Dupont has recently introduced a new Tedlar glazing (400 XRB 160SE) with a life expectancy of 15-20 years as an inner glazing which compares favorably with Kalwall Sun-Lite Premium. According to Felix, "The 'old' Tedlar got a bad name for the following reason: It was being used in water collectors which were allowed to stagnate. The Tedlar couldn't take the high temperatures. Its peak is about three hundred and fifty degrees Fahrenheit, and if kept there too long it would become brittle and cloud. Its operating temperature is two hundred and twenty-five degrees. It will last if you keep it around there and don't allow the system to stagnate. You have to consider the materials that you are using. A lot of

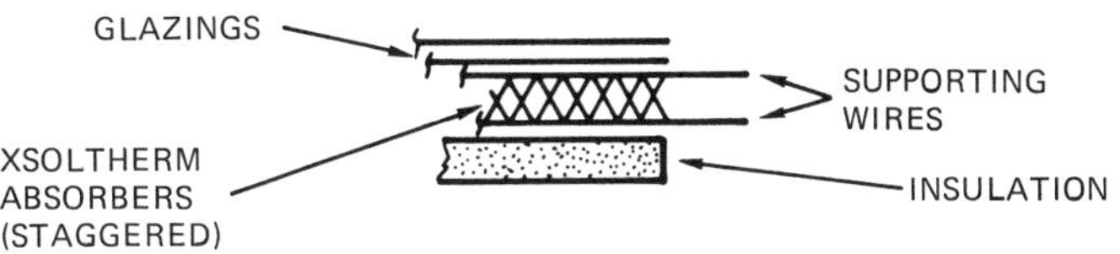

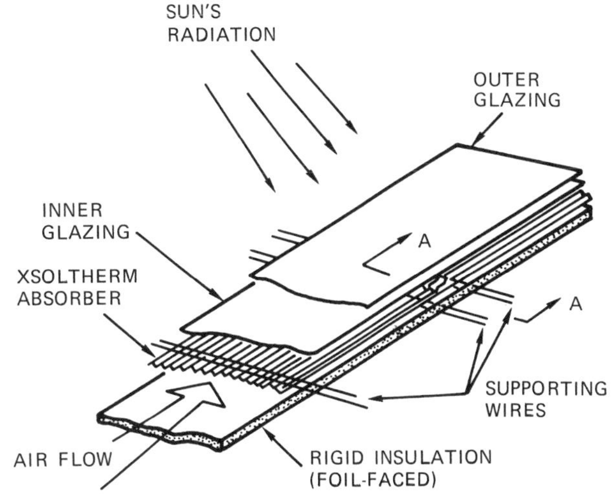

DETAIL OF COLLECTOR PANEL

people weren't too familiar with the materials when they designed their systems."

These components are contained within a 1 x 4 Douglas fir board framework, all of which is fairly easy for the do-it-yourselfer to construct.

Horizontal furring strips were first mounted to the side of the house. The 1 x 4 boards (actually ¾ x 3½″) were ripped into two boards, one ¾ x ¾″ and the other ¾ x 2⅝″. The latter were then drilled with holes to accommodate the absorber securing wires, and then all the boards were given three coats of polyurethane varnish to protect them from the high drying temperatures within the panel. The side panel's boards (¾ x 2⅝″) were then mounted vertically to the furring strips using 1 x 1″ zinc-coated right-angle brackets. These boards were abutted at the bottom end by a horizontal sill plate constructed of two boards separated by an air gap which serves as the cold-air inlet to the panels from a cold-air manifold.

The cold- and hot-air manifolds, running the width of the collector bottom and top respectively, are constructed of conventional lumber and exterior-grade plywood and very carefully lined and sealed with the 0.8″ foil-faced insulation board.

The insulation board is next pressed carefully between the panel sides. The 2 x 8′ sheets are caulked with sealant adhesive where they touch the panel sides, sill, and each other. The steel galvanized wires are then strung tightly through the side panel holes

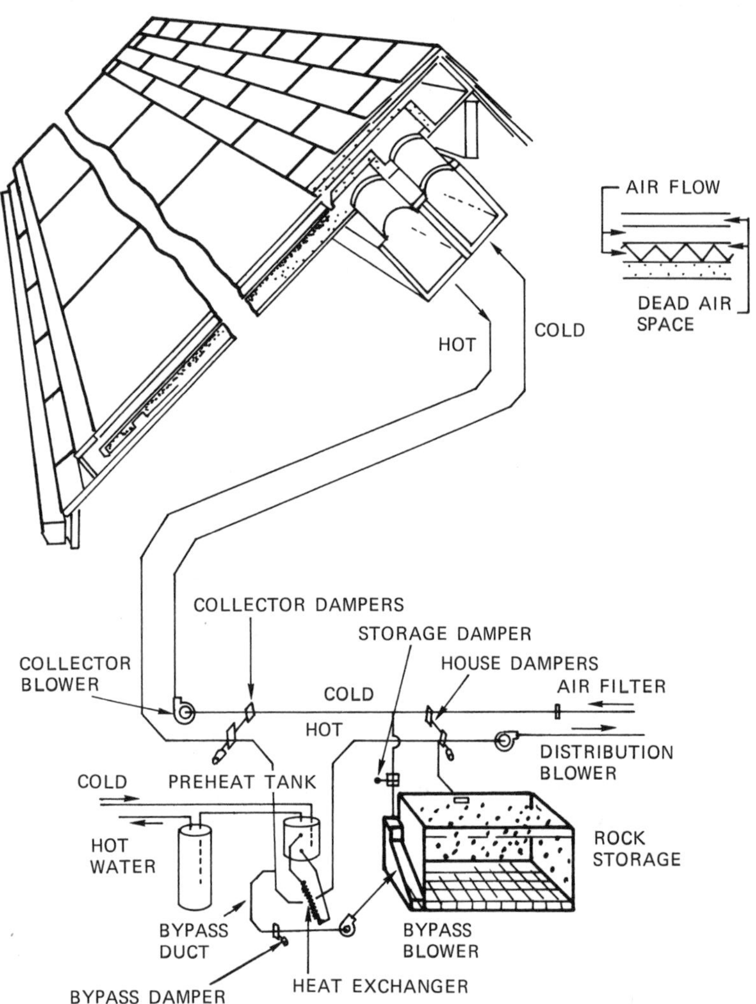

across the entire collector and secured on the outer surface of the end side panels. After the wiring, absorbers were installed from bottom to top and secured by the wires and by stapling the edge corrugations to the side panels. Monsanto Gelva pressure-sensitive acrylic resin adhesive, mounted on double-faced release paper and used as a transfer film, was next taped to the outer services of the panel sideboards and sill board. The inner Tedlar glazing was then stretched the entire length of each panel and adhered to the tape. After the Tedlar was stretched over all panels a ¾ x ¾″ header board was secured against the glazing at the panel/hot-air-manifold interface. As well as securing the top of the glazing and sealing the space between the inner glazing and the hot-air manifold this header board serves as a spacer between the inner and outer glazing. The ¾ x ¾″ sealed strips left over from ripping the 1 x 4 Douglas fir boards were used as additional spacers around the rest of the panel perimeter.

The Tedlar was then shrunk to ensure a tight wrinkle-free glazing using an inexpensive and simple device. A shallow bottomless box 24″ wide (panel width), 18″ long, and 3″ high was made of corrugated cardboard with a 24 x 18″ and 3 x 24″ side missing. With the large open side facing the glazing the "oven" is slowly moved up the glazing while an electric heat gun (or a 1,000-watt hand-held Pro hair dryer) is moved back and forth across the smaller opening. The Tedlar should be free of wrinkles and sags but not drum-taut.

The 4-mil Tedlar outer glazing was then adhered to the spacers, using the transfer film adhesive. A panel trim strip of ⅛ x ¾″ anodized aluminum tightly secures the Tedlar to the dead-air spacer underneath. The outer glazing was shrunk using the procedure described earlier.

The hot- and cold-air ducts connected to the hot and cold manifolds and to the Thermolator (which will be described further on) are constructed similarly to the manifolds.

Storage

The storage bin is a wood-frame box measuring 3 x 6 x 7′ high, located at the rear of the garage and filled to within 6″ of the top with 1½″-diameter rock. The 6″ airspace serves as the hot-air plenum. The frame is tilted inward about 1″ per foot to ease wall loading. All joints are staggered where applicable and all are sealed with silicone to ensure an airtight container. The concrete blocks are spaced ½″ to ¾″ apart on all sides. The cold-air plenum is at one end of the concrete-block ductwork.

Heat Distribution

The thermal regulator, or Thermolator, is the heart of the DIY-Sol heating system. It performs all of the mechanical and control functions of the system and connects the collector, storage, and dwelling ductwork together. It contains the air blower, fiberglass filter, dampers, and the control center. It is hung from the garage ceiling joists just behind the collector. Four thermistor temperature sensors located in the collector and the storage bin plus a two-stage home heating thermostat feed data to the solid-state electronic control center.

Felix describes how the solar system was integrated with the existing forced-air system: "We ran a cold-air stub from the cold-air distribution system of the house to the Thermolator and from there it is blown by a blower through the collector." (The blower is 185-watt and moves 355 cu. ft. per minute.) "There was a house hot-air duct only a foot or two from the Thermolator, so we tapped directly into that. Hot air from the collector is either fed directly into that duct or goes to storage. The two systems are in parallel and can work simultaneously. The Thermolator and ducts are well insulated with foil-backed duct insulation."

As the collector cools in the evening, cold air will settle to the bottom, flow backward through the system, and be replaced by warm house air traveling up the hot-air duct. This reverse thermosiphoning is pre-

Above: Felix's daughter, Tina, hard at work. The swimming pool in the background is solar-heated.

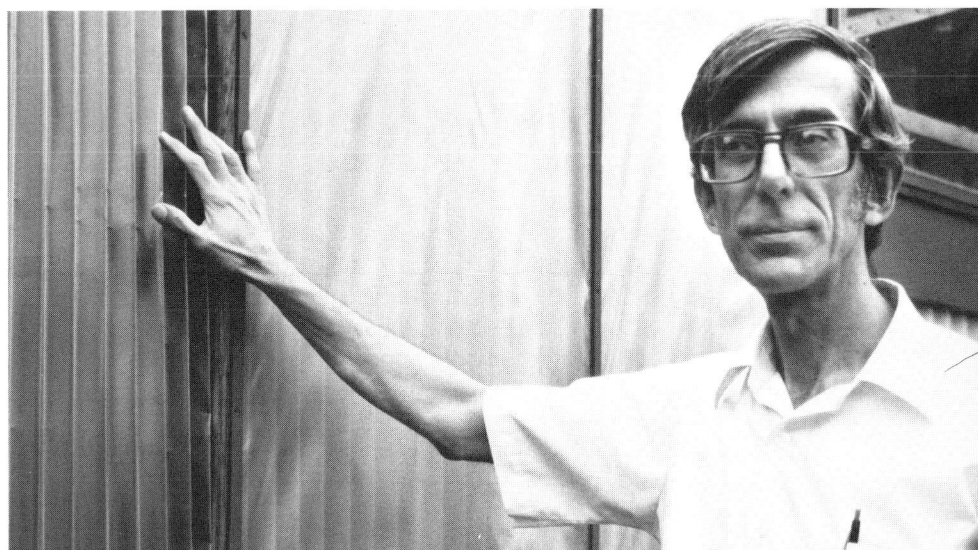

Right: Felix Rapp demonstrates his collector. The Tedlar glazing has been removed from the left-hand side panel to show the deeply corrugated aluminum-foil absorber plate, which has a black selective coating.

The partially constructed rock storage bin is located at the rear of the garage, on the left. Felix is holding the heat exchanger, which connects to the solar domestic hot-water preheater tank, and is pointing to the foil-covered box which houses the heat exchanger.

vented by a damper in the cold-air-supply duct between the blower and the cold-air manifold. For larger collector areas (greater than 300 sq. ft.) Felix recommends that a second damper, connected to the first by the same damper motor, be installed in the hot-air-supply duct.

There are three primary operating modes of the heating system:

1. *Collector to house* (house thermostat calls for heat and the solar collector is warm). Cold air from the house is forced through the collector by the blower and returns to the house. Both of the bypass dampers are closed. If storage is adequately warm the pump is circulating. This mode is actuated by the house thermostat calling for heat and the collector sensor stating that heat is available. This is the condition on cold, clear days.

2. *Storage to house* (house thermostat calls for heat and solar collector is cold). The collector bypass damper is now open, which prevents air from the house reaching the collector, but rather directs it through the rock bin back to the house. This condition exists at night and on cloudy days in cold weather.

3. *Collector to storage* (the collector is warmer than the storage tank and the house thermostat is not calling for heat). The house bypass damper is now open, which prevents air from reaching the house and directs it from the rock bin through the collector and back to the rock bin. This condition exists when space-heating requirements have been met and surplus heat is available for storage. It is also a condition when heat is needed for domestic hot water and the swimming pool, a system which will be described later.

AUXILIARY HEATING

The solar system is totally integrated with the gas-fueled hot-air furnace, and the integration is automatically controlled by the Thermolator. The house had an energy-efficient fireplace but Felix recently installed glass doors.

PERCENT SOLAR-HEATED

It is difficult to determine the solar contribution accurately as the natural gas is also used for cooking and heating the domestic hot water. However, Felix estimates that he is getting between 28% and 30% of his space heating from the solar system. The following table illustrates how natural-gas consumption has changed during the last six heating seasons. In the summer of 1973, 6" of cellulose insulation was added, affecting the figures for the following season.

Inside house temperatures are maintained at 70-72° F. during the day and set back to 65-66° F. at night.

			Collector installed	System complete	System improvements	
Heating season	72/73	73/74	74/75	75/76	76/77	77/78
Degree-days	6306	5989	6177	6046	6775	6708
Natural gas, 1,000 cu. ft.	149.7	124.6	116.0	104.1	112.2	116.9

COOLING SYSTEM

The upper-level attic of the Rapps' split-level house has a peak vent at either end and soffit vents along the west side. The lower level also has west soffit venting. The south gable vent that was covered by the collector has been replaced with an unpowered turbine vent. The attic insulation improved space cooling considerably, but a single air conditioner is still used in the master bedroom and there is a window fan in the kitchen.

Because of the vertical collectors and the high sun angles in summer, plus the fact that heat is supplied to the swimming pool and domestic hot-water heater, no solar cooling vent was installed. In other installations Felix and Jim have installed a solar cooling vent that opens automatically if there is a power failure.

WATER SUPPLY AND WASTE SYSTEM

The Rapp house is linked to the local water supply and waste system. No particular water-conserving or waste-reduction or recycling features have yet been designed into the house.

The Rapps have a domestic hot-water heating system consisting of an air-to-water heat exchanger and a 50-gallon preheat tank. The heat exchanger has six rows of aluminum-finned ¾" copper risers on 1"-diameter manifolds. The preheat tank is a standard Lo-Boy design, electric, dual-element, 50-gallon hot-water tank measuring 31½" high and 26" in diameter. The heating elements are not used.

The tank is mounted on a stand 12" above the top of the heat exchanger. Its hot-water outlet connects to the cold-water inlet of the standard hot-water tank. All pipes carrying heated water are insulated. The heat exchanger is mounted in the air duct between the collector and storage. Hot air passing through the heat exchanger heats the water and causes it to rise by gravity flow. The flow of water is from the bottom of the tank to the bottom of the heat exchanger, up the finned risers, and to the upper part of the tank. This flow continues until the air passing through the heat exchanger is cooler than the water in the risers. The flow is fully automatic, does not require pumps or controls, and does not reverse when the air is cooler than the water. Felix says the two-pass airflow is acceptable for flow rates of up to 450 cu. ft. per minute. Systems larger than that should use a single-pass flow.

Heat for hot water during evening hours or periods of cloudy weather is provided by a separate blower which is mounted with a damper in a bypass duct. The damper and blower are actuated when the preheat tank's lower thermostat closes and a switch in the top of the rock bin indicates that heat is available. An additional switch next to the heat exchanger will also actuate the damper and blower if temperatures near freezing are encountered. The damper and blower do not operate if the collector blower is on.

The bypass blower takes hot air from the top of the rock bin through the collector-to-storage duct. This air passes through the heat exchanger and is returned to the bottom of the rock bin.

ELECTRICAL POWER SYSTEM

Power is received from the regional power utility. When the house was built in 1958 no power-conserving features were built into it, and the Rapps have been so involved with solar projects that they have not made any significant steps toward decreasing electrical consumption, although Felix does plan to take hot air from the rock bin for the clothes dryer. Electric lights are predominantly incandescent.

MAJOR HOUSEHOLD APPLIANCES

Just prior to the "energy crisis" in 1973, Felix and his wife purchased a new air conditioner, dehumidifier, and frost-free refrigerator. None of their appliances can be classed as energy-conserving. They did make an energy-conserving modification to their electric automatic clothes dryer. "The hot-air vent," said Felix, "is exhausted into the house during winter through a home-built Masonite box fitted with a furnace filter. It is now not necessary to use the humidifier, which was always a bit of a nuisance anyway as we always had to be filling it."

COSTS

The completed system cost $1,500, with Felix and Jim Barron doing all the work. This figure includes all material costs. This is in line with the estimated costs for a "do-it-yourselfer" buying many components from DIY-Sol, Inc., and building materials locally. Today for a typical 192-sq.-ft. collector with 65 cu. ft. of rock storage the cost breakdown is as follows: collector, $831; duct and plenum, $53; blowers, $104; controls and dampers, $248; rock bin, $130; water heater, $295; for a total cost of $1,661 or a system cost of $8.69 per sq. ft. For a 480-sq.-ft. collector the total cost is $3,539, or a system cost of $7.37 per sq. ft. The cost of the collector works out to about $4.33 per sq. ft.—one of the least expensive on the market. If the system is installed by a contractor who knows the installation procedures, the installed costs of the complete system averages about $10-12 per sq. ft. of collector.

The increased operating costs are difficult to calculate, as the solar system does not have a separate meter and an estimate of the incremental usage is further complicated by the new appliances that were purchased shortly before the solar system was installed. However, Felix does not think the system uses much electricity, as the blower and water pump are both small. At any rate the power usage relative to the heat gain is insignificant.

CONCLUDING THOUGHTS

Felix has now developed a more efficient *triple*-glazed *two-pass* collector, so he is thinking of converting his present system sometime in the future.

Cool air enters at the top of the collector and flows between the inner and center glazing to the opposite end of the collector. This airflow picks up heat which would otherwise be lost through the outer glazing. The air then passes *underneath* the absorbers to the hot-air manifold. Hot and cold manifolds are therefore located at the top end of the collector with the air turning around at the bottom. This collector is thoroughly described in a supplement to the *DIY-Sol Heating System* manual.

So much interest has now been demonstrated by builders and do-it-yourselfers that DIY-Sol, Inc., has set up dealerships to handle installation work for those people who do not wish to do their own. The company offers a free consulting service for do-it-yourselfers, but the manual is so clearly written and illustrated that the consulting time averages only about four hours per installation.

A big advantage of the DIY-Sol system is that it is available in a kit form "from the simplest system to a large, fully controlled system with most components from one being used for the next. A complete solar-heating kit of 36 sq. ft. is available for under $150. With about $50 of local lumber it will supply over 10 million Btu per year which is equivalent to 120 gallons of fuel oil." This is an excellent, inexpensive way for the novice to become initiated to solar-heating systems.

CHRISTOPHER and MELISSA FRIED

Christopher and Melissa Fried with their young daughter, Heather, moved from Long Island and the security of well-paying establishment jobs to rural Pennsylvania in search of a more self-reliant and healthful way to live. In 1974 they settled on a 9-acre chicken farm that had an existing century-old wood-frame farmhouse and a few outbuildings. They soon became skilled chicken farmers and also learned how to grow, preserve, and prepare most of their own food. They made considerable renovations and restorations to the house in order to conserve energy and to reduce operating costs. The solar collectors and greenhouse which were retrofitted to the south side of the farmhouse are just one of the many changes that Christopher and Melissa made to the old homestead.

LOCATION AND ORIENTATION

The house is near Elysburg, Pennsylvania, and sits on the top of a small knoll, exposed to the prevailing winter westerlies. There are no windbreaks to the west; Christopher has been reluctant to plant one that would spoil the view of the pond. Large maple trees on the south side of the house prevent the collectors and greenhouse from overheating in the summer. There are no large window areas on the south side of the house to take advantage of the winter sun.

The chicken barn and other outbuildings are located downwind (usually) from the house and are too spread out to shelter one another from the elements very well. The buildings, driveway, and pond occupy about 2 of the 9 acres. Except for a marshy area in the northeast corner, the rest of the land is suitable for crops or pasture.

ARCHITECTURAL FEATURES

This two-story 1,700-sq.-ft. structure has nine rooms plus an unheated basement and an attic. The large farm kitchen/dining area on the southeast corner of the main floor catches the early-morning sun. As activities shift to the southwest den in the evening that room is warmed somewhat by the low-angle afternoon sun. Unfortunately, as the house has no windbreaks and originally had no insulation in the walls, this west side of the house tended to be quite cold in winter, especially when westerlies were blowing. The formal parlor on the northwest

ear Elysburg, Pennsylvania
,700 sq. ft. living area

corner of the house is closed up in winter, and heated only for special occasions. Similarly, the door to the mudroom/pantry from the kitchen is kept closed in winter. A one-story workshop on the north end of the house provides some thermal buffering. The second story has four bedrooms and a bathroom. Before the Frieds insulated the house and weatherstripped the windows and doors, the master bedroom with its five leaky windows was often cold during winter storms. Sometimes the bedroom temperature dropped to 45°F. At these times, the family usually all slept in Heather's room on the warmer east side of the house. The wood burner's chimney comes up through a corner of the room and radiates a significant amount of heat.

The unheated basement has stone walls and a dirt floor. The rock storage bin was built in one corner where the coal bin used to be. Christopher put 3½" of foil-faced fiberglass batt insulation between the floor joists.

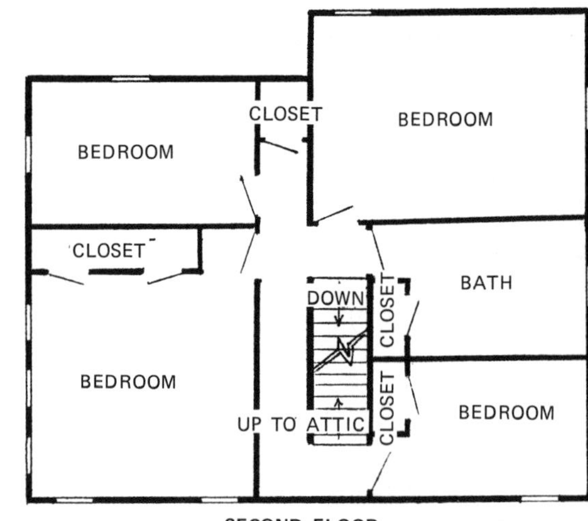

SECOND FLOOR

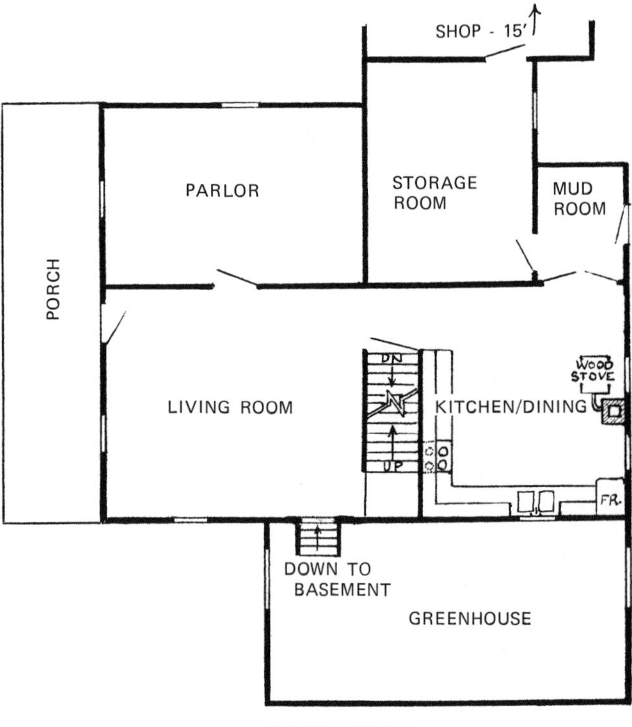

GROUND FLOOR

Exterior Walls

When Christopher and Melissa bought the house there was no insulation in the walls. In the spring they had a contractor fill the cavity between the full 2 x 4 rough-sawn studs with ureaformaldehyde foam insulation blown in from the exterior. Later in the fall when they had to remove some of the plaster from the interior of one of the walls while installing a new chimney, they discovered that in curing, the ureaformaldehyde had shrunk away from the edges of the studs about 3/16" on either side, thus decreasing its insulation value and allowing air infiltration. The Canadian Government Specifications Board recently set standards (51-GP-22MP and 51-GP-24M, both December 1977) for the application of ureaformaldehyde foam which are designed to minimize the shrinkage problem. Anyone considering having ureaformaldehyde blown into walls should be fully conversant with these standards before having the work contracted. The exterior of the house is sheathed with white vinyl siding.

Interior Walls and Ceilings

All of the interior walls are the original 2 x 4 studwalls covered with wood lath and plaster. The ceilings, like those of many houses of this vintage, are much higher than necessary. Those on the first floor are 9' high, and those on the second floor are about 8½'. The ceiling of the second floor is insulated with 8" of pouring wool.

Roof

The gable roof, built by standard roof-framing techniques, has been unchanged except for the addition by the previous owner of asphalt shingles.

Insulation Summary

Basement: R-12; 3½" fiberglass batts between floor joists
Walls: R-20; 4" ureaformaldehyde
Ceiling: R-25; 8" pouring rock wool

Doors

The door most frequently used is on the sheltered east side of the house facing the outbuildings. Both the wooden screen/storm door and the main door are well weatherstripped. One passes through these doors to the unheated mudroom/pantry and then through another door to the kitchen. The house originally had this airlock entrance, but the previous owner took out the partition and door between kitchen and mudroom. When the Frieds took possession they installed two side-by-side doors in the archway to restore the airlock effect. The front door on the cold west side of the house is rarely used in winter. It has an aluminum crossbuck storm/screen door. Christopher is thinking of enclosing the porch to provide a thermal buffer. A doorway at the bottom of the stairs leading to the second floor minimizes heat stratification on the upper level. Tightly fitting doors on all rooms permit them to be isolated from the rest of the house when desired.

Windows

Christopher has weatherstripped most of the original double-hung windows with tight-sealing and permanent thin aluminum spring-metal strips. All windows are equipped with aluminum storm windows. Most of the windows are also equipped with insulating panels made of 1″ rigid extruded polystyrene within a wooden frame. They are simply pressed against the window and are held tightly in place by friction between the edges of the panel and the window frame. They have reduced the radiant and convective heat losses considerably, without any condensation problems.

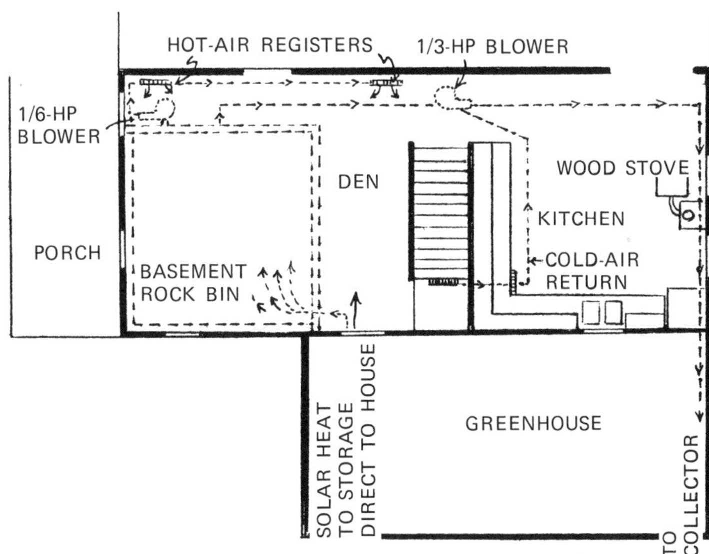

SOLAR-HEATING SYSTEM

The solar system is partially active and partially passive. A passively heated greenhouse was erected on the south side of the house. The base measures 12 x 24′ wide and the south face, sloping at 56° to the horizontal, measures 16′ in length. The bottom 5′ of this sloping surface is translucent to the greenhouse, and the upper 11′ is composed of the active air-type solar collector. The gross collector area is therefore 384 sq. ft., of which about 264 sq. ft. is active and 120 sq. ft. passive.

Salvaged railroad ties were used for the foundation for the greenhouse. The endwalls were constructed of 2 x 4 studs insulated with fiberglass batts and sheathed on the inside with hardboard and on the outside with vertical tongue-and-groove pine boards. The "rafters" are 16′ 1 x 6 Douglas fir boards on 21″ centers. Two layers of 0.025″ Kalwall Sun-Lite Premium (fiberglass-reinforced plastic—FRP) spaced ¾″ apart are used for the glazing. Christopher laid these single-handedly in 16′ lengths. This is one of the main advantages of FRP. It is light and shatter-resistant, and because it can be cut to any required length there is no need for horizontal mullions that cause snow buildup on the collector. The main disadvantage, of course, is that it does not give a clear image.

The absorber plate is composed of 96 0.009″-thick discarded aluminum printing-press plates for which Christopher paid 2½¢ per square foot. He bent the plates so that the absorber has 1½"-deep vertical fins spaced 2" apart on centers. Every 3", he twisted the fin sideways in the direction opposite to the twist immediately before so that the air is forced to delaminate as it flows up the collector. Two plates span the space between the 1 x 6 rafters, and four are stacked end to end to fill the 11′ collector length. The plates are stapled to a horizontal wooden strip placed under the seams and secured to the rafters. The plates were cleaned by etching them with mild acid and then were spray-painted with an oil-base flat black paint. Behind the absorber plate are two Masonite panels, one of which forms the backside of the collector, which faces the interior of the greenhouse. Air travels downward between the two Masonite sections, then turns 180° at the bottom of the collector and travels upward behind the absorber to the hot-air manifold at the top of the collector; from the collector it is distributed directly to the house or to storage.

Storage

The storage bin is a 12 x 12 x 6′-high wood-frame structure located in the basement corner where the coal bin used to be. First 2" of rigid extruded polystyrene insulation was laid on the leveled dirt floor, and then this was covered with ¾" plywood sheathing. Joist hangers were then used to secure the fir 2 x 6s of two of the perimeter studwalls to the plywood floor. The other 2 x 6 walls lean against the foundation. The inside of the studwall was sheathed in ¾" plywood and lined with 6-mil polyethylene vapor barrier. The stud cavities were insulated with 6" fiberglass batts, and the entire bin was bound by two steel cables. The airflow grid at the bottom of the bin is composed of 8 x 8 x 16" three-core concrete blocks laid on edge with a 1" to 1½" spacing between adjacent blocks. Wire mesh (½ x ½" fencing) was laid over the blocks and the bin was then filled with 20 tons (about 4½′) of a mixture of 1½-2"-diameter river rock and crushed stone. All round river rock would have been better because of its lower resistance to airflow, but Christopher settled for what was available at the time. The only problem that the Frieds have encountered with the storage was when the basement was flooded with about 6" of water from overflow from a nearby well during a long late-summer rainy period. The system was retired for the summer during that period; no damage was caused, nor has it seemed to effect the present operation of the system.

Heat Distribution

A thermostatically controlled 1/3-hp blower blows air through the collector, where it is heated and then blown through wooden ducts to storage or directly to the house through a hot-air register located in the bottom half of an enclosed south window of the den. When charging the store, hot air from the collector flows downward through the bin from top to bottom. When heat is required from storage, a 1/6-hp storage-mounted blower reverses the flow through the rocks and hot air is blown into the den through two hot-air registers. A cold-air-return register near the bottom of the stairwell returns room air to the blower.

Hot air migrates to the kitchen from the den through the doorway between them, which the Frieds enlarged considerably to improve circulation and the visual appeal of that area. A small axial fan might later be installed above the archway to improve air circulation between the rooms. Hot air circulates to the second floor by natural convection up the stairwell and through the original operable floor grates.

One might criticize the use of wood for the hot-air ducts; however, Christopher claims that with his low-temperature system no problems have been encountered and he would not hesitate to use wood again. He wanted to use renewable resources as much as possible. Because of the higher insulating value of 1" pine as compared to metal he was able to design the system so that ducts ran in pairs and shared a common partition, thus conserving materials and space.

AUXILIARY HEATING

The first winter in the old farmhouse (1974-75) the Frieds tried burning wood in the existing hand-fired coal furnace located in the basement. Halfway through the heating season they had already burned over five cords of wood, so they switched to a reasonably air-tight freestanding space heater (designed for coal) and automatically halved their wood consumption.

The following winter they switched to an even more efficient barrel stove that Christopher designed and built himself. It is modeled on the downdraft principle. A 4" cast-iron sewer-pipe T was fitted through a 55-gallon drum so that one end opens near the top, inside the drum, while the other end extends down to grate level. The top horizontal opening is fitted with a flapper valve, which is closed during normal operation and opened when the feeder door is open to avoid smoke and flame exiting through the door. The feeder door is salvaged from an old furnace. The firebox was lined with firebrick. The barrel was enclosed within an owner-built metal cabinet. Air intake is controlled by a manual draft wheel, and a thermostatically controlled blower circulates air to the living spaces at 500 cu. ft.

The top two-thirds of the add-on solar greenhouse is an active air-type collector; the bottom third is translucent to the greenhouse.

The wood-frame rock storage bin located in the basement is insulated with 6" of fiberglass.

per minute. Christopher designed the stove so that during normal operation the gases would pass down over the coals to the lower flue outlet and thus achieve more efficient combustion. The Frieds found that this secondary burning effect does not work very well until the stove is operating at a high temperature. Since the heating requirements of the house were such that they were idling the stove most of the time, the temperature within the firebox was generally not high enough to force secondary combustion.

Christopher bought a Suburban Woodmaster circulating wood stove that he intended to use during the winter of 1978-79; however, he sold that and bought a very beautiful, less bulky Cawley-Lemay cast-iron box stove. After a few weeks' trial, he sold this and reinstalled the more effective drum stove.

PERCENT SOLAR-HEATED

In the winter of 1975-76, when the barrel stove was first used and the solar system became operational, the Frieds burned four cords of oak. No monitoring equipment has ever been installed, but Christopher calculated that during the first winter of operation the solar system contributed 20% of the house's heating requirements. Early the following winter (November), the exterior walls were drilled with holes in preparation for the installation of ureaformaldehyde insulation; however, the contractor never arrived until May. As a result the Frieds burned more than four cords of wood and estimate that the solar contribution dropped to 15%. With the improvements that have been made, Christopher calculated that over the past winter the solar system supplied about 25% of the heating needs. The active supplied 20%, and the passive supplied about 5%. They burned three cords of oak, which they expect will be typical for the normal 6,000-degree-day years. Christopher states, "Air infiltration is the home's greatest remaining heat-loss problem. Old homes are notorious for this and plugging the thousands of holes is almost impossible, although we have decided that a reasonable level of energy-efficiency has been achieved."

COOLING SYSTEM

No mechanical cooling devices are used. The large maple trees shade the greenhouse during the hot season. Insulating the house has helped to keep it cool in the summer as well as warm during the heating season. The ample window area and the location of the windows allow for good cross-ventilation. The west den door and the east kitchen door are in line with the large archway between these two rooms. The screened storm doors also facilitate cross-ventilation, a feature particularly welcome when Melissa is baking or preserving.

WATER SUPPLY AND WASTE SYSTEM

Water is supplied from a drilled well and preheated by passing through 40′ of finned copper tubing within the collector's hot-air manifold. Christopher wrapped the insulated glass-lined water tank with an additional 1½″ of fiberglass and lowered the temperature setting to 120° F. from the 170° F. that the previous owner had set it at. He has also insulated all the domestic hot-water pipes.

Blackwater and graywater are disposed of in a standard septic system, and solid wastes such as newspaper, aluminum, and glass are recycled through a community effort. Organic wastes from the kitchen are fed to the dozen or so range-feeding chickens. Chicken litter from the barn is spread on the land for fertilizer.

ELECTRICAL POWER SYSTEM

The farm receives its electrical power from the local utility grid. The Frieds reduced electricity consumption a tremendous amount from what the previous owner had used. The methods for conserving power needed to heat domestic hot water have already been described. Christopher describes the ingenious methods he used to make drastic cuts in power consumption by the chicken operation: "The brooding technique had been, and still is for most farmers in the area, to keep the chicks from one day old to a week and a half old in an area equivalent to about a quarter of the total area of the barn. This didn't make much sense to me, so I made a wood-and-plastic eight-by-twenty-four-foot brooder cover which I suspended from the ceiling and crank down whenever I'm brooding. This electrically heated brooder encloses a volume less than a tenth of the volume of the barn. I proportioned the size of the brooding area to that which the full-grown birds seemed comfortable in. It has worked out very well. We get better results mortality-wise than before, as the heat is much more even and birds don't get chills off in corners. The peeps—chicks—seem a lot happier, and we certainly are, as our heating costs have been cut substantially. The former owner tells me that he used to receive bimonthly electrical bills of a hundred and twenty dollars. Three years later our bimonthly bills are about forty-five dollars, and we have an electric cooking range, which they didn't have, as well as an extra refrigerator. The amount of time that the peeps are kept in the brooder varies with the seasons. Typically, in the fall after one week, I disconnect the brooder space heater entirely. After a week and a half to two weeks I bring them out to about a quarter of the floor area of the barn and separate their section by a piece of plastic from ceiling to floor, therefore still keeping the heat generated by the birds themselves within a small area, and obviating the need for auxiliary heat. I then let the birds decide at what time they want to utilize the whole building and allow them to expand through holes in the plastic. By this time their body heat is enough to heat the whole building. After four to six weeks, depending on the season, there is so much excess heat that barn windows have to be opened in the dead of winter." Christopher has not devised a practical way of storing this heat nor utilizing it to heat the farmhouse (without the poultry odor!). Although the techniques for reducing power consumption described here are specific to a broiler-chicken operation, the ideas can be applicable to a wide range of areas where energy is wasted.

MAJOR HOUSEHOLD APPLIANCES

The Frieds admit that many of their appliances were not chosen too wisely, as they were purchased before they became energy-conscious. The electric cookstove and frost-free refrigerator have no particular energy-conserving features, although the latter was placed against an outside wall where it is exposed to cooler air temperatures than it would be against an inside partition wall. A spare refrigerator and upright freezer are kept in an unheated room, so they consume little power in winter. When selecting a freezer Christopher and Melissa made sure that it was one with a separate heat exchanger on the back rather than one of the "modern" ones that have the heat exchanger integral to the outside walls of the freezer cabinet, thus making it impossible to add additional insulation without defeating the purpose of the appliance. Rigid extruded polystyrene insulation 1" thick was glued to the exterior of the freezer door and 3½" of fiberglass to the sides in order to improve its performance.

The Frieds have an automatic clothes washer and dryer, but the latter is not used often as they prefer to use the outside clothesline and an old-fashioned drying rack next to the wood stove. The forced-drying cycle of the automatic dishwasher is never used.

FOOD SYSTEM

Christopher and Melissa are extremely concerned about the quality of food that they consume. They have thus become almost self-sufficient in terms of vegetable and meat production. They sow ¼ acre of garden vegetables each year, using organic gardening techniques, and grow some strawberries and a few apple trees. Some of the fresh produce is stored in the cool, dark area of the basement where the furnace used to be, some is frozen, and Melissa cans a great deal. In addition, the greenhouse provides three or four varieties of fresh lettuce, spinach, cauliflower, and tomatoes during the cold season. This is possible without the use of auxiliary heat to the greenhouse. Because of its good insulation, double glazing, and the storage capacity of the black-painted, water-filled oil drums and the soil, temperatures within the greenhouse rarely drop below 40° F. In the winter, greenhouse temperatures get as high as 75° F., while during a summer day they sometimes reach 90° F.

Range-fed chickens provide the family's meat and eggs. When they are required to purchase foodstuffs, Melissa and Christopher attempt to purchase high-quality, unprocessed foods whenever possible. One of the highlights of the research which produced this book was when my family sat down with the Fried family for a long and leisurely dinner of farm-fresh foods that had been grown and prepared with understanding and care.

COSTS

The total material costs for the completed solar system were $1,400, of which $750 was for the storage system. Christopher says, "It took me, working alone, less than a week to complete the basic structure; however, I spent many, many hours planning and drawing the details. All the preparation paid off, as everything worked out very well from the start and I didn't have to redo very much."

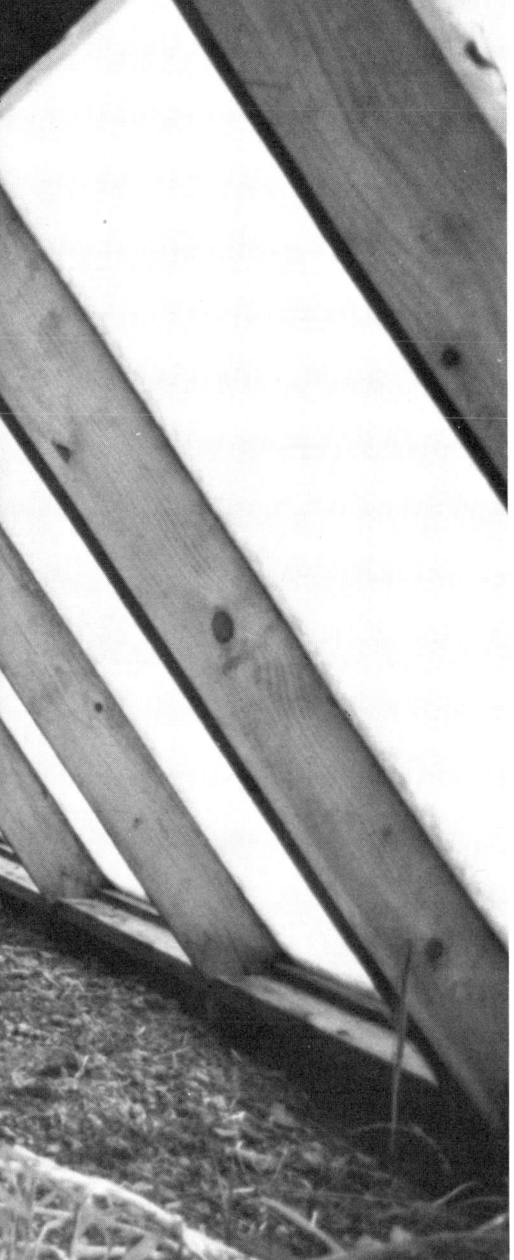

Water-filled drums store passive solar heat and help make it possible to grow lettuce, spinach, cauliflower, and tomatoes in winter.

The kitchen wood-burning stove is the only backup to the solar system. The model shown here has been replaced by an owner-built barrel stove.

CONCLUDING THOUGHTS

As a result of their efforts to achieve a more self-reliant life-style and to use renewable resources to help heat their home, the Frieds became in demand to lecture about and give demonstrations of what they had accomplished on their farm. Christopher describes how this happened: "We got into solar energy out of necessity. I never imagined that I would become involved in statewide educational programs. After I did the solar addition, a few newspapers and TV and radio stations did some stories about our place. We also received a lot of inquiries by phone and letter, and many people stopped by, sometimes without invitation, so I decided it would be rewarding—not monetarily, because it wasn't until recently—to set up an educational program to conduct workshops and media talk shows. I outfitted our van with demonstration water-type and air-type solar collectors, a wind generator, displays of various types of insulation, weatherstripping, caulking, and appropriate literature. The Pennsylvania Department of Community Affairs contacted me and offered me a job conducting a statewide conservation and renewable-energy program. I now travel throughout the state to various fairs, conferences, and educational institutions carrying out what I had first initiated on a small scale.

"What really convinced me of the need to show people alternatives was when Pennsylvania in 1975 aired the concept of an energy park—ten to twenty power plants all clustered in one location, half of which would be nuclear and half of which would be coal-fueled. The environmental and climatic effects would be so incredible that it seemed inconceivable to me how the concept got as far as it did.

"The renewable-energy field is a very promising field of employment. I can't imagine anyone not making a pretty good living at it if he has reasonable intelligence and patience. I'm not looking for a large income, as a long time ago I discovered that money just wasn't satisfying my needs. I wanted an occupation that I would enjoy working in, that was helping people, that I could hope was improving the world situation for my children and future generations, and that would give me a reasonable income. This all relates back to good health, the achievement and maintenance of which has been our main aim."

Madison, Connecticut
2,400 sq. ft. living area

IAN and ELAINE KING

Retrofitting their Cape-style Connecticut home with solar heating was just another progression in Elaine and Ian Kings' efforts to learn and adopt more ways of living lightly on the earth. Ian explains their motivation: "Going into solar heating started with an economic concern—a dissatisfaction with pumping more and more dollars into utility companies that were either unwilling or unimaginative or unable to do anything as an alternative to the wasteful use of nonrenewable resources. Also, do I want to spend that much for electricity? [Their home was solely electrically heated.] Or do I want to do other things for my family with the money?

"Inevitably that brought us down a road to where solar energy made sense to us as a less energy-intensive way of heating our home. The prospect of achieving satisfaction with less energy use and living a simpler, low-maintenance type of life-style—going back to the land, if you will—has appealed to us for a number of years. Ultimately I can envision a home where we could have sufficient acreage and practice woodlot management, and, between wood and solar, be self-sufficient in terms of fuel."

LOCATION AND ORIENTATION

The King home is situated on a 1½-acre site in Madison, Connecticut, in a heavily wooded area. A substantial amount of deciduous growth, in a 60′-high range on property north of the house, protects it from the cold north winds. When Elaine and Ian bought this house for themselves and their four children they were not planning to install solar heating. Fortunately, the orientation of the house (15° west of south), the roof angle (40° from horizontal), the house layout, and the good quality of construction made the building very suitable for a solar retrofit. Earth has been graded high on the north side to better insulate the basement.

ARCHITECTURAL FEATURES

This wood-frame extended Cape-style five-bedroom house has 2,400 sq. ft. of living space, a full unheated basement, and a built-in unheated two-car garage at the basement level. The main living area, composed of family room, kitchen, and dining room, is an open-concept design running along the warm south side of the

FIRST FLOOR

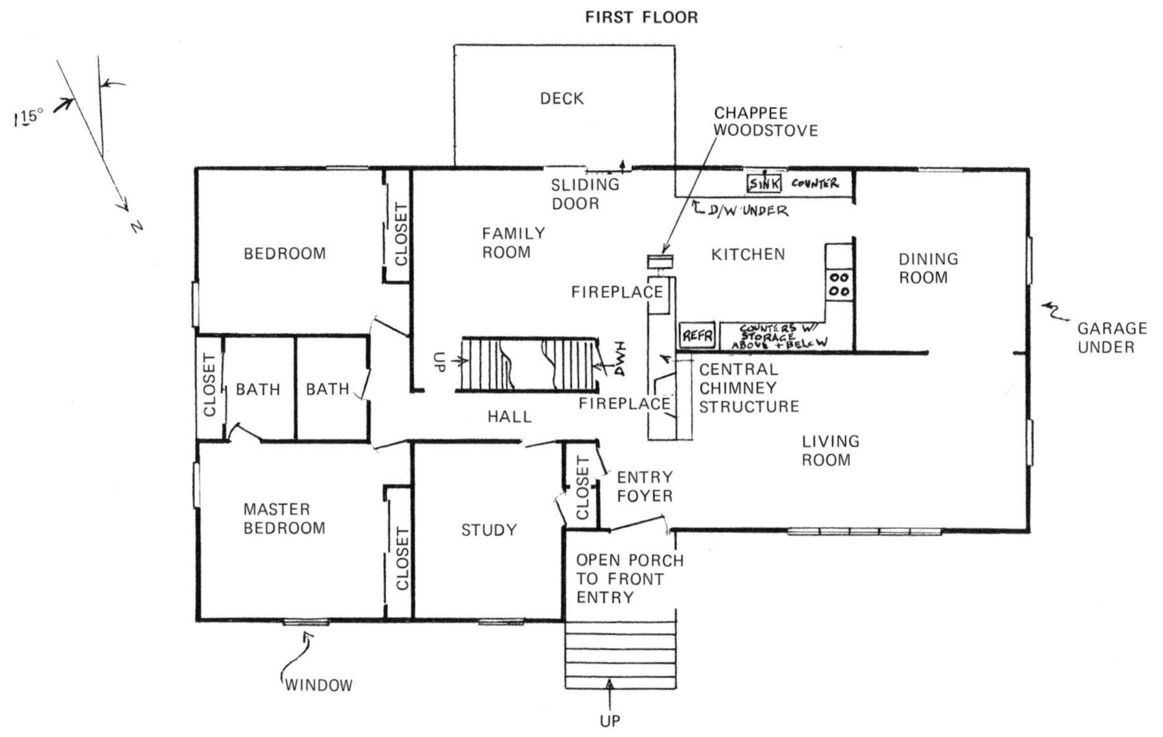

115°
N
DECK
CHAPPEE
WOODSTOVE
SLIDING
DOOR
SINK
COUNTER
D/W UNDER
BEDROOM
CLOSET
FAMILY
ROOM
KITCHEN
DINING
ROOM
FIREPLACE
REFR
COUNTERS W/
STORAGE
ABOVE + BELOW
GARAGE
UNDER
CLOSET
BATH
BATH
UP
DWH
CENTRAL
CHIMNEY
STRUCTURE
FIREPLACE
HALL
LIVING
ROOM
CLOSET
ENTRY
FOYER
MASTER
BEDROOM
CLOSET
STUDY
OPEN PORCH
TO FRONT
ENTRY
WINDOW
UP

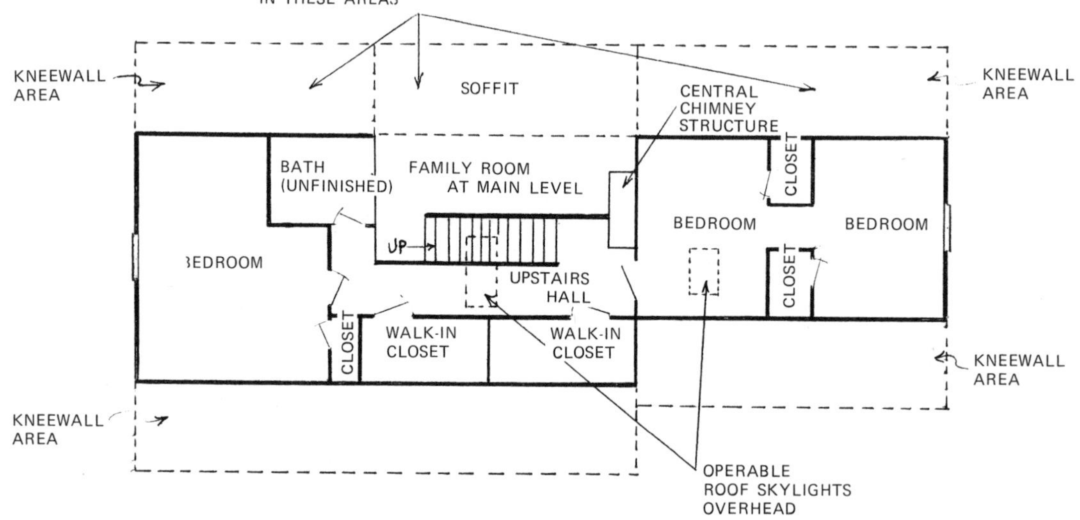

2 8 x 30" SOLAR-HEAT AIR
DUCTS (FULL LENGTH OF HOUSE)
IN THESE AREAS
KNEEWALL
AREA
SOFFIT
KNEEWALL
AREA
CENTRAL
CHIMNEY
STRUCTURE
BATH
(UNFINISHED)
FAMILY ROOM
AT MAIN LEVEL
CLOSET
BEDROOM
BEDROOM
UP
UPSTAIRS
HALL
CLOSET
CLOSET
WALK-IN
CLOSET
WALK-IN
CLOSET
KNEEWALL
AREA
KNEEWALL
AREA
OPERABLE
ROOF SKYLIGHTS
OVERHEAD

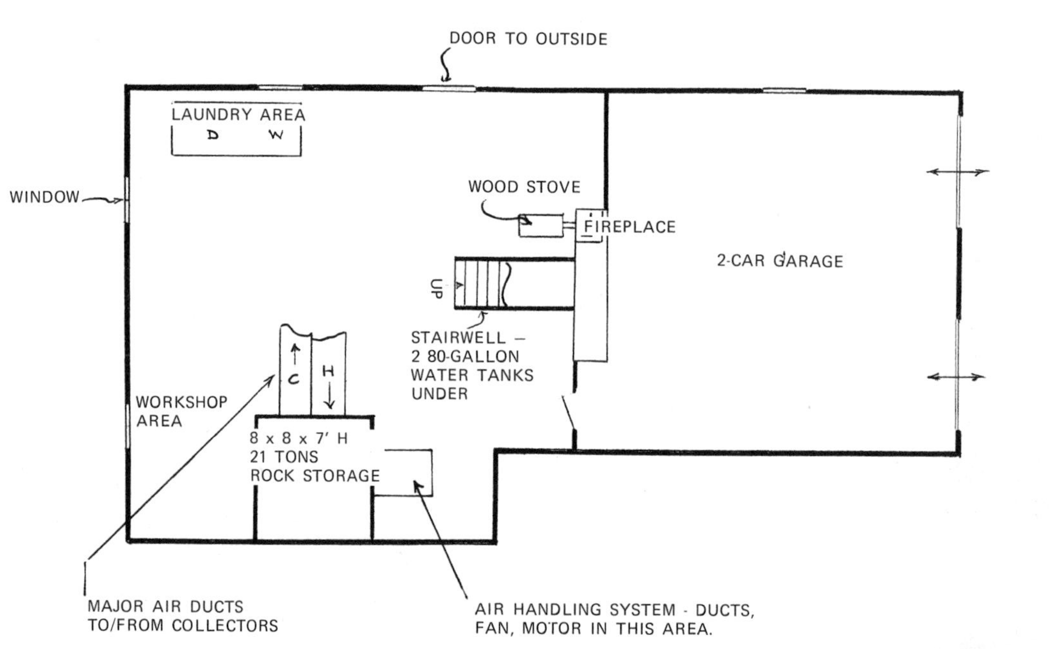

DOOR TO OUTSIDE
LAUNDRY AREA
D
W
WINDOW
WOOD STOVE
FIREPLACE
2-CAR GARAGE
UP
C
H
STAIRWELL –
2 80-GALLON
WATER TANKS
UNDER
WORKSHOP
AREA
8 x 8 x 7' H
21 TONS
ROCK STORAGE
MAJOR AIR DUCTS
TO/FROM COLLECTORS
AIR HANDLING SYSTEM - DUCTS,
FAN, MOTOR IN THIS AREA.

house. The dining room flows into the living room, and a cathedral ceiling extends from the family room to above the second-floor hall, which has an open railing looking down to the family room. These features all help to facilitate good natural ventilation and heat transfer. The two bedrooms on the northeast side of the main floor as well as the unheated garage buffer the weather somewhat. On the second floor, large closets along the north wall provide additional buffering.

The basement foundation walls are of 10″-thick reinforced poured concrete. Standard wood-framing techniques have been used for the main part of the house. Flooring downstairs is oak over plywood subflooring, except for the bathroom and hall, which are tiled. The center hall upstairs is also plywood and oak, and the bedrooms have two layers of plywood plus carpeting.

Exterior Walls

The standard 2 x 4 studwalls have been insulated with fiberglass and sheathed with 4 x 8′ sheets of Texture 1-11, an exterior-grade plywood grooved to simulate rough-sawn vertical boards. The main advantage of this sheathing over boards is that it results in fewer joints and thus fewer infiltration losses. The plywood provides much greater resistance to racking. The exterior paneling and trim have been finished with a spruce-blue Rez stain.

Interior Walls and Ceilings

Standard ½″ gypsum board has been used throughout the house, and this has been painted light colors to help compensate for the small window area.

Three fireplaces were initially built into the house. An airtight high-efficiency French Chappee coal/wood-burning stove now uses the kitchen/family-room fireplace flue. An Ashley is hooked up to the basement fireplace flue.

View from the second-floor hall down to the family room and kitchen.

Roof

Exterior-grade plywood sheathing, building paper, and asphalt shingles over a conventional 2 x 6 rafter frame make up the roof structure.

Insulation Summary

Ceiling: R-20; 6″ fiberglass batts
Walls: R-12; 3½″ fiberglass batts
Basement: The foundation walls were not insulated. Since the basement is unheated, the basement ceiling has been insulated between the joists with R-20 6″ fiberglass batts. All air ducts are insulated with 3½″ fiberglass.

Doors

The front entrance has no vestibule, opening directly into the living room; however, the door is an insulated steel type with an airtight magnetic weatherstripping seal. An aluminum storm door is installed exterior to this. An aluminum thermopane tempered-glass patio door provides access from the family room to the deck on the south side of the house. Considerable condensation occurs on the inside of the aluminum frame in winter, so the Kings are not very satisfied with this type of door. A similar door used to exist on the south side of the basement until one of the boys accidentally broke it. Ian subsequently filled in half the space and installed an insulated steel door in the other half.

Windows

The window area is a modest 176 sq. ft.; however, the open concept compensates. All windows on the north side of the house are Andersen wood-frame thermopane crankout-type casement windows. All others are conventional double-hung wood sash with removable exterior aluminum storm windows. All windows and the patio door have common fiberglass-lined insulated curtains available from Sears or most drapery outlets. Elaine and Ian are now thinking about installing insulated shutters.

During renovations for the solar system two skylights were added to the north roof—one for the second-floor northeast bedroom and one to admit light to the second-floor hallway and down to the family room. These double-glazed acrylic skylights are operable and thus provide good ventilation; however, they seal very tightly.

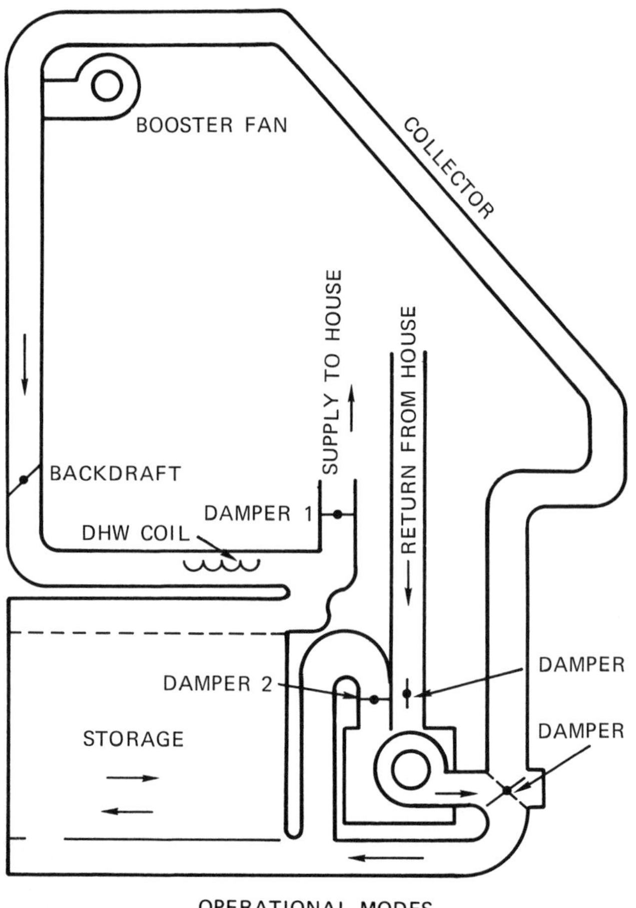

OPERATIONAL MODES

MODE 1: STORING HEAT FROM COLLECTOR
No. 1 CLOSED
No. 2 OPEN
No. 3 CLOSED
No. 4 TO COLLECTOR

MODE 2: HEATING FROM COLLECTOR
No. 1 OPEN
No. 2 CLOSED
No. 3 OPEN
No. 4 TO COLLECTOR

MODE 3: HEATING FROM STORAGE
No. 1 OPEN
No. 2 CLOSED
No. 3 OPEN
No. 4 TO STORAGE

LANDSCAPING

Of this 1½-acre site, 1¼ acres is woodlot, from which the Kings can harvest a cord a year on a sustainable-yield basis. This is a precious resource that they wish to retain. The shrubbery which has been planted around the house was largely designed for decorative purposes; however, the dwarf Albertas and yews which virtually cover the north face of the house provide some protection from the wind. These, some hemlocks, and grass around the house perimeter assist in summer cooling.

SOLAR-HEATING SYSTEM

The George C. Field Co. (see House 5), a well-established building firm in Connecticut, was hired to undertake the renovations. Roy Clark of this company designed the system and oversaw construction.

Collector

The 650 sq. ft. of site-built air-type collector measures roughly 13′ high and 51′ long. As it is laid directly on the south-sloping roof its orientation is 15° west of south and its tilt angle is 40° from the horizontal. There are 26 panels, each measuring 3 x 6½′, arranged in two rows of 13 each. The collectors were constructed in the following manner. A layer of flat galvanized duct metal was applied over the existing roof. The collector fir-wood frame placed over this has oversize dados (rectangular grooves) to accommodate expansion and contraction of the absorber plate and glazing. The flat galvanized-steel absorber plate about 1″ above this base plate is painted on its upper surface with 3M black velvet nonselective paint. Cool air is blown underneath this absorber plate. The collector columns are paired so that cold air enters near the bottom of the first column (west side) from the hot-air manifold, travels upward to the top of the collector, turns, and comes down to near the bottom of the second column, then is ducted to the hot-air manifold and to storage. The same flow pattern occurs in the other columns.

The glazing is double-tempered glass. Both layers of glass were laid and sealed separately so that each becomes a waterproof layer. A butyl caulking compound was used, and although this has worked satisfactorily, Roy Clark feels that the more flexible Tremco-mono sealant might be better. He has noticed that the butyl has dried out somewhat where it is exposed to the elements.

The insulation for the panels is 6″ of fiberglass batts laid between the rafters. Cedar wood is used for the battens covering the joints between the glazings.

Pronounced condensation has occurred between the glass layers of three of the collector panels in the top row. Apart from concerns about efficiency and cosmetics, Ian was worried about moisture getting into the collector substructure or roof and causing damage. Roy Clark will soon replace the three panels under the five-year guarantee.

Storage

The 8 x 8 x 7′-high storage bin is located near the north wall of the basement. Three sides are constructed of concrete cinderblock laid with construction adhesive rather than mortar, and the fourth side on the east is constructed of 2 x 8 studwall framing with galvanized-metal sheeting on the inside, gypsum board on the outside, and fiberglass insulation in the cavity. This studwall would permit easy access if it was decided to change the size of the rock storage or change the storage medium itself. The bottom of the bin and inside of the concrete walls are insulated with 2″ of rigid extruded polystyrene. The storage medium is 22 tons of washed, whole aggregate about 4″ to 6″ in diameter, although some are as large as 8″ or 10″. The stones lie on a cinderblock foundation. Hot air from the collector is forced downward in the bin. When heat from the bin is demanded to heat the house, the flow is reversed.

Heat Distribution

The Kings were fortunate in that the rectangular sheet-metal ducts for the air circulation did not result in much loss of living space. The only useful space lost was half the closet in the first-floor south bedroom, where two 16″-diameter ducts pass. The feeder duct and the hot-air-return duct both run the entire 58-foot length of the house. They are stacked one on top of the other. In the second-floor south bedrooms, they run behind the kneewall, and in the family room they are boxed in at the junction of the cathedral ceiling and the top of the south wall.

A thermistor in the storage bin and one in the collector are connected to a differential thermostat. When the thermostat senses that the temperature of the collector is 20° F. higher than the temperature in storage, the 1/3-hp blower (2,000 cu. ft. per minute) is activated. Typically, this will not come on earlier than 9:00 or 9:15 a.m. and sometimes not until as late as 10:30 a.m. Of course, it will not come on at all if no direct or indirect sunlight strikes the collector.

A thermostat in the first-floor hallway demands heat either directly from the collectors or from storage.

Detail of the concrete-block rock storage bin, forced-air distribution fan unit (lower left), and forced-air ducts.

Small servo motors operate the dampers. A back-draft damper in the collector return duct prevents reverse thermosiphoning. A standard forced-air duct system distributes hot air to the house and returns cold air to the air-handling unit.

In the summer, two pipes with manual control baffles exhaust air up to the north side of the house to the outside—that is, they bypass storage altogether and only exchange heat to the water coil for the domestic hot-water supply. A booster fan driven by a ¼-hp motor was added to the original design, as not enough air was being moved through the system.

AUXILIARY HEATING

The original baseboard heaters supply some backup heating. In some rooms, they are shut off completely; in others they are set at 55-60° F.

The house originally had three fireplaces—one in the basement, one in the kitchen/family room, and one in the living room. Although the masonry chimney is in the center of the house they were all very inefficient, so modifications were first made to these before the Kings decided to go solar. In the basement, an Ashley Imperial C-60 was installed. A ⅛″ steel plate with a 6″-diameter hole in the center was installed in the top of the fireplace and then sealed with stove cement. A similar modification was made to the family room/kitchen fireplace, to accommodate the stovepipe from a small, efficient French stove called the Chappee, which sits midway between the kitchen and the family room.

For the Ashley, only one fire a season is built. The Ashley has a bimetal-spring manually set thermostat which controls the amount of air entering the firebox. This is not run on a very low setting because of the possibility of creosote buildup; therefore, the stove has to be stoked two or three times per day. No additional ductwork was installed for the Ashley. It was placed near the basement stairs and heat was allowed to convect up the stairwell through the open door at the top of the stairs. This arrangement works very well.

The coal/wood-burning Chappee Model 8033 has a small firebox but it provides enough heat for the kitchen/family room and part of the upstairs. This very well-designed stove is lined with high-quality refractory brick and has a heavy-duty shakable cast-iron grate. A built-in heat exchanger allows hot combustion temperatures to be maintained without losing the heat up the chimney. Since the Chappee was installed, the electric baseboard heaters have never been turned on in either the kitchen or the family room. It is used a great deal for preparing soups, stews, and teas.

The two stoves were installed in September 1975. That first winter they burned seven and a half cords of wood (mostly hickory) and 1,500 pounds of coal. The following winter with the solar system installed, only half as much solid fuel was burned.

PERCENT SOLAR-HEATED

The Kings have kept accurate records of electrical consumption since they purchased this home. Using changes in consumption since wood stoves and the solar system were installed, Ian calculates that the solar system supplies at least 60% of their heating and domestic hot-water needs. The following table and Ian's interpretation of it explain how this figure was arrived at.

"In reviewing the above data, I would tend toward rating the system as providing not less than 60% of heat and hot water. No precise measure would be found unless I chose to use electric heat solely as a backup (eliminate wood-stove usage) and corrected the tables via degree-day variation season by season. I do have some conversion values for equating cordwood to kilowatt hours but regard them as somewhat untrustworthy because of a number of variables that enter our equation; for example, our Ashley is deployed in our basement where there was previously no form of heating whatsoever and, a direct comparison of the Ashley and the Chappee, operative across a range of temperatures, to the more precise setting of electric thermostats seems specious. I would judge that the house is maintained at somewhat higher and more comfortable temperatures with wood stoves than that of electric heat when we used it solely.

"An interpretation of the 60% minimum solar support is as follows:

1. An appropriate base would be 37,000 kwh (see totals for calendar 1973 and 1974) since this represents full calendar years where the only means of heating was electrical and is indicative of our use where we began employing simple conservation procedures such as cold-water wash, shutoff of dishwasher before drying cycle, etc.
2. Calendar year 1976 is a poor period of comparison for solar since the system was only operational for about five weeks in that year (system was turned on for the first time in the last week of November 1976). The 21,584 kwh obtained in that year is a larger tribute to wood stoves than to solar systems.
3. Using 37,000 kwh as a base for annual electrical

ELECTRICAL USAGE & COST

		1971	1972	1973	1974	1975	1976	1977	1978
JAN.	KWH		6181	6659	5246	5291	2442	1374	1159E
	$		111.05	135.87	127.23	183.33	86.54	53.66	48.09
FEB.	KWH		7203	5918	4629	4831	1559	1759	1758E
	$		130.19	124.37	116.15	166.82	58.79	66.81	69.93
MAR.	KWH		5866	3543	4105	4699	1675	1606	2955E
	$		110.41	78.91	107.70	163.83	62.55	62.08	110.91
APR.	KWH		2105	2560	2607	2143	1778	1143	1687
	$		43.76	58.26	78.69	79.35	65.69	46.75	66.62
MAY	KWH		1644	1630	1526	1354	1480	1212	1549
	$		36.88	39.87	50.55	53.33	56.63	49.08	62.20
JUNE	KWH		1469	1651	1319	1422	1233	1158	1188
	$		33.67	40.28	48.54	55.36	48.62	47.89	49.90
JULY	KWH		2369	1734E	1192	1279	1255	907	1379
	$		49.88	41.89	46.15	50.05	49.13	38.93	56.92
AUG.	KWH		297	903	1375	1254	1502	1279	1084
	$		12.47	26.85	52.91	49.45	56.86	50.06	45.94
SEPT.	KWH	1350	1223	1238	1670	1368*	1522	1132	951
	$	29.66	29.75	33.89	64.34	53.21	57.31	45.42	41.02
OCT.	KWH	2220	3341	2152	2304	1196	1948	1219	
	$	44.00	70.12	53.46	91.75	47.21	71.33	47.77	
NOV.	KWH	6205	5193	3628	4714	1435	1996**	1602	
	$	113.53	104.83	85.45	179.71	55.21	72.98	61.33	
DEC.	KWH	6505	5301	5025	6175	1821	3194E	1978	
	$	116.28	108.91	117.79	206.63	67.29	111.29	78.19	
TOTALS	KWH	16,280	42,192	36,641	36,862	28,093	21,584	16,369	
	$	303.47	841.92	836.89	1170.35	1024.44	797.72	647.97	
AVERAGE	KWH/MC		3516	3053	3072	2341	1799	1364	
	KWH/COST	.0186	.0199	.0228	.0317	.0365	.0370	.0390	
	$/MO.		70.16	69.74	97.53	85.37	66.48	53.99	

NOTES: "E"—estimated bill by CL & P (Conn. Light & Power—Utility).
* Sept '75 installed wood stoves; usage 8-10 cords wood (or 7½ cords 1500# coal)
** Late Nov '76—solar installation, usage of wood in each of past two seasons 3-3½ cords.

consumption (representative of the standard for this house when solely electric) and 10,800 kwh as the base for annual consumption for lights and appliances (based on lowest monthly electrical consumption of 900 kwh x 12 months =10,800 kwh), then we can make the following calculations:

a) 37,000 -10,800 = 26,200 kwh for heat and hot water.

b) 26,200 x 60% (solar design) = 15,720 kwh displaced by solar.

c) 26,200 - 15,720 = 10,480 kwh (net) for heat and hot water.

d) 10,800 + 10,480 = 21,280 kwh total usage with 60% solar design.

e) but actual usage for 1977 was only 16,369 kwh.

4. When comparing 21,280 kwh (as a 60% design characteristic) to actual billings of 16,369 kwh in calendar year 1977, it's pleasing to note that we are 4911 kwh below that level. In general terms, I would attribute the lower figures to wood-stove usage that gets us below the solar design figure. Some other points:

a) 16,369 kwh for 1977 is slightly understated since our utility estimated our December 1976 bill at 3194 kwh (too high an estimate) and gave us a bill for January 1977 of 1374 kwh, which is corrected to actual usage for the two months (1374 kwh is therefore understated). The average for the two-month period is 2284 kwh, and . . .

2284 - 1374 = 910 kwh

16,369 + 910 = 17,279 kwh - estimated actual usage 1977

21,280 kwh (60% solar) -17,279 kwh = 4001 kwh below

20,800 kwh (65% solar) - 17,279 kwh = 3521 kwh below

b) When I add kwh for the period of July 1977 through June 1978, a total of 18,413 kwh is obtained, which is still 2867 kwh below the 21,280 figure. Our year-to-date figures for calendar year 1978 indicate to me that we will probably be close to the 18,000 kwh level for this year (I suspect that our usage is increasing somewhat in direct proportion to my two teen-aged sons' increased interest in cleanliness via multiple showers per day, which is undoubtedly related to some increased awareness of girls).

5. What does all this mean?

a) I think it means that we are achieving 60% solar contribution to domestic hot water and space heating and maybe more, and beating that design level with supplementary wood-stove use.

b) Our total kwh use in calendar year 1977 is about 40% of what we used in 1972 (42,192 x 40% = 16,876).

c) Our wood usage is averaging 3½ cords per season over the past two years at an average cost of $35 per cord (between what I cut and purchase), so 3.5 x $35 = $122.50. Usage includes some occasional and wasteful wood burning in the living-room fireplace. We have not used coal since the 1975-76 season.

d) It is interesting to note that in the fall of 1977 the solar system provided us with sufficient heat all the way through November, and our first wood-stove usage began in December. This year (fall 1978) is following closely, as I have used the Chappee (only) during two particularly cold nights, following relatively sunless periods so far and don't expect prolonged use to begin until December with wood."

COSTS

The Kings provided the following cost data for their home:

i)	$572.90	interest on capital cost ($6,740 x .085)
	+122.50	wood, 3½ cords @ average cost of $35/cord (between what they cut and purchased).
	+648.00	total electrical cost, 1977
	$1,343.40	total cost, 1977 versus $1,480.00 cost if total electric (37,000 x 4¢/kwh), which is a savings of approximately $137.

ii) There are no property taxes in Madison associated with the solar-system cost.

iii) R. Clark presented the $6,740 cost for the solar system as having a payback in less than 12 years at then-prevailing electric rates.

iv) Ian & Elaine based their decision on a payback period of 5-7 years using electric rate increases of 10-12% per year (they have averaged about 14% a year in the past few years).

v) The Kings were guided in their economic decision by a chart in the Barber/Watson book *Design Criteria for Solar Heated Buildings*, May 1975, a Sunworks Publication. A chart therein from Jesse Denton ("Integrated Solar Power Climate Conditioning Systems," July 1974, Energy Management Center, Univ. of Pa.) relates solar savings per month in current fuel costs to various percentages of fuel rate increase over varying time spans (5, 10, 15, 20 years) at interest rates of 5, 7, 10, and 12 percent to determine an economic limit that is justifiable for capital investment in solar equipment.

COOLING SYSTEM

Because the house is well insulated, overheating in summer is not a problem. The open concept on much of the first floor facilitates cross-ventilation. The operable skylights, particularly the one above the family room, permit efficient exhaust of warm air.

WATER SUPPLY AND WASTE SYSTEM

Water is supplied from a 180′ drilled well fitted with a submersible 8-gallon-per-minute pump. Ten months of the year the water supply is adequate. Twice in the last seven years, however, during very dry summer months when the water table is low, they have drawn rusty or sandy water. Consequently, the lawn or garden is rarely watered during these times.

Domestic hot water is preheated by being passed through an 8′-long stack of finned coils located in the collector hot-air return, near where it enters the rock storage. This stack is three units high by four units wide—a unit being a ¾″ copper pipe with aluminum fins approximately 3 x 4″. Final heating is by an electrical heating element within an 80-gallon hot-water tank. During July this element has been shut off altogether and water heated only by the solar system. Tap temperatures are then typically about 120° F.

In order to conserve hot water, a cold-water wash is used for clothing. A water-saving Nova shower head uses about one-third the water that a conventional shower head uses. The toilets have no water-conserving features.

A standard septic system and leaching field dispose of waterborne wastes.

Newspapers, tin cans, and bottles are saved and delivered to a recycling depot at the local school. Organic kitchen wastes are composted.

ELECTRICAL POWER SYSTEM

Because the Kings are hooked up to the local electrical utility grid and subject to the ever-increasing supply costs, they attempt to conserve electricity wherever possible. The judicious placement of windows makes artificial lighting unnecessary during the day. Fluorescent lighting is used for the bathrooms. Three-way bulbs are used for some lights, and rheostats are used on three of the major systems—dining room, living room, and family room.

MAJOR HOUSEHOLD APPLIANCES

An electric stove with a self-cleaning oven uses less electricity than a conventional stove because of its superior insulation. As mentioned earlier, the Chappee combination coal/wood stove is used a great deal.

A combination upright freezer/refrigerator uses a considerable amount of power. Their old chest-type freezer is more efficient. A fairly new General Electric washing machine permits mini-washes. Elaine uses her clothesline until the temperature gets very cold and then uses the GE automatic dryer, which is exhaust-vented into the basement. The automatic dishwasher is shut off before the drying cycle in order to conserve power.

FOOD SYSTEM

A 16 x 25′ garden provides fresh vegetables during the growing season with enough left over to provide fresh-frozen produce well into the winter. The Kings avoid the use of artificial fertilizers and pesticides, preferring instead to use organic methods. They are motivated by economics and by what they feel is the superior taste and quality of homegrown produce.

COSTS

The total cost of this retrofitted solar system, including all materials and labor, came to $6,740.

CONCLUDING THOUGHTS

Ian and Elaine at this point in time have no criticisms about any of the work or about the design features. In Elaine's words, "Having lived with this solar-heating system for a while now, I feel rather blasé about it. I'm used to it and it doesn't seem innovative anymore. I'm very pleased with the system and with the builder."

Terra Cotta, Ontario
1,990 sq. ft. living area

RIC and SANDRA SYMMES

In 1967 Ric and Sandra Symmes had their house built on Ric's father's pasture farm in Ontario. They added to it in 1972 and then in 1975 they began their first experiment with solar space heating. There were a number of reasons why the Symmeses decided to attempt this project. In 1973 they became involved with the Sierra Club and other groups in a campaign against the installation of an Ontario Hydro powerline that was to run from a generating station in Nanticoke, through their area, around Toronto and to Pickering on the other side of Toronto. Through this effort they became more aware of the problems and damage that hydro facilities were causing and thus resolved to make a personal effort to reduce their own consumption of electricity. (Since 1975 Ric has been chairman of the Sierra Club of Ontario.)

They were also motivated by the OPEC oil embargo and a series of articles on inflation that Ric had read. It became clear to them that a very good thing to do in times of an inflationary economy is to stop buying commodities whose prices are inflated. Ric explains, "If you are buying over a period of time, you are going to pay more than if you can fix your costs at one point. With solar heat you put your money out in front, but ever after the cost of your heat is fixed. In our case the capital cost of the solar addition was low, so I thought it was a good inflation hedge."

Another motivation was curiosity. They were curious to know whether environmentally appropriate ways of supplying energy would really work and whether they could significantly reduce their demands for electricity. Ric first built a device that would cook "hot dogs" and then built a little solar collector to produce hot water. When these two projects worked well he decided to try solar space heating.

LOCATION AND ORIENTATION

The Symmes home is located on 5.9 acres about a mile from Ric's father's home farm in Terra Cotta, Ontario. It was oriented with its long axis running east to west, mainly to take advantage of the view of the pond and the countryside to the north.

Winter winds at this 8,000-degree-day site are from the west-northwest, but that side of the house is buffered by the garage and cedar and juniper trees. There is a heavy cedar bush immediately to the east of the house, protecting it from the occasional bad storm that comes from that direction. Ric and Sandra also wanted to be close to the bush and trees in order to be closer to birds and other wildlife. Being nestled in these woods and at the end of a fairly long lane, the home is very private. Pine trees growing along the edge of the lane will provide a good windbreak in the future.

ARCHITECTURAL FEATURES

Ric and Sandra were influenced a great deal by Rex Roberts' book *Your Engineered House* (New York: Evans, 1964). Following many of Roberts' maxims, they designed the house themselves and acted as their own general contractors both for the main part of the house, built in 1967, and the family room, built in 1972.

The house has 1,990 sq. ft. of living space on one level. A concrete slab serves as the floor and support for the superstructure. There is no basement. Ric and Sandra like this type of design because from a time-and-motion point of view, the house is very efficient. Since Ric is an industrial engineer by training, he is particularly interested in efficiency. Anything that has to be moved can be moved on wheels anywhere in the house. The laundry basket, for example, is literally a shopping cart. There are no stairs in the house, a feature for which Sandy was particularly grateful during pregnancy and now that they have three young children.

Ric acknowledges that other shapes—a cube, for example—are more energy-efficient but cautions that we shouldn't let energy-efficiency be the only criterion in designing a house. "Thought has to be given to the people who are going to live in it."

Rigid panels of extruded polystyrene 2″ thick placed vertically around the perimeter of the floor slab extends down to bedrock. A 2′-wide band of the same insulation was laid horizontally before the concrete floor was poured over it and the packed sand-and-gravel base. A polyethylene membrane was laid over the sand to act as a moisture barrier. There is a small area in the kitchen where the floor is cool, because in one spot the slab wasn't insulated properly from the outdoors. Ric reports that the remaining 95% of the floor remains comfortably warm. The living/dining area was carpeted two years ago for noise control and for a "nice feel underfoot"—not because the floor was cold. The rest of the house has tiles laid directly on the concrete floor. "The disadvantage of slab construction," says Ric, "extends more to utility services. What do you do, for example, when a water or sewer pipe which is buried in the concrete plugs up? I've had no problems, except there are a couple of faucets where the water runs pretty slowly. I don't know yet what I'm going to do about it."

The layout of the house is designed to take best advantage of the view to the north. The kitchen is

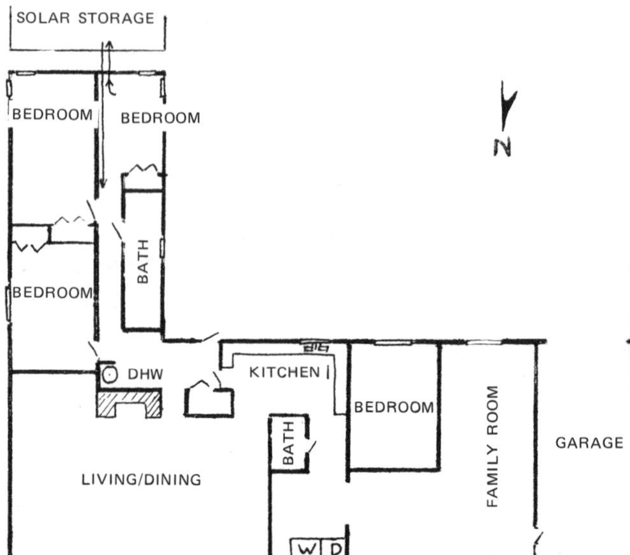

conveniently located in the center of the house. The service inlets and big power consumers are all concentrated in this central area.

The fireplace is centrally located to confine surface heat losses to the living spaces.

Exterior Walls

The exterior walls were built to 1967 electric standards. The standard 2 x 4 studwall has 3½″ fiberglass batt insulation plus exterior asphalt fiberboard. Although the Symmeses preferred the board-and-batten siding recommended by Rex Roberts, they chose the no-maintenance aluminum siding because Ric is away from home a great deal and wanted to minimize upkeep. The inside of the studs has a polyethylene vapor barrier and two ⅜″ layers of gypsum board. Some of the walls are painted, while others have wood panels.

Interior Walls and Ceilings

Standard 2 x 4 studwalls are used throughout and finished in the same manner as the inside of the exterior walls. The 2 x 6 ceiling joists on 16″ centers are similarly sheathed in two ⅜″ layers of gypsum board. The ceiling was strapped and acoustic tile installed. Above the gypsum board is a vapor barrier and fiberglass insulation. The builder put in 6″ of fiberglass, and the Symmeses later added 4″ more.

Sunspot I, nearest the house, on the right, was the first solar retrofit. Sunspot II was recently added to improve the system's performance. They blend in with the house and the rest of the surroundings.

Roof

The 2 x 4 roof rafters, on 16″ centers, were site-built. The roof was sheathed with plywood, tarpaper, and heavy shingles. A 30″ overhang all around provides some protection from the elements. In the winter it allows sunlight to come in the south windows, but it shades them in summer. An excellent feature of the house is its vented ridge. With vented aluminum soffits and the ridge vent running the full length of the roof peak, the house stays very cool throughout the summer.

Insulation Summary

Foundation: R-8; 2″ extruded polystyrene perimeter insulation

Walls: R-15; 3½″ fiberglass batts and other materials

Ceiling: R-35; 10″ fiberglass batts, acoustic tile, etc.

Ric recaulked the whole building in 1978 to reduce heat loss and air infiltration.

Doors

The 1¾″ wood slab door to the front entranceway has a lot of glass in it in order to brighten the hallway. It has a Lloyd wooden storm/screen door, which costs more than an aluminum door but is a better insulator. There is a patio door on the north side of the living/dining area and wood slab doors leading to the garage and out of the family room. The latter two have aluminum storm/screen doors. A recent energy project was to improve the weatherstripping around all the doors. Ric is now considering building an airlock entry from the garage and later possibly one for the front door. He hopes to close off the family room's exterior door for the winter but hasn't yet found a convenient alternative entry for the children when they skate on the pond. Each of the doorways has a cedar bush fairly close by to act as a windbreak.

Windows

Two large 5 x 8′-wide fixed thermopane picture windows and a 5′-wide patio door are located in the living/dining area north wall. Ric makes no apologies for this, as they have a beautiful view to the north. If he were building again he would not change these windows except, perhaps, given today's energy costs, to triple-glaze them.

The other windows in the house are Dashwood wood-frame casement windows. Some windows have three lights of 12 x 32″-high thermopane glass, while others have two. Ric says the quality is extremely good. They close very tightly and have a very good flashing. However, all the wood framing really cuts down on the glass area. If the Symmeses were building again, they would use fewer windows with more glass area per unit. Ric is going to test a couple of acrylic inside storm windows this fall. He is also interested in insulated drapes or shutters, but hasn't done enough research to be able to make a decision regarding their use.

SOLAR-HEATING SYSTEM

In 1975 Ric built 144 sq. ft. of freestanding collector, which he named Sunspot I. The rock storage is contained within an insulated A-frame shed whose south slope accommodates the collector array. Although this worked fine, the quantity of heat which it delivered was totally inadequate for the house's needs and there were a number of things he quickly learned could be done better. So in the summer of 1977, Ric added a similar unit of another 144 sq. ft. of collector sharing the same rock storage. The interior of this second A-frame, dubbed Sunspot II, is used as storage for deck chairs and garden tools. An advantage of using these sheds is that they sit on the ground and can be (as in this case) designed and landscaped to blend in with the house and other surroundings. They were easier to construct than a roof-mounted system probably would have been and the Symmeses don't have to worry about an extra load on the roof.

Collector

The collectors are oriented due south. Sunspot I was tilted 60° but Sunspot II was tilted at an angle of only 45°. Ric chose this lower angle after checking with the local weather office regarding hours of sunlight and percent sunlight for his area. According to his calculations, after he allowed for hours of sunlight—that is, the fact that the days are very short in November, December, and January—and allowed for the low percentage of sunshine in November and December in particular (22% and 26-27% respectively), he determined that there were a couple more percentage points of collecting ability to be gained by tilting the collector back to an angle less than latitude plus 15°—that is, an angle more appropriate to the "shoulder" season. "I have no way of proving these calculations with this system," says Ric. "But I'm very happy with its output."

He recommends that the bottom lip of the collector be 2′ or 3′ aboveground in areas where there is a considerable amount of snow in order to avoid excessive clearing in winter.

Ric considered several types of glazing. He did an experiment with regular glass and discovered that the heat shattered the glass. He also considered fiberglass but opted for thermopane patio-door glass that he bought as seconds because it had appearance defects. He felt it was more durable than fiberglass, has superior performance in terms of light transmission, and with the black absorber plate visible behind, was more attractive. Since maintaining a good seal is important in an air collector, the lower coefficient of expansion of glass was also important.

Each thermopane unit measures 34 x 74″. The first set of eight cost $30 each, while the second set of eight cost $35 each. Ric said if he had to pay the regular price of $93 per unit he would have thought more seriously about it.

The collector frames for Sunspot I are picture-window frames made by a local window maker, and ¾″

quarter-round was used for trim around each glazing. Ric found the trim to be a great snow catcher, so on Sunspot II the glazing has no trim and is slightly above the frames so the snow slides off.

In each case the absorber plate is aluminum roofing painted with nonselective flat black Tremclad paint. "When I built the first unit," said Ric, "I just couldn't find anyone who could sell me a selective paint. Some people will black-chrome metal for you but at a pretty high cost per square foot, and I thought it would be better to spend the same money on more square feet of collector." He has had no problem with deterioration or peeling of the Tremclad after three years of operation on the first unit and one year on the second unit.

In Sunspot I the air travels laterally across the collector from west to east between the glazing and the absorber plate. There are several disadvantages to this design. First, Ric made three slots in each of the wood-frame members separating the eight lights of glass, but learned that they are too small. As a result, there is too much back pressure for the air trying to get through and the volume of air passing is less than it should be. Temperature gain across the collector runs something in the order of 80° F., which is more than it should be for optimum efficiency. Also the greater the back pressure, the more prone the collector is to leaks. Another disadvantage with the front-pass system is that one doesn't get any insulating value from the airspace. As well, Ric found that for some reason the air tends to foul the inside surface of the glass with an oily film which appears to reduce transmission qualities by reflecting light.

In Sunspot II these disadvantages were overcome by using a back-pass system. The air travels behind the absorber plate in a 3½" air passage in the same direction as in Sunspot I. Pipe hangers secured behind the plate break the laminar flow, creating turbulence and some heat loss, but even then the back pressure is very low—about 1/10" of water for the 24' run. The temperature rise across the original collector has not worsened, while that across the new collector is 20° to 30° F. better. Ric now feels that a 2"-wide air passage would have been quite adequate and it would have made the collector box lighter and stronger.

Storage

There are 20,000 pounds of water-washed gravel, ¾" to 3" in diameter, in the 2 x 4 frame shed of Sunspot I. The sloped walls are insulated with 3½" fiberglass batts, and the endwalls have been increased to 7". Ric says that the unit is inadequately insulated and that after doing some calculations, he may add foamboard to the back slope of the shed. He is very happy with stone storage but ideally, he says, it would be best to have the storage within the dwelling, so any heat losses would be to the living spaces. The way it is now, if there are three or four sunless days in a row and the temperature is -10° F., the temperature of the stones drops to -10° F. Then when there is some sun it takes a long time for the stones to heat up to a point where there is usable heat for the house.

In view of this, from mid-November until March 1, Ric sets his controls so that all of the heat that is collected comes straight into the house and is distributed immediately to the living spaces. Fortunately, there is a good balance between what is produced in the collector and what the house needs. On a fairly good solar-heating day the stone storage will get some heat and supply it to the house until about 7:00 p.m., and by 8.00 p.m. the house is using auxiliary heat. Once the ambient temperature starts to get more moderate—approaching the freezing mark and above—the storage seems to work reasonably efficiently.

Heat Distribution

The ductwork into the house for Sunspot I is 6" circular ducts, which worked well for this first unit. Ric feels that it would be more satisfactory with the addition of Sunspot II to have 8" ducts into the house. When he applied the duct tape his intent was only to make sure the joints didn't come apart, so he used the tape very sparingly. He wishes he had used the tape more liberally to ensure an airtight seal at these joints. The ducts are insulated with 3" of fiberglass plus wood and some other materials to about R-15, which Ric feels is less than he should have. He feels it is impractical to rectify these inadequacies the way the system was designed.

He used 8" circular ducts to hook up Sunspot II in parallel with Sunspot 1.

Heat is delivered to the house through a single hot-air register located near the ceiling in the south-wing hallway. The cold-air return is located in one of the bedrooms near the floor on the south wall of the wing.

The two fans in the system were bought from a scrap dealer. Both are 1,400-cu.-ft.-per-minute squirrel-cage-type furnace fans with ¼-hp motors. One is a collector fan which functions when solar heat is available to be collected. When the house's thermostat demands heat, the house-supply fan circulates air out to the collector to be heated and returned to warm the living space. The V-belt-driven fans are located inside the collector unit, and the motors are located outside (with a weather cover) to prevent them from overheating. Ric states, "You need a fairly good-quality motor,

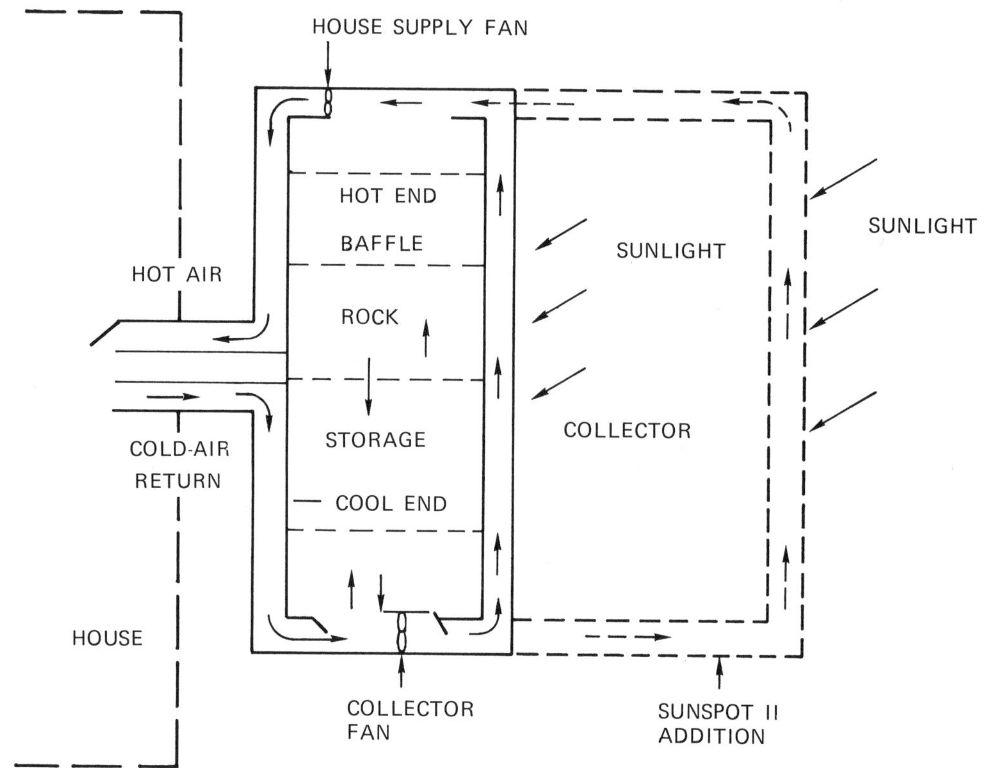

TOP VIEW (Showing air flow)

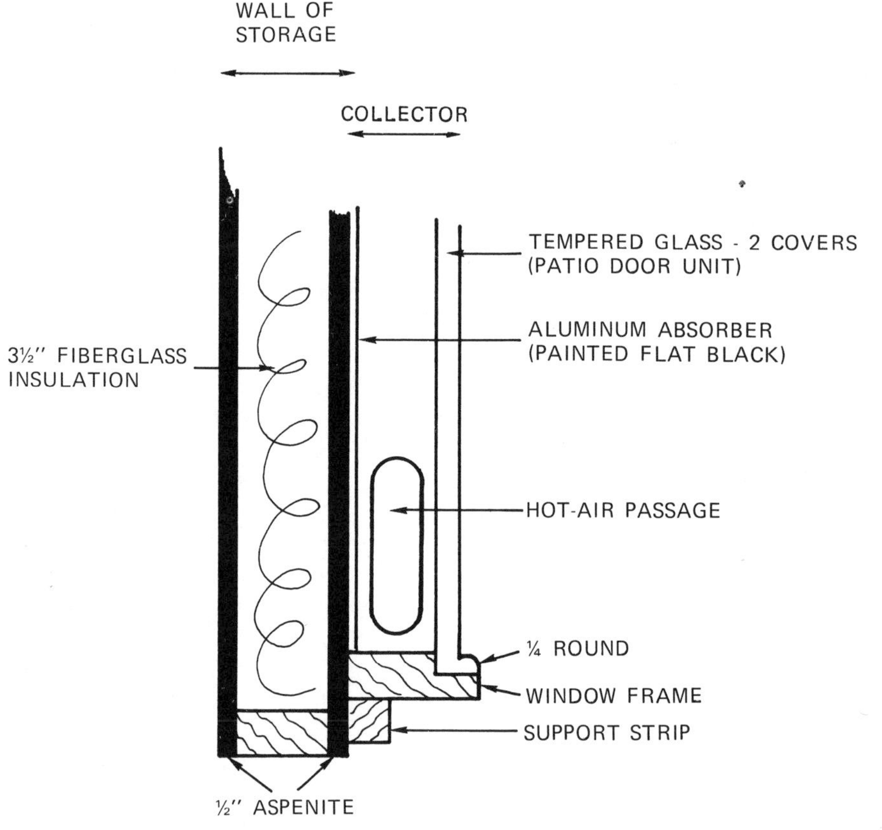

COLLECTOR PANEL, SIDE SECTION VIEW

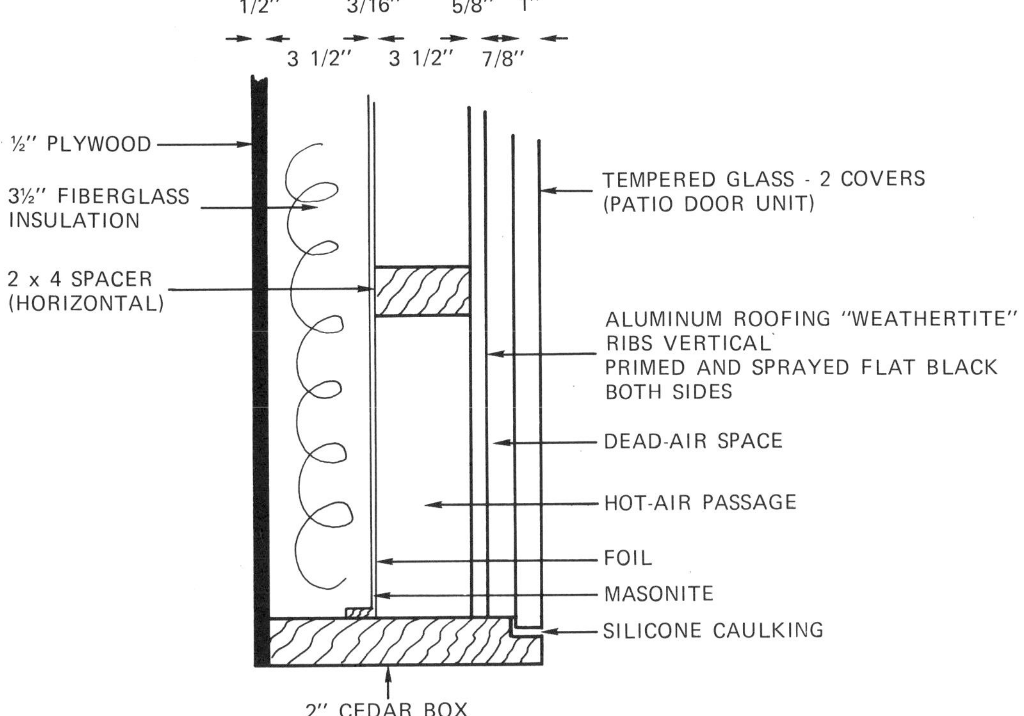

COLLECTOR BOX, SIDE SECTION VIEW

since the unit gets pretty stiff on cold days, but on the whole it works quite well." The system is designed so both fans can run simultaneously.

The original control device for the collection mode consisted of a small wooden box with a glass cover in front of a black plate. Behind that was an airspace that contained a chicken-house thermostat. The box was installed near the top of the shed. The idea was that when the sun shone on the box it would heat up the air within, trigger the thermostat, and turn on the collector fan. This was not a very satisfactory device, as it did not parallel what was going on inside the collector, there being no air change in this control box.

The new control device was installed behind the absorber plate near the top of the hot end of Sunspot II. It is a Honeywell thermostat of the kind which has a probe-type sensor to measure the heat in the plenum of an oil or gas furnace. Installed with no modifications, it essentially opens or closes the hot wire to the collector fan. The point at which the fan comes on or shuts off is manually set. In this case it is set to come on at 105° F. and turn off at 90° F. The turn-on temperature is set 10° F. higher from April 1 to October 15. The house-supply fan is controlled by a 110-volt electric-heat thermostat inside the house in series with a 110-volt chicken-house-fan thermostat located in the rock bin.

Ric had problems with the hot air from the house-supply fan being diluted with cold air coming off the absorber plate, but solved this by installing a solenoid-operated trap door at the collector array's hot-air-outlet port. The solenoid is electrically connected so that only when the collector fan comes on does this trap door open.

As noted in the description of the storage system, from mid-November until March 1 the controls are set so that all heat that is collected comes right into the house, bypassing storage.

One other problem which Ric encountered was reverse thermosiphoning through the hot-air register to the house. He solved this by installing a spring-loaded door on the outside of the register.

AUXILIARY HEATING

The Symmeses primary backup to the solar system is electric baseboard resistance heating. "This is a terrible combination from the point of view of the public interest," says Ric, "because what that means is that I am contributing to putting up the winter peak of demand for electricity and Ontario Hydro has to build generating facilities to accommodate the peak demand." From about the middle of February until November or December they don't use the resistance heating.

The Symmeses were not aware of this problem when they built their home in 1967, nor did they envision adding solar collectors. They decided for first-cost reasons and lack of a basement to install electric heating. The initial installation cost was about $1,000 less than the conventional alternatives, and they did not have the extra $1,000 to spare.

The original massive concrete-and-stone central fireplace had a Heatilator unit built into it, but it was not very efficient, as typically the family would go to bed and in about an hour the fire would burn down and warm house air would go up the chimney all night long and the next morning, or until someone remembered to close the damper. Ric doesn't think the mass effect is very significant, as the Heatilator is insulated from the masonry.

He installed a fan system that draws air from the bedroom wing and discharges it to the living room, dining room, and front hall. Also at the end of September 1978 he installed tempered-glass doors. Ric says he sometimes misses the smell of straying sparks burning the sheepskin rug, but the fireplace seems more efficient, although he has no way of quantifying this. It is safer now and one gets a better view of the fire through the glass than through the screen. The doors are a Brooks unit that cost $114 at Shop-rite. Ric solved the seemingly difficult installation problem by mounting angle iron around the Heatilator within the firebox and securing the doors to the angle iron rather than to the rough stone.

The Symmeses have a small woodlot behind the house plus access to a large woodlot on the home farm, so wood fuel is a very environmentally appropriate source of space heating. Now that the dead elm is gone, they burn mostly maple and some windfall cedar. They have been burning about a cord of wood a season, burning it three times a week. The weekend fire will burn all day Saturday and Sunday, if the family is home, and will heat the central core of the house.

Ric and his father recently designed and had built a tractor-mounted log splitter.

PERCENT SOLAR-HEATED

It is difficult to come up with a precise figure for the amount of heat contributed by the solar system. Ric had to make some reasonable estimates as to what is going on in the house, because all the electrical usage is recorded by one meter. Also, since the winter of 1977-78 had 11% more degree-days than the reference year, 1974-75, an adjustment had to be made to the reference year's electrical consumption.

Ric feels that based on the experience of a friend and other people he has talked to, 43% is too optimistic. "We will just have to assume," he says, "that some of the other energy-consuming steps we have taken, such as installing the storm doors, weatherstripping, and temperature setbacks have had a significant effect." Savings due to recaulking of the house and the addition of the fireplace glass doors do not enter into this figure of 43%, as this work was done after the 1978 heating season. "I would be surprised," says Ric, "if the efficiency is more than thirty-six percent based on the experience of a friend of mine who lives nearby and who has a water system. He has measured it very carefully and knows almost exactly how many kilowatt-hours are saved. His collector efficiency is thirty-six percent."

The Symmeses generally keep the inside house temperatures at 68° to 70°F. during winter days and 63° to 64°F. during winter nights, if they remember to turn all the thermostats back. Each baseboard heater has its own thermostat, so if they miss turning one down it tries to keep the whole house warm. Ric is working on an automatic temperature-setback system but so far he has not found an economic one.

Calculations—Ric Symmes

	Kilowatt-hours
Electrical consumption reference year, 1974 (before solar)	44,800
Less electrical consumption for DHW, lights and cooking (no baby in diapers)	12,000
Plus 11% for degree-day adjustment to 1978	3,608
Electrical consumption, (adjusted) for space heating, 1974	36,408
Electrical consumption, 1978	34,840
Less estimated electrical consumption for DHW, lights and cooking (baby in diapers—more hot water)	14,000
Estimated electrical consumption for space heating, 1978	20,840
Savings in electrical consumption 1978 over adjusted 1974 consumption (i.e., amount provided by solar)	36,408 -20,840 15,568

Apparent percent solar contribution

$$\frac{15{,}568}{36{,}408} \times 100\% = 43\%$$

COOLING SYSTEM

The good insulation, ridge venting, and large overhangs keep the house relatively cool all summer. During hot spells, the Symmeses let the temperature level reach 78°F. or thereabouts. A 5,000-Btu air conditioner can be called into play if required. Generally the air conditioner is used about five days in a year and its fan alone may be used for another five or six days. Since there are no smokers in the house ventilation is not a problem.

The collector is prevented from damage by overheating during the summer by plywood covers.

WATER SUPPLY AND WASTE SYSTEM

Potable water is supplied by a drilled well on the property. The water is very hard and excellent for drinking. They have considered softening the domestic hot water but have not done so yet.

The only serious problem they have had with the plumbing system is that because the vented ridge keeps the attic very cold, water pipes that were installed there froze and burst even though they were under the insulation. Wrapping the pipes with insulation and other measures failed to resolve the problems, so the pipes had to be taken out and installed under the ceiling acoustic tile, between the strapping.

In the spring of 1978 Ric wrapped the 40-imperial-gallon (48 U.S. gallons) hot-water tank with an additional 4″ of fiberglass insulation but has not yet determined the savings from that. One of his next projects is to build some kind of solar-heated domestic hot-water system. He bought some old air-to-liquid heat exchangers salvaged from the back of air-conditioning units and may consider hooking these up to the air collector system, which is idle during the summer.

None of the plumbing fixtures is particularly water-conserving. Since they have their own septic system and no shortage of water in the area, the Symmeses do not see the point in buying new fixtures. Their system is a proven safe and natural way of disposing of wastes and recycling water. When they built their house in 1967 there seemed to be no information on composting toilets.

Ric and Sandy separate all their garbage. Metals, glass, and newspaper are delivered to a recycling depot and anything else that is burnable is incinerated or burned in the fireplace. Remarkably, they put an average of only one garbage can full of things which can't be used or recycled out to be land-filled every three months.

Heat is delivered to the house through a single hot-air register located above the doorway in the south-wing hallway.

ELECTRICAL SUPPLY SYSTEM

The 200-amp service is supplied by Ontario Hydro. The wind regime at their site is very poor for an economic operation of a wind generator. Ric experimented with a Savonius Rotor to pump extra water into the pond from the stream, but when he postponed taking it down for the winter the great wind that sank the freighter *Edmund Fitzgerald* sank his rotor. He plans to build another unit but only for fun—not to save money.

Natural lighting is good in the house. Fluorescent lights are used in the kitchen, bathroom, and family room, and a couple of the incandescent dining-room lights are on dimmers. They tried to reduce consumption by replacing 100-watt bulbs with 60-watt and 60-watt bulbs with 40-watt and by being more conscientious about turning off lights and other appliances when they are not needed.

Ric Symmes displays the ¼-hp motor connected to the squirrel-cage-type circulation fan located within Sunspot I.

MAJOR HOUSEHOLD APPLIANCES

Many of the Symmeses' appliances were purchased before they or many other people became concerned about power consumption. The stove is electric. They now also have a 650-watt (maximum) microwave oven which was chosen mainly because, with three young children, it saves a great deal of time in meal preparation. There is definitely a net energy gain from April 15 to October 15 when the electric baseboard heaters are not on, but in the winter if the electric stove is not operational the baseboard heaters just run more frequently. Sandy has also been cooking in a wok pan recently—an energy-saving and nutritious way of cooking foods.

A good feature of their refrigerator is that there is no freezer compartment within it. The purchase price was therefore less than that of a standard refrigerator and it uses less energy. They have two chest-type freezers.

The automatic washer allows half-washes, and Sandy washes clothes with cold water most of the time. Ric vented the dryer to the inside for a couple of years but under some circumstances the humidity level was so high that he became concerned that he might be jeopardizing the effectiveness of the insulation, so he vented it to the outside again. The clothesline was first installed to the east of the house—a considerable distance from the laundry room. Now that it is installed close to the laundry room it is used extensively, although not in the winter.

FOOD SYSTEM

The Symmeses have a half-dozen apple trees and a large organic garden. In addition the family harvests some edible wild plants and takes advantage of the pick-your-own-fruit and vegetable gardens. In Ric's words, "The whole family descends like locusts and picks large quantities of beans, raspberries, and other produce." Ric is general manager of the Edible Oils and Dairy Division of Canada Packers, so he has considerable insight into the workings of the food industry. He says, "Occasionally we buy a side of beef, but my view is that an individual doing so is really engaging in a speculative activity. If you bet correctly that the market is going to go up, you win; if not, you lose. The cheapest way is to buy features at the chain store as they take a big price cut and allocate the lost money to the other products."

Ric and Sandy are thinking about building a greenhouse. In the meantime Sandy starts a lot of plants for the garden in the family room's large southern windows, and a great deal of produce is preserved in the freezer.

CONCLUDING THOUGHTS

The savings in electrical consumption and the technological innovations and very practical conservation measures that made these savings possible are certainly impressive. But what impresses me more about the Symmeses is their approach to life—their willingness to examine all aspects of their life-style with respect to their impact on the environment, their willingness to share what they have learned, and their commitment to involvement in organizations dedicated to restoring the quality of our natural resources.

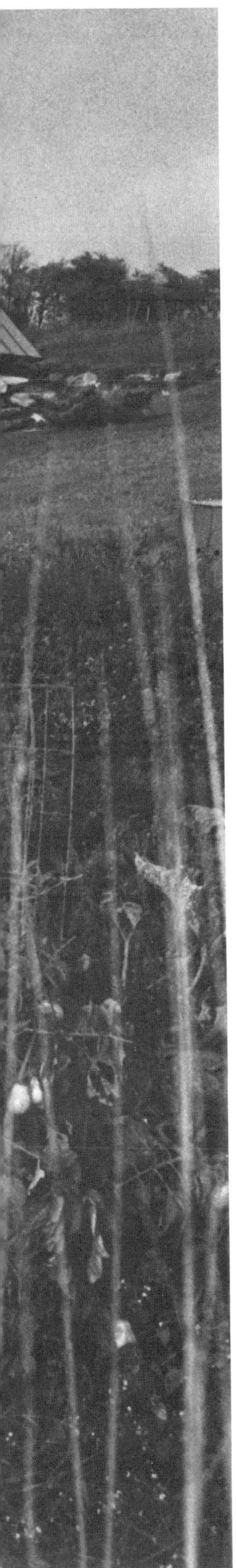

Near Little Compton, Rhode Island
1,350 sq. ft., addition only, including greenhouse

JUNIUS and LOUISE EDDY

In 1974 when Junius and Louise Eddy decided to move their New York City apartment and live year-round in their seaside vacation house in Rhode Island, they soon found themselves face to face with some difficult decisions. First of all, they knew they would need more space; they have six grown children who came to Rhode Island with their families for holidays or summer vacations, and usually wanted to be there all at the same time.

Second, because the house had been so poorly insulated when it was built in 1968, the Eddys realized that if they lived there on a permanent basis they'd be faced with unusually high utility costs. It was an all-electric house, and the electric bills were already high simply for part-time use. In Louise's words, "The original house is beautifully designed, but in practical terms it would have been difficult to conserve energy through insulation without practically tearing down the house and starting over again.

"It seemed to make the most sense," she explains, "for us to build a modest, energy-efficient solar-heated addition that Junius and I could live in during the winter, when we were by ourselves, but then be able to open up the main part of the house when the family or friends were visiting. It was a solution that addressed both of our major problems."

"We were actually interested in doing something with solar, you see, long before we moved up here," Junius adds. "Perhaps because we were living in New York City, our consciences were—in a sense—pricked by the energy and environmental problems. Not really for money reasons, at first, but when we started looking at the electrical bills for that place, dollars and cents certainly entered in. The trouble was we couldn't really get much information on it for a long time."

The Eddys' life in New York was largely centered around the field of education (and the idea of *environmental* education was, during the early '70s, only beginning to emerge as a major priority). Louise had been serving as admissions director for an independent school in the New York area, and Junius was a full-time adviser to a national foundation in the field of arts education. If and when the move to Rhode Island took place, it would mean a significant change in life-style for both of them; she would resign from administrative work, and he would shift to an independent consulting status, working out of his home on a variety of assignments with school systems, arts councils, foundations, and federal agencies.

It all came together for them in the fall of 1974 when they met a young architect named Travis Price at a party in New York one evening. "Until then," Junius says, "we hadn't run across anybody who knew much about solar installations—but Travis had been working for several years on solar developments in New Mexico after getting his architectural degree from the University in Albuquerque. We spent most of that evening talking with him and were impressed with his solar and architectural know-how and his ideas for our addition, and we invited him up to Rhode Island to take a closer look."

The upshot of all this was that, by early winter, the Eddys had hired Price to develop plans for their solar addition. For some of the more technical considerations, Price turned to Everett Barber, a solar engineer from Guilford, Connecticut, who was then president of Sunworks, a solar-collector-fabrication company. (See House 10, built by Barber.) By the summer of 1975, the plans were complete and work on the addition began early in July. Junius and Louise moved to Rhode Island permanently that summer, lived in the main house while work on the addition was going on, and moved into their new "winter quarters" in March 1976.

Living in the original house during most of the 1975-76 heating season proved to be as expensive as they'd anticipated, but it did have one major benefit—they now had almost a full year of electrical utility costs to use as a base year for comparison purposes later on.

LOCATION AND ORIENTATION

The Eddy home is located on 4 acres of open land fronting on an inlet of the Atlantic Ocean near Little Compton, Rhode Island. In order to reduce the wind effect but still retain the view, a system of low coniferous windbreaks is being planned and developed.

The new solar addition faces due south and is protected to the north and northwest by the main house and on the east by being built into the side of a hill. It is thus protected from the prevailing winter northwest winds and the winter storm winds which are typically north and northeast.

ARCHITECTURAL FEATURES

The upper floor of the main house is very energy-inefficient. It has a large open-concept cathedral-ceilinged west-facing living room, adjoining the dining room and kitchen on the northeast side of the building. An inefficient fireplace and large expanses of glass are typical of the lack of concern and knowledge about energy conservation at the time this house was built in 1968. Two bedrooms and Junius's library/study are on the southerly side of this upper floor. A hallway connecting them also leads to the second floor of the addition. The study is integrated into the solar addition.

The lower floor of the main house is composed of a built-in garage at the north and four bedrooms along the west-facing wall. The two southernmost bedrooms were integrated into the first floor of the addition. The walls of these rooms are still poorly insulated, but the owners reinsulated and weatherstripped around the windows.

The addition, which is the main subject of the chapter, is a 1,350-sq.-ft. two-story wood-frame structure including an integrated greenhouse. The greenhouse, 30′ long by 10′ wide, which faces due south, has a potting area at its east end. An open-concept living/dining/kitchen area looks out into the greenhouse to the south and out at the garden and ocean beyond to the west. To the east of the living area is the rock storage bin. The large master bedroom on the second floor also looks down into the greenhouse and overlooks the scene to the west. A bathroom immediately to the north is part of the old house. Several steps lead down to the workshop located above the rock storage bin. This area, though unheated, is so well insulated that it provides a buffer for the living quarters.

The 10″-thick poured-concrete foundation wall is insulated around the outside perimeter with 3″ of sprayed-on polyurethane foam covered with black mastic. Since the addition was built into the side of a hill composed largely of shale (a kind of clay stone that splits readily into thin plates), there had been problems with water running down the hill and against the foundation, thus threatening serious infiltration problems. The whole uphill side of the addition was therefore "French-drained"—that is, a 4″-diameter perforated PVC pipe was laid near the base of the foundation and then covered with crushed stone to within a foot of the surface, or where the topsoil begins. The shale and crushed stone are separated by polyethylene sheeting. The drainage pipe connects to the drainage system under the floor slabs and in front of the greenhouse.

The living/dining-area floor slab is 3″ of wire-mesh-reinforced concrete, mixed with low-density vermiculite aggregate insulation and poured over 2″ of polyurethane foam insulation, a polyethylene vapor barrier,

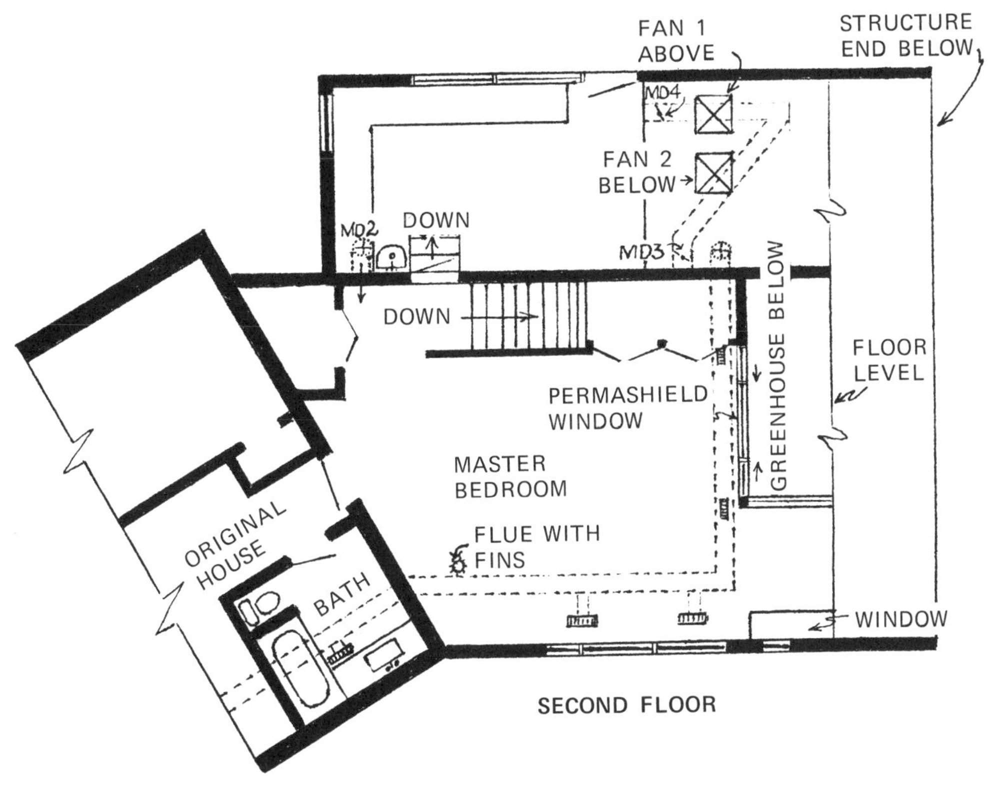

SECOND FLOOR

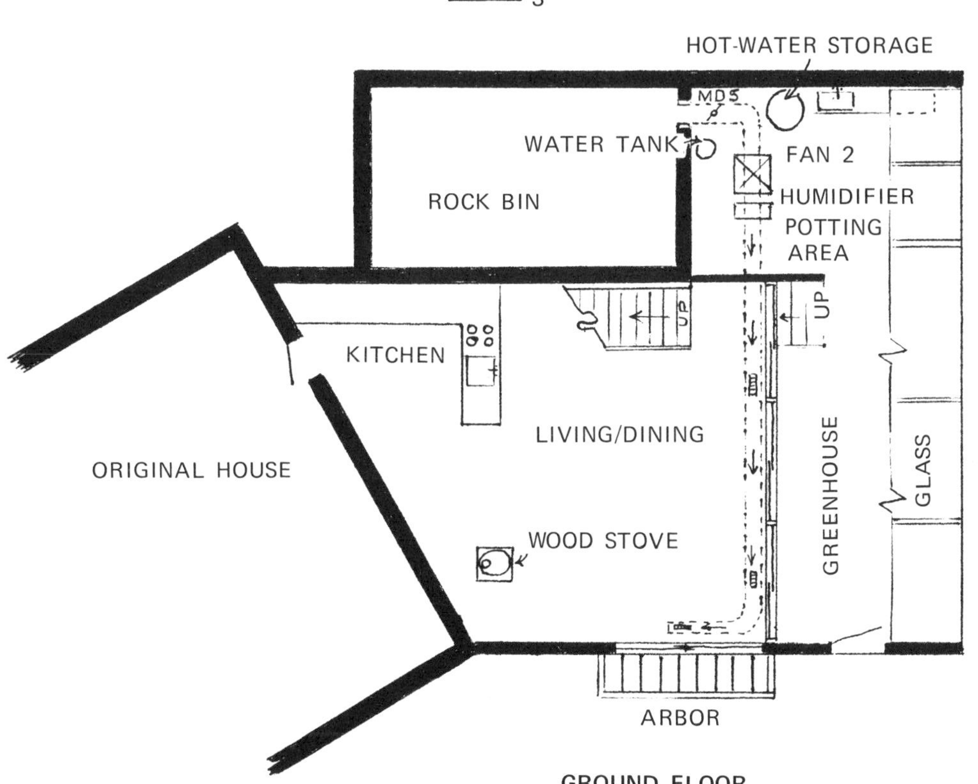

GROUND FLOOR

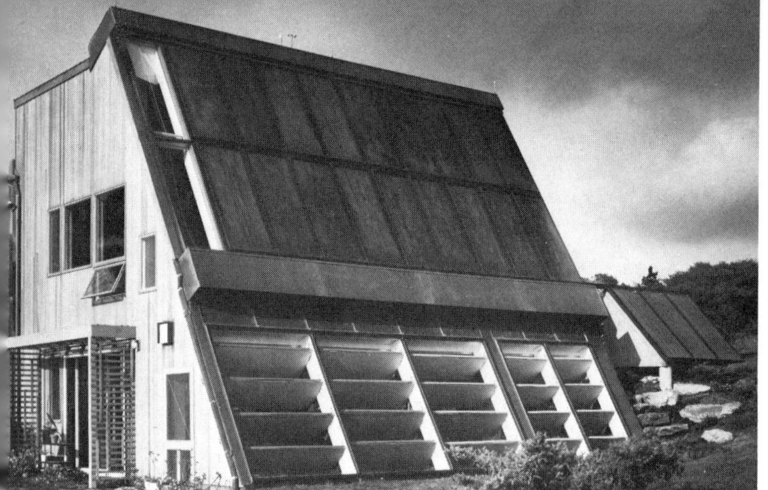

Sunworks air-type collectors cover the upper two-thirds of the south face of the solar addition. Below, the greenhouse receives direct solar gain through the open "Skylids." A thermosiphon solar domestic hot-water preheater is located on the east side of the house.

and crushed stone. Every 5′ a hole was punched through the foam so the concrete would bear directly on the vapor barrier and stone at these intervals. Carpeting adds texture and a feeling of warmth and reduces noise levels. The greenhouse has bluestone over the concrete slab.

The master bedroom has a ⅝″ plywood subfloor over 2 x 10 joists, with a hardwood finish floor as in and continuous with the old house. The 2 x 10s and ⅝″ plywood subflooring in the workshop are covered by another layer of plywood.

Exterior Walls

Standard 2 x 4 studwall construction was used for the main part of the addition, with 3½″ fiberglass batt insulation filling the cavities and 1″ extruded polystyrene panels forming a continuous insulation blanket around the building's interior, immediately under the gypsum board. The greenhouse has a post-and-beam independent structural frame.

The south wall of the greenhouse and the base for the solar collectors has 2 x 12 members sloping 60° from the horizontal and infilled above the glazing with 2 x 6s. This structure is insulated with 6″ fiberglass batts. The endwalls with their 4″ structural members are insulated similarly to the other walls of the addition. The vertical hemlock siding on the east and west walls of the whole addition were treated first with a creosote-type bleaching oil, in order to match the old siding, and later with clear Cuprinol.

Interior Walls and Ceilings

Interior partition walls are of standard 2 x 4 studwall construction. All the addition walls, except exposed concrete walls in the potting shed and greenhouse, are sheathed in ½″ gypsum board, which is painted white in order to optimize the quality of illumination.

Roof

The 2 x 10 rafters of the shed-type roof slope down toward the east. The roof's weather skin is ⅝″ exterior-grade plywood, building paper, and cedar shingles, with copper flashing designed to match the existing roof. The roof is insulated with 6″ fiberglass and has a polyethylene vapor barrier.

Insulation Summary

Foundation walls:	R-26; 4″ sprayed-on polyurethane foam
Floor slab:	R-13; 2″ sprayed-on polyurethane foam
East and west walls:	R-16; 3½″ fiberglass batts plus 1″ rigid panels of extruded polystyrene
South wall:	R-20; 6″ fiberglass batts
Ceiling:	R-20; 6″ fiberglass batts

Doors

The main exterior entrance to the solar addition is through an Andersen thermopane sliding door on the west wall. An entrance on the east side is through the workshop; however, it is rarely used in winter. It has a standard wood exterior door. A thermopane greenhouse door is not used in the dead of winter, when it is covered with bubble plastic. All doors in the original house and the addition are sealed with interlocking metal weatherstripping.

Windows

All of the exterior windows are Andersen double-glazed thermopanes with wood sash. Nearly 50% of the west wall is glazed with the Andersen window wall. Also, an Andersen window wall on the south wall of the living/dining area visually links the greenhouse with the living quarters and permits passive heat gain. The 200 sq. ft. of greenhouse glazing covering the bottom half of the sloping south exterior wall is single tempered glass. This glazing is insulated at night by the Steve Baer-designed self-powered Skylids described in Part I. According to Louise, "They are incredible. It doesn't seem to make any difference that there is no insulation at the joints between adjacent Skylids." Soft fabric secured to the sides of Skylids minimizes convection losses through the cracks between the window frame and the sides of the Skylids and also acts as a lubricant.

From the master bedroom Junius and Louise can look down upon their greenhouse plant and vegetable crop through the wide Andersen Perma-Shield gliding windows. When these windows are opened, hot air is naturally convected into that area. A long narrow fixed thermopane window just to the west of the collector array provides a certain amount of passive heat gain and an interesting view to the south. Two small operable Anderson clerestory windows are the only windows on the colder east side of the room. These and a substantial area of west glazing provide good illumination, ventilation, and passive solar-heat gain when desired. Thin, vertical fiberglass blinds are the only window coverings used at the present time on the lower floor, although a lattice arbor has been constructed outside the living-area window wall, which will have evergreen vines on it for a windbreak. Conventional draperies are used on the master-bedroom windows.

SOLAR-HEATING SYSTEM

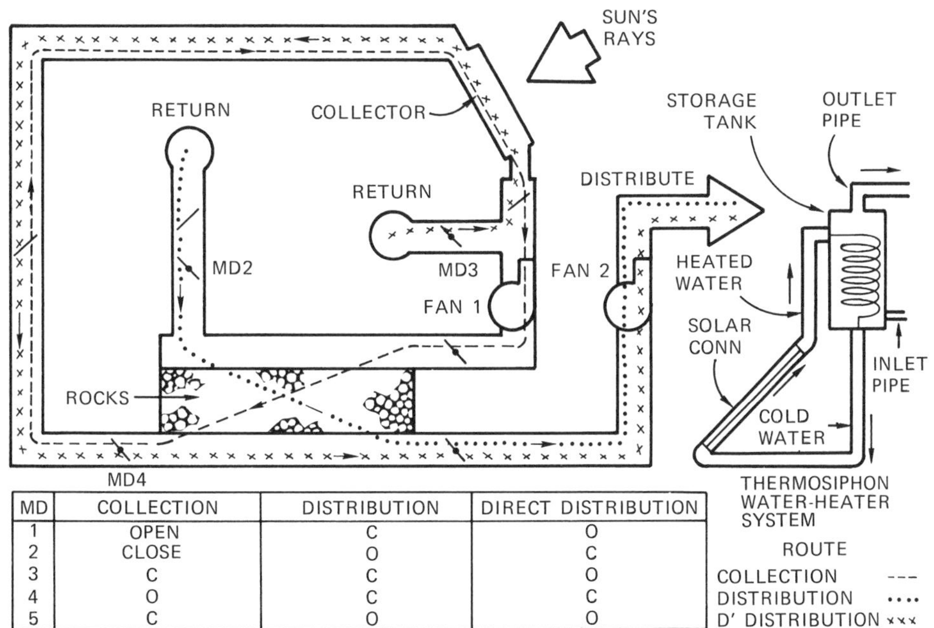

MD	COLLECTION	DISTRIBUTION	DIRECT DISTRIBUTION
1	OPEN	C	O
2	CLOSE	O	C
3	C	C	O
4	O	C	C
5	C	O	O

Good insulation and efforts to minimize infiltration losses account for much of the efficiency of this design. A substantial amount of solar-heat gain is received through the greenhouse glazing and through the south and west glazing of the living quarters themselves; however, it is the active solar system that was designed to provide the bulk of the heat.

Collector

The 18 3 x 7′ air-type collectors (gross area 378 sq. ft., net area 336 sq. ft.) were built by Sunworks, of which Everett Barber was president at the time the system was installed. Being installed on the south wall above the greenhouse, they are oriented due south and are tilted at 60° to the horizontal. The collector glazing is single-pane 3/16″ tempered ASG Sunadey glass, while the absorber plate is a back-finned copper sheet coated with a selective surface having an absorptivity of 0.9 and an emissivity of 0.1. Air makes a single pass behind the absorber and between the back cover of the cedar-frame panels. The panels themselves have fiberglass insulation under the copper; furthermore, they are secured directly to the roof (which is insulated with 6″ of fiberglass) over the plywood sheathing, building paper, and asphalt shingles. Spaces between adjacent panels and under the mullions are thoroughly insulated with fiberglass.

Storage

Passive solar heat is stored in the massive elements of the house such as the concrete floor in the living/dining/kitchen area, the concrete and rocks in the greenhouse, and the gypsum board throughout the house. In the greenhouse a small fan ducts excess heat from the top of the 16′ ceiling to a small rock storage bed 10 x 10 x 3′ deep. Fifty translucent plastic "cider" jugs filled with black-tinted water and Clorox have recently been installed under the greenhouse shelves as added absorptive elements for passive heat retention.

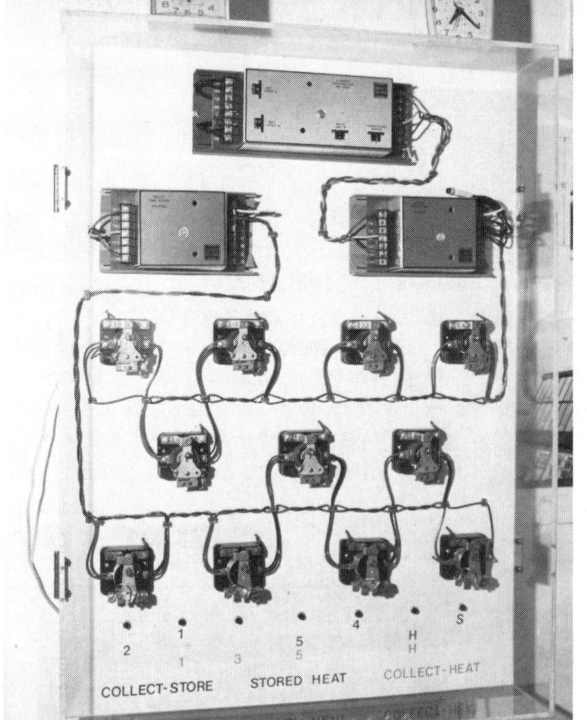

The solar-heating system's control panel was conspicuously secured at eye level on the wall immediately to the east as one enters the living area from the greenhouse.

Integrated with the active solar system is a reinforced-concrete storage bin under the workshop with outside dimensions 12 x 17 x 8′ high and an interior volume of 1,050 cu. ft., including 1″-high top and bottom airflow plenums.

The bin's floor slab has a low-density vermiculite aggregrate insulation mixed in with the concrete. In addition, 4″ of polyurethane foam was sprayed continuously around the inside perimeter and floor of the storage bin. Waterproof gypsum board lines the bin and protects the foam from damage by the 4″-diameter river rock which fills it. The entire family spent a couple of weeks of spare time collecting these rocks from the local beach and washing them by hand.

Everett Barber has calculated that the 4″-diameter stone is the most compatible with the rest of the system, giving the least restrictive flow to air while optimizing heat transfer to storage. The top of the bin is wood-frame with foam insulation sprayed on top. In case moisture enters, the storage bin has a drainage hole connected by PVC pipe to the drain under the greenhouse. Junius explains a concern about this part of the system: "Recently, we have discovered that this drainpipe, which feeds into the French-drain system, may be pulling cold exterior air into the bin during collection and distribution cycles, thus affecting the temperature there somewhat during both the collection and distribution cycles. We don't know this for sure and can't really tell for a while, but Doug, our son, thinks this may be happening and has suggested we dig a hole in the greenhouse slab near where the pit drain emerges and cap it during the winter when there's little chance of moisture building up in the pit. We intend to do this, and in such a way that we can also open it up in the summer, when moisture may be present in the pit, and let any water drain out as before."

Heat Distribution

The collection and distribution of solar heat is through standard air ducts. All but the cold-air-return ducts are insulated with 3½″ of fiberglass. Two fans (one for heat collection and one for heat distribution), five motorized dampers, a differential thermostat, and relays control air circulation. In the collection mode, when the heat sensors (thermistors) in the collector array and the rock storage indicate to the differential thermostat that the temperature of the former is 5° F. warmer than the latter, the collection fan comes on and blows air through the air manifold at the top of the collector array, down through the collectors, and to the bottom manifold, and then to storage, where it heats up the rocks. In the direct distribution mode when the house calls for heat and the sun is out, house air is drawn directly through the collectors in the opposite direction and heated. It bypasses the rock storage by going through the bottom of the pit and then out through volume-control registers in the floors of the living areas. In the heat distribution mode from storage, when the house demands heat that cannot be supplied directly from the solar collectors, relays activate the distribution fan and motorized dampers to draw house air into the top of the rock storage and down to the bottom of the storage, where it is heated and blown through ductwork to the floor-mounted volume-control registers. A humidifier located just downstream from the house heat-distribution fan provides additional climate control.

Regarding operational problems, Junius explains, "The only problems we've had with the space-heating system (we've had *none* with the hot-water system) are, first, that the collection-fan motor burned out last spring, but we learned from Everett that the motor was the wrong size for the size of the fan, and Everett paid for replacement of the correct motor; and second, Everett, Travis, and Doug suggested last winter that we reverse the flow of the collection cycle—bringing it off the top of the collectors, down and under the living-room slab and into the bottom of the pit, up through it, and out at the top of the other end and on to the bottom of the collector panels. This presumably will provide hotter temperatures at the bottom of the pit, from which the ducting for our distribution mode comes. We have made the change this summer, but haven't had a chance yet to determine what difference it will make because we've not distributed more than an hour or so this fall so far."

Greenhouse "Skylids" in the open position.

"Skylids" in the closed position.

AUXILIARY HEATING

A Jøtul 118 box stove is the main backup to the solar-heating system. Junius and Louise found that the Jøtul works well. Typically, the family burns about half a cord of wood during the heating season. Junius's study has solar heat ducted into it but it is at the end of the heat-distribution duct, so it often has to be supplemented with electric heat and/or a small kerosene stove. The two bedrooms have only electric baseboard heating, although the insulated solar ducting runs along the ceilings, with operable registers in them.

PERCENT SOLAR-HEATED

The addition itself, including the greenhouse, is nearly 100% solar-heated. It was first thought that the passive elements of the system would provide between 30% and 40% of the solar-heat gain; however, recent tests indicate that passive accounts for about 65% of the gain in the addition. With a constant daytime temperature of 70° F. and a nighttime setback of 55° F. the needs are typically 90 million Btu per year. Monitoring determined that the active system typically supplies 25% of the heating requirements and the wood stove supplies 5% (based on two-thirds of a cord of wood at 13 million Btu per cord burning at 65% efficiency). Assuming a 5% contribution from lights, electric cooking, and body heat leaves a 65% contribution for the passive system. As mentioned, the Eddys had been using half to two-thirds of a cord of wood per heating season in the Jøtul, but recently, by operating the active system somewhat differently, they hardly have to use the wood stove at all. Junius explained how they improved the efficiency. At first they operated at an average storage-pit temperature of between 110° and 130° F. In the first part of the fall they didn't draw on the pit very much, as they didn't know how long the stored heat would last. When the pit temperature dropped, say 10° F., they wondered if they would get it back, so they tended to use the Jøtul a lot. At Everett Barber's suggestion, they decided to operate the storage in the 85° to 110° F. range by using the stored heat more regularly and found that the system works infinitely better. In the 110-130° F. range, during low or sparse sun conditions in winter, it takes a long time to increase the storage temperature 5° F., whereas, at the lower operating temperature, it tends to heat up much more quickly. "I don't think we are ever going to run out of heat operating in this way," Junius says. "It'll always give us warmer air than there is in the house, and it doesn't go down fast enough to deplete it before another turn of weather in two or three days raises the storage temperature nine or ten degrees."

COOLING SYSTEM

The good insulation in the addition and the interior building mass shield the house from the extremes of winter cold and summer heat. The location of operable windows and doors on opposite walls of the open-concept living spaces leads to good cross-ventilation in summer. In addition, the clerestory windows on the second floor in conjunction with the stairwell leading up from the first floor create a chimney effect for exhausting excess summer heat. By opening the Perma-Shield gliding window between the second-floor master bedroom and the greenhouse, hot air at the peak height of the latter is similarly siphoned off through the clerestory windows by natural convection. It is expected that the arbor, mentioned earlier, will provide an additional cooling effect when the evergreen covers the structure fully. Offshore breezes from the Atlantic further cool the house.

WATER SUPPLY AND WASTE SYSTEM

Water is supplied from a drilled well on the property. The original house had two 70-gallon electric domestic hot-water heaters. When the addition was built, three freestanding 3 x 7′ Sunworks water panels were installed on the bank just east of the greenhouse. They operate on a simple thermosiphon setup, with solar-heated water flowing into a 65-gallon heat-exchange tank located high in the workshop. The bottom of the tank is 2′ above the height of the top of the water collectors. This tank was first linked to one of the original electric water heaters but later was also connected to the second electric water heater so that solar-heated domestic hot water is now supplied to the main kitchen during the summer. Junius describes some of the problems they have encountered and some of their concerns: "Since the electric hot-water heaters are not metered separately from the other appliances, we can't really calculate precisely what the solar contribution of this feature is—nor how much energy or money we're saving. At one point—before we installed our system— we began to have real problems with our well water in terms of mineral deposits on the pipes, so we put in a water conditioner. We learned later than many of the manufacturers of solar *water* systems have become extremely wary of guaranteeing a system for more than five years—even *with* a water-softening system.

"We've become quite concerned about water quality," he continued. "Having read about Cape Cod, where overpopulation has led to overuse of fresh water out of aquifers, resulting in brackish water being pulled out that is polluted with fertilizer and other contaminants from soils, we're more careful now about the amount of water we use and what we put into the waste. For example, we flush the toilets less frequently and take navy showers [that is, water on briefly, water off, scrub with soap, water on and rinse quickly, water off]." The water fixtures themselves are not of a water-conserving design but, clearly, the Eddys are.

Blackwater and graywater are disposed of in a standard septic system. Solid wastes are separated. Organic wastes go into a compost bin near the garden, and the remainder is taken to the town dump, where paper, glass, and tin are placed in separate containers for recycling.

ELECTRICAL POWER SYSTEM

The Eddy home gets its power from Narragansett Electric Company, the local power utility. The height-restrictions covenant governing that residential area at the present time precludes installing a wind generator. A lot of daylight in the addition, through the well-oriented glazing, plus the white-painted walls and ceilings, make artificial light unnecessary during the day. Some fluorescents are used, but Louise dislikes their color rendition, so the Eddys opted for incandescent lights each fitted with a rheostat so the intensity can be controlled.

MAJOR HOUSEHOLD APPLIANCES

Junius and Louise bought their appliances before the power consumption of appliances became a concern and before any energy-conserving appliances were readily available. The stove is electric and the refrigerator is a high-energy-consumption frost-free model. Louise chose an upright freezer rather than a more efficient chest model because she is quite small and could not reach the bottom of the latter.

They use the automatic washer only on sunny days, however, when solar-heated hot water is available. Louise chooses not to use a clothesline because they have so much dampness and salt in the air that it often

The large master bedroom receives direct passive solar-heat gain through the west and southwest corner glazing, and indirect solar gain by opening the windows through which one can look down into the greenhouse.

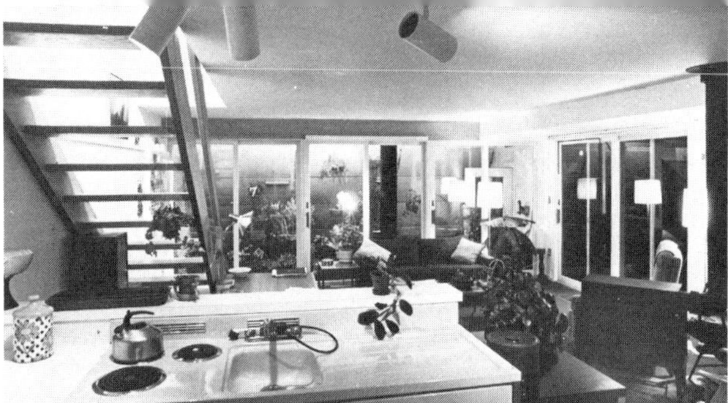

The open-concept kitchen/dining/living area looks out to the solar greenhouse. The Jøtul wood-burning stove is the only backup to the combination passive and active solar-heating system.

takes too long to dry clothes properly, particularly if the house is full of guests. A dishwasher is used in the main kitchen when the Eddy family expands in the summer. The dry cycle is usually turned off in order to conserve some electricity.

FOOD SYSTEM

Food production, preservation, and preparation is one of Louise's fortes. "We produce much of our own food, but I have no illusions about being self-sufficient in food production as it is impossible to do it alone. Junius helps, but because the nature of his work involves considerable travel, he can't always do it. We have a garden and fruit bushes from which we can harvest produce from late June or early July until November. We use manure, compost, and some lime rather than artificial pesticides or chemicals. A gas-driven Roto-tiller was an excellent investment as we constantly use it to renew the land."

The Eddys use no energy in the greenhouse other than solar, except for a small amount of electricity for lights and a small fan for the greenhouse heat-storage system. They use some chemical fertilizers in the greenhouse, but don't use any insecticides unless absolutely driven to it. In the winter, they grow enough tomatoes, lettuce, and herbs to meet their normal needs.

COSTS

As Junius admits, it is a little painful to talk about the costs involved in constructing the addition.

The completed cost was somewhat higher than they'd estimated, of which about $7,000 was for the installed cost of the active solar system (including collectors, storage pit, water tanking, plumbing, ducting, fans, and controls) and $2,100 was for the installed costs of the Skylids. The installed cost of the wood stove was $500. This price, however, included not only the 1,350-sq.-ft. addition but also renovations to a bathroom, two bedrooms, and a study in the original house. It might be argued that a disproportionate amount of money was spent on the active system relative to the amount of the addition's heating needs they have since learned is required for comfort. If wood burning had been the only backup to the solar system, at two and two-thirds cords per year, it would take about 80 years to use $7,000 worth of wood. Apart from the arduous task of chopping and feeding this much wood to the stove, the Eddys' ability to leave the residence for long periods in the winter would have been restricted.

Junius estimates that they are saving close to 50% on their annual electrical bill now—a bill which, if they had continued to live in the original house, would have risen to about $2,400 in the 1977-78 heating season. The costs to run the damper and fan motors are quite minimal. The Eddys' son Doug has estimated during the 1976-77 season, the total cost was about 25¢ per week. Since the 1,350 sq. ft. of the addition gets almost all of its heat from the solar system and the remainder from the wood stove, if Junius and Louise wished or had to "hunker down" only in these rooms, their electric bill would be minimal.

CONCLUDING THOUGHTS

Not tabled in the cost accounting is the satisfaction that Junius and Louise derive from their self-reliance and from sharing their experience so willingly with others, nor the very tangible skills that two of their sons acquired while working on the house. Bill Frederickson, a very skilled carpenter, was hired to do all the finishing work. Another of their sons, Jim, worked side by side with Bill and thus acquired excellent on-the-job carpentry training. Doug worked closely with Travis Price and Everett Barber on the solar installations themselves and has since teamed up with Travis on other renewable-energy projects with the American Institute of Architects, and the Tennessee Valley Authority.

APPENDICES

DESIGN CHECKLIST

A recent book by David Wright, *Natural Solar Architecture, a Passive Primer* (Van Nostrand Reinhold Company, 1978), is an essential resource for anyone planning to modify, design, or build a living space in harmony with the natural environment. In it he has included a checklist or procedural outline which will help the designer to make design decisions in an orderly and proper sequence and thus simplify, in Wright's words, "the process of developing a holistic concept of embracing all of the important environmental aspects." What follows is another checklist which is intended to supplement Wright's list; it is a means for the reader to fine tune his ecological home design.

The checklist contains a list of characteristics against which the designer should measure each of the elements or components of the design, be they doors, windows, landscaping, or whatever. Each characteristic will not be appropriate to each design element, and some characteristics will not be compatible with other characteristics. In any design process there are certain trade-offs that have to be made, but it is important to know what the trade-offs are and why they were made.

CHECKLIST

Design Component		
Characteristics of design component	***Check (✓) if characteristic examined***	***Designer's comments***
1. Minimizes environmental impact during processing, manufacturing, distribution		
2. Minimizes use of resources, particularly nonrenewable resources		
3. Minimizes energy consumption		
4. Optimizes beneficial effects and minimizes harmful effects of climatic influences: wind rain snow hail		
5. Durable		
6. Dimensionally stable under operating conditions		
7. Sufficient strength for function		

Characteristics of design component	*Check (✓) if characteristic examined*	*Designer's comments*
8. Reusable and/or recyclable		
9. Biodegradable		
10. "Childproof"		
11. Fire-resistant		
12. Minimizes environmental pollution		
13. Nontoxic		
14. Nonirritating		
15. Noncorrosive		
16. Vermin- and rodent-resistant		
17. Moisture-resistant		
18. Aesthetically, environmentally, and functionally appropriate to the senses of *all* inhabitants: sight sound smell touch taste		
19. Facilitates maintenance of comfort levels related to. temperature humidity air circulation		
20. Minimizes capital costs		
21. Adds monetary value to the site		
22. Adds recreational value		
23. Eases maintenance		
24. Reduces maintenance costs		
25. Minimizes transportation costs (monetary, energy, and resource)		
26. Facilitates economy of movement on-site.		
27. Adds convenience		
28. Encourages decentralist activities		
29. Other characteristics		

REFERENCES

In the last several years, there have been many articles, reports, and texts written about environmentally appropriate technology It is often difficult, especially for the neophyte, to separate the wheat from the chaff. Several attempts have been made to write annotated bibliographies on the subject and to compile lists of alternative information sources. As well, a number of periodicals are devoted to keeping the reader aware of the latest developments and sources of information. It would be redundant, and out of keeping with the theme of this text, to list all of the information sources related to the field of environmentally appropriate technology, or even solar energy. Rather, I have chosen to categorize a relatively short list of selected references that I and many of the people whom I interviewed for this book have found most useful in our own work. Each of these will lead you to individuals, organizations, and companies knowledgeable in the field of environmentally appropriate technology, and to other related references. The renewable-energy categories have been limited to solar, wind, and wood; however, the interested reader will find within some of the listed references, particularly the access catalogs, information on other forms of renewable energy.

The addresses of those people associated with each building described in this book have been included within the description, except that in a few cases the specific address has been omitted out of consideration for the privacy of the individuals concerned.

Overview

Argue, Robert, Barbara Emanuel, and Stephen Graham. *The Sunbuilders: A People's Guide to Solar, Wind and Wood Energy in Canada.* Renewable Energy in Canada, 415 Parkside Drive, Toronto, Ontario M6R 2Z7.

Brand, Stewart. *Whole Earth Epilog.* Baltimore: Penguin, 1974.

Fine, Richard, Douglas Hart, Joe Umanetz, and Bruce McCallum. *New Energy Sources for Today: The Renewable Energy Handbook.* Prepared and edited by members of Energy Probe and Pollution Probe (43 Queen's Park Crescent East, Toronto, Ontario M5S 2C3). Toronto: Tutor Press, 1978.

Leckie, Jim, *et. al. Other Homes and Garbage.* New York: Sierra/Scribners, 1975.

McCallum, Bruce. *Environmentally Appropriate Technology: Renewable Energy and Other Developing Technologies for a Conserver Society in Canada.* Ottawa: Fisheries and Environment Canada, 1977.

Merrill, Richard, *et al.*, eds. *Energy Primer: Solar, Water, Wind and Biofuels.* Menlo Park, Calif.: Portola Institute, 1974.

Rainbook: Resources for Appropriate Technology. By the editors of *Rain.* New York: Schocken, 1977.

Schumacher, E. F. *Small Is Beautiful: Economics As If People Mattered.* New York: Harper & Row, 1976.

Whole Earth Catalogue; Co-Evolution Quarterly. P.O. Box 428, Sausalito, Calif. 94965.

Site and Building Design

Aronin, Jeffrey. *Climate and Architecture.* New York: AMS Press, 1977; reprint of 1953 edition.

Cole, John N., and Charles Wing. *From the Ground Up.* Boston: Atlantic Monthly/Little, Brown, 1976.

Eccli, Eugene, ed. *Low-Cost, Energy-Efficient Shelter for the Owner and Builder.* Emmaus, Pa.: Rodale, 1976.

Fathy, Hassan. *Architecture for the Poor: An Experiment in Rural Egypt.* Chicago: Univ. of Chicago Press, 1973.

Geiger, Rudolf. *The Climate Near the Ground.* Cambridge, Mass.: Harvard Univ. Press, 1965.

Kaing, M.G. *Five Acres and Independence.* New York: Dover, 1973.

Kern, Ken. *The Owner-Built Home.* New York: Scribners, 1975.

Parker, Harry, and Harold D. Hauf. *Simplified Engineering for Architects and Builders.* New York: Wiley-Interscience, 1975.

Reader's Digest Complete Do-It-Yourself Manual. New York: Norton, 1973.

Shelter. 1973. Shelter Pubilications, c/o Mountain Books, P.O. Box 4811, Santa Barbara, Calif. 93103.

Shurcliff, W. A. *Thermal Shutters and Shades.* 1977. Available from the author, 19 Appleton St., Cambridge, Mass. 02138.

Wade, Alex, and Neal Ewenstein. *Thirty Energy-Efficient Houses You Can Build.* Emmaus, Pa.: Rodale, 1977.

Wagner, Willis H. *Modern Carpentry.* South Holland, Ill.: Goodheart-Willcox Co., 1976.

Solar

American Society of Heating, Refrigerating and Air-Conditioning Engineers, Inc. *ASHRAE Handbook of Fundamentals.* Available from ASHRAE, United Engineering Center, 345 E. 47th Street, New York, N.Y. 10017.

Anderson, Bruce. *The Solar Home Book.* Harrisville, N.H.: Cheshire Books, 1976.

International Solar Energy Society. *Proceedings* of conferences. Contact: American Section, ISES, 300 State Road 401, Cape Canaveral, Fla. 32920, or local chapters. Of special interest to those interested in passive solar systems are the following:

Passive Solar Heating and Cooling Conference Proceedings, Univ. of New Mexico, May 18-19, 1976. Write: Solar Energy Lab (Mail Stop 571), Los Alamos Scientific Lab, P.O. Box 1663, Los Alamos, Calif. 87543.

Proceedings of the Second National Passive Solar Conference, Univ. of Pennsylvania, March 16–18, 1978. Write: Mid-Atlantic Solar Energy Association, 2233 Gray's Ferry Ave., Philadelphia, Pa. 19146.

Montgomery, Richard H. *The Solar Decision Book,* 1978. Available for $10 from Dow Corning Corp., Dept. 2268, Midland, MI 48640.

Nicholson, Nick. *The Nicholson Solar Energy Catalogue and Building Manual* (1977); *Harvest the Sun* (1978); and *Prototype Canada* (1978). Nicholson has built many houses in Canada using air/rock-storage solar systems. The first two books give step-by-step procedures in building these houses. The third includes all the working drawings necessary to build an efficient, maintenance-free air-rock space-heating system and an integrated domestic hot-water system. All three publications are available from: The Ayer's Cliff Centre for Solar Research, P.O. Box 344, Ayer's Cliff, Quebec.

Rapp, Felix, Jr., and James M. Barron. DIY-Sol Heating System, Design and Construction Manual. Available from Felix Rapp, 29 Highgate Rd., Marlboro, Mass. 01752, $15.00.

Shurcliff, William A. "Informal Directory of the Organizations and People Involved in the Solar Heating of Buildings." Available from the author, 19 Appleton St., Cambridge, Mass. 02138, $7.00.

Shurcliff, William A. *Solar Heated Buildings of North America: 120 Outstanding Examples.* Harrisville, N.H.: Brick House Publishing Co., 1978.

Solar Energy Society of Canada Inc. *Proceedings* of the annual renewable-energy conferences held in Ottawa in June 1975, Winnipeg in August 1976, Edmonton in August 1977, and London, Ontario, in August 1978. Contact: SESCI, P.O. Box 1353, Winnipeg, Manitoba R3C 2Z1, or a local SESCI chapter.

Watson, Donald. *Designing and Building a Solar House.* Charlotte, Vt.: Garden Way, 1977.

Wright, David. *Natural Solar Architecture: A Passive Primer.* New York: Van Nostrand Reinhold, 1978.

Wood Heating

Gay, Larry. *The Complete Book of Heating with Wood.* Charlotte, Vt.: Garden Way, 1974.

Ross, Bob and Carol. *Modern and Classic Woodburning Stoves.* New York: Overlook/Viking, 1977.

Shelton, John W., and Andrew Shapiro. *The Woodburner's Encyclopedia.* Waitsfield, Vt.: Vermont Crossroads Press, 1976.

Vivian, John. *Wood Heat: New and Improved Edition.* Emmaus, Pa.: Rodale, 1978.

Wind

Clews, Henry. *Electric Power from the Wind.* East Holden, Maine: Solar Wind Publications, 1973.

Golding, E. W. *The Generation of Electricity by Wind Power.* New York: Halsted/Wiley, 1976.

Planning a Wind Powered Generating System. 1977. Enertech Corp., Box 420, Norwich, Vt. 05055.

Wind Energy Bibliography. Windworks, Box 329, Route 3, Mukwanago, Wis. 53149.

Water and Waste

"Goodbye to the Flush Toilet," *Rain* magazine, April 1976. Available for $1 from Rain Magazine, 2270 N. W. Irving, Portland, Ore. 97210.

Milne, Murray. *Residential Water Conservation.* 1976. California Water Resources Center, Univ. of California, Davis, Calif. 95616.

Rural Wastewater Disposal Alternatives. Report from the Office of Technology, Sept. 1977. Write: State of California, State Water Resources Control Board, P.O. Box 100, Sacramento, Calif. 95801.

Rybizynski, Witold. *Stop the Five-Gallon Flush.* McGill University, Minimum Cost Housing Group, School of Architecture, Box 6070, Montreal 101, Quebec.

Stoner, Carol Hupping, ed. *Goodbye to the Flush Toilet.* Emmaus, Pa.: Rodale Press, 1977.

Agriculture

Jeavons, John. *How to Grow More Vegetables Than You Ever Thought Possible on Less Land Than You Can Imagine.* Palo Alto, Calif.: Ecology Action of the Midpeninsula, 1974.

Kern, Barbara and Ken. *The Owner-Built Homestead.* New York: Scribners, 1977.

Lawand, T. A., R. Alward, B. Saulnier, and E. Brunet. *The Development and Testing of an Environmentally Designed Greenhouse for Colder Regions.* Brace Research Institute, MacDonald College of McGill University, Ste. Anne de Bellevue, Quebec H9X 3M1.

INDEX